The Astors

A FAMILY CHRONICLE OF POMP AND POWER

Other Books by Lucy Kavaler

MUSHROOMS, MOLDS, AND MIRACLES
THE PRIVATE WORLD OF HIGH SOCIETY

For Young Readers

THE WONDERS OF FUNGI
THE ARTIFICIAL WORLD AROUND US
THE WONDERS OF ALGAE

The Astors

A FAMILY CHRONICLE OF POMP AND POWER

by Lucy Kavaler

ILLUSTRATED WITH PHOTOGRAPHS

DODD, MEAD & COMPANY
New York

For my sister Anne

SECOND PRINTING

Library of Congress Catalog Card Number: 66-18348
Printed in the United States of America
by Vail-Ballou Press, Inc., Binghamton, N.Y.

Acknowledgments

The research for a book that spans 200 years in the life of a family begins in the libraries among the yellowing pages of old books, newspapers, and magazines, but it also needs the active cooperation of a great number of people. In receiving this, I have indeed been fortunate, and I should like to express my thanks to the Astors and their many friends and associates. In addition to obtaining first-hand information about contemporaries and near-contemporaries, I have been able to find, still bright in the memories of a handful of very old men and women, recollections of Astors of earlier generations—dead in some cases for better than 70 years. I have spoken with some who danced at *the* Mrs. Astor's famous balls, remember the charm of her all-but-forgotten husband, recall John Jacob Astor III and his kindly Augusta, comforted the homesick wife of William Waldorf Astor, admired the celebrated beauty of the young Ava Astor, and were friends with John Jacob Astor IV decades before the *Titanic* disaster.

Of the American Astors, I should particularly like to thank John Astor, head of the family today, for devoting so much time to telling me of his life and about members of the family, living and dead, known to him. His son, William Astor, was also of great assistance. Ivan Obolensky, son of Alice Astor, was extremely generous in giving his recollections of his mother, his uncle Vincent, and many other members of the family here and in England.

The British Astors were most kind and assisted me in my research in England. I should especially like to thank Lord William Waldorf Astor, the third Viscount, for inviting me to his home, describing his activities, and sharing with me his memories of his grandfather, founder of the British Astor line; his mother and father, Lady Nancy and Lord Waldorf Astor, and many other members of this branch of the family.

Acknowledgments

Thanks are also due to the Honorable Gavin Astor, both for his time and for a most pleasant visit to Hever Castle, seat of his father's barony.

A special word of appreciation goes to Alida Chanler Emmet, last surviving great-granddaughter of William Backhouse Astor, for her reminiscences that go back to the 1880's. Thomas Emmet, her son, also aided me with his knowledge of the family and gave me the opportunity to study the mementoes gathered at the home in Stony Brook, L.I. The Aldrich family, descendants of Emily Astor, kindly welcomed me to Rokeby, the estate bought by John Jacob Astor I for his son and daughter-in-law, where I was able to see family papers and photographs.

Many relatives and friends of the Astors assisted me, in person when possible, by telephone, when it was not, and gave me first-hand information, not otherwise obtainable, about the family. Prominent among these are Mrs. Tracy Dows, Olin Dows, Ashley Chanler, R. Thornton Wilson, Orme Wilson, Jr., and Mrs. Lytle Hull. I should like to thank Raymond Moley for giving of his unique knowledge of the founding of *Newsweek* and his personal understanding of Vincent Astor. Allan W. Betts, Vincent Astor's business manager, added useful information about Astor's last years, business ventures and the Foundation; and Pierre Bultinck told me of his years at the St. Regis under Vincent Astor. Capt. James C. Coggill helped me to trace the Civil War military career of John Jacob Astor III. The Children's Aid Society contributed information on Mrs. John Jacob Astor III; the New York Public Library was helpful in tracing Astor participation from John Jacob Astor I to the present; the Florida State Library and the Jacksonville (Fla.) Free Public Library aided me in tracking down the Florida ventures of William B. Astor, Jr.; the Wisconsin Historical Society similarly informed me as to the fate of John Jacob Astor I's attempts to establish himself in that area; the Waldorf-Astoria made available to me material about the founding of the hotel; and the Office of the Astor Trusts assisted me in tracing the British Astor family.

Marian Hurd Manfredi prepared the intricate chart of the Astor family tree.

In conclusion, I should like to thank my husband for encouraging and helping me all the way.

Contents

Illustrations

Vincent Astor
Nourmahal

Astor Family Tree

In the interest of clarity, it has proven necessary to omit the names of some members of this large family. Those male Astors in the direct line of descent who figure prominently in this book are indicated in boldface type. The marriages of daughters are included, so as to indicate the family surnames of their descendants, but these descendants are not listed individually. In the present generation in the United States and England, listing of children is restricted to issue of the eldest sons of male Astors.

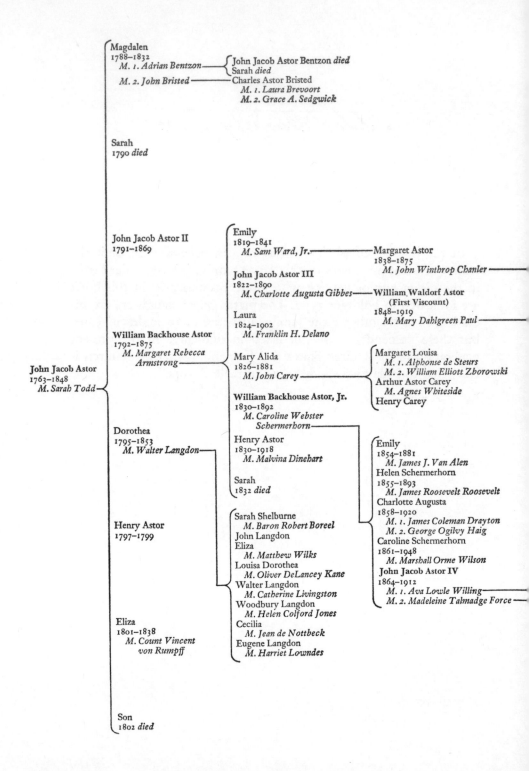

Magdalen
1788–1832
M. 1. Adrian Bentzon ——— { John Jacob Astor Bentzon *died*
                                Sarah *died*
M. 2. John Bristed ——— Charles Astor Bristed
                              M. 1. Laura Brevoort
                              M. 2. Grace A. Sedgwick

Sarah
1790 *died*

John Jacob Astor II
1791–1869

John Jacob Astor
1763–1848
M. Sarah Todd —

Emily
1819–1841
M. Sam Ward, Jr. ——— Margaret Astor
                          1838–1875
                          M. John Winthrop Chanler ———

John Jacob Astor III
1822–1890
M. Charlotte Augusta Gibbes ——— William Waldorf Astor
                                    (First Viscount)
                                    1848–1919
                                    M. Mary Dahlgreen Paul ———

Laura
1824–1902
M. Franklin H. Delano

William Backhouse Astor
1792–1875
*M. Margaret Rebecca
    Armstrong* ——

Mary Alida
1826–1881
M. John Carey ——— { Margaret Louisa
                          M. 1. Alphonse de Steurs
                          M. 2. William Elliott Zborowski
                        Arthur Astor Carey
                          M. Agnes Whiteside
                        Henry Carey

William Backhouse Astor, Jr.
1830–1892
*M. Caroline Webster
    Schermerhorn* ——

Henry Astor
1830–1918
M. Malvina Dinehart

Dorothea
1795–1853
M. Walter Langdon ——

Sarah
1832 *died*

Emily
1854–1881
M. James J. Van Alen
Helen Schermerhorn
1855–1893
M. James Roosevelt Roosevelt
Charlotte Augusta
1858–1920
M. 1. James Coleman Drayton
M. 2. George Ogilvy Haig
Caroline Schermerhorn
1861–1948
M. Marshall Orme Wilson
John Jacob Astor IV
1864–1912
M. 1. Ava Lowle Willing ———
M. 2. Madeleine Talmadge Force ———

Henry Astor
1797–1799

Sarah Shelburne
    M. Baron Robert Boreel
John Langdon
Eliza
    M. Matthew Wilks
Louisa Dorothea
    M. Oliver DeLancey Kane
Walter Langdon
    M. Catherine Livingston
Woodbury Langdon
    M. Helen Colford Jones
Cecilia
    M. Jean de Nottbeck
Eugene Langdon
    M. Harriet Lowndes

Eliza
1801–1838
*M. Count Vincent
    von Rumpff*

Son
1802 *died*

John Armstrong Chanler
  M. Amélie Rives
Winthrop Astor Chanler
  M. Margaret Terry
Elizabeth Ward
  M. John Chapman
William Astor Chanler
  M. Minnie Ashley
Lewis Stuyvesant Chanler
  M. Julia Olin
Margaret Livingston
  M. Richard Aldrich
Robert Winthrop Chanler
  M. Lina Cavalieri
Alida Beekman
  M. Christopher Temple Emmet
Marion Ward Chanler
Son *died*
Son *died*

William Waldorf Astor
(Third Viscount)
1907–
  M. 1. Sarah K, E. Norton ——————— **William Waldorf Astor III**
                                        1952–
  M. 2. Philippa Hunloke ———————— Emily
  M. 3. Bronwen Pugh ————————— ⎰ Janet Elizabeth
                                     ⎱ Pauline Marian
Nancy Phyllis Louise
1909–
  M. Lord Willoughby de Eresby
     (Earl of Ancaster)
Francis David Langhorne Astor
1912–
  M. 1. Melanie Hauser
  M. 2. Bridget Aphra Wreford
Michael Langhorne Astor
1916–
  M. 1. Barbara Mary Colonsay McNeil
  M. 2. Patricia David Pandora Clifford Jones
John Jacob Astor VII
1918–
  M. Ana Inez Carcano

Waldorf Astor
(Second Viscount)
1879–1952
  M. Nancy Langhorne Shaw ———

Pauline
1880–
  M. Capt. H. H. Spender-Clay ——

John Rudolph Astor
1881 *died*

Phyllis Mary
  M. Sir Philip Bouverie Bowyer-Nichols
Rachel Pauline
  M. The Hon. David Bowes-Lyon
Gavin Astor   **John Jacob Astor VIII**
1918–   1946–
  M. Lady Irene Haig ——————   Bridget Mary
Hugh Waldorf Astor   Elizabeth Louise
1920–   Sarah Violet
  M. Emily Lucy Kinloch   Philip Douglas Paul
John Astor
1923–
  M. Diana Drummond

John Jacob Astor V
(Baron Astor of Hever)
1886–
  M. Lady Violet Elliot
     Mercer-Nairne ——

Gwendolyn Enid
1889–1902

William Vincent Astor
1891–1959
  M. 1. Helen Dinsmore Huntington
  M. 2. Mary Benedict Cushing
  M. 3. Mary Brooke Russell Marshall
Ava Alice Muriel
1902–1956
  M. 1. Prince Serge Obolensky ———— ⎰ Ivan Obolensky
                                         ⎱ Sylvia
  M. 2. Raimund von Hofmannsthal ——— Romana
  M. 3. Philip Harding ———————— Emily
  M. 4. David Pleydell-Bouverie

John Jacob Astor VI
1912–
  M. 1. Ellen Tuck French ————— **William Backhouse Astor**
  M. 2. Gertrude Gretsch —————   1935–   ⎰ **William Backhouse Astor, Jr.**
  M. 3. Dolores Fullman   *M. Charlotte Fisk* ————   1959–
                                    Mary Jacqueline   ⎱ Caroline Fisk

"He dined here last night and ate his ice cream and peas with a knife."

The name of the guest described in that sneering remark has come through the years to stand for refinement, exclusivity and wealth. It has become a word, as well as a proper noun.

Who is society? Most Americans answer that question with two or three names. The first one given is almost always "Astor." It might be the widow of moody Vincent Astor, or the children of the various marriages of restless Alice Astor, or British Lord Astor or the exile Baron Astor of Hever. Tabloid readers suggest John Jacob Astor VI, natural prey of the society columnists, or his sedate son William. Some people offer the name without having a specific Astor in mind at all. It has gone beyond the individual and has become a symbol.

No doubt, the legendary Mrs. Astor, who believed—and history has proved her right—that she needed no first name to identify her, has helped to forge this popular American image. Surely everyone knows that she and her social prime minister, Ward McAllister, created the term, the "400."

This plain, overdressed woman with dyed black hair (Caroline or Mrs. William to add the all-but-forgotten first names) made Americans in Chicago, San Francisco and in the small towns of Montana and Wisconsin vividly aware of glittering balls, fabulous nine-course dinners and glamorous debutante cotillions. She was the codifier of the laws of society and, to this day, social families follow a way of life that is essentially a modern version of her rules and rituals.

But the Astors were a social power long before Caroline came on the scene to rule the gilded era of the late 1800's.

High society, as members of the inner circle will assure you earnestly, is made up of families that are "old." By this they mean that the family has been prominent in America for many, many generations. The Astors are an old family: John Jacob Astor I landed here in 1784 and had made his first quarter of a million dollars by 1800. But many families are older by far—the De Peysters, the Van Cortlandts, the Van Rensselaers, the Jays, the Livingstons.

This makes no difference at all. Mention the other great names and someone is sure to ask you for a fuller description. This one is descended from a Dutch patroon, that one from an aristocrat who received a land grant from the King of England. Astor is the name that needs no explanation, that has become the synonym for society. Its only rivals are Whitney and Vanderbilt. Of these three, Astor is the "oldest." Indeed it is the only one of these great society families to have entered the inner circle before the Civil War, selected by social historians as the dividing line between old society and new. This may explain why it is the first half of the painfully cute name "Astorbilt," but it does not tell how the Astors rose into high society so quickly themselves.

"It's easy if you're an Astor." This cliché is heard wherever there are wistful people striving for acceptance in exclusive clubs, the "right" private schools, children's dancing classes, debutante balls, charity benefits, private subscription dances, *Blue* books, *Green* books and the *Social Register* (in which the name of the present head of the family, incidentally, does not appear).

The cliché could have been coined a century and a half ago. The Vanderbilts struggled for social recognition for many years . . . J. P. Morgan was frowned on in his day as *nouveau riche* . . . the Rockefellers needed the skillful guidance of public relations . . . but John Jacob Astor I, son of a smalltown German butcher, was invited to the most exclusive homes in early nineteenth-century America. And the fact that the peas may have slipped from his knife was mentioned only behind his back, and did not stop his hosts from issuing return invitations. This was a tribute not only to his wealth and influence, but also to something in the personality and character of that brilliant, dynamic man. It was easy for *that* Astor.

His descendants, aided both by his example and his money, found it easier still. And when the Astors decided to invade England, they moved with incredible speed right into Burke's *Peerage* and the Queen's circle.

But the Astor name means more than society. The social connotations have made us forget the dominant role the family has played in exploration, trade, shipping, real estate and in the city of New York.

The fur trade from which young Astor wrested his first fortune was of inestimable importance in opening up Western and Canadian wildernesses. In a search for new markets, he expanded trade between this country and the Orient. Both of these enterprises contributed to the growth of the port of New York.

The Astor imprint is strongly on this city. John Jacob Astor I was the first man to grasp what New York might become and to invest in its future. What is more, he passed his vision on to his children and grandchildren.

No other family has ever owned so much of a modern city— owned it in the most literal sense, too. Countless blocks, thousands of residences, scores of commercial buildings, miles of waterfront property, acres of vacant lots, hotels—all, all belonged to the Astors.

Possession of land and houses led to the possession of power and the family became a potent force in both national and city politics. The expatriate Astors across the Atlantic are influential in British politics as well.

This, then, is the dynasty of power and elegance that the Astor family has become. To understand how it got this way, one has to go back to the beginning—to a German immigrant who worked hard and went to bed early in the naïve conviction that "good habits make any man rich."

2

The Man Who Made Money

On a cool day in the autumn of 1962, Baron Astor said goodbye to his tenant farmers in the tiny English town of Hever and set off for France.

"This is sad for me," he said at the London airport. "I leave England with deep regret."

Lord Astor of Hever was being forced into exile for the strangest of all crimes: he was too rich. This could have happened only to an Astor.

A change in the British tax law made the family's tremendous American holdings subject to an 80-percent death duty. If Lord Astor, a man in his late seventies, were to die in England, his heirs would lose a fortune.

The exiled Briton quite suitably bears the name of the man responsible for his problem. The Baron is John Jacob Astor, the fifth of that name. Numbers six through eight are also living. Only one of them, the sixth, is an American. In an odd switch, this is the one who is poor today—by Astor standards only, to be sure.

"The American Astors are now just ordinary millionaires, like thousands of others," he muses in the spacious living room of his seventeen-room Fifth Avenue apartment.

Contrary to popular belief, the American part of the fortune has not been squandered on girls and gin; it was deflected by the late Vincent Astor and put into an Astor Foundation devoted to good works. This idea would have stunned the first John Jacob Astor, who once donated twelve pieces of nankeen to an orphanage. That was the kind of charity he understood; real money was to be passed on intact to your sons.

The making of that money was his ambition, and in fulfilling it he created a legend. Brilliant, bold, daring, vigorous, possessed of financial genius—this is how he was viewed by most of his awe-struck contemporaries. Cold, calculating, crafty, unscrupulous, unprincipled, grasping—this is the image held by those who competed with him in the fur trade, export-import, or real estate. Warm, loving, sentimental, charming, vital, magnetic—this is how he was known to his friends and family. Crude, vulgar, ill-mannered—this is the opinion held by the Old Guard society of his day. Each of these images is true, but even putting them all together does not give a complete picture of the complex, contradictory nature of John Jacob Astor, who rose out of poverty to become the richest man in America and to found one of society's greatest dynasties.

His story, like that of the typical Horatio Alger hero, began humbly, in his case on June 17, 1763, in the small German village of Walldorf, where his father ran the local butcher shop, and, from what one can gather, not too well.

"The father could not have been much of a butcher" is the apt comment of young William Astor, John Jacob I's great-great-great-grandson. "Otherwise why did so many of his children leave home?"

Two of John's older brothers preceded him in his search for a better life, George going to London and Henry to New York. The father, a cheerful beer drinker, completely lacked his sons' drive to make money, but no one could say that he lacked drive: he fathered twelve children by two wives. The second wife, John's stepmother, just to add the Cinderella motif to the Horatio Alger theme, was unkind to the children of her predecessor. Working by day with the stinking carcasses of his father's butcher shop (John's schooling was terminated when he was fourteen; no healthy boy could waste any more of his life learning his letters) and returning at night to the unpleasant atmosphere of his home hardened his character, yet left him with a great yearning for the warmth of a loving family. By the time he was seventeen, he could stand it no more and started on the journey that was to make him a multimillionaire, a word that had not yet been coined.

As the Revolution was raging on the North American continent, he went to England to work in his brother George's music store. He learned a good deal about music and took up the flute. This interest never left him; sixty years later he would recall the songs of those early days and all but weep at the memories they brought forth. Still, England was not as hospitable to John Jacob as it was to his descendants when they arrived 110 years later with a hundred million dollars in their pockets. When John's discontented nature drove him on three years later, he had saved only enough to pay for a steerage passage to America, with five English pounds left over, a good suit, and seven flutes. That may be legend, though, because the story of this period of his life was pieced together long afterward from the vague scattered memories of others.

Astor was not yet twenty-one years old on the spring day in 1784 when he reached a New York different in almost every particular from modern concepts of what a city should be. There were no police, no firemen, no street lights, no running water, no street cleaners, and no public transportation.

Crime, rampant in those lawless years, was discouraged only by the night watchman, picking his way with difficulty through the dark streets, crying the hour "and all's well."

If a man did not own a horse and carriage, he walked, and walking in New York of the 1780's was not for the infirm. Just outside the few residential and commercial blocks lay swamps, woods, fields, and farms. Planks were thrown over the ditches that pitted the dirt paths. What is now downtown New York was a pleasant countryside with little ponds, lofty trees, rolling hills, and a scattering of farm houses and church steeples. To get to Brooklyn, one had to row across the river in a boat.

The filth throughout the city was such as to disgust the fastidious; even on the better residential blocks, pigs rooted around in the garbage. Dust, ashes, leaves, and manure were pushed to the center of the streets. After a rainstorm, women trailed their skirts through rivers of foul-smelling mud. Cleanliness in a city without running water was a luxury for the rich only. There was as yet no reservoir, and housewives ran to the public pumps at the street corners for their drinking water. The "Tea Water Pump" in what later became the business district was the source of the city's best water.

For years it was peddled through the streets in casks labeled TEA WATER—2 ¢ A PAIL.

The population of less than 30,000 was roughly equivalent to that of Hackensack, New Jersey, or Jefferson City, Missouri, today. Still, if one attempts to see New York through Astor's eyes, it was a crowded, immense, cosmopolitan city. And the spirit of growth was there. The successful conclusion of the Revolutionary War had fired the citizens with enthusiasm to make more of their young country and of this city. This attitude was matched by the boundless ambition of John Jacob. New York was his natural spiritual home, as sleepy Walldorf or tradition-bound London never could have been. The combination of the man, the time, and the place were right; Astor needed America to fulfill himself, and the young growing country needed the dynamism of men like him.

John was welcomed to New York by his brother Henry, who, in the tradition of the family, ran a meat stall in Fulton Market. Henry and his wife, Dorothea were childless and would have liked to take John into their home. They were a wealthy couple already —and were to become even wealthier—because Henry, displaying considerable foresight, was investing his earnings in New York real estate. John decided against remaining with his brother; he had not left Walldorf to become a butcher in New York.

At the beginning, though, it was a moot point whether Astor was stepping up or down, for with only a strong back to offer an employer, his first job was peddling a heavy tray of cakes and cookies through the pitted streets of New York. His next was even more unpleasant—beating the dust and bugs out of furs and then packing them into bales. Wages were two dollars a week and board. The task, which would have been repulsive to anyone not accustomed to the bad smells, blood, and mess of a butcher shop, appeared to Astor as a steppingstone to the glorious future he never for a moment doubted was to be his.

Robert Bowne, his employer, soon began to send John into the wild country north of Albany to trade with the Indians. He struggled through the forests alone on foot, carrying on his back a pack weighted with his supplies and the cheap cloth, tobacco, and bright jewelry that the Indians would accept as payment for their beaver, otter, and musquash (muskrat) skins. The trip back was even more arduous, with the neat pack replaced by bundles of reeking animal pelts. Death was always near at hand; if he were to wander off the ill-marked trails, he might easily stumble into territory occupied by hostile Indians. But John Jacob was not a man to dwell on such possibilities; it was his way to consider only the positive. And he soon found that he enjoyed bargaining, inducing the Indians to part with valuable furs for a trifle of their worth.

His ability became so obvious to Bowne that within a year, Astor was sent on a business trip to London, where his eyes were opened to the facts of fur trade life in the 1780's: a good-sized beaver skin bought from the Indians for a bit of cloth could be sold for forty shillings, a profit of about 900 percent.

John came back from these wanderings to his room in Widow Todd's boardinghouse. Where Astor was on the way up, the Todds were on the way down, poor relations of the powerful and social Brevoort family. The daughter, Sarah, who helped with the housework, was a slender girl, with great big eyes in a thin face. Although his job was exhausting, John was too much his father's son not to have enough energy for love at the day's end. In one of the best moves in a career noted for good moves, John married Sarah Todd. She had two major assets: a $300 dowry and her Brevoort connection. Astor used the money, his first real capital, to open an odd little store where he sold pianos and flutes, in addition to the furs that were to make him famous. As for the Brevoort family connection, this was later to prove extremely valuable to the Astors in their rise to the upper rungs of the social ladder. Neither of these was his reason for marrying Sarah.

Long afterward one of their grandchildren asked him why he had married Sarah, who had become a strict and sometimes cross old lady. John Jacob thought for a moment and answered: "Because she was so pretty."

No one ever expressed similar sentiments about him. His was a strong face, but never a handsome one. The nose was too big, the eyebrows heavy, the eyes small and piercing; and only the thick, fair hair could be described as attractive. (Less that ten years later, when Astor was rich enough to have Gilbert Stuart paint his portrait, he felt that the first version was not flattering enough and insisted that the great artist do another.) Although he was five feet nine inches tall, a good height for a man of the eighteenth century, his square, stocky build made him look shorter. And he was fat before he was middle-aged. But his looks were never the important thing about him. The man was so full of life that it was stimulating to be in his presence. His vitality and drive either attracted or repelled immediately.

When questioned recently about his distinguished ancestor, John Jacob Astor VI remarked: "I've never felt I had anything in common with John Jacob Astor I. He was extroverted and aggressive. But I do feel a real kinship with his wife. She was very shy, and she passed that quality on to her children."

Sarah was not too shy to hold her own against her aggressive husband. She was better able than he to judge the quality of furs, and he knew it. In later years he would ask her for an opinion when a particularly important fur deal was pending. Sarah would study the furs and quietly tell him what they were worth. Her charge for this service: five hundred dollars an hour. John paid her bill promptly and without complaint. He was, perhaps, amused by her businesslike demand, and it had no effect on the warmth of their relationship.

When first married, the young couple worked together as a team, living modestly in rooms right over the store. Sarah was as vigorous as anyone but her husband, and quite capable of managing the shop while he went out to trade for furs in upper New York State and Canada.

John's journeys for Mr. Bowne had shown him that furs were the commodity on which a fortune could be made. As a dealer in musical instruments, he might, like his brother in England, become fairly well-to-do, but there would be a limit to how far he could go. The supply of pianos and flutes and the demand for them were both moderate. On the other hand, most of North America was still a wilderness through which roamed millions upon millions of animals. An energetic trader could obtain countless beaver, otter, seal, and muskrat skins from the Indians. And he could sell every one with ease in an era when houses were poorly heated and traveling was done on foot or in chilly horse-drawn carriages.

One might assume that this self-evident fact would have propelled many ambitious men into the fur trade, but *no* other American exploited its potential in the way that John Jacob did. The business was simply too repulsive, dirty, and dangerous to appeal to gentlemen born to wear clean linen and shoes with silver buckles. They could and did hire middlemen, but anyone who had not dealt with Indians and white trappers personally was ill-equipped to make profitable use of agents. Most men were also put off by the complications and frustrations of the fur business. The British, smarting from their defeat at the hands of the former colonists, stacked the cards against all North Americans. The law was that any furs bought in British territory, which included Montreal and most frontier posts, had to be shipped to London and only then sent back to New York.

None of this flustered Astor. He was no gentleman. If there was money to be made, he would make it, no matter how difficult, strenuous, or abhorrent, the work involved might be. He had staggered beneath a heavy pack for Bowne's benefit; he would do it for his own. Knowing how cheaply the Indians could be induced to part with their furs, he was convinced that even after sending them to London and back, he could still make a good profit.

Before long, this backbreaking business began to pay off, and John Jacob started to look around for investment opportunities. His brother Henry gave him a piece of good advice: buy land. As a matter of fact, Henry just happened to have a few lots on the Bowery Road available. In less than two years John put exactly $6,898.75 of the earnings from his store into real estate. It was just a sideline to him. Only hindsight makes it appear important.

Forty years were to pass before Astor was to say wistfully: "Could I begin life again, knowing what I now know and had money to invest, I would buy every foot of land on the island of Manhattan."

While the Astor fortune was growing, so was his family. Although running the shop with quiet efficiency downstairs, Sarah managed to bear eight children upstairs. Five of them lived, a fairly good record for the period. Three years after giving birth to a daughter, Magdalen, Sarah produced the eagerly awaited son, who was proudly made his father's namesake. It soon became clear, however, that something was very wrong with John Jacob Astor II. Most written accounts of the time refer to him as an imbecile. In the absence of intelligence tests and psychiatrists' reports, it is hard to be sure just what was the matter with the youth. Descriptions of his behavior, though, point strongly to his having been insane, rather than a moron. Throughout his life, John Jacob II had periods of lucidity, and there were times when he was clearheaded enough to write some poetry.

Like most parents with sick or defective children, the Astors never gave up hope that the boy would one day become normal. For years John Jacob I kept this son at home and insisted that he be treated as if nothing were wrong with him, an obviously impossible demand. Astor's unquenchable optimism is revealed in a somewhat touching postscript to his life: there is a clause in the will increasing the inheritance for John Jacob II, should he ever change, despite the fact that he was 57 years old during his father's last illness.

But John Jacob I was not to be cheated of his heir. William Backhouse Astor was born in 1792 to carry on the Astor name and, in time, the family fortune. Two daughters, Dorothea and Eliza, followed. To them, Astor showed one of the other sides of his multifaceted nature. He was warm, loving, even doting—but, inevitably, with his personality, overpowering. If his children never showed more than a modicum of their father's brilliance, perhaps it is because he did not let them. "Father knows best" was the policy of the home, and at least in terms of building a fortune, it was the right one. It has often been said that the Astors made and kept more money for longer than any other family in American history. The statement is true but incomplete. The Astors made and kept this money by dutifully following the orders of John Jacob I.

As with the hero of a Horatio Alger novel, Astor relied princi-pally on hard work to raise himself from rags to riches. But the parallel is even closer in that John, like the storybook figure, needed a stroke of luck. His lucky break was not the rescue of an old millionaire or stockbroker, but the passage of a treaty with Great Britain, ending the awkward back-and-forth fur game. According to this agreement, negotiated by statesman John Jay in 1796, furs bought in Canada could be sent directly to New York without first going to England.

"Now I will make my fortune in the fur trade!" exclaimed Astor when he heard the news.

The modification of restrictions stimulated trade in New York and was of the utmost significance to the growth of this city. No single person, however, was benefited quite so much as Astor. Hundreds of thousands of skins poured over the border to his storeroom. John Jacob no longer traveled himself; although only in his early thirties, his health had been affected by the excessive exertions of his youth. The agents he hired were not left on their own initiative any more than were his children. Astor ran the business with an iron hand. At his instigation, his men went ever deeper into the wilderness to set up trading posts where the Indians could bring the pelts of the animals they had trapped. Fur traders and missionaries, went a saying of the time, go where no white man has ever been before. It is all too easy to see which of them had more of an influence on the Indians.

Four years after the treaty was signed, Astor was worth a quarter of a million dollars, a tremendous fortune for 1800, a time when a whole family could live comfortably on $750 a year. Unable to forget the poverty of his youth, he remained careful about personal expenditures. It was only at this point that he decided he could afford to move the store away from home. After waiting an additional three years just to be sure that this extravagance would not prove ruinous, he took somewhat larger quarters for his family, too. He did not lose his head even then and only moved down the block to 233 Broadway, and kept some of the rooms for his office. Two establishments were possible; three were simply wasteful.

Astor put every penny he earned to a definite use. This inherited trait inspired his great-great-grandson, Vincent Astor, to say a century and a half later, "Every dollar is a soldier to do your bidding."

In the early years of the nineteenth century, John Jacob launched a two-point program to turn his money into more money: first, to find a new market for his furs, and second, to diversify the stock carried in his store. At that time, silks, spices and tea were scarce and valued commodities. If he were to sell furs in China, he could invest in these desirable products on the spot and have his ship return to New York with a cargo even more valuable than the original one.

No one else had attempted such a plan, because it was clearly impossible with the British East India Company in full control of trade with the Orient. Astor, to whom the impossible was merely a challenge, went to England and inveigled the company into giving him permission to take ships into any of its ports. To explain this surprising action by the British, Astor's competitors later insisted that he had pull—an old friend from Walldorf was working for the company. No such friend has ever been found; any pull John Jacob may have had was surely financial. And the East India Company probably underrated him. Selling furs to the Chinese must have struck anyone but Astor as akin to selling ice to the Eskimos. After all, northern China and nearby Russia both contained vast numbers of fur-bearing animals. But if any man could break into that Chinese market, Astor could do it, and he did.

He bought a share of a ship, then a whole ship, then a fleet of ships, and within a few years was the dominant figure in the China trade. His very best furs, first checked by Sarah's trained eye, went to China. He called upon his trappers to furnish so many of the sea otter pelts favored by the wealthy citizens of Canton and Shanghai that the species faced extinction. Astor was indifferent; his profit on the silks, tea, and spices sold in America was tremendous.

Even then he was not satisfied with the fortune he was making. Discontent was a key element of his personality. It had taken him out of Walldorf and then London, had lifted him from a start as a street peddler to the possessor of hundreds of thousands of dollars, and still that was not enough. There was always a way for an alert man to earn a little more. Astor's ships broke their journey at the Hawaiian Islands to take on food and water. What might Hawaii have to offer a rising tycoon? It did not take John Jacob long to figure that out. Sandalwood was plentiful there, and so he instructed his agents to buy it—cheaply, of course—and add it to the cargo. This lovely wood became popular both here and in China, and Astor's monopoly of the sandalwood trade endured for nearly twenty years. Toward the end of that time, he branched out into opium, which his ships picked up in Smyrna. He gave up on the drug traffic after a few years, however, probably not for moral reasons—Astor's moral code was never known to interfere with business—but because the profits were not large enough to be worth the risk.

His powerful position as a shipper was not maintained easily, but obstacles only stimulated him. He liked to quote the homily "Make the best of things," which invariably worked, because Astor took whatever action was needed to make them best for him. At one time during the uneasy period preceding the War of 1812, an embargo kept all American ships locked in New York harbor. Astor did not fight the government decree openly; he was growing older and craftier. Surely there must be some way to get a ship from New York to China. John Jacob dispatched a Chinese mandarin, Punqua Wing-chong to Senator Samuel Mitchell of New York with the perfectly reasonable request that he be returned home for his father's funeral. Mitchell sent a letter to the President, describing the mandarin's plight. Thomas Jefferson kindly gave his permission for Punqua to be taken home on the American ship *Beaver*. The name alone might have been a hint to the observant that a fur merchant was owner of the ship, but no one noticed the connection until the loading of a huge cargo of fine furs began. Astor then pointed out blandly that it would be ridiculous to send out a big ship carrying only a single Chinese gentleman. The other merchants and shipowners rushed to write letters, sign petitions, and issue complaints. It was too late. Jefferson had approved the sailing of the *Beaver*, and sail it did—and return, too, with a cargo of tea and silk and sandalwood and spices. As it was the first ship to come to New York in more than a year, Astor was able to raise prices on everything and earned more than $200,000 from that one voyage.

A few years later rumors of another impending blockade sent John Jacob into fast but efficient action. Staying on the dock himself to direct the operation, he was determined to get one of his ships loaded and out of the port over a single weekend. When he sent the workers home at ten o'clock on Saturday night, he ordered them to return first thing Sunday morning—with the exception of one very religious man. "You go to church," said Astor, "and pray for us poor sinners hard at work."

His wife Sarah would have been horrified if she knew; religion was the comfort and mainstay of her life. Astor seldom attended church himself, excusing his absence on physical grounds: "I cannot sit in church. I have a painful disorder that prevents me." (A fistula, medical reports of the period indicate.) By then John Jacob was no longer a member of the Lutheran church of his boyhood, and what little churchgoing he did was to the Reformed, which was somewhat more highly regarded socially, though not on a par with the Episcopal.

By the time Astor was in his late twenties, he had grasped the importance of going where the money was and getting acquainted with men of prominence. He became a Mason, joining Holland Lodge No. 8, which counted Henry Livingston and George Clinton, first governor of New York, among its members. In 1792 he bought a share in the Tontine Coffee House (ostensibly for his tiny daughter Magdalen), which was frequented by members of the Merchants Exchange. He was often to be found there himself, eating raw codfish and drinking a glass of red wine. Learning that such eminent personages of the day as General John Armstrong II, war hero and politician, patronized Mrs. Keese's boardinghouse at the corner of Wall Street and Broadway, he made a point of dropping in. Through the friends he made there, he was introduced to Stephen Van Rensselaer, then lieutenant governor of New York, and Aaron Burr. All of these connections assisted him immeasurably when the time came for him to use them. Most political figures and businessmen were members of the inner circle of the society of the period, yet they did not bar Astor. His social and business activities became ever more closely interrelated, an incredible accomplishment for a man of his origins.

The Old Guard of New York society was made up of descendants of the original Dutch settlers of New Amsterdam and members of wealthy English, Scotch, Irish, and Welsh families. They still lived like the landed gentry of Europe, protected by their wealth from the rigors of life in the new country. A veritable army of servants and slaves—slavery in New York was not abolished by law until 1826—saw to their comfort. The old-world standard was maintained: either one was born a gentleman or not.

It would be natural to assume that Astor, a butcher's son with poor manners and a strong foreign accent, would never be welcomed into the company of such gentlefolk as the Livingstons, De Peysters, Beekmans, and Morrises. These and other leading families had founded the New York Society Library in 1754 for the exclusive use of people like themselves. Reading in the eighteenth century was, after all, a pasttime for gentlemen only. And yet in the late 1790's, Astor was invited to subscribe to this fashionable library.

How was this boorish businessman able to breach the wall separating the Old Guard from other people? John Jacob's wealth, of course, made the first wedge. His wife's Brevoort connections widened the opening, although Sarah seldom had either the time or the inclination to accompany him to social affairs. But perhaps most responsible for Astor's swift rise into the world of gentlemen was his fascinating personality. Despite the accent, John Jacob I was a lively and interesting conversationalist. And those who were impervious to his charm sensed even early in his career that here was a man who would surely wield great power.

Not all of those who invited him to dine accepted him as a gentleman. Oldest of the Old Guard, Stephen Van Rensselaer, was silent on the subject. Albert Gallatin, Secretary of the Treasury under Jefferson, told his intimates that there were no two ways about it: Astor was simply not of his class. This appraisal did not, however, prevent Gallatin from spending a lot of time with John Jacob anyway, both in business ventures and socially.

At one dinner party Astor wiped his fingers on the sleeve of the lady seated next to him.

"Oh, Mr. Astor," fluttered the hostess. "I must have forgotten to give you a serviette [napkin]."

Although John's manners were not suitable for high society, they were no worse than the average. An etiquette book of the time found it imperative to advise that "nothing but sheer necessity can excuse any teeth picking at the table" and "it is not 'comme il faut' for gentlemen to blow their noses with their fingers."

Sometimes an invitation to dinner was motivated by the emotion described in the bittersweet saying "It's as easy to fall in love with a rich girl as a poor one." Astor, ever the indulgent father, took his spoiled temperamental eldest daughter, Magdalen, along on several of his trading missions to Montreal. Samuel Bridge, an English merchant, asked them to dine, confiding in his diary: "A Miss Astor from New York (her father who is at present here is said to be worth £200,000—the report says he will give this daughter £25,-

ooo)." Despite this temptation, Bridge did not marry Magdalen.

For this he was much envied by the man who did, Adrian Bentzon, a one-time governor of the Virgin Islands. At the wedding in 1807, Astor declared him to be the ideal son-in-law and, as the supreme accolade, allowed Bentzon to serve as a business representative. Adrian lacked only one attribute to deserve fully that adjective *ideal:* the ability to get along with Magdalen. Always a self-centered girl, she became embittered by the tragedies that touched her life. Her eldest son, named John Jacob Astor, in an attempt to make up to her father for his disappointment in her brother, was tragically drowned in an accident. A second child, a daughter, died in infancy.

After this there was little hope for the marriage. Adrian not only made love to another woman, he virtually shouted his adultery from the rooftops. In other nineteenth-century families, marriage had to be endured, no matter how miserable husband or wife might be. Not in the Astor family. The situation was insupportable, so John Jacob set out to correct it. His darling Magdalen could not be left with an admitted adulterer. Separation was no solution, because it would prevent her from finding another—hopefully more pliable—husband. What she needed was a divorce, and her powerful father got her one.

New York society was shaken, but Magdalen was unperturbed. With her father's backing, there was not the slightest possibility of her remaining a grass widow, and indeed another husband was found within the year. This time it was an Englishman, the Reverend John Bristed. (Unkind tongues whispered that no one in New York was willing to take Magdalen, no matter how rich her father was.)

Bristed soon fled back to England. "It is impossible to stay with that maniac!" he exclaimed, as he boarded the ship.

He had stayed with her long enough to father a son, Charles Astor Bristed, who was to be the comfort of his grandfather's old age.

But Astor's real comfort in life was always business. Because even the highly profitable China trade was based on furs, by 1808 he decided that it was time for him to become *the* power in the fur trade. *Monopoly* was one of his favorite words—provided it was his. He had been buying most of his skins in Canada, but new frontiers were opening. Lewis and Clark had completed their successful expedition through the Far West in 1806, and suddenly the young nation's attention was focused on this immense unexplored territory. Its significance was clear to all men of vision, and Astor saw it from his own particular viewpoint, that of the businessman. The moment was at hand, he believed, to gain possession of the valuable animals in the wild country west and northwest of the Great Lakes. To go after these, John founded the American Fur Company. This brought him into direct competition with the British-run North West Company, which dominated fur trading in the area. Competition, of course, was something Astor thrived on.

He decided to establish a fur empire—a chain of trading posts along the Missouri and Columbia rivers and their tributory streams—with a capital to be named Astoria situated at the mouth of the Columbia River. Astor was coming to enjoy power and saw himself as the Alexander the Great of the business world, with Astoria as his Alexandria.

Although checkers, not chess, was his game, John Jacob considered all possible countermoves to every move he made. He therefore decided to befriend the Russians also gathering furs in the northern wilderness. His ship, he suggested, could supply their traders as well as his own on its annual trip to Astoria. In this way, he would have only the British pitted against him.

Two expeditions set off on the hazardous westward journey to the mouth of the Columbia River, one by land and one by sea. By then Astor was friends with every leading political figure in the country, starting with the President, and it seemed only natural for James Madison as a favor to ask the Navy to give a leave to Lieutenant Jonathan Thorn so that he could command John's ship, the *Tonquin*. It was to be the most unfortunate favor ever done Astor.

Early in the voyage, Thorn's treatment of the crew was so cruel that Alexander McKay, one of Astor's partners, exclaimed to the mate: "I fear we are in the hands of a lunatic!"

Thorn brought the *Tonquin* to the mouth of the Columbia River, got the building of Fort Astoria underway, and set off to begin his disastrous fur-trading negotiations with the still savage Salish Indians. It was then that McKay's fear was proven true.

When the chief demanded a high price for the skins, Thorn hit him in the face with an otter skin. McKay tried to remonstrate, but in vain. The lieutenant was unable to view red men as thinking human beings. When the canny Indian chief suggested an exchange of furs for knives, Thorn jumped at this favorable arrangement.

Astor, who had first-hand experience at dealing with Indians, had given Thorn one piece of advice before the *Tonquin* sailed: "Don't let too many Indians on board at a time."

Thorn would not take advice from a civilian. When enough Indians on board had knives, they turned on the white men and hacked them to ribbons. Two Indian braves seized the hapless Mc-Kay, lifted him high over their heads, and dropped him overboard. He fell into a war canoe loaded with squaws who killed him with cooking utensils. Thorn, at last realizing what he had done, went down fighting gallantly.

The tragic news reached Astor on a night when he planned to go to the theater, one of his favorite diversions. He refused to change his plans.

"What would you have me do?" he asked a friend who expressed dismay at his seeming coldness. "Would you have me stay at home and weep for what I cannot help?" (This careful phrasing probably owes a debt to Washington Irving, who has given the account of this incident to posterity; the language is too refined for Astor.)

This was his attitude in all adversity, and it stood him in good stead, for the reports coming from the land expedition to Astoria were not much better. The travelers struggling through forests and deserts endured nearly two years of unbelievable suffering, hardship, and hunger so great that they killed and ate their horses. Some were massacred by hostile Indians, and others drowned in a mistaken effort to journey down the Snake River by canoe. In 1812 the emaciated, exhausted survivors straggled into Astoria.

As soon as they recovered their strength, they took part in the building of the trading post and fort there. They made a small schooner of fir timbers, and still thought kindly enough of their employer to name it the "Dolly" after Astor's daughter Dorothea. The schooner sailed up the Columbia River, and trading posts were set up at places that later became Boise, Salem, and Spokane.

At last it looked as if Astor's dream of empire might become a reality. And then for the only time in his life, history played him false. The War of 1812 broke out at the critical moment in the building of the new enterprise. Despite monumental efforts by Astor to get a ship there in time to defend it, Astoria fell to the British, and the Union Jack was hoisted above the fort that Astor's men had so laboriously and painfully constructed.

To render John Jacob's defeat complete, his agents at Astoria knuckled under to the British North West Company. More than $200,000 worth of furs was sold for less than $80,500. Otter skins valued at five dollars apiece went for fifty cents.

This has gone down in history as Astor's one great defeat. It was not the nature of the man to be defeated. "While I breath and so long as I have a dollar to spend I'll pursue a course to have our injuries repair'd," he wrote to an associate. "And when I am no more, I hope you'll act in my place; we have been sold, but I do not dispond." (The spelling is Astor's.)

He went on from that low point to one success after another. As for Astoria, even there his efforts were not in vain. After the war, Astoria was returned to the United States by the Treaty of Ghent. It helped to establish the American claim to the Oregon country, which became a state of the union in 1859.

In later years Astor was to look back on his dream of empire with few regrets, proud of the role he had played in opening the West. When he was old, he asked "Vashington Irving" to write the story of this great doomed venture. "It was a magnificent enterprise," wrote Irving. And the failure was not Astor's fault.

The war years did bring Astor one other disaster, however, or so he viewed it. While visiting his prominent friends, the Albert Gallatins, in Washington, his daughter Dorothea, then seventeen years old, fell madly in love with dashing Colonel Walter Langdon. Gallatin, aware of what counted, immediately warned her father that the suitor had no money. John Jacob was appalled. He loved Dolly, but this was really too much. Completely confident himself, he simply could not imagine what Langdon meant to the girl who was usually unkindly called "this fat German Dolly." Her mother, the one person who might have influenced Astor, remained silent. Faced with her father's opposition, the young couple eloped.

For many years Astor would have nothing to do with them. This did not succeed in cooling their ardor; they produced eight children. Any number of sugary stories about the reconciliation have been passed on in the family, and some of them may even be true. John Jacob was a German, and sentimental. The most frequently told of these stories takes Astor to a party at the house of a friend where a pretty little girl is romping about merrily. Something about her face brings a lump to his throat.

"What is your name, little girl?"

"Sarah Sherburne Langdon," she lisps prettily.

He looks into her eyes and gives a deep sigh. "For your sake, I shall have to forgive your father and your mother."

The reconciliation meant that the Langdons could buy an estate, Hyde Park, and that the colonel could live like a gentleman on his father-in-law's bounty.

Astor could well afford such largesse by then; his setback at Astoria had caused him to falter but a moment on his road to financial greatness. Once the war was over, he went right back into the fur business, like a rider who has been thrown once and is determined to show the horse who is boss. His American Fur Company became one of the most powerful in the country. Just as his grandson's wife was to be known simply as *the* Mrs. Astor, so was his fur company known to John Jacob's contemporaries as *the* Company.

Dirty, unscrupulous, immoral, inhumane, and inhuman—that was the fur trade of the time, and Astor, seeing only profits not human beings, was the master of it. The American conquest of the West owes a great debt to the fur companies, with their hunters, trappers, and agents, but some of the guilt for the debasing of the American Indian must be borne by them, too. The law forbade the sale of liquor to the Indians, but "the American Fur Company," charge reports of the period, "was above the law."

"He who has the most whisky generally carries off the most furs," groaned Colonel J. Snelling, who had the hopeless assignment of keeping liquor out of the area west of Detroit.

All the fur traders leaned heavily on liquor in their dealings with the Indians, but, as in everything, Astor was better at making use of it. His agents actually operated their own still. The Indians, befuddled, lost track of fur prices. In any event, they were charged so much for the liquor and worthless merchandise being offered as barter that they were sometimes in debt to *the* Company. One year Astor reported that the Winnebagos, Sacs, and Foxes owed him $50,000, and this was at a time when a pack of beaver pelts was valued at $180. The Indians were not even cheated with good liquor. One agent wrote down his recipe: alcohol cut with water and pepped up with red pepper and tobacco. It cost him five cents a gallon to make. The Indians paid fifty cents for a small bottle.

Astor and his fellow rulers of the fur trade were no kinder to their white workmen, the *engagés*, hired for $100 a year until John Jacob decided that $250 for three years was more than enough. The labor they performed was so backbreaking that few survived for long, whatever the pay. Their immediate employers, the traders, were kept so deeply in debt to the company by means of the inordinate prices charged them for supplies that they sometimes had the *engagés* murdered when the time came to pay the wages owing.

John Jacob's prominence in the fur business was not due solely to unscrupulous methods coupled with financial genius; it was also a result of his ability to make and use influential friends. The most important growth years for the American Fur Company fell during the administration of James Monroe. The statesman was often in need of money, and Astor was always ready with a loan.

"It may not bee convenient to repay me the Sume Lend to you nor am I particularly in want of it," went a letter from Astor to the President. (Three years after Monroe's term of office expired, Astor demanded repayment, quite unmoved by the fact that the ex-President was so short of money that he had to sell some of his slaves. By then, though, John Quincy Adams, whom Astor had been courting assiduously for some years, had assumed the Presidency.)

While Monroe was still President, Astor expected and obtained special favors. As he once told his son, "To give something for nothing is to weaken the giver." Contemporaries declared that measures virtually written by Astor were regularly introduced into

Congress. There was even a loophole in the liquor law, permitting whisky to be provided for "boatmen." A law barred Canadians from the American fur trade, a pro-American piece of legislation that sounds natural enough, but that in practice was passed for Astor alone. And when John Jacob found that he needed Canadians for the heavy labor, he simply asked Monroe to exempt them, so that the law in effect only prohibited Canadian entrepreneurs from operating here.

Monroe delegated the authority for dealing with all complaints against the American Fur Company to Governor Lewis Cass of the Michigan Territory. A study of the books of the American Fur Company reveals a curious payment of $35,000 to Cass. No hint is given as to what he was paid for, but he clearly never spoke an unkind word to Astor's agents.

With such aid, *the* Company took over many of the trading posts of its competitors. The United States government, however, was also maintaining trading posts at which no liquor was sold and the rights of the Indians were zealously guarded. It was not quite so easy for private companies to compete with their own government's trading posts. The best thing to do, then, was to abolish them. Before long Senator Thomas Hart Benton of Missouri, who just happened to be lawyer for the American Fur Company, was addressing Congress in favor of free trade. Astor brought both direct and indirect pressure to bear on other legislators, and in 1822 the government decided to close its trading posts.

John Jacob went on and on, engulfing his competitors. Soon buyers from all over the world were coming to his spring and fall auctions. On a single day, 550,000 muskrat skins were sold. When he finally disposed of the American Fur Company in 1834 in order to devote himself exclusively to real estate, it had earned two million dollars for him.

A few years ago a book describing how to make a million dollars in real estate in one's spare time was widely read by would-be tycoons. Had that book appeared one hundred and fifty years earlier, only one man could have been the author. At that date real estate was a spare-time activity for John Jacob Astor. When one considers the amount of property he acquired, it becomes clear that what he did would have been a full-time job for anyone else.

There are many ways of making money in real estate, and Astor tried almost all of them. One system is to lend money to landowners who happen to need some ready cash. For a number of years Aaron Burr and John Jacob were neighbors on Broadway. Every schoolchild knows the story of how Burr shot Alexander Hamilton in a duel and had to flee the country; few, however, know where Burr found the money for his escape. It came from his kind neighbor, Mr. Astor. In return, Burr turned over the lease to a huge tract of land in what is now Greenwich Village. This property became one of John Jacob's greatest sources of income.

Mortgage foreclosures are another method for increasing landholdings, and in this way Astor obtained a large farm far above city limits from a debt-ridden whisky distiller. Some years after the foreclosure, the Eden family, heirs of the original owner, discovered some question to Astor's title and appealed to the courts for redress. The Edens may have had the right in the case, but John Jacob had too much political power for any judge to care to say so. The case dragged on for twenty years, until Astor thought of a face-saving way out of the dilemma for everyone. He offered the heirs nine thousand dollars for their claim, and they took it gladly. The Eden farm lay on what was to become Broadway from Forty-second to Forty-sixth Streets. Fifty years after Astor's death, this land was worth twenty million dollars to his heirs.

By the time John Jacob was in his late forties, he was so powerful that those seeking his goodwill came to him with tips, hints, and secret information. One lawyer pointed out that through a legal quibble, a huge tract of valuable land in Putnam County might become available. It had been confiscated from Roger and Mary Morris during the American Revolution, because they were Tories. The tip was that the state had no right to confiscate the land in the first place, because the Morrises held only a lifetime lease on the property. Upon their deaths, it was to go to their three children, who could not be penalized for the political sins of their father. Mrs. Morris was still alive, but Astor, always a man to look ahead, went to the children and bought up their claim for $100,-000. With this in his pocket, Astor settled down to wait for old Mrs. Morris, who was then approaching eighty, to die. She refused to oblige, lingering until 1825 to the age of ninety-six. Astor marked her demise by sending eviction notices to the seven hundred families who had bought farms from the New York State government. These farmers had improved the land and had built houses, barns, and cottages themselves. Nonetheless, John insisted that they were trespassing and that he had the right to take over their homes without paying them a penny. The defense was presented in court by such impressive legal talents as Daniel Webster and Martin Van Buren, but no one could win a case against a man whose circle of friends took in the White House. A plan was worked out by which John Jacob was to give up the land in return for $520,000 in New York State stocks paying 5 percent interest a year. In other words, only the state was the loser.

"Real estate," says a modern speculator, "is just a commodity. Buy it cheap and sell it dear."

This philosophy was Astor's during his early years. Land might have been a part of the inventory of his store or cargo of his ships. Even then he had figured out the key way of extracting the ultimate in profit from a given piece of land. He seldom confided his business policy in anyone. On one occasion, though, in a particularly expansive mood, he told a friend how he operated: "Buy the acre; sell the lot." This policy is still an effective one, as any builder of suburban housing developments could tell you.

Gradually he began to change as he observed how the city was growing. It was no longer the small town of the 1780's, with its population of 30,000. On the first of May, Astor would go down to City Hall Park to see what was going on. Custom had made this the annual moving day in New York, and from all over the city scores of people carrying their possessions would gather in the Park to wait for a house. No one knew where they came from or where they had lived before. Perhaps relatives had sheltered some of them; others may have settled in huts as squatters on the swamplands and forests around the city. Every year at this time they appeared by the thousands. While trying to find homes for them, the city officials would lodge them in the jail. If a house was even half-finished, people would move into it. Officials reported that there was not a vacant house in the city. And yet in a single year 1,969 buildings had gone up.

Leaving the Park, Astor would walk slowly through the city, his squarely built body grown fat and flabby. It was still not easy walking for any man, but now one of the hazards was that of falling into the excavation for a new house. Compared to the city of his youth, however, there were many cobblestone-paved streets. Canal Street had been laid out and went far beyond its start on the rolling fields given the city in the 1790's by John Jay. Bloomingdale Road (Broadway) was extending northward through what had been woods only a short time earlier—nicely cutting through several pieces of Astor property and increasing their value considerably. The Bowery Road led out of the city to distant Harlem. On the East Side, four short avenues, A, B, C, and D ran east of First Avenue. The East Road connected Fifth Avenue with Bloomingdale Road at Twenty-third Street. All this growth had been made essential by the increasing population of the city, from 33,000 in 1790 to 96,000 in 1810 to 124,000 in 1820. Houses went up as fast as builders could work, and stores, banks, and warehouses to serve the people's needs were founded one after the other.

Today it seems obvious that this was only the beginning. But at the time each expansion was considered to be the last. To paraphrase a popular song, most people thought that the city had gone just about as far as it could go. Why, there were farms and country estates in what is now the East Seventies. No one could possibly live there and commute to work in the city. The shortage of homes would be solved by putting up more houses in the residential district below Canal Street.

Astor, always impervious to outside influences, was not affected by this popular view. The boy whose father had given him no guidance had grown into a man who relied on no one but himself. He had seen what furs and international trade—both of which he dominated—had done to stimulate the growth of New York as a commercial center. Packet boats were by this time going regularly from New York to Liverpool, Le Havre, Savannah, Charleston, and New Orleans. In 1820 John Jacob fully expected New York to become what it is today. Using the money he was earning in furs and the China trade he was able to buy land and make history work for him.

He perceived that there was little point in selling land, no matter how big the profit seemed to be. Eventually, it would be worth more than the best price any of his contemporaries could offer him. What is more, the way a piece of land looked today was no indication of the way it would look tomorrow. An arid stretch of farmland would in time become the site of a home, store, or business, and while still a farm, it could not command the price being charged for a lot with a building on it.

With this in mind, Astor sought land that looked worthless and was priced accordingly. He bought dozens of lots on lower Broadway for $200 and $300. It was this vision that made possible the Astor dynasty. Money can be dissipated; land remains.

"Buy and hold. Let others improve." This became Astor's new motto.

The way he devised to get others to improve his property was extremely simple. Astor would give the tenant a long-term lease, usually running for twenty-one years. If the tenant wished to build a house on the land—and he almost always did—he could do so at his own expense. When the lease ran out, Astor had the right to buy the house at its estimated value, and because he was popular and/or generous with politicians, the valuation invariably turned out to be very low. John Jacob often preferred to renew the lease at a rent far higher than the old one; after all, the building made the property so much more valuable. Eventually he made it a condition of the lease that the tenant build a house on the land. He was a strict landlord; it was never wise to fall into arrears on rent payments. Astor knew what was owing him on any given day—at any given hour, whispered some of his tenants.

John Jacob loved his holdings, and kept close watch on each of them. "The roll-book of his possessions was his Bible," asserts one of his biographers.

He liked to spend the little spare time he allowed himself in looking over his properties. Pulling the reference book out of his pocket, he would check what he had paid for a piece of land and calculate what it would be worth now. The difference seldom failed to bring a smile to his thin lips.

During his lifetime he put about two million dollars in real estate. His tenants and the city government helped him to double, redouble, and double again the value of his investment.

Being a shipping tycoon as well as a real-estate investor, John

Jacob felt he had better get the rights to waterfront property. When New York's port facilities became inadequate—and he never doubted that they would —he could build docks and charge for their use. The city, he was also sure, would be obliging enough to extend his property by filling in the river where it was shallow. In this way he would have some lots that had not even existed before. As his descendant, John Jacob VI, has said, Astor was not shy. He did not hesitate to ask for whatever he wanted.

City officials were extremely generous in giving Astor waterfront rights for the smallest possible sums. Nevertheless, he would sometimes have second thoughts and petition for more favorable terms. The rent he was paying might be reduced, or perhaps he might be allowed to forego all payments for a period of say thirty years? The municipal authorities were quite happy to agree. This was an era when money could buy power blatantly. A popular story of the time has a young man being offered a political job: "It's worth $600 a year—besides stealings." In order to gain power, Astor did not need to be a politician. He just needed to control politicians—and he did. Which party? It did not matter. If a man was useful, he was a friend.

Astor's belief in the eventual value of New York land was absorbed by everyone who came into close contact with him. His half-sister Elizabeth, a plump, golden-haired girl, who had also left Walldorf for New York, married a porter employed by her rich brother. This porter, John Gottlieb Wendel, saved every penny he could, and following his employer's example, invested it in land. Wendel so thoroughly indoctrinated his family with the Astor principle of holding onto property that his grandson some years later hung a sign over his office saying NO REAL ESTATE FOR SALE. By that time, the Wendel holdings had increased in value to fifty million dollars. Wendel's consuming worry became his sisters. Surely unscrupulous treasure hunters would try to marry them for their wealth. He warned them against this in such frightening terms that they died multimillionaires and virgins still. Ella, the last of them, died in 1931 clutching seventy-five million dollars to her untouched bosom. The only creature she had dared to love was her dog.

John Jacob Astor I, to whom their fate can ultimately be traced, never considered money as a substitute for love. The tragedy of his life was the condition of his eldest son. In the early 1820's he took John Jacob II to Paris, hoping that French doctors could do what American had not. At home a doctor-companion was with the unstable young fellow every moment. Whenever he became boisterous, the doctor would quiet him with a firm admonition, "Astor, be a man." Things were no better in Paris, and John had to be sent home, where for a time he was confined to an institution. Eventually his father built a special house for him at Ninth Avenue and Fourteenth Street. A high fence protected him from the curious, some of whom crossed themselves as they went by.

John Jacob I found his greatest consolation in the company of his youngest and favorite daughter, Eliza. Even today the incredible sweetness of her face lights up the faded portrait of her that remains. Her eyes are glowing, her mouth so gentle that it is impossible to imagine her saying an unkind word. She accompanied her father on many of his trips and acted as hostess at the villa, Genthod, he maintained in Geneva. Her presence was quite essential to Astor, because being a doer and talker, he hated to travel alone and Sarah considered Albany about as distant a place as any decent wife could be expected to go. Magdalen and Dorothea had children of their own to care for, and William Backhouse was needed at home to mind the store. Travel was necessary for Astor, who had to see for himself what possibilities for profit were untapped in Canada, the Great Lakes region, or Europe; only then could he assign duties to underlings.

On one of the trips he performed the fatherly duty of arranging a marriage for Eliza with Count Vincent von Rumpff, minister of the German Free Cities. Gossips said that she was really in love with a Vermont dentist, Eleazar Parmly, but that her father had wanted a much grander marriage for her. He had whisked her off to Paris and forced her to marry von Rumpff. In the meantime, her mother had tried to foil John Jacob and to help the young lovers. She had sent for Parmly, had given him a thousand dollars to cover his expenses, and told him to leave for Europe and save Eliza. Alas, he had arrived too late! The facts do not back up this romantic story. The panting young lover arrived in Paris not a few days, weeks, or months too late to seize his beloved in his arms, but two whole years after her marriage.

The one undeniable fact is that John Jacob was delighted with his new son-in-law. Von Rumpff got him entree to the courts of the lesser German princes, had him presented to Charles X and to Louis Philippe, and arranged for him to attend the coronation of Ferdinand II at Naples. Astor did not really understand New York society. Acceptance by the Old Guard meant rather little to him. He was pleased when he succeeded in arranging an inner-circle marriage between his son William Backhouse and the daughter of prominent John Armstrong. But the social connotations of that union did not seem exciting to a man dazzled by the glamor of royalty. When he was received at European courts, Astor felt that he had really arrived socially.

As for Eliza, was she happy? If not, she never said so. She became very religious, establishing Sunday schools for children and inviting guests to what she called "religious soirées." The first hour and a half of these evenings was devoted to reading the Bible and praying, the balance to refreshments and lighter conversation.

One day Eliza received from a friend in New York a parcel wrapped in a religious newspaper. Glancing idly at the paper, she observed that it reported on a sermon preached in New York. If John Jacob Astor gave a promissory note, the minister had said, no one would hesitate to take it, because they would have faith in his word. People should have the same confidence in God. Eliza cut out the clipping with her little scissors and sent it to her father. He was desolate when she died, childless, at the age of thirty-seven.

Eliza's demise followed a number of other deaths in the family. In 1832 Astor went abroad—this time for his health, rather than his business or social life. Although his mental vigor was unimpaired by the passing years, his physical strength was breaking down. The change of scene had not helped him, he complained moodily on the ship returning home. The news that was awaiting him was hardly of a type to make him feel better. During his absence his wife Sarah had died. The same fate had befallen his daughter Magdalen, one of his granddaughters, his brother Henry, the butcher, and his half-sister Elizabeth.

Unable to live alone, Astor took his grandson Charles Astor Bristed into his home. He invited Washington Irving to come and stay with him while writing the story of Astoria. For the most part, though, he buried his grief in his business, working with the dogged zeal to which he attributed his success.

"The man who makes it the habit of his life to go to bed at nine o'clock usually gets rich," he advised his quiet son William. "Of course, going to bed does not make him rich—I merely mean that such a man will in all probability be up early in the morning and do a big day's work . . . it's all a matter of habit and good habits in America make any man rich."

For all his brilliance, he had the methodical mind of the German and appeared to feel that his daily habit of breaking his working day after lunch to play three—never two or four—games of checkers and to drink one—never more—glass of beer was also behind his incredible wealth.

As he grew older, he began to live a little more comfortably. Summers were spent at his country estate—a lovely house with lawns sloping down to the water's edge—at Hellgate (now Eighty-eighth Street and Second Avenue; the East River came farther inland then than now). He had left his modest home at Broadway and Vesey Street for a finer one on Broadway near Prince Street, and had it filled with works of art to which he paid scant attention. The skin of an otter hanging on the wall meant much more to him. His piercing eyes would soften as he looked at the fine fur, and every so often he would stroke it gently. "How soft and beautiful it is!" he would murmur. To him the otter was a symbol of the business that had laid the foundation for his immense fortune. He never forgot that without furs there would have been no real estate.

John Jacob Astor became a millionaire by 1830 and a multimillionaire soon afterward. The great depression of that decade, the panic of 1837, impoverished thousands and enriched a handful of men, among them Astor.

"Two hundred and sixty houses have already failed, and no one knows when it is to end," wrote Captain Frederick Marryat, the British novelist, who visited New York at that time. "Had I not been aware of the cause, I should have imagined that the plague was raging. Not a smile on one countenance."

That last sentence cannot be wholly accurate. Astor at least had cause to smile. His name appears in sixty mortgage foreclosures. He took over a farm on what later became an incredibly valuable piece of East Side Manhattan property for twenty thousand dollars. But he seldom needed to pay so much; an entire block in Harlem became his for two thousand dollars. The panic went on, and John, one of the few men in New York with ready cash, was able to buy property all over the city. Desperate landowners were willing to sell at any price. Astor bought some lots for such low figures that the courts later insisted that he pay a little more.

Where money was concerned, John Jacob was never softhearted, but the panic did lead to one of his very few gestures of financial kindness. Gerrit Smith, the son of a former associate, was lent $200,000 to save him from bankruptcy.

By the time the panic was over Astor was so rich that he could hardly remember another way of life.

"A man who has a million dollars is as well off as if he were rich," he consoled a less fortunate friend.

Still, the panic did do him some harm. It gave him New York, but took away his chance of owning the West. During the 1820's and 1830's, while operating his nationwide fur business, he picked up considerable property around St. Louis, as well as territory in Wisconsin, Ohio, and Illinois. Gradually the dream of empire, lost for a time in the misfortunes that befell Astoria, awakened again and he determined to found a city in Wisconsin that would bear the proud name of "Astor."

But Wisconsin was not New York, and settlers were not eager to buy building lots from him, particularly as he persisted in the belief that any land was valuable if he owned it. The panic of 1837, so helpful in New York, was disastrous in Wisconsin. To turn "Astor" into a going community required investors with capital, not mortgage foreclosures.

In time "Astor" simply became a part of the city of Green Bay, proving that John Jacob could not function as a long-distance empire builder. As a final ironic twist, the State Historical Society of Wisconsin today reports that there is no documentation of the town's ever having existed. All records were destroyed in a fire. The only connection between the Astors now and that long-ago dream is through Charlotte Fisk Astor, wife of John's great-great-great-grandson. She is a native of Green Bay.

Astor's disappointment was considerably modified by the success he was meeting in all other areas. Unquestioned ruler of Manhattan real estate, at the age of seventy he decided to go into a new business, that of hotel owner.

When planning the building of the Park Hotel (soon renamed Astor House), he went to dinner with a friend at another new hotel.

"This man will never succeed," said Astor.

"Why not?"

"Don't you see what large lumps of sugar he puts in the bowl?"

Despite this niggardly attitude, John Jacob was determined to make his the finest hotel in the world. He set out to buy the entire block front on Broadway between Vesey and Barclay Streets, where he had lived for a quarter of a century. Many of the neighbors objected to the erection of a commercial hotel in such an exclusive section, but only one home owner put his objection in a form that mattered to Astor—that is, refusal to sell. This man, Coster, held out in a manner that would have done Astor himself credit. He finally agreed to sell for $60,000, nearly twice the valuation of the house and land. Even then, he would not move out. The wreckers came and began demolishing the buildings on the block until only the Coster house was left. The workers came and asked Astor what to do.

"Just start tearing down the house anyhow," he said, "and—by the way—you might begin by taking away the steps."

Once this snag was out of the way the hotel went up, six stories high and with three hundred bedrooms. Astor felt that ten "bathing rooms" would be more than enough, but was talked into seventeen. His yielding was as usual apparent, not real; the gentlemen to whom he was leasing the hotel found themselves footing the bill.

The furniture of the bedrooms was of black walnut, considered the last word in elegance. A bowl and pitcher and free soap were placed in every room. An attendant was always on duty to take hats and coats; another brushed the shoes of guests. Space on the lower floors was rented to five tailors, a barber, a wigmaker, a jeweler, a trussmaker, and nine other shopkeepers. The dining room tempted the most demanding guest with stewed kidneys in champagne sauce, corned leg of pork, roast loin of veal, boiled chicken and pork, and a perfect soft vanilla custard that was admired as far north as Twenty-third Street. The wine list boasted sixteen different sherries and twenty Madeiras.

From the day it was opened in 1836, the Astor House became a center for politicians and visiting celebrities. Abraham Lincoln, Henry Clay (Astor once lent him $20,000), Jefferson Davis, Jenny Lind, Edgar Allan Poe (he got the idea for "The Mystery of Marie Roget" there), William Thackeray, and the Prince of Wales (later Edward VII) were just a few of the guests. The foreigners were somewhat dismayed by their view of New York. Charles Dickens stood on the steps before the main entrance and was horrified by the sight of pigs gobbling up the garbage.

American citizens took the dirt more philosophically. Daniel Webster was undismayed. "If I were shut out of the Astor House, I would never again go to New York," he declared.

When Davy Crockett stayed there, he was amazed to hear how much Astor had spent on the hotel. Assuming that the money came out of the fur business, he exclaimed: "Lord help the poor b'ars and beavers! They must be used to being skun by now."

Some of the guests might have felt that they, too, were being "skinned,"with the daily rate of two dollars, American plan. James Gordon Bennett soon began to list the arrivals at the Astor House in his new newspaper, the New York *Herald*. "Anyone who can pay two dollars a day for a room must be important," he told his staff. Bennett was one of the first editors to realize that gossip about society sells newspapers.

Astor wanted his hotel to last forever. It stood for only eighty years. But for hotels, "forty years in America is like 300 in Europe," according to an articulate modern hotel manager. One half of the Astor House was torn down when the subway was being constructed. John Jacob would not have minded too much: the subway increased the value of Astor property by then in the hands of his descendants. Vincent Astor, in fact, was so rich that he was able to indulge himself in the ultimate of luxuries—he maintained an unprofitable hotel, because he liked to go there for lunch. In this, he most certainly did not resemble his great-great-grandfather, who would never have held on to anything that did not bring a profit.

As Astor grew old, the thoughts of those around him turned to the charity he might be doing. A study put out by the New York *Sun* had named him the richest man in America, with a fortune of twenty million dollars. Cornelius Vanderbilt's wealth was at that time a mere one and a half million dollars; department store tycoon Alexander Stewart had two million dollars; the Goelets, with a big chunk of New York real estate, were put down at two million dollars also.

A minister called on John Jacob, seeking a contribution for a worthy cause. "You are indeed fortunate to have such a great fortune," he began confidently. "It increases your ability to do good."

"Oh, the disposition to do good does not always increase with the means," replied Astor coolly, an attitude shared by many men of wealth. Even in the enlightened 1960's, a *New York Times* reporter tracked down the fact that fifteen modern millionaires are contributing less than five hundred dollars a year to charity.

John Jacob was not at all concerned with what others thought. On another occasion he refused to give to a charity, claiming that he simply did not have the money.

His secretary, Fitz-Greene Halleck, who took a perverse delight in needling his employer, spoke up: "If you're out of money, Mr. Astor, I'll endorse your note for a few hundred."

John Jacob's one great charity was the Astor Library, which was to be the basis of the New York Public Library. The money for this was wheedled out of him with dogged persistence by Joseph Green Cogswell, a merchant who had once been a schoolteacher.

"He is not a mere accumulator of dollars, as I had thought," Cogswell wrote to a friend the night he met Astor. "He talks well on many subjects and shows a great interest in the arts and literature."

During the course of that evening, the scholar had put forward the idea of a public library, and Astor had agreed. Between the word and the deed, however, many weary years were to intervene. Cogswell was burning with enthusiasm and could hardly wait to get to work, and Astor was in no hurry at all. There was, luckily, a weapon for Cogswell to use as polite blackmail. John Jacob, always gregarious, could not bear to be alone, particularly at night, because he suffered greatly from insomnia. Cogswell came to live with him.

He read to Astor, whose eyes were failing, and sat up at night to discuss immortality, which had become a favorite topic of conversation. The subject of the library was much less appealing. At last Cogswell threatened to leave. Faced with the loss of his valued companion, John Jacob capitulated. Cogswell began to buy books; they soon filled five cases.

Astor purchased only one work for the library himself, Audubon's *Birds of America* series. The price, set at one thousand dollars, was high, even for John Jacob. The rumor, unproven but persistent, is that Audubon had a great deal of trouble collecting his money.

During his last years, Astor was finally living like a millionaire, spending much time at his Hellgate country estate. He affected huge silver buckles on his shoes and an ermine cap. The dinners that were served in his home were princely, starting with oysters, washed down by Moselle wine, followed by a main course of turkey, quail, canvasback duck, or *filet de boeuf aux champignons*.

Still, for all his wealth, waste continued to anger him. "He would never fail to reprove me for taking more butter on my plate than I could eat," recalled his grandson Charles Astor Bristed.

In similar vein, he became enraged when another grandson's wife drew near to the fire wrapped in her furs, careless or ignorant of the fact that heat ruins the valuable skins.

His love of music remained strong to the end. "You are my singing birds," he would say sentimentally to his grandchildren when they performed for him during the family's regular musical evenings.

Usually at twilight, he would painfully make his way out to the terrace, supported by two servants, and watch the night boat going down the East River. But the time came when even this was too much for him. As he could not exercise, efforts to keep his circulation going consisted of tossing him in a blanket.

He became unable to digest most foods, and so his doctors prescribed human milk, and a wet nurse was found for him. Many years later the same diet was ordered for another multimillionaire, John D. Rockefeller, Sr., suffering with a strange stomach ailment. Apparently millions of dollars are hard to digest.

Despite the failing body, Astor's mind remained clear. Those about him insisted that he still knew to the penny what rent was owing on each piece of property. As a result, a story began to be circulated that by now is most often presented as fact. According to this anecdote, his agent came to report on the rent collections and found John Jacob being tossed in his blanket. Nonetheless, Astor immediately remembered an aged lady who was late in paying her rent.

"Has she paid yet?" he gasped.

"She can't," replied the agent. "She simply doesn't have the money."

"She must pay!"

The agent went to Astor's son and asked for advice. William Backhouse calmly counted out the money for the poor woman's rent and told the agent to bring the receipt to his father.

John Jacob was elated. "I knew you could get it, if you only went about it in the right way."

Death finally took Astor on March 29, 1848. The newspapers had a field day. Most of them praised him to the skies. Not so James Gordon Bennett of the *Herald*. To him, Astor was "a self-invented money-making machine." He took particular exception to the fact that barely one fortieth of the twenty-million-dollar fortune was left to charity. But Bennett was just a voice crying in the nineteenth-century wilderness. Social conscience had not yet been awakened. Other reports of the time express surprise that a millionaire did so much. Astor was lauded immoderately for bequeathing $400,000 to the Astor Library, his only really large benefaction. He also left $50,000 for the building of a home for the poor of Walldorf, Germany.

A rather strange fate befell this home. In the 1930's a visitor to Walldorf discovered that the building had been taken over by the Nazis as a barracks for members of the Bund Deutscher Mädchen ("Organization of German Girls"). This group was made up of teen-age girls who pledged themselves to bear children for the Fuehrer—in particular, the children of SS men and high Nazi officials.

It was the only bequest not used exactly as Astor had intended. The force of his personality was so great that not only his money but also his wishes were passed on to his heirs. For many generations they lived as if his hands were directing them.

3

This Is the Way the Money Grows

"He could climb to the top of a high hill, look down at the city of New York spread out in front of him and cry, 'This is mine, all mine!'" exclaimed a foreign visitor to New York a hundred years ago.

The "he" at that time needed no further identification. It could be only one person: William Backhouse Astor, son of the man who had made the money.

To follow his history is to trace the history of a city as much as that of a man. There are no legends about William's wresting a fortune out of a wilderness, outsmarting Presidents with trumped-up mandarin stories. But if he was not an interesting personality in his own right, he helped to create an interesting time. His influence on the New York that made his family wealthy was tremendous. Without him, Astor control of the real estate would have dwindled. The spread of the unwholesome tenements through the city was encouraged by William's acquisitive nature together—for he was not an evil person—with a total lack of imagination. The "money-making machine" John Jacob was accused of inventing was really his son rather than himself.

Those who did not know William well envied him. But one of his few close friends said of him, "He sat in his office as if it were a house of detention to which his father had condemned him for life."

William never rebelled, or even tried to rebel; he was conditioned to fill the role of heir from early childhood. Many biographers add a spurious touch of excitement to their accounts by describing William's early life as one of hardship and privation, with his afterschool hours devoted to beating the raw beaver and muskrat skins in John Jacob's dusty storeroom. It is a bit difficult to make this dramatic image stick, considering that Astor had earned a quarter of a million dollars by the time this son was eight years old. And far from setting the boy to beating furs, John Jacob set to making him a gentleman. As even in the early 1800's attendance at the right schools was the first step taken by those who were to rise into society, William was sent to one Reverend Smith's boarding school in Stamford, Connecticut, where his classmates included scions of such good old families as the Roosevelts, Gouverneurs, and Delafields. He needed all the social advantage a refined education could give him, because John Jacob was not Pygmalion enough to bestow charm upon him.

Although different in almost every way from his dynamic father, William's character was, nonetheless, formed by the loving, overpowering nature of John Jacob. Perhaps the only time in his life when he was free of his father's domination was during the years he attended the University of Göttingen in Germany. For all the Astors' involvement in the growth of America, the German heritage remained strong through another generation. John spoke German to his children all his life, and William was to do the same with his.

By the time William entered the university, his father's international reputation was so great that wellborn Christian C. J. Bunsen (later Baron von Bunsen, ambassador to Britain) was elated at being selected as tutor.

"My own studies . . . are necessarily somewhat interrupted in consequence," he wrote to his sister, "but, on the other hand, I have occasion to improve in English and such a mode of life is in more than one respect useful to me."

William, who possessed an earnest and scholarly mind, applied himself conscientiously to his studies. As an Astor, and with the sponsorship of Bunsen, he mingled with the intellectual set of the university. In later years he liked to impress associates in New York with reminiscences of philosophical discussions with Arthur

Schopenhauer, whom he remembered as a moody young man with a poodle.

Returning to distant America for vacations was obviously impossible, and free time was spent touring Europe. And so it was that the outbreak of the War of 1812 caught William far from home. With the Napoleonic Wars also raging on the Continent, John Jacob became frantic.

"William is no more!" he exclaimed in a moment of despair.

When he discovered that his grief was premature, Astor swung into action. He wanted his boy safe at home. True, New York harbor was blockaded, and no ships were being allowed to get through, but rules were something that Astor felt applied to other people. He had broken blockades before, and he could do so again; it was simply a matter of bringing his Chinese-mandarin stunt up to date. This time he found French General Jean Victor Moreau, who was burning with desire to fight against Napoleon. How could he return to Europe? On Astor's ship, the *Hannibal*, of course. As John Jacob could not resist the pleasure (and profit) of getting furs out of blockaded New York right from under the noses of the British enemy, the ship left the harbor carrying both the general and a valuable cargo of furs. On the way back, William was a somewhat unwilling passenger, displeased at having been forced to cut short his European adventure.

After the war, John Jacob, showing his customary indulgence where his family was concerned, sent William back with permission to spend whatever he wanted. William kept an itemized record of all travel expenses, noting down every cup of coffee. It turned out that he was a chip off the old block when it came to the careful use of money.

"He spent only $10,000!" His father could not get over it. "I thought he would certainly spend $50,000."

Perhaps such a mature young man was already capable of taking his place in his father's office. John Jacob was looking for a partner and manager. He had offered the job to Albert Gallatin, and been refused. A legend persists to this day that Gallatin would not work for a man whom he did not consider a gentleman, but it is far more likely that he realized a partnership with Astor could never be a real one. There could be no question as to who was boss, with John

Jacob keeping absolute control of every one of his innumerable business ventures. An obedient son was just about the only person who could work with such a man.

William accepted the offer without question and set about helping his father in the demanding task of increasing the wealth that was someday to be his. Traveling days were over, and forty years were to pass before he would see Europe or Christian Bunsen again. Perhaps, as has been said, he was a prisoner in the office, but prisoners sometimes grow fond of their cells. If William was unhappy there, he was probably not happy anywhere else. But then, no one, even in his own time, knew very much about William's dreams and ambitions; he spent most of his life in the shadow of his colorful father. John Jacob's personality was so vivid that still today it leaps from the pages of old documents and letters. In contrast, records and memoirs of his contemporaries tell more about what William owned and did than what he was. Descriptions of his character stress the negative and colorless. At least, pictures can tell us what he looked like. An old miniature treasured by his last surviving great-granddaughter reveals the surprising fact that he was a handsome boy, with fresh coloring and soft, wavy brown hair. The years were not kind to his looks, however, and by the time he reached manhood, his features had taken on a heavy Germanic cast.

"William was the richest and least attractive young man of his time," said a contemporary, with brutal frankness.

He had not been lucky enough to escape the Astor nose or the small eyes. His one physical asset was that he was tall and powerfully built, a trait that has been passed on from him to succeeding generations of male Astors. In his case, though, this was counterbalanced by his unfortunate habit of slouching. His father was hardly the matinée idol of his day either, but, as we have seen, what he lacked in good looks, he made up for in vitality. His son, on the other hand, was phlegmatic and sluggish, showing so little emotion that he was generally believed to be a cold man. That was not an altogether accurate evaluation, since he was capable of deep feeling for a few of the people closest to him. Although dominated by his father, he inherited his mother's reticence and shyness. Unsociable by nature, he did not have much to say for himself.

None of these qualities kept him from being the most eligible bachelor in America. New York society was busy guessing what lucky girl would get him, which really meant, of course, who John Jacob would decide was a suitable bride. William met the girl who was to win him on one of the rare occasions when his father let him go to Albany to discuss real-estate legislation with Judge Ambrose Spencer. The judge's house guest that day happened to be Margaret Rebecca Armstrong, a rather plain eighteen-year-old with thin, tight lips that made her seem prim. William hardly noticed that, though, being struck by the beauty of her complexion, which had the soft, lovely coloring of a fresh peach. His father was equally struck by her background, which would pass the scrutiny of a *Social Register* committee in any era. Her grandfather General John A. Armstrong, a fighter in the French and Indian War, so distinguished himself as a brigadier general in the Revolution that the state of Pennsylvania struck a medal in his honor. Her father General John A. Armstrong II, whom Astor had met years earlier when cultivating the rich and powerful, had similarly achieved fame in the Revolution and the War of 1812. His brilliant career encompassed service as Secretary of State of Pennsylvania, U.S. Senator, U.S. Minister to France and to Spain, and Secretary of War. As for Margaret's mother, her family tree was shared by two of the country's most distinguished families—Livingston and Beekman.

"The Astors . . . and other present leaders have attained their station largely through the infusion of aristocratic blood into their line through marriages with the old families. Their wives made them," reported society's Mrs. John King Van Rensselaer haughtily in her study of inner-circle ways made some forty years ago. She singled out William Backhouse Astor for special attention in this connection, and although oversimplified, her statement has considerable truth in it.

Despite this high society background, Margaret was not the sophisticated woman of the world to lord it over her *nouveau* in-laws.

"She is really just a country girl," remarked a socialite of the time.

She was also a deeply religious girl, which appealed to her

fiancé, because this was the one area of William's upbringing dominated by devout Sarah instead of John Jacob. William read the Bible regularly, marking the passages that meant the most to him, and on Sundays he attended church both morning and afternoon.

John Jacob was so pleased by the impending marriage that he was willing to swallow his pride to bring it about. General Armstrong was the author of "Notices of the War of 1812," an inflammatory document charging Albert Gallatin with treason and insisting that Astor had been deeply involved with his friend. This bit of unpleasantness was calmly overlooked.

The wedding took place in society's favorite Episcopal Church, a significant indication of the family's steady climb into the inner circle. And before the marriage was consummated, a settlement, devised with care and foresight, was signed. Although at that time, in 1818, John Jacob had still to make his first million, he was sure he would do so. Thinking in dynastic terms, he wished to take no chance that the bulk of the fortune be deflected into another family by the uncertainties inherent in married life. After all, his own Magdalen's marriage was breaking up, so what confidence could one have in husbands or wives? Astor suggested that the bride give up her dower rights in return for a specific sum of money. This policy was dutifully (and, as it turned out, luckily) followed by several generations of Astors.

After arranging this most suitable marriage, John Jacob looked for a most suitable social address for the young couple. The rich were living below Chambers Street, the best addresses being around the Battery and on Broadway up to about Cortlandt Street. The Battery was the favored place for wellborn New Yorkers to take their Sunday strolls. Few cared to go driving, as dust rose from the partly paved streets to swirl in great clouds about the heads of anyone in the carriage. The house selected by Astor was on Broadway and White Street, a spacious, even elegant, block, with painted brick houses and a flagstone sidewalk, kept scrupulously clean by servants. Most home owners were quite unaware of the difficulty of obtaining water, because there was always someone else to run to the corner pump. Milk was delivered to the door by men carrying large tin cans suspended from a yoke across their shoulders.

Once settled in his new home with his wife, shy William relaxed sufficiently to give her a pet name—"Peachy," a tribute to her complexion. That is one of the few touches of human sentiment to be found about him in the family documents. For the most part, he lived up to his father's dictum: "Good habits make any man rich." William set his life into a pattern and followed it doggedly until four days before his death at the age of eighty-three. He got up early and took care of his personal correspondence before eating breakfast. This meal was served to him at nine o'clock. Then he walked to the office, arriving by ten. At the end of his day's work, he walked home. The walk was both for economy and exercise. William did not believe in wasting a penny. He spent very little on his clothes—too little, some members of his family complained. As a result, he often looked sloppy, particularly because he was of the type in whom muscle inevitably gives way to fat.

It is not surprising that Margaret escaped from the tedium of life into wildly imaginative fiction. Her first baby, born just a year following the wedding, was named Emily after the heroine of Ann Radcliffe's popular novel *The Mysteries of Udolpho*. Three years later came the necessary son, John Jacob III, known as junior. (No one ever thought of using the term for the true junior, his insane uncle John Jacob II.) The family grew to include two more daughters, Laura and Alida. In 1829 an unbroken line of Astors was insured by the birth of William Backhouse, Jr., and a last son, Henry, was born in 1830. William, it was soon observed, played favorites. He adored his firstborn, Emily, and favored his eldest son as heir apparent, while rather ignoring the rest.

His most meaningful relationship was with his father and, this being the case, necessarily with his father's business. He did not bring new vitality, drive, or daring into John Jacob's enterprises. That was probably just as well; his father had more than enough for two. But no piece of work was too small for him as a young man or ever after. Every detail of each of his father's activities was interesting to him. He checked and rechecked every expenditure. Was it really necessary? Could the job be done more cheaply? He inspected furs, investigated tenants, kept track of every dollar owing.

"He knew the rent rolls by heart" admitted one of his rival landlords.

John Jacob could say with pride that William's high-priced education had been one of his soundest investments.

"William was really no better than a head clerk—a very good clerk, and a trusted one—but an underling, nonetheless," commented a friend long afterward.

This was even true of the American Fur Company, the only enterprise in which his father granted him the title of president. It was a gesture of kindness; it did not mean that the older man was delegating authority to the younger. John Jacob did all the planning, and William kept the books. The son, a religious man, was more distressed than the father by the sale of liquor to the Indians. He even tried to do something about it and appealed to the Hudson's Bay Company to join in a pact to exclude liquor from the Indian Territory. This well-meaning effort fell through, possibly because John Jacob was not behind it. His good impulse stifled, William left the running of the company to his father. As if to prove that the son was president in name only, John personally arranged the terms of sale when he decided to get out of the fur trade.

It was the same with the hotel business, which was ostensibly William's bailiwick: he had been given the Astor House for "one Spanish milled dollar." Still, when the leases were signed, the name John Jacob Astor appeared on each.

"William did not seem to resent this," said a contemporary. "He was very fond of his father. John recognized William's shortcomings as a man of action, but he loved the boy dearly."

The father traveled to find new markets and expand old ones, to buy and use influence. William stayed at home and took care of the business. John Jacob knew that he would return to find everything as he had left it. The books would be in order, the payments up to date. In his father's position, William would never have made the fortune in the first place. Once it was made, he succeeded in doubling it.

"Take care of what you have. That is what makes the money grow." This was the policy that ruled William's life.

He was helped, of course, by the growth of New York. This

was foreseen by his father, who made most of the major real-estate purchases. But if Astor had confidence in New York, William had confidence in his father and bought some land cautiously, always following John's advice. Astor declared that the city was expanding northward, and so one day in 1826 William, his nervousness concealed behind his unemotional manner, agreed to pay the Thompson family $25,000 for a huge plot of inferior farmland. His father was right, of course. Eventually Fifth and Madison Avenues were cut through the Thompson Farm, which covered Thirty-Second to Thirty-Fourth Streets, and its value skyrocketed. Fifteen years later, William sold a single lot—no Astor cared to sell more—at auction for $1,200. One of the men who was present at the auction reported that "a universal titter went through the room," because the price was considered ridiculously high. It was just as well that William did not agree and held on to the bulk of the property, which remained in the family until the twentieth century.

Although he had to wait until he was middle-aged to inherit his father's millions, William became a millionaire himself long before that. Some of his money was earned through opportunities thrown his way by John Jacob; the rest came from his Uncle Henry, the butcher, who selected William as his heir. And should anyone doubt that a butcher could amass a fortune, let him consider Peter Widener, founder of the prominent Philadelphia family, who also started as a butcher boy and made his first fortune in meat, or Chicago society, which, wags say, rests on a base of four hooves.

The possession of the butcher's money sent William in search of a new address. It was already time for him to move. Lower Broadway was fast dropping in the social scale for a reason that even John Jacob had not foreseen. The appalling sanitary conditions of the city, which had never concerned him a whit, were responsible. In 1819 and again in 1822 devastating yellow fever epidemics had swept through the heavily populated southern part of the city. Flight was the only way then known for frightened New Yorkers to escape the ravages of this disease. Greenwich Village, which had been rural, was hurriedly built up. Washington Square, a former potter's field, was filled in to make the Washington Parade Ground, because Sunday strollers eschewed the Battery for fear of infection.

The first person William consulted in his quest was naturally his father. John had just the piece of property, it turned out, on Lafayette Place. William built his mansion there of red brick, and another house was constructed on the corner lot at Art Street for his sister, Dorothea Langdon, and her family. Their father considered taking that site himself, but could not overcome his superstitious fear that corner lots were unlucky for him. To make certain that Lafayette Place would really be the right place for the right people, Astor sold all the remaining lots to successful merchants or bankers. On Sundays, New Yorkers used to drive down Lafayette Place to stare at the mansions and wait for the Astors to come out, like modern tourists watching the front doors of the Beverly Hills palaces of the movie stars.

The ownership of this fine new home did not keep the Astors in the city during the summers. It was customary for well-to-do families to escape the heat and the epidemics that accompanied it (the best neighborhoods were not so contagion-proof as all that). For this purpose, John Jacob had given William and Margaret the wedding present that she desired above all else—her family home in Dutchess County to use as a country estate. The Armstrongs were living there, but no one could refuse Astor, who just kept on raising the price until General Armstrong conceded: "I simply could not turn it down."

The estate had been called *La Bergerie* (sheep farm), because Napoleon Bonaparte had urged Armstrong to raise sheep there and presented him with merinos as a gift. Margaret, ever the romantic, renamed it "Rokeby," after a poem by Sir Walter Scott. If there is any single place that can give a sense of the continuity of the history of the Astor family, it is Rokeby. Still in the possession of John Jacob's descendants, Rokeby is filled with the pictures, papers, books, and furnishings of the generations that followed him. Even today it remains magnificent in its very disrepair. Renovating would mean replacing the irreplaceable, disposing of the threadbare upholstery and what remains of the delicate, flowered wallpaper hung in the early years of the nineteenth century.

Margaret's brothers, who had expected to inherit the place, were enraged when it went to the Astors. The eldest, Horatio, insisted that he be given the furnishings, and the Astors yielded on this point.

"The furniture did Horatio no good anyway," William observed later. "His house burned down five years after he got it, and everything was lost."

A visit to Rokeby reveals that the real losers were the Astors, who replaced the lovely French Empire furniture with heavy, dark, ornate Germanic pieces.

Big as it was, the house did not seem large enough to William. The Astors retained the European sense of family, and it never occurred to William that he might turn his relatives out. His father-in-law and a bachelor brother-in-law, Kosciusko Armstrong, remained as permanent tenants. To house these relatives as well as his own family, William added an entire wing, topped by a tower from which a glorious view of the Hudson could be seen.

His own bedroom was in the new wing, while Margaret's was rather far distant, in the older part, an arrangement apparently based on poor planning rather than any frigidity in their relationship. The marriage appeared to be a happy one. Exceedingly capable in running his business, William was inefficient when it came to his own home; nor did he trouble to consult his wife about the practical aspects of housekeeping. Although the dining room was on the ground floor of the original house, for example, William had an enormous kitchen placed on the second floor of the new wing. This meant that food had to be carried from the stove all the way across a long pantry and then sent down by dumbwaiter. Waited on by a retinue of servants, William probably did not notice how awkward it was.

By the time he reached the plans for what was to be his favorite room, a huge, octagonally shaped library, he had begun to worry about the amount of money he was spending. Economy might have been the eleventh commandment as far as William was concerned. He decided to save a few dollars by avoiding the traditional oak paneling and having the plaster ceiling painted to look like wood. A scholarly man, William in later years liked to sit by the fireplace in the library, with Margaret across from him. His reading, however, according to his family, was usually limited to German encyclopedias and dictionaries, of which he had a large collection.

One shelf, of gardening books, was Margaret's. Gardening was her delight, and even in the city, she kept the windows of her sitting room filled with plants. She was pleased by William's decision to follow her father's example and run part of Rokeby as a farm.

When her eldest son some years later hired a man for the grounds, he was to state firmly: "My mother is a good deal of a farmer. You are engaged for her, not for my father."

Recognizing her love of flowers, William once gave her a choice: "Should I give you money to establish an orphanage, Peachy, or to build a greenhouse?"

Margaret thought it over. "I would dearly love to have a greenhouse," she replied. "But as I am a good Christian woman, I know that the orphanage should come first."

"That is the right answer," returned William. "You shall have both."

William's lack of *joie de vivre* kept Rokeby from being as lovely a house as it might have been. A cousin who visited pointed out that the drawing room with big French windows opening onto spacious lawns was hardly ever used. Instead the family gathered in a cluttered "little home parlor." The dining room, she went on gloomily, was hung with family portraits by "mediocre artists." Nonetheless, the general effect of the high-ceilinged rooms with their rich, if heavy furnishings was then, and still is, singularly impressive.

At Rokeby and in their home at Lafayette Place, the William B. Astors took the place in society to which his money and her birth entitled them. Despite his celebrated frugality, William allowed himself a few luxuries. A surprisingly ostentatious touch was the keeping of servants in livery. And although his appearance and dress did not really show it, he had a valet. Some years later this same valet was hired by President Martin Van Buren; apparently his lack of success in making a Beau Brummel out of Astor was not held against him. In a gesture quite unlike him, William bought a complete set of goldplate dishes and had them kept on display on the sideboards. They were frequently in use, for the Astors entertained regularly.

Their parties were surely even stiffer than the great formal balls given a generation later by their daughter-in-law, *the* Mrs. Astor. William possessed no social graces himself. Because he never drank more than a single glass of wine, no artificial stimulant loosened his tongue. His wife came from a distinguished background, it is true; but she, too, lacked the personality of a polished hostess. Nevertheless, the inner circle of New York did accept invitations to the home of the young Astors; their guest lists included such notable old names as Brevoort, Jay, Schermerhorn, Duer, and Stuyvesant. And if these Old Guard couples were bored, they were too well-bred to show it. The Astors were invited in return to the homes of other social leaders. In 1830, for example, the big social event of the season was a fancy dress ball given by Mrs. Charles Bruguière. William and his wife were present. One cannot help wondering if the comparative anonymity a costume bestows upon its wearer helped stiff William to unbend.

During those years when he was moving heavily through the social life of the city, William's main interest was real estate. Sales were infrequent. As a rule, William held to the policy of renting out the land. When he first joined his father, rents ranged from $50 to $87.50 per lot per year. Gradually, property values rose. In the year 1825 alone, five hundred new business establishments were opened, along with twelve banks and ten marine insurance companies. Thirteen hundred sailing vessels entered New York harbor each year bringing immigrants and cargoes from all over the world. In 1832 the New York and Harlem Railroad Company ran horse cars between Prince and Fourteenth Streets, giving the city its first public transportation. Two years later steam trolley cars took passengers all the way to Yorkville, and ferries connected Brooklyn with Manhattan. The neighborhood below Canal Street was so built up that gaslights illuminated the streets of that section at night.

By the 1840's the father-and-son team was able to rent a single lot for $175 a year on a twenty-one-year lease. If there was a house on the land, of course, the rent rose accordingly. Any issue of *The New York Times* today carries advertisements of apartments at rents of well over one thousand dollars a month. Even Astor would not have believed this possible. John and William, charging every cent the traffic would bear, had to content themselves with from $600 to $1,400 a year for both land and house. And people at the time were complaining about skyrocketing rentals. Why, back in

John Jacob Astor I, the driving, dynamic butcher's son, who became the "richest man in America" and founded society's great dynasty.

Hellgate, country estate of John Jacob Astor I, situated on what is now 88th Street and Second Avenue.

Brigadier General John Armstrong, distinguished military forebear of the Astors, who fought in the American Revolution and later became Secretary of State of Pennsylvania.

William Backhouse Astor, as a boy, from an old miniature.

William Backhouse Astor, as an adult, who became "landlord of New York," and doubled the fortune left him by his father.

John Jacob Astor II, whose incurable mental condition was the tragedy of his father's life.

Eliza Astor von Rumpff, the youngest and sweetest daughter of John Jacob Astor I.

John Jacob Astor III. His vast fortune brought him "nothing but a certain dull anxiety."

William Backhouse Astor, Jr., overshadowed forever by the forceful wife who refused to use either his first or middle name.

The Mrs. Astor, ruler of society's gilded age.

The Mrs. Astor stood
beneath this portrait by
Carolus Duran while
greeting her guests.

The art-gallery ballroom where *the* Mrs. Astor entertained the "Four Hundred" at society's most celebrated balls.

the 1820's, $300 a year was a rent a rich man would pay for a good house on a good block.

At that date, however, New York held but 125,000 people. Ten years later, the population had risen to more than 200,000; by 1840, it had topped 300,000. The housing shortage, severe when John Jacob first watched the homeless congregating in City Hall Park, had become steadily worse. The pressure on housing had been intensified by a terrible fire back in 1835, which leveled hundreds of buildings to the ground, seven hundred of them in what is now the financial district. Of course, every fire was disastrous in a large city with no running water and only volunteer firemen to drag the engines and pump the needed water out of the East or Hudson River. Just one man was posted atop the City Hall to spot fires, sound the alarm, and then send the volunteers to the blaze by waving a lantern in the appropriate direction. Rebuilding, therefore, had to compete with new building.

This municipal misfortune made the fortune of any man who owned land. Lesser entrepreneurs were desperate to get their hands on a piece of ground, any piece at all. The main reason for leasing a lot from the Astors or the Goelets, Stuyvesants, Rhinelanders, Schermerhorns, and other big landlords was to put up a house and rent it. The more people the house could hold, the better. On this principle, the nineteenth-century tenements went up. So did the Astor fortune.

William had been the most eligible bachelor of his day, and his children were the most sought-after marriage partners of theirs. Sam Ward, Jr., son of a noted banker and a descendant of two former governors of Rhode Island, set his sights high, on William's eldest daughter. Emily was as unlike an Astor as it was possible for a child of this family to be. Her father's long face and phlegmatic manner did not dampen her high spirits, and she went through life with a smile. With reddish-gold hair, sapphire-blue eyes, and the pleasingly plump figure that was considered ideal at the time, she was her parents' joy and her grandfather's pet. He would listen for hours to her beautiful coloratura soprano voice.

Shrewd Sam quickly realized that he had to win not only the girl and her father but also her forceful grandfather.

"He was full of jokes for the old man," one of his many friends recalled. "He once brought a ventriloquist to the estate at Hellgate in secret. Sam told me afterwards that he wanted the performer to make old Astor believe he had a cat in his belly."

Sam was so successful at pleasing his grandfather-in-law that the young couple received a house on Bond Street as a wedding gift. John Jacob could not bear to be parted from Emily for long even after she was married. In his late seventies by then, Astor could not endure the strain of traveling around the city and issued directives on both business and personal matters from his Hellgate estate. Every few months, the summons would go out, and Sam and Emily would pack their bags and set off on the tiring journey to Eighty-Eighth Street.

Emily's younger sister Laura, a plain young girl, found this favoritism hard to endure. It was particularly irksome during the summers, when she was living together with her parents and the young Wards at Rokeby. Cheerful Emily, who could not bear to see a sad face, soon discovered that the best way of comforting her sister was to promise to bring back a ring or a bracelet. That may be why Laura throughout her life retained a passion for jewelry.

The marriage of Emily and Sam was as short as it was happy. She died of fever after childbirth in 1841 when she was just twenty-two years old. The family never fully recovered from her loss. The Astor men at least had their business to bury themselves in, but Margaret lacked this distraction.

"Mother became a different woman," her surviving children observed. "From a genial person, she changed into a stern, quiet one. She could never bring herself to mention Emily's name again."

Doctors insisted that the grief-stricken woman take a walk every day. She would not go alone, so her two younger daughters accompanied her, all three swathed in heavy crepe veils reaching to their feet.

Handsome, dashing Sam had loved Emily, but he was not the type to mourn forever, and he was soon married again to one Marie Angeline "Medora" Grymes, described by the family as a "showy and fascinating Creole." It did not take much to be considered "showy" by the conservative Astors, it is true, but Sam should have thought twice before allowing himself to be so fascinated.

Sam's sister Louisa was visiting the Astors at Rokeby when news of the second marriage arrived. For once William lost his composure and flew into a rage all the more terrifying because it was so unusual. "Order the carriage for Miss Ward at once!" he shouted.

John Jacob was just as furious as William. To add insult to insensitivity, Sam blandly settled the Bond Street house, gift of his first set of in-laws, upon his second wife.

"The affair sticks deep into the old gentleman's gizzard," Astor's nephew, Henry Brevoort, wrote at the time. "He views it as a sort of impeachment of his accustomed sagacity."

The outraged John Jacob retaliated by demanding that Emily's small daughter, Margaret "Maddie" Astor Ward, be sent to the Astors. Although the arrangements for this were as usual made by the old man, it was the William B. Astors who took the child into their home. Although the door was closed to Sam and his second wife, Peachy, always a good woman, let Maddie make brief visits to them.

As if touched by the Astor curse, Sam's luck turned bad: Prime, Ward & Company, the banking house he had inherited from his father, crashed, an event followed quickly by Medora's departure for her native New Orleans with their two sons. Ward made and lost several fortunes thereafter, winning back and losing his beautiful wife coincidentally each time. She eventually departed permanently for Nice, and both the boys died there. The one consolation was that William, once over his initial rage, relented and permitted Sam to come to the house to see Maddie. The circumstances of the repeated separations were such, though, that her relationship with him remained stiff and formal, disappointing to emotional Sam.

Maddie was an extremely pretty child, who became deeply religious under the Astor influence. "Whenever I went to see her, I would find her sweeping her room," Ward told one of his granddaughters years later. (Anyone who knew Sam well realized that this cryptic remark was an allusion to a poem of George Herbert's:

> Who sweeps a room as in God's sight
> Makes that and the action fine.

The pure and lovely Maddie grew up to marry handsome John Winthrop Chanler, a Tammany politician whose family came from the South. His legacy to his many descendants was to be charm, good looks, and to some, a streak of eccentricity. In the Astor family, a mention of the Chanlers brings a shake of the head, a smile, and an "Oh, those Chanlers!"

Members of society's inner circle like to say that all the really good old families are related. This inbreeding is in keeping with the practice of European royalty. Three years after Emily's death, her younger sister Laura added her mite to this legend by marrying Franklin Hughes Delano. It was quite a catch for so plain a girl. A dazzled female relative has remembered him as "one of the best-looking men of his day." At the wedding at Rokeby this girl was so overcome that she backed into the French windows and nearly fell out onto the lawn.

Both John Jacob and William were delighted with this match and outdid one another with largesse. A story went the rounds of New York society that Astor handed his granddaughter a check on her wedding day. When she looked at it, she saw that it was for a quarter of a million dollars. More sober accounts made it a trust fund of $200,000. In addition, the grandfather presented the young Delanos with a townhouse on Lafayette Place, which was so rich with Astors that Art Street on the corner was renamed Astor Place. William then bought them an old Dutch farm, "Stein Valetje," right next to Rokeby and added to it many acres of his own land. This was not a family in which it was easy for an incoming groom or bride to escape the in-laws.

Although Delano had been a partner in a shipping firm before his marriage, he resigned from this position. Occasionally, thereafter, he dabbled in real estate, joined in a shipping enterprise, or assisted his wealthy in-laws in their ventures. The Delanos, particularly Laura, collected art of varying degrees of merit, porcelains, and jewelry—always jewelry. When they were older, the couple moved to Europe, and Franklin died there. The closely knit family looked for a way to comfort Laura. They decided to send her great-nieces, the Chanler girls, to spend a month with her each summer. Laura used to take the children out driving with her, giving each of them a bag of pennies to throw to the beggars following the carriage.

The Delanos had had everything, but it was nothing in the end, since they were childless. There was a niece, however, Sara Delano, who was to become the mother of Franklin Delano Roosevelt. When Franklin was born, Sara wanted to name him Warren. Her family talked her into naming the child after "Uncle Frank, who was so good to us all."

The youngest of William's daughters, Alida, was married to John Carey, Jr., an Englishman. The Astors were always partial to British ways, a fact that sometimes offended Americans. Unkind gossip got back at them with the rumor that he had come here to marry an American girl with a fortune. If so, Carey picked rightly. Alida brought him $200,000 in cash and another $100,000 in real estate.

During all these years William's sister Dorothea Astor Langdon lived right next door to him in the spirit of family closeness fostered by John Jacob. As the decades passed, she grew steadily fatter. Dolly lacked the personality to be a social leader, but many of them must have envied her. When it came to performing what society considers a woman's most important task, Dolly was incomparable: her children made brilliant marriages.

One daughter became a baroness; the eldest son, Walter, in the social tradition of inbreeding, found a Livingston for his bride; another married into society's noted Jones family. The older ladies of this family were social arbiters for many years, well known for their staunch refusal to accept anyone new. After the death of one of these aged matrons, her grandson sold her house to a woman who had been considered a newcomer. He confided: "I assure you I was actually afraid to give my consent to the lease. I felt I might be visited by Grandmamma's reproachful spirit." Nonetheless, the Joneses accepted the Astors gracefully. This high society bride, by the way, was the one who enraged her grandfather-in-law by sitting too close to the fire in her furs.

Members of society would have you believe that not only the *good* old families but also the *rich* old families are related. The Astors have done their best to make this part of the legend come true as well. There is even a connection between the Astors and fantastically rich, fantastically mean Hetty Green.

It can be traced to Matthew Astor Wilks, son of Dolly's prettiest daughter Eliza. When he was sixty-five years old, Wilks fell in love with Sylvia Green, Hetty's daughter, who was twenty-seven years his junior, Sylvia was surely the poorest of all little rich girls, and nobody had less fun. Marriage to a balding, elderly bachelor might not be considered delightful by many, but to Sylvia, it spelled happiness and freedom from her mother.

Hetty was not impressed by the Astor relationship. "I intend to see that my daughter makes no mistakes," she announced. "I want to know Mr. Wilks better."

When Wilks agreed to waive his claim to the Green fortune, Hetty decided that she knew him quite well enough, and the marriage took place.

To return to Dolly Langdon, only one of her eight children inherited the rebellious nature that had prompted her own elopement years earlier. This girl, Louisa, while out for a drive with her sister Eliza, remarked innocently that she needed to buy something at Peiser's dry goods store. "I'll just be a minute," she told her sister. "You wait for me in the carriage."

Eliza waited, but her sister did not come back. Finally, she went into the store, where the clerk informed her that Louisa had come in, walked through the shop, and gone out the back door. There was nothing to be done on the spot, so Eliza went home to lunch.

Just as the pudding was being served, the message arrived: Louisa had eloped with Oliver DeLancey Kane. History repeated itself promptly. Her father, Colonel Langdon, was not softened by any recollections of the years when he had been ostracized by John Jacob Astor. Refusing to listen to the pleas of his tenderhearted wife, he announced that he was washing his hands of the wild young pair. With John Jacob too old to be bothered in this crisis, William, Louisa's uncle, was called upon to add his bit to the general censure. Although barely middle-aged, William had, with true Astor foresight, already made his will. He immediately cut Louisa out of it. Colonel Langdon died in 1847, before Louisa's lisping children could appeal to his better nature. William had time to relent, and he restored some of his bequests. Louisa was returned to the family circle in the last year of her grandfather's life.

William was fifty-six years old on that March day in 1848 when his father died. His entire life had been a preparation for this event. His late father, too, had devoted years of thought to it. John

Jacob's will had been worked and reworked and changed again until Astor was satisfied that the fortune would last, not only through William's day, but would be there for William's sons, John Jacob III and William Backhouse, Jr., and for their sons in turn.

When Astor first drew up his will, he left William the bulk of his fortune in the form of a life trust. A board of trustees carefully selected by the father would help William to administer the estate and would see to it that he did not give it away or squander it. With his uncanny ability of staying ahead of his time, John soon realized that this will was not foolproof. It might be legislated out of all usefulness and cease to protect his millions. Laws were being passed limiting trusts to two generations, and the future might bring stricter rulings.

Nine years before his death, John Jacob came up with a leapfrog system of leaving his wealth. It was extremely simple: William was to get one half of the fortune outright, with the other half held in trust for his children. Upon William's death, his children would get that trust fund outright. William in turn would put in his will —his father told him to, so, of course, he did—the requirement that they hold the original half of the fortune, plus anything additional William had earned, in trust for their children. In other words, the half of the fortune to be held in trust was alternated from one generation to the next. This meant that the laws limiting trusts did not apply.

John Jacob I intended this system to go on forever. It lasted through only three generations. Then John Jacob IV left the entire fortune to his son Vincent, outright, and Vincent went on to leave it to a charitable foundation.

Head of the house at last, William displayed a side of his nature that no one had even thought existed. He had been considered a stingy man, a penny pincher. Once all the pennies were his, however, he showed liberality in a number of ways. He discovered that his father's former secretary, Fitz-Greene Halleck, had been left an annuity of $200 a year. Upon questioning the man, it turned out that Halleck had once remonstrated with his employer, "Of what use is all this money to you, Mr. Astor?" he had asked. "I would be content to live on a couple of hundred a year for the rest of my life, if I was only sure of it."

Halleck had been indulging in poetic license. A former poet, he had put his muse aside to take a high-salaried job with Astor. John Jacob, who sometimes had a rather cruel sense of humor, had inserted a clause in his will leaving Halleck exactly that amount. William had no sense of humor at all; he could not see the joke. His logical mind simply told him that it was unfair. To the relief of the unfortunately witty Halleck, he raised the annuity to $1,500.

His next move was to take a hand in a lawsuit that had been dragging on for many years. One of John Jacob's early business associates, a man named Ogden, had died during a trading mission to China. When Ogden's relatives came to ask for his share of the business, they were coldly informed that all documents were lost. The Ogdens went to court, but all cases against Astor had a way of dragging on interminably. William had not meddled earlier, but with the old man dead, he quickly came to terms with Ogden's heirs. The affair was settled for a figure guessed by contemporaries at $200,000.

"William B. Astor is the best man in the United States to have charge of a colossal fortune," came praise from a writer of the period.

The newspapers were heralding his father's one great benefaction, the Astor Library, but it was William who packed Cogswell off to Europe to buy books. The Library was to be erected on two of the less valuable lots on Lafayette Place. John Jacob had left $75,000 for the building, a sum that was inadequate even at mid-nineteenth-century prices; William quietly added money for shelves and arches. With his push behind it, the Astor Library opened in 1854, holding more than 80,000 books. These were not to be circulated; the Library was for research only. This was not just an example of Astor snobbism. The idea of a free public lending library was not yet current. In New York people well educated enough to read for pleasure—a minority—bought their own books or were members of the New York Society Library.

It did not take schoolboys long to discover the Astor Library. Cogswell was horrified by the large number of untidy youths pouring into his sacred rooms. "Youngsters out of school read trashy books by Sir Walter Scott, Charles Dickens, and James Fenimore Cooper," he declared ruefully. He consoled himself with the thought that "even this is better than spinning street yarns."

One day Cogswell went into the Library and discovered school-boys copying English translations of the Latin and Greek works they were studying. The old scholar was appalled. He insisted that the minimum age for use of the Library be raised from fourteen to sixteen. After all, no mature sixteen-year-old could stoop so low as to use a "pony."

By the time the Library had been open for a year, it was clear to everyone that it needed to be enlarged. William bought three lots next to the building for another wing. Contributions to the Library continued throughout his life. Following his father's lead, it was made the main benefaction in his will, too.

Along with the benefactions, lawsuits, real estate, and money, William inherited the problem of his insane brother John Jacob Astor II. William investigated the arrangements his father had made. Shocked to discover that his brother's physician-companion was being paid $5000 a year, he fired the doctor and hired a lower-priced guardian instead. His brother, he was sure, would never know the difference. This lack of imagination and ignorance about insanity played him false. As soon as John Jacob II realized that the doctor was gone, he flew into a rage. A big, powerful man, he broke windows and threw furniture about. When he had exhausted himself, he lay on the bed and cried. William was not a cruel person. Upon discovering how deeply his brother felt, he asked the doctor to return.

"I'm not coming back," replied the physician. "I'm a free man for the first time in years."

When William offered to raise his salary to $10,000, he agreed to go back. It would be nice to think that he might have cared a little for his charge anyway. The face of John Jacob II looks out of his portrait with an expression of intolerable sadness. All his father's money had not saved him from the tortures of his own mind.

William's feelings about his brother were no doubt related to a problem much closer to his heart. In addition to John Jacob III and William Backhouse, Jr., there was another son, Henry, who was hardly known outside of the immediate family. In fact, *The New York Times*, as that part of the news it decided was fit to print (or perhaps was all that it knew), wrote, "There was a third son, but on account of a marriage of which the family did not approve, he has not been recognized for many years, and the public generally does not know of his existence."

It is true that Henry's marriage was not approved, but this son was a problem long before that. "Henry was not insane; he was just queer," his family was careful to point out.

A special little house was built for him on the grounds at Rokeby, and he lived there all year around until his unexpected marriage to Malvina Dinehart, whose father had worked as a gardener for the Astors. William was by then so far removed from his father's humble beginnings that he considered Malvina a "peasant," and said so. He hastened to cut Henry's share in his will down to $30,000.

Henry's only comment on his family's reaction was quite sane: "Money counts for little in this world, compared with love and life."

He did not have to do without money either, despite being all but cut out of his father's will. His grandfather had already left him some property, including a one-quarter share of the Eden Farm, on Broadway in the Forties, and the income from this was rapidly going up.

Henry bought two hundred acres at Copake, New York, and built a house with its own private race track and a room paved with silver dollars. Six feet tall and muscular, with a flaming red beard, he was easily the most colorful character in Copake. He was a heavy drinker and flew into violent rages when drunk. In other moods, he would put on a surplice and preach sermons, striking a bell with a crowbar to emphasize his points. It came as no surprise to anyone when he got into serious trouble by hitting the four-year-old daughter of a neighbor. Her family sued for $20,000. The Astors paid up, but took control of his property away from Henry. From then on, it was managed by his eldest brother.

John Jacob III did not do such a bad job. When Henry died at the age of eighty-eight, his property was sold at a huge real-estate auction for $5,159,075. This is the kind of fortune that belongs to a disinherited Astor. It was a mere nothing, though, compared to the immense wealth accumulated for his brothers by their father.

A catch phrase is often attached to the names of well-known

people. John Jacob I was the "richest man in America"; William became the "landlord of New York." Real estate was his passion. He left the management of the Astor House to the leaseholder, Colonel Charles Stetson—checking all expenses and repairs, naturally. Although a heavy stockholder in the Delaware & Hudson Railroad and many other major enterprises, he was never actively involved in their administration. Land was another matter. There was not a rock on a lot or a brick on a wall that was unimportant to him. He watched over these possessions from the office of the Astor Estate on Prince Street.

The Astor Estate sounds impressive, but there was nothing impressive about the office. It consisted of but two rooms. In the first of these, one or two clerks were checking figures, and John Jacob III was hard at work on the books. Like his father before him, he was being trained in the business. The second room, which was plainly furnished, was William's office. Unlike other big executives, he was not protected from interruptions by a secretary or staff. Anyone could go in to see him. Not many dared.

"I would walk into his office, and he would look up without speaking," remarked a businessman of the period. "He would look at me, but ask no questions. It was up to me to tell him what I was there for. And it was clear that he would like me to do so in as few words as possible. Then he would answer with equal brevity. He seemed to value each word as if it were a dollar."

Every dollar, of course, went into buying more real estate, not to improving what he had. His tenants and the city would do that for him. Corner lots, for example, were a particularly good investment.

"The corner of a block is the first part to be improved," he explained one day, as he took his son through the city to view their property.

If the tenant or the city did not remove rocks, cut roads, or put up houses, Astor would wait. His lots could stand weed-grown and ugly in the midst of a fine residential or commercial area. Sooner or later, somebody would break down and hire the laborers to do some work—somebody else, not William. He was in no hurry. If you hang on to New York City land, the value has to go up, no matter how little you do to it.

Following his father's example, he bought lots both where the city was and where he thought it was going. In the 1850's, when Central Park was being laid out, William began to concentrate on land south of its Fifty-ninth Street boundary. Entire blocks from Fourth to Seventh Avenues became his, yet then, and for the next quarter of a century, the Fifties were too far uptown to be considered residential. When the Jones family in the 1870's built mansions there close to the shanties of the squatters, they were viewed as peculiar. William bought up lots on Sixth Avenue from Sixteenth Street all the way to Fortieth Street. His possessions extended into the slums around Tompkins Square, along First Avenue and Avenues A and B, and on the densely populated blocks east of the Bowery. They stretched from downtown to uptown, from East Side to West, in every ward, practically on every avenue or street, farm or wooded area.

And while he was buying (or holding onto his father's) land, the need for housing was increasing. In the late 1840's the potato famine in Ireland and the political troubles in Germany drove thousands from their homes. Immigrants poured into the United States at a rate of 300,000 or more a year. So many of them settled in New York that by 1850 nearly half of the city's population of better than 500,000 was foreign-born. Homes had to be found for all these people. And on one Astor lot after another, the tenements rose, and with them rose the city death rate. It climbed from one in 41.83 in 1815 to one in 27.33 in 1855.

Most of the new tenements were not put up by the Astors themselves. The building was done by the men who rented the lots. These sublandlords, who were required to improve the land, put up the building, and pay the taxes, were in a particularly difficult position. There was only one way for them to make a profit, and that was to squeeze a great many families into each building and to charge high rents.

When it came to repairs, Astor was not involved. William never forgot the day his father had nearly fired an agent for presenting a bill for eighty-seven cents for repairs. Could not the fool see that the leaseholder should have paid this sum, John Jacob had fumed! Following this example, William made his sublandlords responsible for repairs, a policy that encouraged them to do as few as possible.

The buildings would deteriorate, of course, but that would only add to their value, as many sublandlords had the foresight to predict fairly early in the century. A rundown tenement would go to the very poorest people, who would pay rent for a part of a room. No amount of overcrowding would be too great for this group. In time, some of these tenements were to sink so low that derelicts paid three cents for the privilege of spending a night in the hallways, sheltered from the cold.

Astor knew that the tenements existed. He kept a careful eye on the value of each piece of property. But the use of the sublandlord made it possible for the owner of the land to escape a sense of responsibility. After all, it was not up to him to control the greed of the sublandlord. William was not imaginative, and far more perceptive men were allowing the tenements to go up on their property. He saw these houses only as a source of income, never as a source of tragedy. As income producers, they were most satisfactory, yielding on the average 15 to 20 percent on the investment. This was more than William could say for his lots and houses on the fashionable West Side, where yields seldom topped 6 or 7 percent.

A typical tenement in the mid-nineteenth century was four to six stories high and twenty-five feet wide and took up from sixty-four to ninety-five feet of a one-hundred-foot lot. The outside of the buildings often had some pretensions to elegance, with carved stone entrances, arched doorways, and cornices, a startling contrast to the squalor within. The original plan was for four families to live on each floor of a tenement, but the great waves of immigration soon made that scheme seem like the height of luxury. Most apartments were shared by several families, despite the fact that only the living room deserved the name of "room," being twelve feet long by ten feet wide. The bedrooms were no larger than a clothes closet in a modern home. Many sublandlords discovered that a second house could be fastened onto the rear wall of the tenement, a practice that cut down on the already insufficient light and air. Each outdoor privy had to be used by so many people as to be utterly repulsive. Until well into the 1860's pigs rooted in the garbage thrown into the gutters, their main competition for the rotting scraps of food being hungry slum children. The few street cleaners employed by the city seldom ventured into the poorer neighborhoods. Those streets were impassable in bad weather anyway.

It is not surprising that many tenants made use of the one escape that was easily available—liquor. One valuable room on the first floor of many tenements was occupied by the liquor store. Unscrupulous shopkeepers offered gin, known to the immigrants as "Monongahela schnapps," at six cents for half a pint. As it cost twenty-five cents a gallon to make, it is easy to see why the liquor store concession was a real political plum. The landlords as a group observed a hands-off policy. To have faced the problem would have forced them to face up to the appalling conditions of the tenements.

"The very dogs and cats would, if unmolested, prefer the open street," the Reverend Peter Stryker declared from his pulpit in the Thirty-fourth Street Reformed Dutch Church, after a visit to the slums. "The . . . tenement houses . . . are a standing reproach against our rich men who ought, for the sake of humanity, to be using their surplus funds in erecting cheap and comfortable residences for the poor."

The thought never entered the minds of Astor and the other major landlords. For that matter, hardly anyone else listened to the outcry of a few ministers, doctors, and reformers. In those days there was a vast chasm between the rich and the indigent. William had never been poor, and he did not understand poverty. Why, his father had landed in America with but five English pounds in his pockets, and look what he had made of himself! Surely any hard-working young fellow could do the same. If a man was poor, it was because he was lazy. There was nothing pitiable about it. William walked through the city of New York as if he had blinkers on.

On the firm foundation of his tenement property, Astor built his fortune. The city administration, under Democratic Mayor Fernando B. Wood, helped him whenever it could. By the middle of the nineteenth century, politicians had learned that slum landlords were a candidate's best friends. The huge populations of the tenements could be rounded up by political henchmen on Election Day. Immigrants were taken to vote before they were naturalized. Waterfront rights were handed to Astor and the other big real-estate owners for a token thirteen dollars a foot. Taxes were kept low, and property improvement and housing were left to their discretion.

The lesser local politicians were paid off by being allowed a free hand in running dives, brothels, and gambling establishments in the worst neighborhoods. The new, small police department had no choice but to look the other way at the fences buying stolen goods, the young girls selling hot corn—and themselves—on the streets, the lodging houses where mothers and daughters accommodated male customers at the same time and in the same small room. Crime flourished in the Five Points section of the city east of Broadway, where one block was given the expressive and accurate name of "Murderer's Alley."

William Astor, immersed in his ledgers, Bible, and family life, appeared oblivious to all this. His heavy, slow-moving figure made its way from Lafayette Place to his office and back home again. Mayor Wood's political maneuverings were of little interest to him, so long as they increased the value of the Astor property. As for Wood, the Tammany mayor was a most agreeable man to know. Tall, dark, and handsome, with a big black mustache, he was always fashionably dressed and at home in any drawing room. He favored the drawing rooms of the very rich.

Astor's acceptance of Wood was not shared by less affluent New Yorkers, who raised an outcry about the corruption. The Republicans tried to get the police department out from his control, so that it could be used to fight vice. Wood's supporters countered with a mass meeting for the Mayor at which William, despite his shyness, was honorary vice-president, along with such other notables as Peter Cooper, Horace Greeley, and Cornelius Vanderbilt. Wood kept control of the police department.

In 1856 Wood wanted to run for re-election but was opposed by those of his fellow Democrats who were sickened by his lack of ethics. A testimonial for Wood was drawn up. His enemies insisted that he wrote it himself; that made no difference. The important thing was the names that were signed to it. William B. Astor's was prominent among them. When Wood was re-elected, Astor and his fellow landlords were rewarded with low tax assessments and additional waterfront rights.

As Civil War clouds gathered, pro-southern Mayor Wood offered the proposal that New York become an independent city. This position led presidential candidate Abraham Lincoln to observe wryly that this was hardly the time for the front door to detach itself and set up housekeeping. William Astor thought his powerful political friend was going too far, but he was worried about the impending insurrection. Although he was studious by habit, he was never capable of understanding large issues. His sons urged him to support Lincoln, but they could not influence him. William ran his family according to the Germanic tradition, as had his father before him. He treated his wife and children kindly, but never considered their opinions worth having. And so he wrestled alone with the new problems facing him as a man of influence and power.

He studied the troubled national situation with only one thought in mind: what will war do to business? His conclusion was that it might cause real-estate values to depreciate. He, therefore, opposed Abraham Lincoln in the campaign for the Presidency and poured thousands of dollars fruitlessly into the Fusion opposition to Lincoln in New York.

A month after Lincoln's election, Sen. John Crittenden of Kentucky sponsored a compromise designed to prevent civil war. Slavery was to be written into the Constitution as an amendment. Astor seized on this as the perfect solution. An old rumor has it that William was so enthusiastic that he took a copy of the bill to the office of the New York *Herald*. A meeting was then held by Astor and thirty other business leaders urging the acceptance of this amendment.

The firing on Fort Sumter in April 1861 brought an end to hopes of compromise. William accepted the inevitable with good grace, and, to the relief of his sons, promptly announced that he was a loyal citizen of the Union and would stand by it to the end.

The result in terms of real estate came as a relief to William. His dark forebodings proved faulty, and wartime inflation pushed rents to high levels. By the time the Civil War was over, William's political affections had been won by the Republicans. He threw his support to Andrew Johnson and then got solidly in back of Ulysses S. Grant, who became a fast friend of the family.

One war measure that infuriated stolid William was the imposition of an income tax. In 1865, with an income of $1,300,000, he was handed the largest tax bill of any individual in the United States. As the Civil War was over, William decided that there was no need for him to remain silent about this outrage. He called in his confidential lawyer, Charles F. Southmayd, insisting that there must be some legal way out. Southmayd was the right person to ask.

"His whole life was devoted to defending property," declared a man who knew him well. "He never married. For that matter, I don't think he ever even knew a woman intimately. He didn't care for sports or art or literature. The law and the business activities of his client were enough for him."

This legal paragon prepared a brief and, self-effacing, agreed that one of the other lawyers for the Astor Estate, William Maxwell Evarts, would do a better job of presenting it to the Supreme Court. And the Court duly found that the income tax was unconstitutional.

Saved from this drain on his fortune and solidly entrenched in society, William, nonetheless, disliked references to the humble origins of his family. John Jacob I had commissioned portraits of his parents, in which they were portrayed as poor peasants selling fish, game, and flowers. Sold after John's death, the pictures were bought back into the family by William's niece Eliza and hung in her Lafayette Place home. When William noticed this, he promptly requested that the paintings be given him. As he appeared even more somber than usual, she asked why he wanted them. "To burn them," he replied coldly.

His attitude only amused Eliza, who like all of John Jacob's grandchildren, felt perfectly secure socially. New York's high society had changed so markedly during these two generations that the Astors were "old society." The example of John Jacob Astor I had encouraged a group of newly wealthy families to try to break into the inner circle. They were aided by one of the strangest of all social arbiters, Isaac Hull Brown, the hulking three-hundred-pound sexton of Grace Church, who for thirty-five years acted as a sort of social secretary, public relations man, and adviser. He claimed to know everyone who passed by, and would mutter, "Old family, good old stock," about one, or, "Ah, here's a fellow who intends to dance his way into society" about another. An unsure hostess giving a party would head straight for Brown. He would check her invitations list, adding names himself where necessary. If the hostess had a son, he could suggest a young belle with a fortune. If bachelors were needed, he had a little list.

Where Brown is found
To fashion's eye is hallowed ground.

So went a popular rhyme composed by a cynical social climber.

Even Brown did not hesitate to endorse the Astor family's position in the inner circle. In fact, William's nephew, Charles Astor Bristed, had become the model of the Old Guard socialite. Charles popularized the term *the Upper 10,000* by writing a book with that title about society. The term, coined by a fashion magazine editor, described the group later known as the Four Hundred. This number would have suited the exclusive Bristed better. He explained to his readers that the ten thousand "is an exaggeration, for the people so designated are hardly as many hundreds." Like others of his set then and since, he deplored the fast-growing practice of inviting vast numbers of people to a ball. One could not be certain of whom one might meet, and it took a quarter of an hour to thread one's way through the ballroom to the dining room.

What did American society in the mid-nineteenth century look like to a young Astor? "A set of exquisites—daintily arrayed men who spend one-half their income on their persons and shrink from the touch of a woollen glove." In his book, Charles described the man of society as one who "dabbles in literature, in business, in everything but politics—talks metaphysics one minute and dances the polka the next." The author went on to add that he was given to "foppery in dress and general sybaritism of living." (He was most certainly not using his hard-working uncle as an example.) After his book was published, Charles spent the rest of his life denying that he was the prototype of the hero of his work, while enjoying the fruits of his social position.

The men of the inner circle associated with the few whom they considered their equals (a small group that included the Astors) in men's clubs, fashioned after those of England. The Hone Club had as members the oldest of New York's Old Guard, and the Kent Club had the gentlemen-lawyers. The Union Club, which leased William's old house from him, was strictly social, but "somehow," said a member disapprovingly, "financiers seem to be the strength of the club." Many of them shared William's careful way with a dollar and stakes for card games were not allowed to exceed twenty dollars. The New York Yacht Club was founded for the sportsmen of the time. (In order to gain acceptance for his yachtsman son, James Gordon Bennett tempered his harsh attitude toward society in the New York *Herald*.) The Century Club was formed for those gentlemen interested in letters and the fine arts (plus a few who were interested mainly in money).

"William was a member of three or four clubs, but a habitué of none," was the conclusion of Francis Gerry Fairfield in a nineteenth-century study of clubs.

There was little in social life that appealed to William; he found it painful to tear himself away from his work for any reason. Despite his European education, he went abroad only once. In 1857 he took his wife on the "Grand Tour" of Europe. Traveling in solid comfort, they experienced but one night of excitement in Italy, when the volcano Vesuvius threatened to erupt. The proprietor of their hotel awakened all the guests and asked them to move to a safer place. Everyone complied immediately, except for the Astors. William B. Astor was seen pacing up and down in front of the hotel, waiting for Margaret. Upon being urged to make his wife hurry, William replied with his customary brevity: "My wife is a general's daughter. She cannot be made to feel frightened."

Emerging from this episode unscathed, they journeyed to Göttingen, to visit William's erstwhile tutor, who was by then Baron von Bunsen. "I will call him 'du' [the familiar form of 'you' in German] just as in the old days!" von Bunsen burst out sentimentally.

William did not give him very much of an opportunity to say anything. The Astors dashed in and out of Göttingen as if pursued. A long itinerary had been mapped, and being a methodical man, William did not mean to miss anything of importance. On the other hand, who knew what was happening to the business at home? Could his eldest son, a mere stripling of thirty-five, be trusted? He was glad to get back.

For all that she was a general's daughter, Margaret was not really more adventurous than her husband. The world that mattered to her was the narrow, feminine one of home, children, her garden, the church, and the charities she sponsored.

"There are perhaps ten times the number of women in good society in New York who interest themselves in the support and direction of moral objectives and benevolent institutions than could be found in any city of the same population in Europe; and while their husbands are busily engaged in their mercantile or professional vocations, a good portion of the wealth they acquire is directed by the benevolent influence of their wives into useful and charitable channels." So wrote James Silk Buckingham, a British visitor to America during the nineteenth century.

Charitable contributions in Europe must have been low indeed, if Margaret Astor's donations are to be taken as an indication of what these praised Americans were doing. (They probably can, because all period accounts refer to Margaret as a particularly public-spirited and generous woman.)

"Mrs. Astor gave us our first gift—fifty dollars," said Reverend Charles Loring Brace, founder of the Children's Aid Society.

The Dutchess County orphanage, given her along with the greenhouse, it will be recalled, housed and educated fourteen girls. Margaret's largest single contribution was one thousand dollars, and it went to the New York Women's Hospital, which also received a regular annual donation of one hundred dollars a year. These figures could hardly be described as a "good portion" of her husband's one-million-dollars-plus-a-year income. Still, she did as well as she could in a time when benevolence was not in style. A bowl of soup or a jar of jelly brought to a starving family was still considered suitable charity for a lady. And Margaret, unlike many rich matrons, did not satisfy her conscience with giving money, instead of time and interest. For many years she was secretary-directress of the New York Women's Hospital, served on the board of the Association for the Relief of Respectable Aged, Indigent Females and was a patroness of the Methodist Church near Rokeby.

With all of society's gaiety available to her, this was her life. She died in 1872, fifty-four years after her marriage to William. The usually stolid, unemotional man was terribly upset by her death. Unable to endure the sight of the home where they had been together, he moved to a house on Fifth Avenue. He was irritable and at times seemed to be bordering on senility. The only thing that gave him pleasure was to have Emily's daughter, Maddie Chanler, read the Bible to him.

A great-grandchild, Margaret Chanler, used to come into his room to try to cheer him up. "Grandfather, if you will whistle 'St. Patrick's Day in the Morning,' I will jig it," she would say to him, but he would only answer sadly that he did not know the tune.

William died in 1875, having lived for eighty-three years. For a good number of them, he was the richest man in America. His property stretched over the map of the entire city, and his power was commensurate. Still, the general public knew him only as a name; he never allowed a reporter to interview him.

His family dutifully followed the casket to the graveyard. His will gave his sons and grandsons the bulk of his fortune, but all were remembered generously. Sweet Maddie received Rokeby and an estate worth five million dollars. She was never to enjoy any of it, because she died of pneumonia caught in that chilly cemetery. Maddie left eleven children and a heartbroken husband.

*

4

The First Aristocrat

Shortly after the end of World War II, handsome young Thomas Emmet, great-grandson of Emily Astor, was stationed with the United States Army in Germany. Finding himself near Walldorf, he decided to visit there. His first stop was at the town hall, where he made known his relationship to Walldorf's best-known citizen.

The officials were delighted; they had been making great efforts, they told him, to trace the background of his ancestor. The name of the father of John Jacob Astor I (Johann Jakob) was clearly written in the church book, as was that of the grandfather, Felix Astor. But when it came to the mother, that was another story. The name was scrawled and the ink so faded that it was impossible to make out all the letters. Some readers thought it said "Vorfelder," and others "Vorberger." The trouble was that there did not seem to be enough letters for either. The Germans finally decided that the name was really "von Berg." As proof, they pointed out that there had been such a family in the eighteenth century; the descendants still live near the town of Bruchsal.

"This means that John Jacob's mother was of noble birth," they explained to Emmet. "She came from a family of impoverished aristocrats."

What is more, says Emmet, the story around Walldorf has it that as a boy, John Jacob was known as *der Nobbele,* "the little nobleman."

This account would make the dimly remembered mother of John Jacob I the first aristocrat in the Astor family. Outside of

Walldorf, however, most people have given the title of "first aristocrat" to tall, distinguished John Jacob Astor III.

"Work hard, but never work after dinner." This was the aristocratic advice regularly handed out by the grandson of one of the hardest-working men of all time.

John Jacob III took his position in the world for granted. "He had the air of reserve and dignity, the bearing which marks the man to whom by nature, place and honor belong," declared the Reverend Morgan Dix, a nineteenth-century rector of Trinity Protestant Episcopal Church and descendant of the man for whom Fort Dix is named.

The British magazine *The Spectator* went even further by pointing out in true Anglophile spirit: "That indefinable air of vulgarity that attaches itself to some of the greatest of American millionaires did not attach itself to Astor."

His confidence and natural air of superiority were fostered by his father, who gave him favored-son treatment all his life. Like any member of royalty, William was always aware of the law of primogeniture. This attitude is clearly shown in his will, which was made long before his death. Money was to be divided equally between his two sons, but the elder was to get a much larger share of the incredibly valuable real estate. Even when they were boys, the father completely ignored the fact that William Backhouse, Jr., was by nature better endowed than his brother.

John went to college at Columbia, where he "failed of distinction," according to a harsh report uncovered recently in an old issue of *Harper's Weekly*. (His brother, on the other hand, maintained an outstanding college record, graduating second in his class.) Nonetheless, members of the family decided to send John to Göttingen to receive his education in Astor style. They were still Germanic enough to call him Johann among themselves. His grandfather and father cudgeled their brains to come up with the best man to accompany him. Sam Ward, who had not yet in 1839 appeared on the family's blacklist, urged that they consider his friend Henry Wadsworth Longfellow. The idea was appealing, but was hardly realistic, a common failing of Sam's ideas. Longfellow was at this time a professor at Harvard University, with a tremendous reputation of his own. Even an Astor's millions could not induce him to drop everything and act as a companion to a callow youth.

Unlike Longfellow, Joseph Cogswell was all too available. He was hovering over the family at this time, trying to further his dream of the library. It probably was not much fun for John to go abroad with an aging scholar, but he was not given the option to refuse. In this German family, the father's word was law. Young Astor and Cogswell spent two years at Göttingen. Cogswell came out of this with $60,000 for the library, and John came out well enough prepared for a year at Harvard Law School.

His father did not wish him to become a practicing lawyer. The Astors employed most distinguished legal talent, but William Backhouse wanted his son to have a smattering of knowledge about deeds and leases, water rights and legislative acts. To obtain practical experience, John followed his year at Harvard with another in a law office. By 1843, at the age of twenty-one, he was considered ready to meet the Astor fate at the office on Prince Street.

John Jacob III was the first of the Astors to be bored by the business that held both his father and grandfather enthralled. He quickly realized that the best way to cope with the dullness was to keep his working hours to a minimum. The son accompanied the father on his walk to the office each morning at nine, knocked off at noon for lunch, and then worked again until three. It cannot be denied that John worked hard during the bankers' hours he kept. Despite his poor showing at Columbia College, he proved a surprisingly apt student to the thorough and sound teaching of his father. As the Astor fortune continued to grow, John decided that his short hours were somehow responsible. This led him to the pronouncement quoted earlier.

Strangers found young Astor rather intimidating. He stood six feet tall in an era when many men were half a foot shorter, and he had a commanding presence as well. His keen light gray eyes were striking against the dark, ruddy hue of his complexion. Possessed of the thick hair of the Astor men, he allowed himself a flowing mustache and sideburns. His manners were courtly and formal, not calculated to put others at their ease. Only his family recognized that he had inherited the shyness and reticence of his father and grandmother. His inborn feeling of superiority was of no help in finding subjects to talk about. He was comfortable with only a few good friends. It was, therefore, fortunate that his grandfather had been careful to surround his children and grandchildren with what members of society would describe as the "right" kind of people. The neighbors on Lafayette Place were either rich or refined.

The Gibbes family, originally from South Carolina, fell into the second category. "The Gibbes were proud, but threadbare," said a friend.

Indeed, they were so proud that they claimed descent from King John of England. They were not so threadbare, however, that they could not live up to the standards expected of them by society. The father, Thomas S. Gibbes, was one of the founders of the exclusive Union Club. The daughter, Charlotte Augusta, had attended the fashionable finishing school run by Mme Chagaray.

Because he had grown up with her, Augusta—she seldom used her first name—was one of the few girls with whom John was at ease. Physically, she was almost his exact opposite, being small, blonde, and frail. Her long nose kept her from beauty, but she had great charm, and everybody who met her was drawn to her.

"The better sort have been regaled by a good wedding . . . attended at the house of her father by all the fashionable people of the city." This entry appeared in 1847 in the diary of Philip Hone, one-time mayor of New York.

The match, as was true of most at that period, had been arranged by the two sets of parents. But those who knew the couple say the marriage that resulted was a happy one.

A lavish wedding was expected of members of society. It was not necessary to follow it up with day-to-day extravagance. Augusta had won the hearts of her friends with her charm; she delighted her new in-laws with her careful management of money. She was not the girl to spend money that was not yet hers. Everybody knew, of course, that John Jacob III was to be a millionaire. As a young man, however, he was dependent upon his father.

"As long as William Backhouse lived, Augusta and her husband practiced extreme simplicity of household management," reported a curious neighbor. "Her dress was plain and so was her home."

John Jacob III applauded her economies. He kept track of the household expenses as if expulsion to one of his father's tenements would result from the smallest extravagance. He used public transportation rather than his own carriage when distances were too far for him to walk.

This careful couple produced only one child. Luckily for the dynasty, it was a boy. By this time, in 1848, the Astors, in royal fashion, were regularly naming children either John Jacob or William. Because John Jacob III was getting a bit tired of being called Junior, he favored William for the new baby. The problem here, though, was that both his father and his brother bore the name William Backhouse. To prevent confusion he then decided to add his grandfather's hometown as a middle name, and his son became the first William Waldorf Astor. (The reason for the dropping of an *l* from Walldorf has never really been explained.)

The intention of avoiding difficulties with the mail was completely foiled some years later by the forceful woman whom his brother married in 1853. Caroline Schermerhorn not only insisted that her husband drop the "Backhouse," she went on to assert that first names were altogether superfluous to a truly important Astor. She was in this regard referring more to herself than to her husband, who was kept in the background by both his father and elder brother.

"Whenever he would come to the office, they would make him feel unwanted" is the view expressed recently by his grandson John Jacob Astor VI. "He was a proud man, and so he did not push himself in."

The fact that William Backhouse, Jr., drank heavily was certainly a contributory factor in his exclusion. But those who loved William —and for all his failings, there was something appealing about him —declared it was his father's cold attitude that caused him to drink. Whatever the interpretation, he was never active in managing the property.

Although, like a young Prince of Wales, John had to wait for his father to die before becoming absolute monarch, he did make a number of important investments in real estate earlier. In fact, he liked to keep a large sum of ready cash on hand. "You never know when you'll see a good buy," he told one of the clerks in the Estate office. "I want to be able to pick up a bargain on the spot."

William allowed his more daring son to do so, because he remembered his own brilliant youthful purchase of the highly profitable Thompson Farm. Even as a young man, John had grasped the sense of the family policy of buying undeveloped land in outlying districts. As he pointed out to one of his friends, sportsmen had gone hunting on Murray Hill when his father was a boy and now one building after the other was being erected there. The other powerful landlord family, the Goelets, was buying up all the land it could lay its hands on from Union Square to Forty-seventh Street. The city's northward expansion was continuing unabated; a few hardy souls were settling in suburban Harlem. Perhaps some day people would even venture as far uptown as the wilds of the "Annexed District."

That rural area had been in the possession of the influential Morris family for the better part of two centuries; Lewis Morris, son of the original settler, had been granted the title of lord of the manor of Morrisania in 1697. But his descendants had not prospered, and the Morris holdings shrank acre by acre. On a winter's day in 1853, John Jacob III had his horses hitched to his carriage and made the long and uncomfortable journey out of town to buy what was left of the Morris estate. He looked over the wooded hills, so confident of the future of the area that, on an impulse, he bent down and roughly marked on the cold, hard ground the places where building lots should go. This purchase was of the type his grandfather had made in his day. The Annexed District is now known as the Bronx.

This success did not excite him. How could it? Success is not exciting to one who has never failed.

As his father grew older, John Jacob took over more of the active management of the Estate. In buying he showed more foresight than William; as a landlord, he was slightly more liberal, but in basic policy they were as one: "I will not sell my land," said John, "I will not put up buildings on it. One thing and one thing only will I do—lease it for twenty-one years."

At least the leases he negotiated gave somewhat better terms than the old Astor leases, and he did encourage tenants to improve property—within reason. His true opinion of the houses put up by the sublandlords, though, is evidenced by his refusal to get fire insurance in a city still dependent on volunteer firemen.

"It is cheaper to lose a whole block of buildings by a fire every once in a while than to pay insurance premiums," he would explain his position to his few intimate friends.

This would sometimes put him in mind of a story his father used to tell. William Backhouse dashed home one day shouting, "Father, one of our houses on the Bowery is on fire!"

John Jacob I was studying the floor carefully and did not answer. William repeated his dramatic statement. His father bent down and picked something up. "Now that I have found the five-dollar bill I had dropped, you may tell me about that house. A bill in the hand is more important than a house in ashes."

John Jacob III, who was not a subtle man, would hasten to assure his listeners that this story was not really true. It had been told him to drive home an attitude that a good businessman should never forget.

Astor was indeed a good businessman, and immigrants were continuing to pour into the city. People needed houses, and he was providing them. By 1860, the population was packed into the East Side tenements at a density equivalent to 290,000 people to the square mile, with the Astor Estate as the chief beneficiary.

And Astor, proving his right to the title of the family's first aristocrat, was as prominent in society as in business.

"Socially," remarked a British magazine writer, "he is at the top. Why, he is as well-known in the United States as the Duke of Westminster is at home."

No one questioned his right to participate in preparations for the visit of the Prince of Wales (later Edward VII) to this country in 1860. The Prince had decided to travel incognito, using the name of Baron Renfrew, but he was not so incognito as to object to having a ball given in his honor. The fear of gate-crashers at the ball was such that each door was guarded by a gentleman of undisputed social pre-eminence. If he did not recognize a guest, admittance was denied. John Jacob III quite naturally was one of these honored guards.

Still, knowing the social elite is not necessarily amusing, and Astor was bored. One year was much like another to him, taking over the business from his aging, plodding father. The approach of the Civil War fired his senses as no well-planned long-term lease or canny real-estate purchase had been able to do. Revealing surprising independence of mind, he supported Lincoln in the bitterly fought election campaign of 1860. His father was opposed to war altogether, and Mayor Fernando Wood, whose good will was worth thousands of dollars, was pro-southern. John Jacob III, by then a man in his late thirties, was sufficiently involved in the Astor Estate political maneuverings to understand the danger of antagonizing Wood and his Democratic henchmen. The one person who agreed with John wholeheartedly was his southern wife. Augusta, an intelligent woman of unusual character, weighed the issues involved and came out strongly in favor of the Union. She was later to do more than just talk and encouraged the recruiting of a regiment of Negro troops to which she presented the colors herself.

Her husband was at his desk in the office of the Astor Estate when the word came that Fort Sumter was besieged by southern troops demanding its surrender to the state of South Carolina. Although he never showed emotion outwardly, John Jacob was tremendously excited by the realization that this meant war. What was his part in it to be?

His initial move was conditioned by his Astor training. He became one of the first—his friends insisted that he was the very first—major contributors to the Union cause. Astor's financial support was valuable to the government, not only for the obvious reason, but also because of the effect it had on the Rebels. A letter found in *Confederate Annals of the War* describes a conversation with Robert E. Lee. "New York is furnishing the Union government with large sums of money," said Lee. "Astor is reported to have offered $10 million."

There is no evidence to prove that he actually gave such a huge amount, but he was undeniably vigorous in supporting the efforts of the Union Defense Committee. Thanks were not always his reward. A month after the start of the war, for example, he offered to send "rifled cannon" to Fort Pickens. Secretary of War Simon Cameron replied curtly that he did not want these cannon and would Astor please not ship any to Fort Pickens.

A civilian's role in the war was clearly unsatisfactory. John Jacob III decided to enter the army. Enlistments and commissioning of officers was somewhat informal in those early days of the

Civil War. The Adjutant General later reported that Astor was never formally appointed or commissioned in the army. Chances are that he simply had a uniform made for him and reported to headquarters in late November of 1862.

With his imposing bearing and superb health, John Jacob looked magnificent in his uniform. Although he appeared every inch a soldier, the heir to the Astor millions was as raw a recruit as any to be found in the army. His years in the Astor Estate office could hardly be counted as military training. Nonetheless, John was promptly given the rank of colonel. It was an era when no gentleman was expected to fight as a common soldier. Even later when the draft went into operation, payment of $300 could exempt a man from service.

First assigned to Washington, D.C., it never occurred to Astor or anyone else that he might live there in an army camp. He rented a fine house and quickly hired a chef, steward, and valet to take care of him. The new colonel was to serve as an aide-de-camp to Major General George Brinton McClellan. This dashing young officer was a personification of the glamor of war in an era when war was still thought to be romantic. It has been said that no general was ever so loved by his soldiers, and Astor, too, was under his spell. McClellan gave John Jacob a particularly sensible assignment for a man of his background.

"I have made it Colonel Astor's duty to remember and keep recorded all information in regard to transports, so that I may always know the exact condition of the transports and their locality," wrote McClellan as he embarked on his unfortunate campaign on the peninsula.

Every ship, ferryboat, schooner, barge, and tugboat available was being gathered to carry McClellan's troops down the Potomac to the peninsula lying between the James and York rivers. From there they were to march toward Richmond. It was still early in the war, and plans were being changed from one day to the next. Astor was the very man to keep a clear head no matter what was going on. In his apprenticeship to his father, he had learned how to transform a tangled mess of information into a concise record. But he wanted action, and this, too, was granted him, and he followed his general up the peninsula.

"I was present at the siege of Yorktown and at the Battle of Williamsburgh, and took part in the Seven Days' fight or battles near Richmond," reported Astor later, adding, "These have been the only exciting years of my life."

His father worrying about him every second did not share his excitement. "Where is Johann now?" he would mutter in German.

The family, gathered in the octagonal library at Rokeby, was silent while William carefully read the accounts of the battles and studied the maps. He flatly forbade his younger son to join the army at all. William, Jr., who had organized a regiment among the farmers of Dutchess County, was longing to fight. He was never able to withstand bullying by either his father or his wife, and so he stayed home, while John was participating in the making of history.

One of the soldiers who was with Colonel Astor in battle was amazed by the man's coolness: "If I had been the heir to the Astor fortune and estate, I would have run away, if I had been hanged for it."

The Union Army was firmly convinced that the Rebels picked off officers first. Some officers put on privates' uniforms to save themselves. John Jacob III never dreamed of doing so; he would maintain status no matter what the cost. It pleased him to observe that his general had a gentleman's regard for property and protected homes and possessions of the Rebels after a battle. This attitude, which aroused Astor's respect, won McClellan many enemies.

One day an old friend of Astor's turned up in McClellan's camp. It was Fernando Wood, pro-southern and a leader of the Copperhead movement in the North, but too shrewd to pass up the opportunity to ally himself with as popular a man as the General. Wood suggested that McClellan might make an excellent presidental candidate in 1864. The youthful McClellan was too flattered to realize that he should not be seen with Wood at all. Astor, accustomed to observing the success of Wood's wily methods, was equally surprised by the violent objections that followed the meeting.

Despite his customary accuracy, Astor was exaggerating when he described his army service as the "only exciting years" of his life. He served but eight months. By then he was forced to realize that he had hitched his wagon to the wrong star. McClellan's career was foundering, because of his failure to win the war. This caused Astor to lose his enthusiasm for army life. As he had never been formally commissioned, he was never actually discharged. He simply resigned from the army in July of 1862 and went home. The following November McClellan was relieved of his command.

John Jacob III remained friends with his former general and urged McClellan to assume the presidency of the New Jersey Railroad and Transport Company. This offer was not made merely out of charity—no Astor could desert common sense so far—McClellan happened to be well qualified for the job. Before the Civil War, he had been president of a railroad, with an amazing salary, in 1861, of $10,000 a year. The former general, however, wanted to run for President of the United States in 1864, so he refused. It was not a wise decision, because he lost badly.

Toward the end of the war, Astor was brevetted brigadier general, an honor roughly equivalent to being given a medal. He preferred to be known as Colonel anyway. A few years later he applied and was accepted for membership in the Military Order of the Loyal Legion of the United States, an organization of former Union Army officers. The letters of recommendation appended to his application are flattering. A careful reading of these yellowed letters, however, casts some doubt on the sincerity of the glowing sentiments expressed. General John McAllister Schofield, Secretary of War under Andrew Johnson, for example, admits that he had no "personal knowledge" of Astor and based his recommendation only upon the man's "general reputation"—showing that in the military as well as in the social world, "it's easy if you're an Astor." John Jacob used to enjoy attending meetings of the Order. These gave him the opportunity to recall his army days. Perhaps it is a measure of his life that those eight months were all he was ever to know of excitement. Thirty-eight years later *The Spectator* was to write, "There is something pathetic about the death, or rather the life, of John Jacob Astor."

When Astor returned to New York in 1862, he found that clubs as well as families were being torn apart. He was horrified to learn that the Union Club was accepting the resignation of Confederate members instead of expelling them. In protest against what they viewed as a namby-pamby way of handling the situation, he and other ardent supporters of the North formed a new club, the Union League. It backed Lincoln and the Republican Party, a political allegiance it has maintained ever since. Augusta Astor, true to her Union loyalties, became active in the committees formed among wives of Union League members. (Nonetheless, it did not occur to Astor to cancel his membership in the Union Club. Why, his family had always belonged to it; the Livingstons—and his grandmother was a Livingston—along with two or three other really old families dominated the Club.)

The upheaval at the Union Club, although taken with extreme seriousness by members of the Old Guard, was, of course, but a minor manifestation of the changes being brought about by the war. The country was being shaken to its foundations, even in places far from the battlefields. Rebellion was in the North as well as in the South. The rumblings of discontent rose until in July of 1863 the slum dwellers rioted against the unfair Draft Law, which exempted the rich from military service. For five days the rioters held off the police. Fifty buildings were burned, and several hundred people killed or wounded. The Draft Riots frightened city officials and mobilized public opinion. Perhaps something should be done for the poor.

A Citizens Association was formed. John Jacob Astor III quickly realized that he was a citizen himself. He had himself put on the committee, along with another friendly citizen, his brother-in-law, the handsome Franklin H. Delano. The Association decided that a group of doctors should inspect the tenements.

None of the physicians who went on that tour was ever to forget what he saw. Five families shared a single room, taking turns at the two beds. Staircases were so rickety that it was frightening to use them. Tenants rented cellar space only six feet high. The rooms upstairs were but seven or eight feet high, for that matter, and many had no light or ventilation of any kind. Children were sent out into the streets at night to get a breath of air. Filth and vermin were everywhere. The sick lay with the well. Although the construction of the Croton Reservoir had brought running water into the city as early as 1842, it was certainly not apparent to slum dwellers. Even the newer buildings on the Astor lots along First Avenue had only backyard privies. At best one might find "school sinks" where water was turned on once or twice a day. An appalling stench from the garbage-filled gutters pervaded the air.

These findings horrified all New Yorkers, including the landlords. The doctors made haste to point out that it was impossible to control the ever more virulent and widespread epidemics of smallpox, cholera, and typhoid in the crowded, squalid slums. All agreed that what was needed was a city Board of Health, and in 1866 one was organized.

The following year the first Tenement House Act was passed by the city legislature. It ruled that no building could take up more than 60 percent of a lot. What is more, it decreed that windows—46,000 of them—be cut in the inner rooms and that cellars were not to be rented as living quarters.

Astor, Goelet, Rhinelander, and the other landlords read this Act down to the small print and raised objections to almost every clause. These men were not inhuman; they most certainly did not approve of the conditions in the tenements. They were quite sincere in wishing that cholera, typhoid, and smallpox be eradicated. What they simply could not see was that the terrible condition of the tenements had very much to do with them as owners or builders. It was caused by the tenants, who were dirty, shiftless, drunken, and careless. The view that poverty was a man's own fault was still the prevailing one. The head of a family should go out and get a good job, instead of making his wife and children share living quarters with others. As for improvements, these were simply wasted on such people. Time and again, a landlord would put up partitions and build indoor privies only to have the tenants take them apart and sell them piece by piece. Filth and vermin were not brought into houses by the landlords. Garbage collection was not in their province.

The new Board of Health summed up the problem accurately: "Some of the tenements are owned by persons of the highest character, but they fail to appreciate the responsibility resting on them."

This was certainly true of Astor, who was a most honorable and upright man and religious besides. In church he handed around the collection plate. In his office he opposed every measure that might improve the condition of the poor.

The landlords and building contractors worked diligently to take the teeth out of the Tenement House Act. John Jacob III did not even accompany Augusta and his parents to Rokeby for the summer, remaining in town to put in his few but vital hours. The Astors never consulted their wives on business matters, so the reason for all this industry was not made clear to Augusta. This may have been just as well for the happiness of the marriage, because she was quite capable of seeing the tenants' side of the issue. After five years of effort Astor and his colleagues induced the legislature to hold new hearings. The decision was that the Act itself should not be rewritten, but that the Board of Health be given the power to modify it. This sounds as if the landlords had lost, but in practice, the reverse was true. The members of the Board of Health were merely men, not supermen. They tried to force the powerful landlords to live up to the Act, but in many cases they failed. Officials stood by helplessly while tenements were erected occupying ninety feet or more of a one-hundred-foot lot, blocking out the light and air of all neighboring buildings.

Every few years the outcry against conditions in the slums would become so great that a new committee of investigation would be appointed. But a study of lists of committee names reveals that they were seldom so new as all that; the Astor name appears time and again. One of the few practical results of any of these investigating committees was the design for a "model" tenement, which was followed for years thereafter. It provided a simple, economical and unappealing solution to the problem of ventilation—an airshaft five or six feet wide running down the center of a building. This provided some air for the inner rooms, at least on the top floors (decaying debris settled at the bottom of the shaft, forcing tenants on lower floors to keep their windows shut), but it guaranteed eternal darkness to all these rooms.

With things going so well, John Jacob III objected to any change that might rock the boat. He even fought the proposal for a subway under Broadway, and influenced his son, William Waldorf Astor, to do the same. The landlord lobby succeeded in postponing this kind of transportation for several decades. Its most convincing argument was that the buildings would collapse as a result of the digging. Justice does not always triumph. When the subway finally came, the buildings not only stood firm, but increased in value immeasurably.

The only changes sponsored by Astor were minor. He was willing to contribute to the $260,000 fund being collected by the Improved Dwellings Association to put up a number of good houses. Each room was to have a window, and indoor bathrooms were planned. The profit on these houses was limited to 5 percent. This development had virtually no impact, however, on the housing problem in New York.

Aided by the corrupt city government, the landlords were able to block slum clearance measures for years. John Jacob Astor III, knew full well what friends in high places could do for him. The dapper Fernando B. Wood had been of invaluable aid first to his father and then to him for many years. Eventually, however, Wood's power in New York declined, as the knowledge of his corruption spread. Although he lost control of the city, Wood never really fell very far. In 1867 he took off for Congress, where he was to expound the views of his wealthy friends for fourteen consecutive years.

By that date New York City had become the fiefdom of William Marcy "Boss" Tweed, ruler of Tammany. Nor could this politician's influence on state politics be described as having been negligible. He served a term as state senator, and for a time controlled the State Democratic Assembly. In 1869 he was able to make John T. Hoffman, one of "his" men, Governor. On the city level, it was Tweed all the way. He controlled the Mayor, A. Oakey Hall, whom he liked to call "Elegant Oakey"; the Comptroller, Richard B. Connolly, whose nickname of "Slippery Dick" he did not like to hear; and the City Chamberlain, Peter Barr Sweeney. These men were known collectively as the Tweed Ring.

Tax rates were set by the city; property valuation was set by the city; water rights were given away; tenement house legislation was enforced (or not) by the city. A businessman not in favor with Tweed was unlucky indeed.

Although quite a snob by this time, Astor forced himself to overlook the fact that Tweed had not been born a gentleman. The Boss was the son of a chairmaker, and had started in politics at the bottom, as a volunteer fireman. Nonetheless, he had acquired, along with his power, a palatial home on Fifth Avenue, a stable, and a yacht. He possessed real estate, and was a director of many corporations, among them the Erie Railroad, this last being due to his friendship with robber barons Jay Gould and James Fisk.

Absolute power has corrupted better men than Tweed and his Ring, but few have ever been quite so venal. In two and a half years these officials robbed the city of forty-five million dollars. If you add the amount lost by such practices as tax reductions for Tweed's friends, the figure rises to two hundred million dollars. A contractor hired for a municipal job was told that he must submit two bills, one to the city and one to the Ring. In this way twelve million dollars of the taxpayers' money was appropriated for a new city courthouse, which cost but three million dollars to build.

Despite his power, word of the utter corruption of Tweed's Ring began to spread. *Harper's Weekly* attacked with cartoons; *The New York Times* tried to arouse the populace. They were not successful. Tweed was popular with the man in the street; he had charm and he was generous. The Tammany Boss had the good sense to give back as donations to charity a few dollars of the millions he stole.

Still, with the elections of 1870 coming up, Tweed was concerned about the increasingly unfavorable reports of his activities. It would be wise to quiet them once and for all. He needed the cloak of respectability. With this in mind, he gathered a group of the most respected men in the city and asked them to form a committee to investigate the city's books. His good friend John Jacob Astor III agreed to head this committee.

Astor was known as an upright and honest man. Although he enjoyed Tweed's favor, there was not the smallest doubt of his personal incorruptibility. Wanting low taxes is not public-spirited, but it is certainly not corrupt. When Tweed came to him with this infamous suggestion, Astor accepted the commission as a business necessity. John knew, of course, that Tweed, like Wood before him, had done a number of unethical things. That was politics, however, and politics was a dirty business, not fit for a gentleman. Astor personally would have nothing to do with it. Somewhat later, for example, when President Rutherford B. Hayes offered him the ministry to England as a reward for campaign support, he turned it down flatly. Political morality, he believed, was on a lower level than business morality, which was on a lower level than personal morality.

Astor, along with five other leading citizens, put his name to a report that was to be known later as the "Whitewash of the Ring." In it was the declaration that all financial affairs of the city "are administered in a correct and faithful manner." One can only assume that John Jacob, whose ability to add was second to that of no man, either did not look at the books at all or was given a doctored set.

The report was released to the newspapers two days before the election of 1870. The weight given to the names of its signers was such that Tammany won again. (It is interesting to note that only fourteen years after this, the temper of the times had changed to such an extent that support by rich men was to spell political disaster. When James G. Blaine lost his bid for the Presidency, his supporters believed that he had ruined his chances by attending a dinner held for him by Astor, Carnegie, Gould, and other tycoons.)

The backing of the wealthy saved Tweed once. Then he went on to ruin himself. Flushed with the success of his coup, the Boss made the mistake of quarreling with one of his underlings—a man with access to the correct books. In July of 1871 a complete set of the city records was delivered to *The New York Times*. It ran in daily instalments for three weeks, revealing such staggering thefts as fourteen million dollars taken on a single April day.

This exposure finished off the Tweed Ring. A committee of seventy, on which John Jacob III did not serve, was named at a citizens' mass meeting to handle the prosecution of Tweed and his Ring. The master politician eventually died in jail.

The scandal worried Jim Fisk and Jay Gould, who were happily making a good thing for themselves out of the Erie Railroad. With Tweed's kind assistance, they had sold five million dollars of fraudulent stock. Although the attempt to cover himself with respectability had not helped Tweed much in the end, Gould and Fisk thought they might have a try at it themselves. They reorganized the board of directors, taking on such highly regarded men as Astor, August Belmont, and Levi P. Morton. Astor's good name, oddly enough, had survived his involvement with Tweed. He had

little effect on the management of the Erie. Gould and Fisk continued their chicanery until it drove the railroad into bankruptcy and
subsequent reorganization.

For all his brilliance in the management of real estate, Astor was
singularly ill equipped to deal with the robber barons. As a rule he
bought only the safest gilt-edged securities—Delaware & Hudson,
New York Life and Trust, United States Trust, bank stocks, New
York City sinking-fund bonds, Valley Coal, Columbus & Hocking
—but every so often he was tempted by a riskier venture. It was
usually a mistake.

Some years before the Tweed scandal, for example, he became a
major stockholder of the New York Central Railroad. Cornelius
Vanderbilt wanted it, and wanting and having were synonyms to
him. He observed that only the Hudson River Railway made the
run between New York and Albany. At this transfer point passengers and freight changed from or to the New York Central. Vanderbilt bought the controlling interest in the Hudson River Railway and promptly ordered the employees to refuse to connect
their trains to the Central or to take on freight. The passengers had
to walk the half-mile distance between the two railroads, loaded
down with baggage. The stock of the Central dropped steadily.
Astor and his fellow stockholders finally gave up and turned over
the New York Central to Vanderbilt.

The only time when Astor was not completely routed by the
unscrupulous tycoons of his era was in the case of Western Union,
and even this could not be described as an Astor coup. John, a director of the corporation, and his fellow board members refused to
allow Jay Gould to join them. This did not stop Gould, who
gained control by a series of manipulations. He did not, however,
force Astor out, and the family retained its interest in Western
Union for the next two generations.

Win, lose, or draw, such business deals were insignificant to a
man whose fortune rested on the soil of New York City. In the
years following the Civil War, the Astor Estate's profits rose
steadily. The first chapters of the tenement story had been written
while his father and grandfather were in charge. During the stew-
ardship of John Jacob III, yet another chapter was to be added, as
the tenements spawned the sweatshops. These manufacturing

operations, whose very name came to stand for oppression and exploitation of the worker, were run in private houses, so as to evade the laws regulating factory labor. No more imaginative than his forebears, Astor did not consider himself involved in what went on in buildings erected and run by others on land that he owned. The sublandlords sought sweatshop operators eagerly, because they could be charged many times the rent asked of ordinary tenants.

The sweatshop operators and the sublandlords (sometimes they were one and the same) were heartily loathed by the poor. The slum dwellers seldom realized who really owned the buildings. One day a doctor visiting a tenement stopped to talk to the tenant of a small, dark inside room. All the time they were chatting, the man, his wife, and twelve-year-old son kept on at their work making cigars. On an impulse, the physician asked if they knew who owned the house. "Astor," replied the cigar maker bitterly. The doctor commented later that this was the only time he found a tenant who knew the name of the top landlord.

Rents were never cheap in the tenements, and they moved steadily upward. In a display of nineteenth-century fair trade, Astor, Rhinelander, and the other major landlords one year raised all rents by 10 percent. Profits frequently amounted to 30 percent of the investment, and 40 percent was not considered unusual. Some houses brought in profits of 100 percent.

By the 1880's, only a few years after the death of William Backhouse, the Astor Estate's income amounted to about five million dollars a year. John got half of this, and, as a result of the somewhat unfair will, his brother received a third. The other relatives divided the rest. John Jacob III sat at his desk while his agents came in to bring the reports of the rentals collected. The keen eye of one of them noticed his employer writing and rewriting a telegram one day. Astor was trying to find a way to save a word. And his estate was then worth eighty million dollars by the most conservative estimate.

A visiting businessman once commented rather fulsomely to him that it must be wonderful to have control of such a fortune.

John stroked his flowing side whiskers and replied somberly; "Money brings me nothing but a certain dull anxiety."

He had a lot to be anxious about. The account of the Astor

Estate holdings was kept in big flat ledgers. A study of them indicates the staggering extent of the possessions. You could pick almost any block in the city at random and find an Astor lot or building. The family owned property on such streets and avenues as Amsterdam, Barclay, Barrow, Bleecker, Bowery, Broadway, Broome, Cooper Square, Clarkson, Crosby, Dey, Duane, Elizabeth, Front, Gansevoort, Grand, Greene, Greenwich, Harrison, Houston, Hudson, John, King, Lafayette, Lenox, Leroy, Liberty, Macomb, Madison, Mercer, Nassau, New, Park, Park Row, Peal, Pine, Prince, St. Nicholas, South, Vesey, Wall, Washington, West, White, and Worth.

Other Astor real estate was to be found on Avenue A and on every avenue from First through Eleventh, with the exception of Second. As for numbered streets, Astor lots lay on 3rd through 8th Streets, 11th, Little 12th through 20th, 25th through 30th, 33rd through 36th, 39th through 52nd, 54th through 56th, 74th through 76th, 79th, 90th through 96th, 107th, 117th, 125th, 129th, 130th, 150th, and 185th Streets. The Estate owned the Astor House, Astor Building, Schermerhorn Building, Exchange Court, Guaranty & Indemnity Building, Oriole Building, and Rogers Peet Building. Even this is not a complete listing; the Astors owned at least 2,500 houses and commercial buildings. What is more, it does not cover the extensive holdings in the Bronx.

John Jacob Astor I and his sons and grandsons had indeed been correct in assuming that the city would grow, chiefly northward, but in all other directions as well. In many ways the new sprawling New York was a much uglier city than it had been in the days of the first of the Astors. Overflowing refuse barrels spewed their repellent contents on every street corner. Sidestreets were narrow and filthy. Even the tree-lined blocks were pretty only in the spring, because the mere handful of street cleaners employed by the city lacked time to rake leaves, and few home owners bothered. Houses had gone up so fast that beauty had been sacrificed. Rows of identical buildings stood side by side on Broadway as a result of a tradition of speed and economy that was to be displayed again in the twentieth century in low-priced suburban developments. Only Bryant Park, like Washington Square a former potter's field, and Central Park, running from 59th to 110th Streets, recalled the bucolic loveliness of earlier days. However, any stroller who looked around would see the ramshackle cabins of squatters on the nearby hillsides.

It was possible to get even farther uptown by public transport, but this was hardly a pleasure trip. Horse-drawn coaches took the traveler northward to Grand Central Station, where a locomotive would be attached for his journey to the suburbs. He would bump slowly past the country estates of the rich and the contiguous cabbage and poultry farms of the poor.

The owners of so much of this valuable land had by then abandoned Greenwich Village, which was no longer really fashionable. In fact, Astor Place, which had been the scene of a slum riot back in 1849, had never lost its nickname of "Massacre Place." Both John Jacob III and his brother William Backhouse Astor, Jr., had settled into mansions on Fifth Avenue on the block between Thirty-third and Thirty-fourth Streets. This area quickly became the place to live, as is revealed by a glance at the yellowing crumbling pages of *Phillip's Elite Directory*, precursor of the *Social Register*. The listings show John Jacob III at 338 Fifth Avenue and William, Jr., at 350, next door to August Belmont and social hopefuls Vanderbilt and Gould. Such stores as Tiffany's, Gorham's, Lord & Taylor's, and Altman's soon followed their rich clientele uptown.

Modern millionaires on Fifth Avenue would be stunned at what their predecessors had to put up with. The street was badly paved with irregular blocks of stone. A drive to Central Park or to the Croton Aqueduct left the traveler all shaken up. In fact, one society doctor refused to let the more delicate ladies go driving at all. None of this affected the prestige of a block occupied by the two leading Astor families.

The office was also moved uptown from Prince Street to 21-23 West Twenty-sixth Street, where a discreet bronze plaque was simply lettered ASTOR ESTATE. During the move, John Jacob III came down to superintend the packing. To the surprise of the workmen, he insisted that all old books and documents be burned.

"He did it to save the cost of moving them," muttered one of the workmen. John's care over minor expenditures was well known by then.

His friends, though, believed he did it because he was afraid that the records might fall into the hands of reporters. He had a terror of publicity.

"He was even afraid to write letters," remarked one of his associates. "I only had two or three from him in all the time I knew him. He begged me to burn them after I finished reading them."

This attitude had been instilled in him by his father. When John Jacob I had died, William Backhouse Astor deliberately destroyed fifteen packing cases filled with old papers. A part of history vanished in the flames.

This secretive attitude has resulted in a spate of contradictory reports about members of this family. There is no agreement even about basic facts. Some biographers maintain that John Jacob Astor I left a fortune of twenty million dollars, and others put it at forty million dollars. (The former figure is the likelier.) Still today, the managers of the Astor Estate shudder when asked the simplest questions about the holdings of the British Astors. And the private lives of the family are subjects for the wildest conjecture.

But this reticence has had positive advantages, too. It is one of the reasons why the reputation of John Jacob Astor III remained unblemished, despite his association with questionable personalities. Even the reformers were somehow unable to put two and two together and make it add up to Astor. In Jacob Riis' slashing denunciation of tenements, *How the Other Half Lives*, for example, the name is mentioned only once. And then it is to praise Mrs. John Jacob Astor III for charities performed during "her noble and useful life."

Whatever can be said against the way in which the fortune was earned, there can be no question that Augusta Astor really tried to apply as much of it as possible to doing good. A magazine writer of the period described her aptly as a "woman of exceptionally beautiful character." In her case, the Astor dislike of waste was translated into the action of sending the food and flowers left over after each of her dinner parties to patients in Women's Hospital.

"Augusta really wanted to help everyone," a friend said of her. "Elizabeth Chanler, one of her great-nieces, suffered for years with a serious hip ailment. Whenever she was having a bad spell,

Augusta would drop everything and rush to her side."

Her kindness also extended to people with far less claim on her. If her dressmaker looked upset, she would find out what was the matter and then do something about it.

In terms of money, her largest public benefaction was $225,000 for the Astor Pavilion, first building of the Memorial Hospital for the Treatment of Cancer. Her pet charity was a project run by the new Children's Aid Society to send destitute boys from the slums to foster homes on farms in the Midwest. This was one of the few attempts of that time to cope with the appalling circumstances of the lives of the children of the tenements. With whole families starving in overcrowded rooms, boys roamed the streets hunting for something to eat, sell, or steal. A future of hunger and crime awaited them. Inadequate as it was, the Children's Aid program saved at least a few. Later charges of improperly checked foster parents and "slave" labor tend to ignore the fact that nothing better was then available. During her lifetime, Mrs. John Jacob Astor III paid the way for about 1,500 of these youngsters. (Not even Riis mentioned her family's role in creating this army of street arabs.)

As a group of boys was about to leave, Augusta would appear at the train station, a small frail figure almost overbalanced by a large hat pinned atop her coronet braids. She would rush up and down the lines of boys, the jeweled cross she wore on a chain around her neck swinging wildly, as she made sure that each had received her gift of a coat, hat, scarf, shoes, and gloves. One day she noticed that something was missing.

"And your Testaments, boys?" she asked.

They were quite willing to go without the Bibles, but she would not hear of it. While they stood waiting, she dashed over to Bible House to get the books.

John Jacob III, who was public-spirited in anything not connected with business, supported her in these ventures and after her death contributed handsomely to the Children's Aid Society for a school to be run in her memory.

The Wood and Tweed administrations, which he also supported, were noted, among other things, for allowing prostitution to be practiced unchecked. Augusta was one of the moving spirits behind the Midnight Mission, one of the most naïve but well-meaning efforts to counter prostitution ever to be made. The women running this mission went out on the streets themselves each night and picked up the prostitutes, who were plying their trade. They asked the unfortunates to come in to the mission for something to eat and a few moments of prayer. Then refreshed, the girls would go back on the streets. The hope was, of course, to influence them to abandon their way of life. Augusta had a slightly more practical mind than her fellow do-gooders and arranged for the mission to set up a dormitory where the girls could sleep alone. And if they earned nothing, at least they spent nothing.

But to portray Augusta as an earnest dispenser of charity is to miss all the spontaneous gaiety and charm of her nature. After the mourning period that followed the death of her father-in-law in 1875, Augusta emerged as one of the city's leading hostesses.

"Augusta's parties contained a mixture of the best elements of New York—surrounded by all that wealth and taste could add to originality of concept," according to a memoir of the 1870's.

Possession of a great social name did not guarantee an invitation to this Mrs. Astor's parties; wit and intelligence were the prerequisites. Literary and political figures inspired the sparkling conversation she appreciated (and could not count on her husband to provide). A natural iconoclast, she welcomed people who were not being accepted by the set dominated by her sister-in-law, *the* Mrs. Astor. Edwin Booth, younger brother of the man who had assassinated Lincoln, was being ostracized by everyone else in society. Augusta Astor had him to dinner and gave him the place of honor on her right. Actresses, too, were not considered suitable guests in the drawing rooms of "respectable" women. Socialites loved the theater, paying an exorbitant price of one dollar for an orchestra seat or seven dollars for a private box, but the prevailing view was that stage people should stay where they belonged. Augusta stunned society with a reception for the Italian tragedienne Adelaide Ristori, who was no longer young or beautiful but was still at the height of her acting powers.

The excitement produced by the presence of such dazzling personalities bypassed John Jacob. He was relaxed only at small dinner parties, and guest lists at his wife's balls, as was customary in the 1870's, often numbered three hundred or four hundred people. At the larger affairs he stood in the background, a remote, elegant figure, occasionally exchanging a remark with one of the business friends whom Augusta thoughtfully invited for this purpose.

One might ask why a thoughtful wife insisted on giving the balls in the first place. The fact is that John, like many tycoons then and since, wanted to maintain a prominent position in society and was pleased that Augusta was capable of playing the required part. For all his carefulness with the money he inherited, he never said no to a request for funds for party-giving. He even urged his wife to hire a truly superior chef, and the cuisine at the Astors was known throughout the city. The wines served at their table were of the very best, and no gentleman had cause to criticize the brand of cigars. Members of their social set liked Augusta better than John and persisted in saying that it was she who had made him a connoisseur. There seems no reason, however, to question a man's ability to like fine food and wine. This diet, although gentlemanly, was not good for his health, because he had a tendency to gout and in later years suffered from a heart condition. He looked so well with his red face and erect posture that few people realized why he took to moving so slowly when he was old.

In his own way Astor always enjoyed the social prestige that his name gave him. When asked to give his occupation on membership application forms, John Jacob III simply wrote in his flowing script, "Gentleman." Astor was welcomed as a member of the city's most exclusive clubs and was a founder of others. He was a leader of the group of Union Club members who could not tolerate the way that the *nouveaux riches* were being accepted.

"What is needed is a club that places family background first," they stated and, to this end, started the Knickerbocker Club.

By the mid-1870's it was hard to find a New York club whose membership list did not contain the names of the Astors or their relatives the Kanes, Langdons, Wilks, Bristeds, Chanlers, and Brevoorts. The importance of this family in New York society was such that almost all memoirs of the period describe the activities of one or another of them. DeLancey Kane, for example, John's cousin (Dorothea Langdon's grandson) started New York's Coaching Club and made it fashionable for young sports to drive four-in-hand carriages down Fifth Avenue. Kane (whose sons were in

their turn to be the *enfants terribles* of society in the 1890's) startled the inner circle of his day by operating a public coach, the
"Tally Ho." It left from the Hotel Brunswick at Fifth Avenue and
Twenty-sixth Street in the morning, got its passengers to the country club in Westchester in time for lunch, and then returned them
to New York for dinner. To accomplish this incredible feat of
speed, horses were changed several times. To the surprise of the
conservative Old Guard, Kane's social reputation was only enhanced by this commercial venture.

"The Marquis of Blandford drove his coach as a public vehicle
between London and Dorking," Kane would explain if anyone
raised an eyebrow.

Augusta was amused by the doings of her young relative, because
she had innate sympathy for anyone trying to be different. In her
own way, she broke with tradition by starting a literary circle at a
time when literary people were considered rather bohemian. Of
course, as an Astor was involved, the Old Guard made haste to
claim that the group was patterned after a club that had been popular two centuries earlier in old New York among the wives of the
Dutch patroons. The women of the Van Rensselaer, Van Cortlandt, Phillipse, Beekman, and De Peyster families, society of that
day, had all been members of a literary club, The Rose. Augusta,
displaying her erudition, adopted as a name for her nineteenth-
century counterpart the *Causeries du lundi* ("Monday chats")
from the title of the weekly literary essays published in France a
few decades earlier by the critic Charles Augustin Sainte-Beuve.
Each of the forty prominent society matron members was required
to write a paper, story, or poem and read it aloud to the group.

Despite her interest in things of the mind and spirit, Augusta was
a completely feminine woman, even a bit frivolous. She simply
could not resist a beautiful piece of lace and, because John indulged
her, bought much more of it than she could possibly wear. (The
Metropolitan Museum of Art in New York has it now.) Another
great weakness, like that of her sister-in-law, Laura Delano, was for
jewels. Her favorite earrings contained four diamonds, each the
size of a teardrop, surrounding a perfect ruby as big as a hazelnut.
Augusta attended the great formal balls resplendent in three hundred thousand dollars' worth of diamonds. A tiara perched on top

of her blonde braids; necklaces hung to her slender waist; rings and bracelets adorned her delicate hands and arms.

This was an era in which rich people were expected to look it. The customary Astor secretiveness makes it impossible to find out just how much the Astor ladies spent on clothes and adornment. The father of a young belle in their social set was not so reticent. He reported spending twenty thousand dollars to outfit his daughter for a single New York season. This outlay covered a wardrobe that included forty-five gowns, seven coats and cloaks, forty-eight lace-embroidered chemises, and twenty pearl-encrusted hairnets.

Nearly as much was required for the summer social season. Resort life had become established as society's warm-weather way of life, and Augusta joined the inner-circle group that was making Newport, Rhode Island, a social summer capital. This seaside community had long been known for its healthful climate. In 1783, George Washington had urged an ailing nephew to go there. Until the mid-nineteenth century, Newport was popular with Southerners trying to escape the heat. The resort was very quiet then, as can be seen by the form of exercise most popular with the Southern belles. Chairs were attached to each end of a "joggle board," a sort of seesaw. Young ladies would joggle one another up and down by pushing with their pretty little feet.

Newport had become considerably livelier by the time Augusta settled down for "the season" at her French château "Beaulieu" on Bellevue Avenue. Each summer she gave a tremendous ball to which invitations were eagerly sought. These dances were on the grand scale, but they possessed an air of gaiety, nonetheless. This spirit was notably lacking in the ponderous affairs given by Augusta's dignified next-door neighbor and sister-in-law, *the* Mrs. Astor. The difference lay in the natures of these two women.

"Aunt Augusta was not a heavy woman," says her one surviving great-niece, Alida Chanler Emmet. "She was not heavy in body, and not heavy in spirit."

Alida, now in her nineties, is one of the few living people who can still remember John Jacob Astor III and his Augusta. She is the last of the children left motherless when Maddie Ward Chanler caught her death of pneumonia at the funeral of William Backhouse Astor. The father, John Winthrop Chanler, soon followed his wife to the grave.

With a touch of the typical Chanler insouciance, he remarked, "Children, never listen to a lady who refuses to stop playing croquet when the grass is wet." A week later he was dead of pneumonia.

Alida and her nine brothers and sisters (one of the original eleven Chanler children had died by then) were left Rokeby and the bulk of their mother's large estate. The children and their possessions were guarded by an elderly spinster cousin and a group of trustees. Although their grandfather, Sam Ward, was still alive and certainly the logical person to take charge, he was not even named as a trustee. The recurrent bitterness between Sam and his first wife's relatives had cropped up again after Maddie's death. Sam, who had expected a sizable bequest, had been cut off with an annuity of $1,000. Unable to control his temper at this slight, he had lashed out bitterly at the Astors and Chanlers, with the result that he was barred from his grandchildren even more rigorously than he had once been separated from his daughter. And so it was John Jacob Astor III, their great-uncle, who took the place that might have been Sam's, as chief trustee. It was not an altogether happy arrangement as far as the children were concerned. Another man might have become a substitute father; John Jacob did not have the gift for warm human relationships.

Alida finds it hard to describe her great-uncle at all, although his death from angina pectoris did not take place until she was in her teens. When reminiscing, she sometimes confuses him with William Waldorf Astor, who succeeded his father as trustee and displayed similar cold correctness in his dealings with the Chanlers. Aunt Augusta, on the other hand, is a warmly treasured memory. And Augusta predeceased her husband by three years.

Margaret Chanler Aldrich, an older sister who survived until 1963, remembered John Jacob Astor III much better. She had found him kind but stern. It was very hard to get money out of him, she recalled. Although the income on the Chanler estate amounted to seventy thousand dollars a year, he objected to the cost of the stones needed to complete the solid hand-set wall that surrounds much of Rokeby.

Shielded from the outside world by that wall, money, the Astors and other trustees, the Chanlers grew up in seclusion at Rokeby. After one of the boys died at St. Paul's School in Concord, New Hampshire, all his younger brothers and sisters were tutored at home. The atmosphere was very religious; on Sundays, tennis and croquet were strictly forbidden. ("It was a dull life," comments Alida; "we were bored with it long before it ended.") It was hard to tame the Chanlers. The boys used to take the dogs out to the servants' porch at the back of the house and wrestle with them on Sunday afternoons.

The Chanlers were so different from the Astors that it is hard to believe that they, too, were descended from William Backhouse Astor. The family tends to blame all peculiarities on the Chanler heritage, and yet the Astor closet holds some skeletons, too, notably John Jacob Astor II and the erratic Henry in the next generation.

Whatever ancestor may have been at fault, solid, stolid John Jacob Astor III was totally unable either to understand or to cope with these charming, attractive, unstable relatives. Astor loved his Augusta quietly and soberly; it was impossible for him even to imagine the emotions driving John Armstrong "Archie" Chanler, who went mad for love when his wife, Amélie Rives, author of the sexy (for that period) novel *The Quick and the Dead*, became infatuated with Count Pierre Troubetskoy.

"Archie had such a great heart that when he saw what had happened, he said to his rival, 'I give you my wife, because you love one another,' " his sister Alida relives that old tragedy. "Can you think of another man who would do that? It was too much for him. It drove him out of his head."

Archie was confined in the Bloomingdale asylum. Here, too, authorities were quite unable to control the Chanler spirit, and one Thanksgiving Day he escaped. Realizing that he would otherwise have to spend his life in hiding, he eventually went voluntarily to a hospital where he was adjudged to be sane. But when he attempted to get the estate to raise his allowance, he found that the New York courts did not accept the certificate of sanity issued in another state.

"How can I be sane in Virginia and insane in New York?" he asked in helpless fury. (A similar legal impossibility exists in the family today. John Jacob Astor VI is married to Dolores Fullman in Florida and is not married to her in New York.)

Archie was so angry at his family for not supporting him in his suit that he took a strange kind of vengeance against them: he changed his name to Chaloner.

His brother, Robert Winthrop Chanler, had not a whit of his great-uncle's carefulness with a dollar. He cheerfully signed over his entire fortune—which by then had appreciated to more than one million dollars—to his bride, opera singer Lina Cavalieri. Within the week love vanished and she left him. Luckily for young Chanler, the more sober Astors prevailed. The trustees of the estate refused to recognize the agreement, and Lina got a settlement and a divorce. Archie could not resist showing his unholy glee at the mess his brother had gotten himself into. He sent a wire: "Who's loonie now?"

While the Chanlers lacked the Astor common sense, they were far more creative, and Bob went on to become a successful artist with a highly decorative, imaginative style. Unfortunately, most of his work has been lost, because he devoted his greatest efforts to painting murals in the homes of members of society and both murals and mansions have been demolished. One of the few remaining examples of Robert's art can be seen in his old bedroom at Rokeby, where he amused himself during a sleepless night by covering the walls with brilliant orange poppies and gloomy-looking black crows.

Many of the Chanlers had an artistic streak, and the family, at Archie's urging, established the Chaloner Prize, providing scholarships for three years of study in Paris to young American painters and sculptors. Archie induced his great-uncle William Astor, Jr., to contribute $2,500 and his uncle William Waldorf Astor to give $1,500. Great-aunt Laura Delano was called upon for $1,000. With his customary flair, Archie made a bet with a cousin that the first of them to die would leave $25,000 to the competition. (Archie won.)

Another brother, William, found an outlet for the family high spirits in a life of adventure. His guardians, recalling that John Jacob III had profited from a year in the law school, had attempted to tame William by sending him to Harvard. It was in vain, and he quit in his sophomore year. William was much happier exploring Africa, where he discovered a waterfall to which he gave the family name, a new antelope, *Cervicapra chanleri*, five new reptiles, and a new species of insect, *Chanleri l. astoria*. His days as an explorer were brought to a premature halt by a mutiny of his porters, who were not enjoying the safari as much as William was.

"Father had the family problem of stuttering, but he improved a great deal in Africa," says his son Ashley Chanler. "He always said it was because he did so much yelling at the porters."

With this improved diction, he was able to serve a term in Congress, the first of the Chanler boys to follow their long-dead father into politics. His brother, Lewis Stuyvesant, the most prominent of his generation of Chanlers, became lieutenant governor of New York. As a youth, Lewis was psychic, a trait common among the Chanlers. Archie used to receive messages from a deceased Confederate officer, and Lewis often heard a dead servant, Jane, sweeping in the room above him at Rokeby at night.

All the three girls left orphans by Maddie Chanler were debutantes, brought out by their doughty great-aunt, *the* Mrs. Astor. Alida still trembles at the memory of her overwhelming debut at Newport; *the* Mrs. Astor was not much help.

Of the great aunts, Augusta, dead by the time of this debut, had been by far the more popular with the Chanler girls. Augusta lavished affection on them; she never had a daughter of her own, and her only son, as was the Astor tradition, was dominated by his father.

All of the sisters were beautiful, having inherited the Chanler rather than the Astor looks. The loveliest of them was the eldest, Elizabeth, who lived up to the promise shown in her infancy when her young mother had mused, "The bud is so beautiful, one wonders what the open flower is to be."

John Jay Chapman, the distinguished essayist and poet, selected as a husband for Elizabeth was a member of the intellectual Boston set centering about William James. Chapman's temperament was as notable as his intellect. One day he thrust his hand into the fire and burnt it so badly that it had to be amputated. The only reason he would give for this irrational act was that he felt remorse at having beaten a man who had "insulted" a young girl. The Chapmans later spent many years in England, becoming a part of the Astor expatriate circle. Elizabeth arranged to have her younger sisters, Alida and Margaret, presented to Queen Victoria at her last "drawing room."

Alida married C. Temple Emmet, descendant of a lawyer who had represented John Jacob Astor I. Members of the family like to remark that Emmet was the man who got Astor interested in real estate, but they smile when they say it.

Her sister Margaret, an ardent Suffragette, was much more like the Chanler boys in her ambition and energy. During the Spanish-American War, she set up base hospitals in Cuba and Puerto Rico and later worked to establish an Army Nurse Corps. Although the attractive Chanler family had produced few spinsters, it looked as if Margaret was going to be one. In the role of old-maid aunt, she offered to arrange the debut of a niece. At this coming-out ball, held seventeen years after her own, Margaret met Richard Aldrich, music critic of *The New York Times*.

Aldrich took no chances of anyone's accusing him of being influenced by his spirited wife. "Please never refer to what we have heard until I have written my criticism," he adjured his wife, as they took their seats at a concert.

In the end, it was Margaret who inherited Rokeby. She reached the age of ninety-two. In her last years she took pride in the fact that she could remember half a dozen people born in the eighteenth century. Because her son had died before her, she willed Rokeby to her grandchildren, the oldest of whom was a Harvard senior at the time.

Margaret, a strong-willed woman, refused to receive anyone who had been divorced. She was thus virtually cut off from most of the Chanlers and Astors.

5

"The" Mrs. Astor and the Society Establishment

She was neither beautiful nor brilliant; her manner lacked charm, and her conversation wit. The husband, whom she professed to love, ignored her, fleeing from her side into a world softened by alcohol, pretty girls, and good fellowship. But no one seeing her standing in purple velvet, with her small plump body held stiffly erect to counterbalance the weight of a fortune in jewels, could have missed knowing that he was in the presence of one of the great personalities of an era.

Certainly, Ward McAllister sensed this in a moment. "I then, for the first time, was brought into contact with this grande dame and at once recognized her ability and felt that she would become society's leader," he wrote of their initial fateful meeting.

Caroline Webster Schermerhorn Astor was well along in her thirties by then and was moving inexorably toward the throne she was nearly ready to assume. In her own mind, at least, she had always been the crown princess of society, prepared for her role even before her birth by generations of distinguished forebears. Her family was firmly established in Dutch-ruled American society for 150 years before John Jacob Astor I disembarked from the *North Carolina* and made his way to New York. Jacob Jacobsen Schermerhorn had come from Holland to Beverwyck (Albany today) in 1636 and had quickly obtained a large estate and amassed a goodly sum of money. By 1845 his descendant, Abraham Schermerhorn, Caroline's father, was listed in *The Wealth and Biogra-*

phy of the Wealthy Citizens of New York as worth half a millon dollars. Even better in society terms were the family's relationships with the prominent Van Cortlandts, Barclays, and Beekmans. All of Abraham's children made brilliant marriages—to a Jones (the right one, of course), Suydam, Irving, Welles, and Bayard—and the Schermerhorns were welcomed by the Astors when the time came to find a husband for the youngest, Caroline.

And what could be better than a wedding that brings together a rich family with one that is richer, and a newly social family with one that has a long and distinguished pedigree? Such unions are blessed in the society heaven. In later years the friends of William Backhouse Astor, Jr., wondered why he had ever agreed to marry this dull, homely girl, with the big nose, small mouth, and heavy jaw, who was still unclaimed at twenty-two. After all, William was not only the heir to a great fortune, but was a bright and charming young man besides. His grandson and always his apologist ("I named my son after him") John Jacob VI, who has had considerable experience with unhappy relationships, attributes the marriage to William's extreme youth. Only twenty-three at the time, young for a husband if not a wife, William probably wanted to assert himself in the family, says his grandson, and show that he was no mere boy. As for Caroline, united with the most pleasing personality of the stolid Astor family, the marriage seemed almost too good to be true. On the surface, everything appeared perfect. After his brilliant showing at Columbia, William had traveled extensively in Egypt, Palestine, Turkey, and Greece and had developed an abiding interest in their art and literature. The trip had broadened his horizons in an era when most rich men, his brother included, had little to talk about outside of business. His cultured taste and polished manners were a striking contrast to the heavy cold correctness of his father and brother. No, Caroline had no way of knowing in advance that she had gotten a second-best Astor. No one warned her that nothing William was or did could make up in his father's eyes for the fact that he was not the eldest son. It was enough to drive a man to drink—and it did.

Caroline showed considerable forebearance with her husband's failings; it was, one must realize, an era when women suffered in silence at the animal nature of man. She exhibited far less equanimity about the secondary position accorded her by the family and the social set of New York. They took it as a matter of course that the universally popular Augusta as wife of the eldest Astor son outranked her. Even during the years when the John Jacob III's lived comparatively modestly, everyone persisted in considering them by far the more important couple. What solace could be drawn from the fact that Mrs. John Jacob III laughed at the idea of careful stratification in society or the family? It did not seem funny to Caroline.

Wherever she could, she made her forceful personality felt. Lafayette Place, she insisted, was becoming déclassé; all sorts of people were moving in, and commercial establishments were going up nearby. It was really no place to bring up children, and Mrs. Astor planned, indeed had to have, more, because she had so far produced only a daughter. After carefully weighing the real-estate holdings of her husband's family, she settled on the old Thompson Farm at Thirty-fourth Street and Fifth Avenue, the one daring purchase her father-in-law ever made. Nagged by Caroline, William summoned up his courage and asked his father for half of the property. Once suggested, it was so obviously an ideal place to live that John Jacob III and Augusta promptly decided to build themselves a mansion on the other half of the plot, giving Caroline the satisfaction of having for once imposed her will on the entire Astor family. Twin four-story red brick houses went up side by side, joined by a garden and protected from the eyes of the curious, of whom there were many, by a high wall.

In the northern of the two buildings, which was in time to be the scene of the most famous balls in American social history, Caroline led the life of the young society matron, neglected somewhat but not completely by her husband, if three more daughters and a son can serve as evidence of occasional attention. And it was in motherhood that Caroline found herself. None of her detractors, and there are many, deny that this stiff, dignified woman was capable of warmth, tenderness, love, and unique loyalty so far as her children were concerned. Caroline's children adored her, and this total adulation brought out the best in her demanding nature.

"She was one of those women to whom one instinctively applies the adjective 'motherly' in no matter what walk of life they may be placed," wrote Elizabeth Drexel Lehr, wife of the man who was to be Ward McAllister's successor.

William fathered this brood, but did not dominate them; the role of Germanic head of the house was not for him. He quickly learned that he had exchanged the patriarchy ruled by his father for a matriarchy ruled by his wife. Discouraged, he responded again in the only way he knew—withdrawal. He built a magnificent sailing yacht, the *Ambassadress,* and spent as much time on board as possible. An estate, Ferncliff, was established in fashionable Dutchess County near Rhinebeck, and William, when not leading the gay life, devoted his energies to administering a farm and breeding racehorses. In the late spring and early autumn, when neither New York nor Newport was in season, Caroline would join him there and entertain the local gentry. (Her standards of who constituted society were not as rigid there, it was said.) At Easter time William frequently accompanied her to Europe; he always loved to travel. For the most part, though, the relationship of husband and wife became a standoff: as he pushed her out of his life, she, in turn, pushed him out of the lives of their children, allowing him to assert himself only during crises, engagements, and weddings, when a father was essential.

Society matrons today, when asked why they devote so much time to charity balls, luncheons, club affairs, and committees for subdebutante and debutante parties, reply, to a woman, "I do it for the children." Mrs. Astor, similarly motivated, rose from what no one but she considered social obscurity to the position she intuitively felt should be hers in the early 1870's, when her daughters approached the age to be introduced to society and concomitantly find husbands. It is hard to imagine that Caroline (or her modern counterparts) would have been restrained in any event, but the added incentive was all that she needed to arouse her to yet greater efforts. At that critical moment she met Ward McAllister, and social history was in the making. McAllister had the dream and Caroline Astor the means and the desire to make that dream reality. The two of them placed an imprint on society that it bears to this day.

Time has dealt cruelly with McAllister; he was of a type that is remembered at its worst. His pomposity, his unwitting ability to make the remark that almost demands satirization, have caused him to come down through history as a bit of a joke. But his longing to create a society in America comparable to that of the European aristocracy was "so ardent, so sincere that it acquired dignity," said one of his contemporaries; "it became almost a religion."

McAllister, born just four years before his patroness, in 1827, in Savannah, Georgia, never lost his lazy, southern drawling speech, but it was in the North that he found his métier. At the age of twenty he visited New York and was introduced into social circles by a godmother who was expected to make him her heir (which she did not). Like a nineteenth-century F. Scott Fitzgerald, he awakened to the starry-eyed realization that "the very rich . . . are different from you and me." When Ward did receive a legacy of but one thousand dollars, he spent most of it on a costume for a fancy dress ball, an extravagance that delighted him in retrospect for the next forty years. But his funds were not sufficient for social New York, and so he journeyed to San Francisco, where his father and brother, anticipating ample business as a result of the 1849 gold rush, had opened a law office. Luckily for the clients, Ward was not required to practice law; his assignment was to entertain contacts, which he did with tremendous flair. Dinner parties, at which he served roast turkey with the tail feathers reassembled and fastened back on, were costly but brought in the business. By the time McAllister wearied of San Francisco, he had earned enough money to return East and to take himself a meek, retiring wife, Sarah T. Gibbons, who was never heard to object to, or for that matter encourage, any one of her husband's flamboyant ideas. The couple took the Grand Tour of Europe together. No one has ever been able to find out what Sarah got out of it, but Ward's observations of European aristocracy served him as raw material in planning the society he was to help create in America. In England he dined with the chef of Queen Victoria and was invited to look upon Her Majesty's table set for dinner.

"And then I was told to go." Another man might have objected to such peremptory dismissal, but not McAllister. It only kindled his deepest admiration, and besides, "I saw all I wanted to see."

Upon his return to the United States in 1858, he bought "Bayside Farm" at Newport, where he knew he would be surrounded by the cream of society. He began to entertain on a scale that would have done credit to an Astor. For an afternoon's *fête champêtre*, he did not hesitate to hire a flock of sheep and a few cows. Even more important, as he wrote later of his party-giving, "I map it out as a general would a battle, omitting nothing, not even a salt spoon; see to it that I have men on the road to direct my party to the farm."

Being of good family himself—he was a cousin of the mercurial Sam Ward, who had married lovely Emily Astor—he had little trouble in attracting the inner circle to these carefully engineered affairs. By the late 1860's, even before the McAllister-Astor entente, he was beginning to be recognized as a social arbiter in Newport in the summer and New York in the winter. Caroline Astor, for her part, was not yet *the* Mrs. Astor, but the moment when she could legitimately claim that title was fast approaching.

It has often been asked just what Mrs. Astor and McAllister did that no one else had done. With unbelievable concentration, they organized social behavior into an elaborate set of rules and rituals and produced a Napoleonic code of society, making it clear just what it was and detailing who was in and who was not. This clear-cut legislation, oddly enough, was seized upon by the outs as well as the ins, because it showed them exactly what to strive for and made it possible for them to know when they had arrived.

Of course, the time itself was peculiarly right for Mrs. Astor and her prime minister. In the early years of the nineteenth century there was no need for such codification. The population of this country was comparatively small, and everyone knew who was high society and who was not. The definitive stratification of European society had not yet been lost, and those who belonged to families that had been prominent in the Old World received what they were convinced was their due in the New World, too. Naturally they knew how a gentleman should live—not only in terms of home, estate, dress, and servants but also in use of leisure. They formed men's clubs from which outsiders were rigorously excluded by virtue of the black ball, joined the New York Society Library, hunted, attended the National Horseshow from its inception in 1833, and enjoyed private subscription dances. Members of this group might seemingly accept a John Jacob Astor I, but privately they sneered at his manners and never really considered him as one of them. Astor's sons and grandsons did better, but there is no doubt that their wellborn wives increased their social mobility.

The democratic spirit of this country only gradually permeated all aspects of life. For a time it was enough to have "no taxation without representation" and the Bill of Rights. Ambitious men, like John Jacob Astor I, were content with an economic equality in which it was possible to rise as high professionally as one's talents would take one and earn great sums of money. The new democracy did not extend to a feeling that one must live in the style of Old Guard society and be accepted by it. For that matter, rather little was known about the way the inner circle really lived. Today anyone literate enough to read the tabloids is barraged by a never-ending spewing forth of details about the Paris-original ballgown, the yacht with El Grecos in the lounge, the formal dance with two orchestras and big-name entertainers, the *quiche Lorraine* at dinner, and the ten-thousand-dollar debut with champagne flowing from the fountain. It is hard to realize that James Gordon Bennett was displaying a rare degree of journalistic foresight when he began to list names of Astor House guests in his New York *Herald*. That was in the 1830's, and before then, newspapers carrying reports about society went only to the very people being written about both in England and here. The gossip columns did not appear for some years thereafter. The poor and even the moderately well-to-do had only a hazy idea of what went on in the high-ceilinged rooms in the mansions of the rich.

Not many had the leisure to devote much thought to the subject anyway while facing the rigors of life in America during the first half of the nineteenth century. Work was backbreaking and never-ending for those not waited on by a large retinue of servants. That, rather than slovenliness, was why sidewalks in all but the very best neighborhoods were hardly ever swept, and why any garbage refused by pigs rotted in the gutters. Even maintaining minimal standards of personal cleanliness was a time-consuming occupation before the opening of the Croton Reservoir in 1842. The family wash—with all the long underwear, voluminous nightshirts for both sexes, innumerable petticoats, and mud-spattered skirts and pants—was done in rainwater collected on the roof. The water had to make do for baths, too, and so these tended to be infrequent, and in dry seasons whole families would use the same bath water one after the other. This was hardly a procedure calculated to make them welcome neighbors at the book-lined shelves of the New York Society Library, even if they knew how to read and wished to do so.

Now the *nouveaux riches*, like the poor, have always been with us. Others besides the Astors did get rich in the growing, young United States, and occasional attempts were made to scale the wall around the inner circle. In the early years of the century, the City Assembly, a private subscription dance, accepted only the oldest of old families, and even then, there were enough aspiring members left over to make possible the formation of the New Assembly. This group quickly overcame its second-best status by setting its admission at so high a price (three dollars per person) that some members of the City dance transferred in order to show that they could afford the tariff. As a result, there was some mingling, but it was really of oldest and old families, rather than of old and new.

The Civil War changed all that; its impact on society in the South has been studied in exhaustive detail, furnishing the raw material of which best sellers as well as scholarly works are formed. But life in the North, too, was altered in myriad ways. The war, as William B. Astor, Sr., had learned, was not necessarily bad for business. Although some members of the inner circle were reduced to aristocratic penury, fortunes were made or increased. It all depended on what the individual was buying, selling, or owned. The population grew, both as a result of renewed immigration from Europe and the influx of people from the South. It was no longer possible to know everyone in New York society or even to know everyone rich. For the first time the expression *social climber*, or another term of the time, *silver gilts*, began to be heard, and regularly, too. Many were no longer content to line the streets between four and five in the afternoon to watch the society matrons take their drives; they wished their horses to trot beside Mrs. Astor's.

In New York appeals for aid were made to Sexton Brown, aging and monstrously fat, but still a factor to be reckoned with. The private subscription dances, such as The Assembly (no longer City or New, but simply The), were inundated with requests for invitations. The committees running the affairs tried to hold the line, but were sometimes foiled. A story of the time, probably apocryphal, has it that a banker received an invitation to the Assembly after threatening the committee head with financial ruin. He attended the dance and found himself virtually alone on the floor at Delmonico's, because the Old Guard stayed away in a body. Members instead formed the "Cheap and Hungries," a dance group for people who abhorred the former and knew nothing of the latter. Even here it soon became necessary to keep the names of members of the invitations committee secret.

As if all this were not bad enough, a postwar lack of restraint led to excesses by people who were either young, naturally wild, or had no social position to lose, and parties took on an aspect that at times verged on the orgiastic. All inhibitions could be relaxed at balls where masks concealed the faces of hot-eyed men, and women who encouraged advances by daring to show their legs in short dresses. Along with such comparatively innocent goings-on, vice was uncontrolled and moral standards low in a city ruled by Boss Tweed. Depravity and its practitioners came dangerously close to the world inhabited by the inner circle and infiltrated it at weak points. Dance halls patronized by an unsavory lot flourished in the vicinity of Thirty-fourth Street and Sixth Avenue, a stone's throw away from the mansions of the Astors. Gambling was wide open in the neighborhood near the Fifth Avenue Hotel, and one of the most famous brothels of the time, kept by Irene McReady, was located at 4 East Fourteenth Street, not far from the Academy of Music, which was (also) attended by the elite. Mme Restelle, an abortionist, set herself up in business on Fifth Avenue and found such a large clientele among the rich and social that there was virtual panic when, with the law in hot pursuit, she committed suicide in her bathtub, leaving her confidential list of clients for the police to find. If they found it, though, they never used it; someone—no facts as to his identity ever leaked out—suppressed or destroyed it.

For all the efforts of the Old Guard this was a disorganized period, with elements of grace, refinement, and Victorian correctness and, at the same time, crudity, corruption, and depravity. A mother with a daughter to bring out into society had ample cause for worry. And it was into this world that Mrs. Astor and Ward

McAllister stepped, pulled together the more settled older elements, and endeavored to oust or best the newcomers.

The first step in this was to make it abundantly clear just who was really society in that season of 1872–73, when Mrs. Astor's eldest daughter Emily had turned eighteen. McAllister suggested that a subscription dance organized far more rigorously than any in the past was the simplest and best way to tell the world who "had the right to create and lead society." The prototype for such an organization was Almack's in England, where society matrons arranged balls to which only the leading families were invited. In the American adaptation, Ward urged that men rather than women should be dominant, and Mrs. Astor tactfully concurred— provided, of course, that she should have a voice in deciding which men were to be allowed to be dominant. Then began a period of worry, work, tracing of lineages, and making of lists. (McAllister was not yet known by his eventual nickname of "Make-a-list-er," but it was clearly coming.) An executive committee met with him daily to wrestle with the weighty selection problem. In the end they came out with the announcement that the Patriarchs were to number but twenty-five men. These gentlemen were not all there was of society, but they (and their wives) knew everyone who was worthy of inclusion, and they would have the right to invite the other insiders to the Patriarchs' ball. Each Patriarch could ask four ladies and five gentlemen, including himself, to each ball. In addition, a committee could invite up to fifty "distinguished strangers," so as to include visiting royalty or socialites from other cities.

The original group of Patriarchs contained a rather heavy concentration of Astors, Schermerhorns, and their connections, which surely came as no surprise to anyone in the fashionable Thirties on Fifth Avenue. In addition to William Astor (Caroline had already induced him to do away with the Backhouse middle name, which she felt possessed no cachet at all, and was well on the way to doing away with his first name, too) and John Jacob Astor III, we find Eugene A. and Maturin Livingston, Lewis Colford Jones, Benjamin S. Welles, W. C. Schermerhorn, and Walter Langdon. Later, when vacancies occurred, McAllister and Mrs. Astor checked the backgrounds of applicants, although, of course, they really knew everyone who counted already. McAllister liked to say that he insisted on a pedigree of four generations in society, but as usual he was exaggerating, and he slipped from that ideal a number of times. Certainly the male side of the Astor family would not have been included according to that criterion.

Neither of the arbiters was likely to be lenient where Jews or Catholics were concerned. Mrs. Astor was in this view reflecting the temper of the times and her social station, but she was never a woman to place ideas above the individual. Once she accepted someone, it was forever, and so a friend, Ellin Dynley Prince, dared to confide her love for James Speyer, a Jew. Torn between passion and her desire to retain her place in society circles, Mrs. Prince asked: Would anyone receive a Jew and a Jew's wife?

Mrs. Astor did not hesitate: "I don't think we have any alternative, for we are all so fond of you. Marry him, my dear, if you want to. I for one will invite you both to my parties and I think everyone else will do the same."

Mrs. Astor and the would-be Mrs. Speyer did not need to *think*, they *knew* that with Caroline's sanction, everyone else would do the same. This action was an exception, to be sure; still, there were others. Years later, in 1898, Mrs. Astor again shocked New York society by entertaining Baron Oppenheim, a nephew of the rich and powerful Rothschild family. In general, however, Mrs. Astor was not one to lower the social barricades erected against Jews, and she might well be turning over in her grave, as today's Old Guard haughtily murmurs, if she knew that a synagogue now stands on the site once occupied by her mansion. During the heyday of the Patriarchs, the committee did not consider extending an invitation to even so notable a Jew as August Belmont, who was married to a Christian.

Aware that all the other society matrons were as concerned as she about the problem of introducing their daughters to this Patriarch-dominated society, Mrs. Astor and McAllister organized the Family Circle dancing classes for young girls. Ward jubilantly described these as "Junior Patriarchs," and they were indeed a preparation for marriage to the very kind of man who was destined to become a Senior Patriarch. McAllister had a personal stake in the classes—his daughter Louise, a plain girl in need of careful social launching. The Family Circle was held at first in private homes, then moved to Dodsworth, which later became Delmonico's. Mrs. Astor and McAllister thus put the seal of approval on affairs held in public halls. The Archibald Gracie Kings, themselves Patriarchs, went so far as to hold their daughter's debut at Delmonico's.

The point was not where the debut was held, but which parties the young lady was asked to attend during her *season*. "To Mrs. Astor, a deb whom she did not invite to her parties was not a deb at all," says Mrs. Tracy Dows, one of the last survivors of those long-ago debutantes.

According to the thinking of Mrs. Astor and her followers, the difference between the "ins" and the "outs" of society was solely one of family. Ostentation and what would today be considered vulgarity were displayed by all rich people, not by newcomers only; understated elegance was not in style. At one dinner party in the 1870's, for example, each male guest received as a favor a cigar rolled in a hundred-dollar bill, with the host's initials inscribed in gold. At another a thirty-foot-long pond with four swans brought in from Brooklyn's Prospect Park was set up in the center of the floor at Delmonico's. The swans, sad to relate, behaved very badly, although they had been drugged. Caroline Astor was not up to such shenanigans, but she did not encourage quiet restraint. In her home, as well as in the homes of the *nouveaux riches*, every wish was attended to by a large staff of servants attired in blue livery, which was a "line-for-line" copy of the uniforms worn at Windsor Castle. Dinners lasting three hours or longer were served on heavy gold plates; Mrs. Astor's were rumored to have cost three to four hundred dollars apiece (although after her death, an appraiser insisted that they were plated). At parties the table was decorated with hundreds of Gloire de Paris roses, which cost her a dollar apiece, or with orchids, the choice of McAllister who always urged the most expensive item possible. Following both her own and her friend's inclinations, Mrs. Astor frequently wore a corsage containing roses *and* orchids.

As for the menu, French cuisine predominated, and nine-course meals were served by those who could afford them. When Mrs. Astor followed McAllister's advice, a typical menu included: Tortue claire; mousse aux jambons; salmon (but only in spring or summer; terrapin was the winter choice); filet de boeuf with truffles, not mushrooms; riz de veau à la Toulouse; pâté de foie gras en Bellevue with artichokes sauce Barigoule; Sorbet, flavored with maraschino, not with rum; Camembert cheese with biscuits; Pouding Nesselrode.

(The spelling for the above, and the mixture of languages, are taken directly from a menu suggested by McAllister.)

Champagne was served from the fish course to the roast, and Mrs. Astor needed no urging to pour vintage wine costing fifteen dollars a bottle at dinners for three hundred people. After the beef, the appropriate red or white wine accompanied each course, with the gentlemen receiving an added bonus of Madeira after the ladies had withdrawn.

Caloric intake was restricted by pocketbook only, and exercise for most consisted of the ritual afternoon drive in a carriage drawn by a pair of fine horses. Mrs. Astor's figure as a result could hardly be described as willowy, and McAllister had a decided paunch. Young society matrons, except for those with high metabolism or small appetite, could approach the eighteen-inch waistline demanded by fashion only by means of rigorous lacing. Luckily human flesh is malleable, and what went in at the waist overflowed above, to help form the desired thirty-six-inch bosom, and below to hips, which were ideally so ample that those who refused the *riz de veau* and only nibbled at the *pouding* had to resort to padding.

Dress was as extravagant as cuisine, and Mrs. Astor often appeared in elaborate gowns designed by Worth.

"She was a really homely woman . . . no looks at all," says her niece, Alida Chanler Emmet.

This failing did not cause her to adopt inconspicuous attire. She would appear regal in white satin embroidered with pearls and silver, trailing a train of green velvet, or in black satin embroidered with roses, or in her favorite purple velvet trimmed with pale blue satin and embroidered with gold paillettes. Her gowns were so heavily encrusted with beading and jewels both front and back that it was impossible for her to lean back in a chair, which had the practical effect of enhancing her queenly posture immeasurably. Mrs. Astor's dignity was such that people who did not know her well were terrified by her.

"I only remember her in evening clothes covered with diamonds," murmurs an old lady recalling that golden era.

"Mrs. William Astor wearing less diamonds than usual . . ." so began a sly item in the *Herald*. . .

Well, if you had them, you wore them; that was the rule for Caroline and most other rich ladies. A single diamond necklace containing 204 stones valued at about $60,000 was frequently clasped about her neck, as was another worth around $80,000, which displayed a veritable explosion of 282 stones arranged in a sunburst effect. A favorite among her jewels was a stomacher (a big brooch worn on the bosom rather than the area named) that was supposed to have belonged to Marie Antoinette. For a ball, Mrs. Astor would fasten on jewel after jewel. At one affair an observant guest totaled the gems she was wearing: a triple necklace of diamonds, a diamond stomacher, a twelve-row fall of diamonds over the bosom of her dress, and a diamond tiara and diamond stars in her hair. Mrs. Astor's own hair was too scant to hold very many diamonds, so she usually wore a wig. This, as well as her own thin hair, was dyed a raven black. Although at that time dyed hair was associated with actresses and kept women, Mrs. Astor could get away with it. Her position in society was so secure that if she did a thing, that automatically made it all right.

By her attendance she made Monday *the* night at the opera. Even today, with the Patriarchs all but forgotten and Mrs. Astor a faded memory to a handful of aged men and women, the Monday after the opening remains society's night at the opera. Actually, when the opera first opened at the Academy of Music in 1854, the Astors were not among the high society subscribers—an oversight, which they corrected a few years later. By the time that newcomers, such as the fast-rising Vanderbilt family, realized that Monday at the opera was a social necessity, no boxes were available. The Academy of Music held only eighteen boxes in all—not even enough for the Patriarchs—and bidding was said to go as high as $30,000. With the push of the *nouveaux riches* behind it, a new opera house, the Metropolitan, was built with a triple tier of boxes. This turned out to be too many for society music lovers, and after the initial season of 1883–84, the top tier was removed. The remaining two were quite adequate, not only for the Astors, Roosevelts, and other society families, but for the Vanderbilts and Goulds as well. In fact, one newspaper reporter rather sourly remarked that the air was perfumed with "the odor of crisp greenbacks." The glittering display quickly gave the boxes of the Metropolitan the name of the Diamond Horseshoe; one lady box holder had a special high chair built for her so as to be able to show more of her bosom. Let no one think that she wished to reveal her cleavage; she merely wanted to offer a better view of her diamonds. Still, Mrs. Astor's followers, ever loyal, insisted that the Horseshoe was named after her. Box Number Seven was hers, a fact known by every operagoer, because the management considerately distributed clearly marked diagrams. These also revealed that Mrs. Vanderbilt had succeeded in capturing neighboring Box Number Six. Thus directed, opera glasses from all over the house were focused on Mrs. Astor, her gown, her jewels, her rather coarse features, and her escort, who was more often Ward than William. She would not leave her seat during intermission, remaining there to receive her many sycophants. But Mrs. Astor could seldom stay to the end of the last aria, whether sung by Marcella Sembrich or Christine Nilsson. She had to leave to prepare for the Patriarch or Assembly balls, which were held on Mondays also. It was indeed society's night.

And rivaling those great group social events was Mrs. Astor's own major ball of the year, held on one of the first three Mondays in January each year in the great ballroom of her home at 350 Fifth Avenue. In addition to this ball, she gave an endless procession of dinners, parties, and lesser balls, many of them attended by several hundred people. The arriving guests would be greeted by the queenly Mrs. Astor standing alone or with her grown children beneath a portrait of herself painted by Carolus Duran. They would then head toward the famous art gallery–ballroom through masses of flowers that transformed the entire mansion into a greenhouse. In the ballroom the pictures, like the jewels and gowns of the ladies, were overpowering, hung one on top of the other, as if in a museum, rather than a home. Culture was never a strong point of the Astors, but by following the conventional taste of the time, they did not go wrong with paintings by Jean François Millet, Constant Troyon, and others of the French Barbizon school.

It would not have mattered much, though, if they had hung cartoons or travel posters. No one had eyes for the pictures, or for the great candelabras that William had found on a trip to Italy, or for the marble Psyche at one end of the room; everyone was looking at the raised platform on which was an oversized divan covered with red silk cushions—the "Throne." A buzz of whispers would go through the room as those lucky enough to be asked to join Mrs. Astor on the Throne moved to that place of honor. This invitation was the ultimate compliment; it was impossible to rise higher socially in that milieu. And it was taken with a deadly seriousness. At one of the balls, Mrs. John Drexel, whose antecedents were unquestionable, burst into tears when she was passed over. Sobbing loudly she walked the entire length of the dance floor, conscious of the eyes of the murmuring crowd, and summoning a blue-liveried servant to fetch her cloak, she departed. On the balcony the orchestra of John Lander, the society band-leader of his day, concealed from view by banks of flowers, hurriedly came forth with "The Blue Danube."

Endurance was a requirement of social affairs of the nineteenth century, not only at the interminable dinners, but at the dances that lasted half the night. The high point, however, took place while everyone was still comparatively fresh at 1:30 A.M., when the german, or cotillion with its intricate figures, was performed. Those gentlemen who were skilled at leading the cotillion were sought after by all hostesses. The guests were rewarded with favors for their efforts—boutonnieres for the men, and brooches, bracelets, necklaces, or long jeweled hairpins for the ladies.

Sometimes with an undercurrent of malice, a departing guest would express surprise at William's absence; he was out on his yacht, was he not? There would be a hush while others in the crowded room waited to see how Mrs. Astor would react. Caroline never lost her regal composure: "Oh, he is having a delightful cruise. The sea air is so good for him," she would remark imperturbably. "It is a great pity I am such a poor sailor, for I should so much enjoy accompanying him."

William was one of the great yachtsmen of his day, possessing first a sailing yacht, *Ambassadress*, and later the largest steam yacht of the period, suitably named the *Nourmahal* ("Light of the

Harem"). Conveyed by one or another of these boats, William liked to put the length of the continent between him and his wife. While she was occupying herself with ruling New York society, he was living on board his yacht, anchored off the coast of Florida. Founding the Florida Yacht Club, he became its first commodore. This was before Florida was adopted as a winter playground for the rich, and the governor was overjoyed to have a representative of so prominent a family there. Despite his drinking, William treated everyone he met with old-world courtesy and was every bit as sought after in Florida as his wife was in New York. It did his ego a world of good. The governor, looking for ways to keep William happy, invited him to join the military staff. Astor responded in a manner calculated to keep the governor happy: he paid for a company of soldiers to be assigned to search the Everglades for hostile Indians, who were believed to be lurking. The state topped this gesture by giving Astor a grant of eighty thousand acres.

Although William kept his hands off real estate in New York where first his father and then his brother consistently downgraded his business acumen, he felt confident enough in Florida to pay ten thousand dollars for a large plot of ground in Jacksonville. There he erected the three-story Astor Building, with his name on top in iron letters. Showing what looked like Astor foresight, he bought fourteen thousand acres in Orange County, near Jacksonville, for a mere $7,500 and discussed the planting of the largest orange grove in the world. Nearby he built a fourteen-room hotel, a store, and a large dock, and the resulting town was promptly named Astor in his honor. But somehow, nothing ever worked for William. Any other Astor would have made a fortune; certainly many citrus growers eventually became wealthy in that very county. But William's groves were never particularly lucrative, and the docks were nearly destroyed by fire. His land declined in value so markedly that when it was finally sold by Vincent Astor in 1938, it brought but $3,100. Still, the towns of Astor and Astor Park remain as a tribute to the Astor who hated New York's formal society.

Nonetheless, William had enough of a sense of family, an Astor trait, to return whenever something he considered important—

definitely not his wife's parties—occurred.

Caroline would take each of these opportunities to tell her friends: "Dear William is so good to me. I have been so fortunate in my marriage."

Such an event was the engagement of their daughter Emily in the winter of 1875–76 to James J. Van Alen. Although he had been a cavalry commander in the Civil War and was an investor in the New York Central, Van Alen's father was known about town as a playboy. William, possibly because he had a similar reputation, objected mightily. "Damned if I want my family mixed in with the Van Alens!" he swore through his mustache, and the next thing he knew, he had been challenged to a duel. The prospect of these two gentlemen wielding pistols with their unsteady hands terrified New York society, and William was eventually induced to send a letter of apology. He even steeled himself to give the bride away at church and to stand by his wife's side during the home reception, but late in the afternoon he reached the limit of his always limited endurance and fled to his yacht to set sail for Florida at once. But Emily's hard-won happiness with Van Alen was not fated to endure; she died young in childbirth, leaving three motherless babies. Her father-in-law, exhibiting just the kind of trait that William had objected to, soon afterward had a nervous collapse while on board an ocean liner. A gentleman to the last, he jumped over the side to his death, still holding a walking stick in his neatly gloved hand.

A universally approved match was made in 1878 by a younger sister, Helen Schermerhorn Astor, who married James Roosevelt Roosevelt (yes; this Roosevelt made his name doubly sure), providing the Astors with a second connection with the powerful Roosevelt family. James was the stepson of Sara Delano Roosevelt and half-brother of Franklin Delano Roosevelt. The third of Mrs. Astor's daughters, Charlotte Augusta, named after her aunt, married James Coleman Drayton of Philadelphia the following year. This left the Astors with just two young children, Caroline and John Jacob IV, at home.

Mrs. Astor's life by then followed a seldom-varied routine of New York in winter, Paris or London for Easter, New York again or the estate at Ferncliff in late spring and autumn, and a cottage in

Newport in the summer. Surely by now everyone knows that a Newport cottage is in truth a French château or Italian Renaissance mansion, costing several million dollars to build, and as much or even more to fill with marble sculpture, Aubusson carpets, paintings of the Barbizon school, imported mirrors, cut-glass chandeliers, and heavy carved furniture. The homes of society's great names lined Bellevue Avenue and Ocean Drive. Mrs. Astor's cottage was Beechwood, a showplace even before it sheltered her illustrious head. And right nearby was Beaulieu, the French château owned by the John Jacob Astor III's. Beaulieu was so carefully constructed that even the hallway offers a glorious view of the Atlantic Ocean.

There has never been—and never again can be—a place like Newport in its days of glory. On all sides could be seen evidences of the honest, unabashed conviction of its chosen people that they were truly superior. Streetcars were routed away from the homes of the prominent by royal Astor edict. McAllister, who was kindly although pompous, urged anyone endeavoring to enter society to start with Bar Harbor; Newport was just too difficult.

"If you were not of the inner circle," he wrote in an odd little book that gave advice on entering society, "and were a new-comer, it took the combined efforts of all your friends backing and pushing to procure an invitation for you. For years whole families sat on the stool of probation, awaiting trial and acceptance, and many were rejected."

There was indeed no place where a newcomer was made to feel more totally inferior, inadequate, and unendurable. The natives were even worse off, because they hardly existed at all in the eyes of the summer elite; one socialite called them "Our Footstools" in a quite audible whisper. Even their beach, Easton's, was known to everyone as "The Common Beach." The insiders bathed at Bailey's Beach, protected from the possible invasion of the unacceptable by a watchman clad in a gold-laced uniform. This guardian of privilege would pass strangers only if they were armed with a letter of introduction. The sportier society maidens and matrons appeared at Bailey's arrayed in heavy flannel bathing suits with skirts hanging to below their knees, stockings, bathing shoes, and a straw bonnet to protect their delicate complexions. When wet, the suits were so heavy as to constitute an actual hazard in the water, but modesty was, of course, the primary consideration. Other athletes among the inner circle played tennis at the Casino, feeling incredibly agile without their corsets. Through most of the 1880's, though, heavy petticoats were still worn beneath a tennis outfit that consisted of a long tight gown with a flounce at the bottom.

Those who eschewed more active sports strolled slowly in the morning along the Horse Shoe Piazza of the Casino where a string band was playing. After a morning's fun, the socialites gathered for a luxurious luncheon party served by Mrs. Astor and such rival hostesses as Mrs. John Jacob Astor III, Mrs. Stuyvesant Fish, Mrs. August Belmont, Mrs. Ogden Goelet, and Mrs. Hermann Oelrichs.

Just because they were at the beach did not mean that proper dress was neglected. Mrs. Astor and her fellow matrons and their daughters wore a different dress for each occasion all summer, requiring a wardrobe of at least ninety gowns. Parasols were matched to each daytime dress, as were the feathers of the great-brimmed hats that topped coiffures made bouffant by "rats," chignons, switches, or, as in Mrs. Astor's case, a wig. The summer's heat was considered no reason to abandon white elbow-length kid gloves in daytime or evening, and a popular lady might run through three or four fresh pairs a day. (It was not until late in the following decade that standards relaxed enough to allow ladies to take off their gloves for the "informal picnics" of the Clambake Club. Even then they kept gloves on until the moment when the clams were brought to the table in tin basins.)

The fashion show of the day, when natives and newcomers could feast their eyes on the gowns worn by Mrs. Astor and her followers, took place after the lavish luncheon. A resplendent parade of ladies in carriages driven by liveried coachmen set off down Bellevue Avenue at three o'clock every day when the weather was fine. The matrons would nod or smile at one another, seemingly oblivious to the stares of the onlookers. Protocol was followed as rigidly as at a state dinner. No one would dare to overtake the carriage of a lady of superior social rank.

The days, filled with dressing, bathing, dressing, tennis, dressing, lunch, driving, resting, and dressing again were as nothing to the Newport nights. During the 1870's the week-night affairs were somewhat marred by a manpower shortage, because husbands whose wealth was not inherited went back to the city on Mondays to work. The problem was kindly solved by the United States Navy in 1880, when it opened a war college and torpedo station at Newport. McAllister, by some process of tortuous reasoning, felt that he was responsible for this naval order. In any event, he was sure that the decision was based on the need for dancing escorts. Balls costing in the tens of thousands—some reaching $200,000— were held nightly at one or another of the cottages. If anything, the battle of hostesses was fought more vigorously than in the winter. Society matrons poured small fortunes into transforming their cottages into flowered bowers, engaging dance bands to play all night, ordering chefs to prepare nine-course meals starting with *pâté de foie gras*, purchasing ancient imported champagne and wine, and obtaining fantastically expensive favors. Parties were so elaborate that an intimate evening at home with Mrs. Astor found one dining with a hundred other guests. Without the help of servants, no lady could possibly have had the energy to arise after nights like those and once again begin the ritual of lacing the corset, donning the petticoats, fastening the endless buttons of the close-fitting dress, slipping into the long gloves, and securing the large hat needed for the first outing of the day.

In a place where social position was taken as the only thing that mattered, Caroline Astor flourished—and fumed. She was accustomed to putting up with her older sister-in-law, Augusta, and practiced a certain laissez-faire, but when her nephew, William Waldorf, installed his bride at Beaulieu as a rival, she felt that the time had come for a showdown. She was, she decided, *the* Mrs. Astor, and she duly eliminated the "William" from her calling cards. When the patroness list for the Casino ball appeared with her name as Mrs. William Astor, she wrote a blistering letter to the ball chairman, insisting that she had been insulted. Her friends were told that all mail was henceforth to be addressed to "Mrs. Astor, Newport," and instructions were accordingly issued to the postmen. Mrs. John Jacob Astor III was only amused by these pretensions and cheerfully continued to use her full name, but her son who lacked both humor and humility was enraged. He insisted that his wife, shy, beautiful Mary Paul, was *the* Mrs. Astor, and he, too, issued orders to this effect to friends and postmen. This maneuver resulted in a good deal of mixed-up mail, but nothing else. Mary did not have either the character or the desire to battle her doughty aunt; she would have liked to please her husband if he had not made it so difficult for her to do so. Caroline Astor won a decisive victory for all time. When she went out to dinner she was given without question the seat at the right of the host. McAllister called her his "Mystic Rose," and the gossip columnists called her "the Queen," but the name by which she was then and forever after known to the world was "*The* Mrs. Astor."

With Mrs. Astor in firm command, acceptance by the inner circle meant acceptance by her. And so would-be socialites schemed and bribed her friends and servants to procure for them invitations to her balls. A rumor was current then that fifteen-thousand dollars paid into the right hands would get one into Mrs. Astor's annual ball. Just being seen there, in theory at least, solidified a newcomer's social position. But families that really wished to infiltrate the Old Guard wanted acceptance and recognition from Caroline herself; nothing less would serve their ambitions. Of all who tried, few were as wealthy or as gifted in campaigning as Mrs. William Kissam Vanderbilt, born Alva Smith in Mobile, Alabama. With her husband's vast riches and her own drive, she meant to leap over the barricade and land right in the midst of Mrs. Astor's inner circle.

"The Vanderbilts only went to Newport because the Astors were there," according to a malicious whisper of the time.

Wherever the Vanderbilts went, they moved with a flair. Their cottage, the Breakers, was the most extravagant and elaborate at the resort, built at a cost rumored to be as high as four million dollars and furnished for an additional five million dollars. Everyone in Newport—except Mrs. Astor, and so that meant no one—knew that they were there. Alva's parties were so lavish that a sly anecdote was told about a woman arriving unexpectedly at the home of a society matron, "I meant to go to the Vanderbilts," she said, "but on the way I decided I wasn't dressed well enough and so I came here." The Newport assault on Mrs. Astor was just one of the sorties planned by the determined Mrs. Vanderbilt. In order to live in the high society style, she engaged Richard M. Hunt, *the* architect of the 1880's, to design a mansion for her at 660 Fifth Avenue.

He was not asked to look for economical short cuts; unlike William B. Astor, Sr.'s false paneling at Rokeby, everything was to be of the best. With such encouragement, Hunt ran the bills up to three million dollars, and his clients were only delighted with him. At the sight of the grandeur of this mansion, McAllister's susceptible heart melted, and he invited the Vanderbilts to the Patriarch Ball. *The* Mrs. Astor did not follow his example; there are some matters in which even a prime minister cannot influence a queen.

No one has ever known whether it was kind fate smiling on Alva, blind chance, or a skillful plot that led to her ultimate triumph. Her weapon, at least on the surface, was no different from the ones she had been using all along—a magnificent fancy dress ball, this one to serve as the housewarming for her new mansion. The debutante and subdebutante set in New York to which young Carrie Astor belonged, all unaware of its parents' hidden motives, threw itself wholeheartedly into preparations. The young girls decided to perform a quadrille in star formation, and rehearsals began weeks in advance of the ball. Carrie, well aware of the grace of her slender little figure, was dreaming of how she would look in the dance when the blow fell. Mrs. Vanderbilt said blandly that the girls would have to find a substitute for Carrie; Mrs. Astor had never called, and so her daughter could not possibly be invited. Well, where her children were concerned, Mrs. Astor was as weak as any other mother. Caroline's tears moved her where Alva Vanderbilt's extraordinary effort had not.

"I think the time has come for the Vanderbilts," she said and, fastening on her large hat with the ostrich plumes, went to pay the necessary call.

The overjoyed Mrs. Vanderbilt abandoned all restraint in arrangements for her party and turned the second floor of her mansion into a tropical forest with eleven thousand dollars' worth of flowers ordered from Klinder's, which had a monopoly of the high society trade. One hundred and forty dressmakers worked around the clock for five days, it was said (no one troubled to ask why they could not have been given more notice) to make 150 costumes at a price of $500 to $700 apiece. The New York *World* estimated that $250,000 had been spent on the ball, and even if that is journalistic license, it surely does not exaggerate by more than, say,

$50,000. Mrs. Vanderbilt did not begrudge so much as a penny, no matter what the cost. Mrs. Astor deigned to smile at her from the neighboring box at the Metropolitan Opera. And the following season, in 1884, at last came the invitation to Mrs. Astor's own famous ball.

Acceptance of the Vanderbilts did not ease the lot of others striving for social recognition. Alexander T. Stewart, the five-foot-tall department store tycoon, lived right across the street from the Astors in a mansion filled with Carrara marble and decorated with ceilings painted by Italian artists specially brought to this country for the job. As far as Mrs. Astor was concerned, he and his wife simply did not exist. Throughout her life she refused to recognize the Goulds or the Harrimans, and those who knew them insist that the Morgans never tried for her favor. A family that did, the Richard Thornton Wilsons, had the right tools with which to work their way into the magic circle of those invited to dine on *the* Mrs. Astor's gold plate—their children. In 1877, one daughter, May, moved the Wilsons several steps up the ladder of society by marrying Ogden Goelet, whose family were fellow, though not equal, landlords of New York with the Astors. And then a son, Orme Wilson, fell in love with Carrie Astor. Luckily for her, young Caroline bore no resemblance to her mother; blonde and slight, she was also by all odds the sweetest of the Astor children. Still, there were those who could not believe that so desirable a match could be made for any but crass or social-climbing motives. For their part, the Astors were not as delighted as the Wilsons by the suggested engagement and raised all sorts of objections. They said that Orme's father would have to settle half a million dollars on the young couple, a figure that the Astors would then match. The inequity was apparent to the least astute; half a million dollars was a moderate sum to William Astor, whereas it was about half of Wilson's total holdings. The groom's father, after considerable soul searching, finally agreed. Despite Wilson's capitulation, Mrs. Astor remained unenthusiastic until the spring day when she saw the young lovers coming out of church together, hand in hand, looking at one another tenderly. At that moment she became convinced that Orme loved her daughter truly and not just for money and social position. From that day on she threw herself wholeheartedly into plans for one of New York society's greatest weddings, and the bride walked down an aisle set up in the huge ballroom at 350 Fifth Avenue, her little feet cushioned from the hard dance floor by a three-inch-thick carpet. An altar banked with roses was placed in front of the ebony fireplace familiar to all members of the inner circle. The wines and liquor flowed so freely that General Ulysses S. Grant, an honored guest, got drunk and burned himself by putting the lighted end of his cigar in his mouth. Fortune has a way of beaming at those on whom it has already smiled, and the newlyweds received about a million dollars' worth of gifts.

The Wilsons were indeed fortunate in this marriage, because Carrie proved to be a lovely and gentle wife to Orme, and the Astor connection proved an excellent investment for his whole family. They were invited to join the Patriarchs and in time came to play a dominant role in New York society.

Having presented three daughters to her inner circle friends, Mrs. Astor could do no less for her son. A lavish reception for eight hundred guests introduced John Jacob IV into the high society world of 1887, and if his success is to be measured in the same terms as a female debutante—that is, a brilliant marriage—it was a triumph. Four years later came the wedding to Ava Lowle Willing, a devastating beauty of Philadelphia and Newport, whose family claimed descent from Alfred the Great, Henry I, Edward I, Henry III, and Henry IV of England, and Henry I of France. The Astors converged on Philadelphia in a body for the wedding and filled the Bellevue Hotel to overflowing. John Jacob IV and his immediate family enjoyed comparative seclusion away from the throng of relatives, in the Stratford, where they and their servants occupied eighteen rooms. The very rich groom gave his fairly rich bride a diamond tiara on which to fasten her veil, and his mother proffered a four-inch-large lover's-knot also made of diamonds.

Possibly affected by the love in bloom around him, William Astor returned to his wife's side during that winter. She took full advantage of this opportunity to still society's wagging tongues by giving a series of dinners in his honor as if he were a visiting dignitary—which, in a sense, he was.

Newspapers from coast to coast took full cognizance of his comings and goings, and of all else that went on in the mansions lining

Fifth Avenue. Mrs. Astor, like most of her family, hated and feared publicity—as she grew older she would not go near the Fifth Avenue windows of her home unless the curtains were drawn— but, unlike her predecessors, was quite unable to avoid it. Gossip columns about society nourished and were nourished by the grow- ing public interest in the activities of the inner circle. The most avidly read of the gossip sheets was *Town Topics,* a revised version of the old *American Queen, A Magazine of Art, Music, Literature and Society,* which had been run by Louis Keller. In 1882 Keller sold the magazine to Colonel William D'Alton Mann, a flamboyant figure who affected a Biblical white beard, a severely cut dress coat, and a flaming red tie, which was more indicative of his character than the other two. Mann was quick to relegate art, music, and literature to the editorial background and to concentrate on society —particularly society's secrets and scandals. The former owner of the magazine, Keller, was just as interested in society as Mann, but from quite another angle. He felt that a simple list of names of members of society was enough to hold fascinated readers, and he was right, as the success of the *Social Register,* which he founded in 1887, was to prove. But Mann was right, too, in his view that the misbehavior of the rich and social is a firm foundation on which to build circulation. The *Social Register* was for him but a source of names about which he could make news.

Mann's method of avoiding libel suits was simple and effective. The love affair, unfaithful wife, philandering husband, illegitimate child, or orgy would be graphically but anonymously described in one thrilling news item; it would be followed by a bland account of a party given or a trip taken by the very people whose names had been left out of the preceding paragraphs. The most un- schooled reader was well able to put two and two together. But Colonel Mann was no advocate of freedom of the press; he was willing to suppress any item at all. The socialites involved, politely informed of the impending publicity, were given every opportu- nity to make it worth Colonel Mann's while to keep the news out of the paper. Thus, the corrupt roué, instead of being exposed to the world in *Town Topics,* appeared in those columns as a model gentleman. To supplement his income, the charming colonel also published *Fads and Fancies of Representative Americans* at a cost of $1500 a copy. Who would buy it? Why, any prominent citizen who wanted a favorable write-up, even, or particularly, if he did not deserve it.

Other publications wrote about society without resorting to blackmail, filling columns with news of parties and other social events, hostesses, dress, jewels, resorts, and trips much as they do today. Such reports appeared in daily newspapers not only in New York but also in small towns throughout the country. Mrs. Astor, "the Queen," and Ward McAllister, "her Prime Minister," were national institutions; everything they did, wore, and said was duly noted in Wichita, Chicago, and San Francisco (where McAllister's brother was a notable society leader). A debutante visiting an aunt in Montana was able to impress ranchers and their wives by telling them that she had attended one of Mrs. Astor's balls. Her listeners were better able to describe Mrs. Astor's green velvet, gold-embroidered gown than she, possibly, the girl confessed, because she was nearsighted. John Lander, the dance band conductor, and Elisha Dyer, most popular cotillion leader, would have had no trouble obtaining invitations to parties in Detroit or Los Angeles, where they were as well known as any local celebrity.

In the newspapers of the nation the doings of what came to be known as the Four Hundred were carefully chronicled. The origin of this term has been disputed, but there seems little question that McAllister brought it into popular usage. In addition to living the society life, he wrote about it, and his articles, which were widely reprinted, were chock full of anecdotes about the Four Hundred. How did he arrive at that figure? Some said he meant the number that could fit into Mrs. Astor's ballroom, a statement that could only have been made by those who had not been there, because the vast room held double that crowd on many occasions.

On March 24, 1888, McAllister, who never knew when to keep his mouth shut, explained the term to a persistent New York *Tribune* reporter: "If you go outside that number," he said, "you strike people who are either not at ease in a ballroom or else make other people not at ease."

Coming from McAllister, who was far from a distinguished-looking figure himself, with his little paunch, thinning hair, unimpressive Van Dyke beard, and carelessly worn clothes, it was more than most contemporaries could endure. By that single statement McAllister labeled himself forever as a pompous fool. Of course, he was quite unable to see this and went right on using the term. Pressed for the names, he hemmed and hawed, but eventually, in 1892, gave *The New York Times* the official list of those invited to Mrs. Astor's ball. It included the Chanlers, Vanderbilts, Mills, Livingstons, Goelets, Fishs, Delafields, Cushings, Jays, Rhinelanders, and De Peysters. But by a peculiar quirk of fate, Mrs. Astor gave a particularly small ball that year. And so the famous Four Hundred list contained but 220 different names; the figure can only be raised to 309 by counting each "and Mrs." as a separate entry.

Whether 200, 300, or 400 rightly belonged in the inner circle, its center was Mrs. Astor. She reigned as undisputed queen. And it was when she was at the height of her powers that she was struck by a blow that might have unseated a lesser monarch. Her daughter, Charlotte Augusta Drayton, after leading a model life as wife and mother for ten years, was swept off her feet by an uncontrollable passion for one Hallett Alsop Borrowe. Before the fascinated gaze of a nation of gossip-column readers, Augusta left husband and children—with a true Astor touch, she paid him $12,000 a year to take care of the children—and fled to Europe with her lover. There, detectives hired by Drayton reported seeing a brown-haired lady with a fair complexion and innocent blue eyes in the company of Borrowe in the St. Pancras Hotel in London. The description, to the surprise of no one, fit Augusta. The one consolation New York society could find in this affair was that the lover was a man of impeccable background, vice-president of Equitable Life Insurance, and a member of the best clubs.

Drayton, belatedly determined to save face, crossed the ocean and challenged Borrowe to a duel to be fought in France, but somehow this duel kept being postponed. During the interval, someone— rumored to be either Borrowe himself or Drayton's second—was cad enough to sell Augusta's steaming letters to her lover to a newspaper for five hundred dollars. The negotiations dragged on interminably until at last the duel was referred to a French court of honor. It handed down a decision that Drayton had no right to challenge his wife's lover, saying brutally, "There is no longer any honor where there has been traffic, when honor has been conditionally sold." The fact was that in addition to the sum given him for maintenance of the children, Drayton had accepted five thousand dollars a year as payment for a silence he did not even keep. The dishonored husband returned to the United States, where he divorced his wife on grounds of "cruel suspicion as to her marital fidelity." Despite Augusta's attempts to get her children back, the court awarded them to Drayton. She captured the attention of two continents with the drama of her great love affair with Borrowe, but Augusta had not inherited her mother's constancy. Free of Drayton, she did not remain in Borrowe's arms. Instead, she was seized by desire for a handsome and rich young Scotsman, George Ogilvie Haig, and in time, married him.

And what were her parents doing while this scandal was raging? That was the question New York society was asking. William, who probably understood matters of the heart best, nonetheless played the stern father and warned Augusta that if she did not return to Drayton's bed and board, he would cut her out of his will and have all her possessions, up to and including her childhood toys and wedding dress, sold at auction. These threats had no effect at all, but he carried out at least the first of them. In the midst of the crisis when the family was gathered in Paris, William suddenly exclaimed, "I've got an awful pain." Two days later he was dead. When the fifty-six-page will was read, it was learned that Augusta's share of his estate was to go to her children. Although she was a woman who could clearly get along without an inheritance, her brother later, possibly at the urging of their mother, reinstated her.

The Mrs. Astor, during the entire scandal, showed her true mettle, remaining loyal to her daughter, no matter how sordid the details being revealed daily. Nothing could induce her to abandon this daughter. Her posture was a little more regal, her bejeweled head held a little higher; that was all. These were black years for her. While Augusta's love affair was being lived before the eyes of the world, Mrs. Astor lost first her husband and then a year later, her daughter, Helen Roosevelt. Accepting these blows of fate, Mrs. Astor rallied to Augusta's side with even more vigor. While the divorce suit was being fought, she received guests at a huge reception at Beechwood, in Newport, with her daughter standing beside her. Later she "rocked society to its foundation," as the saying went, by holding a reception for Augusta and the *second* husband. William Randolph Hearst's *Journal,* playing the story for all it was worth, hastened to run "A Sermon on Society," criticizing Mrs. Astor for her lack of morals in accepting her black sheep daughter and so sanctioning adulterous behavior.

While these dark threads were woven through the fabric of her personal life, she glittered in the gilded age of the 1890's. After having made Fifth Avenue in the Thirties the place to live, she went on to shift the center of society farther uptown. There were two reasons for her move: her house at 350 Fifth Avenue had become too small for her ever-growing entertainment requirements; and worse yet, her obstreperous nephew, William Waldorf Astor, smarting under the ignominy of having failed to make his wife *the* Mrs. Astor, had decided to remove to England and have his house right next door made into a hotel. And so a mansion at Sixty-fifth Street and Fifth Avenue was designed for Caroline by Richard M. Hunt, who had followed his Vanderbilt triumph with assignments for the Goelets, Belmonts, and Gerrys. Done in a style described by some anachronistically as "modern Renaissance" and by others as a "French château," it was a double house, divided by a removable partition, the idea being that the William Astors were to live in the northern half and the John Jacob IV's in the southern. Unfortunately, William was never to live in or see the completed house, because he died before the plans left the drawing boards. However, things being as they were, he might never have seen very much of it anyway. By the time it was finished, Mrs. Astor had invested $1.5 million in the house and another $750,000 in furnishings selected to make each room represent a different period.

Heavy as these expenditures seem for an era when whole families lived on a few dollars a week, they were moderate for a woman in her position (at least by Vanderbilt standards). This was, after all, before income taxes or social consciousness on the part of the rich.

"Up to this time," wrote McAllister in 1890, "for one to be worth a million dollars was to be rated as a man of fortune, but now, bygones must be bygones."

A butler in the home of a society leader received $75 a month, and footmen who consented to powder their hair were paid $55.

Nor did these wages lead socialites to make do with small staffs. Society matrons Mrs. Ogden Mills and Mrs. Elbridge Gerry liked to say that they could invite one hundred guests to dinner without hiring so much as an extra footman. The chef of an Astor, a Vanderbilt, or a Fish could command $100 a month and 10 percent of the food bills—often $500 a month to the butcher and $125 to the grocer.

Although the rich, particularly after the depression—or panic, as it was then known—of 1893, were given to saying piously that displays of wealth had disappeared, it is hard to imagine where they had got to. At Newport, Mrs. Pembrooke Jones allocated $300,000 for a single season's entertainment. And an all-too-plausible story went the rounds that one hostess invited no one whose personal fortune could not be totaled in seven figures. Mrs. Astor by then had found it incumbent upon her to remodel her cottage, Beechwood, so that it could boast the largest ballroom in Newport.

Social life was so time-consuming that even Mrs. Astor became concerned. She was careful always to leave herself time to devote to her family, a grandson, Orme Wilson, Jr., recalls. To solve the problem, she called upon the services of a special assistant, who was to be the prototype of a new breed of women—the social secretary, a personage far more social than secretarial in manner, lineage and influence. Maria de Barril was nearly as demanding and fully as snobbish as her chief client, Mrs. Astor. In fact, she told her friends that *she* had investigated Mrs. Astor before consenting to work for her. Miss de Barril was the niece of the gentleman who had sold Beaulieu to John Jacob III, and hers was a wealthy family —until the panic of 1893. After financial calamity struck, Miss de Barril was forced to put her contacts to commercial use. She swept through Newport and New York in dramatic gowns and huge ostrich-feathered hats, clanking as she went, because of the heavy dangling jewelry that she always wore. At Newport, she joined her clients in the afternoon driving parade, appearing in a black carriage drawn by a pair of glossy black horses. It was almost an act of condescension for her to prepare invitation lists, order flowers, and arrange for musicians, menus, and caterers to serve others. Her Spencerian backhand writing became known to everyone in or on the fringes of society, and social hopefuls knew they had made it when the distinctive envelope was delivered to the door. One of this secretary's secretaries learned to imitate her hand, and with that as her chief recommendation, was later hired by Miss de Barril's successor. Juliana Cutting, descendant of an early real-estate partner of John Jacob Astor I. (Astor with his customary adroitness had maneuvered this partner out of the profitable Eden Farm, but Cutting managed to build up a sizable fortune, nonetheless, as well as a high position in society.)

Despite the thrill engendered by the sight of Miss de Barril's Spencerian writing on an envelope, the social events of themselves were heavy and dull.

"I went to my first society dinner party and I was bored to death," a debutante confided in her friends. "I amused myself by grading the people at the table in terms of dullness from one to ten, with one being the absolute peak of deadliness—and hardly a guest fell below three."

"As a society it seemed flat and arid," wrote Mrs. Winthrop Chanler in her memoirs of the 1890's. "The 400 would have fled in a body from a poet, a painter, a musician, or a clever Frenchman."

Yet the power of Ward McAllister, who to many epitomized that society, was slipping from its height of the 1880's. As was his way, he contributed to his own decline by publishing in 1890 a book, *Society As I Have Found It*, that did not find favor with society. Instead of being the gossipy volume everyone had hoped for, it turned out to be a how-to book, telling how to rise in society in such exhaustive detail that the reader even learned how to finish a dance floor and select turkeys (the feet are the giveaway of age). All advice on launching a girl or a family in society was quaint and utterly humorless. He completed the ruin of his reputation by falling afoul of Chicago society when he issued snide comments on the occasion of the 1893 World's Columbian Exposition being held there. When he died in 1895, only five Patriarchs attended his funeral. Still, there were those who saw behind the pomposity and snobbishness. At the mention of his name an old lady's face lights up: "He was so nice," she says. "A real aristocrat."

Kindly or not, McAllister and the world he symbolized had aroused enough dissatisfaction, even in the inner circle, to make possible the rise of a man like Harry Lehr, always the amusing, but slightly vicious, life of the party. There was nothing pompous about his rejoinder when asked how a newcomer could advance into society: "Try to get invited for a week or two on someone's yacht." Lehr liked to consider himself the successor to McAllister and always attributed his rise to Mrs. Astor. "She made Harry Lehr," he often said.

Lehr approached her, as he approached all of society, as a comedian. The wealthy Baltimore family into which he was born became impoverished when he was a boy, and Harry determined to get the money back, but not, definitely not, by anything so dull as work. His big opportunity came when he was invited to the Elisha Dyers at Newport on a night when Mrs. Astor was there. She was as always aglitter with diamonds, and so he seized a huge bouquet of flowers out of a vase and thrust them upon her, saying, "Here, you look like a walking chandelier." His manner was so merry and he was so young—younger than her son—that Mrs. Astor was charmed, instead of being offended. She invited him to lead her next cotillion, and he began, as he put it, "to scale the heights."

Within weeks he had gained the title of "society's court jester." His braying laugh became his trademark, and the Newport *Morning Telegraph* wrote: "Haven't you heard 'Harry' Lehr's laugh? Everyone has." Socialites laughed right along with him, and he began to live without money just as well as if he had it. Playing his powerful connections for all they were worth, he stayed at the Waldorf, dined at Sherry's and Delmonico's, was dressed by Wetzel, traveled on the railroad, and even sent cables—for nothing. Black, Starr and Frost did not go quite so far as to present him with jewels, but they were perfectly willing to lend him any he wanted. His only steady source of income was $6,000 a year paid him for ostensibly acting as a representative of a French champagne importer.

Aware of the uncertainty inherent in this kind of life, he set out in search of security in the form of a rich wife and settled on oh-so-unlucky Elizabeth Drexel Dahlgreen. A more sophisticated woman might have been scared off by Harry's high-pitched voice, soft, blond plumpness, effeminate mannerisms, and propensity for female impersonation, but Elizabeth was dazzled by him. Determined not to risk his hard-won position in society, he took Elizabeth to lunch with the most powerful foursome in the city: Mrs. Astor, Mrs. Stuyvesant Fish, Mrs. Hermann Oelrichs, and Mrs. Oliver H. P. Belmont (the former Alva Vanderbilt, who had by then divested herself of William K.). Elizabeth had the misfortune of pleasing everyone with her pretty face and agreeable manner. At the conclusion of the luncheon, the women looked at one another and smiled in agreement. "We four are going to take her up," Mrs. Oelrichs assured Lehr. "We will make her the fashion. You need have no fear."

On her wedding night Elizabeth learned the fatal flaw in the prize she had captured. Harry coldly informed her that he had married her for her money and that nothing would induce him to touch her. In utter sincerity he pointed out that the marriage would be to her advantage, too, because he could give her a "wonderful position in society." For the twenty-eight years of their unconsummated marriage, Elizabeth had this as her sole consolation.

Although Mrs. Astor had made him, Lehr was really much more in his element arranging parties for Mamie Fish, who was prepared to put up with anything but boredom. He brought a circus elephant into her Seventy-eighth Street mansion designed by Stanford White and had guests feed the animal peanuts as they danced by. One banquet was given for an exclusive list of one hundred dogs, and at another, male guests were instructed to dress as cats and were then handed white mice to present to the giggling, shuddering ladies. The Lehr-Fish prank that staggered society took place at a dinner in honor of a visiting Prince Del Drago. The prince was late, so the other guests were already at the table when he arrived on Lehr's arm and was carefully led to the chair usually occupied by Mrs. Astor, who was mercifully absent. Del Drago turned out to be a nice little monkey neatly dressed in a full set of evening clothes.

Mrs. Astor murmured about the methods some people would employ in order to achieve notoriety and attract a following. But irrepressible Mrs. Fish had the last word, saying with deceptive kindliness, "Mrs. Astor is an elderly woman."

And it was true, although only the lined face revealed the passage of time; Caroline's superb posture and black hair (well, it had been dyed for years) were unaltered by age. But she had lost the ability to keep the tight control on society that had character- ized her during the previous twenty years. McAllister was no longer there to help her, and even their joint effort to organize so- ciety, the Patriarchs, faded away in 1897. Society had become much harder to control in any event, with the gradual loosening of re- strictions on the things that one could or could not do. Whereas for years a lady might dine only in a carefully selected number of homes, it became quite permissible for the most delicately nurtured to go to a restaurant. Under Lehr's prodding, even Mrs. Astor in pearls and white satin sampled the filet de boeuf at Sherry's. The first time she did so was news, and one reporter wrote hysterically, "But I never dreamed that it would be given to me to gaze on the face of an Astor in a public dining room."

Even at home, Mrs. Astor was far less stringent in her require- ments. She went so far as to give a dinner for Mrs. Potter Palmer, who although Queen of Chicago society, had previously been snubbed as a hotelkeeper's wife. As the years went by, Mrs. Astor's balls departed so far from the Four-Hundred concept that in 1904, twelve hundred guests attempted to waltz in the enormous ball- room at 840 Fifth Avenue. One newspaper in distress wrote, "She Lets Bars 'Way Down and Asks Even the Edge of the Fringe of Society." It was really too much for Caroline; she gave up and slipped off to don her voluminous frilled white nightgown and get into bed while the dance band was still playing. Left to themselves and an army of servants, her guests proceeded to spill drinks on her sofas, burn tabletops with cigars, and strike matches on the walls. This no doubt accounts for the condition of her fur- nishings when after her death an appraiser from W. & J. Sloane ex- claimed at them in horror.

Her followers remained blind to any change in her or society and went on insisting that everything was just the way it had been from the first days of her reign. An Episcopal clergyman, the Rev- erend Charles Wilbur de Lyon Nichols, went so far as to write in an incredible publication, *The Ultra-Fashionable Peerage of Amer- ica, with a few appended Essays on Ultra-Smartness*, that an invita- tion to Mrs. Astor's ball put one in the Four Hundred, whereas a dinner invitation from her placed its recipient among the "ultra smart" 150. "Not to have dined at Mrs. Astor's virtually debars one from eminent leadership in that surpassing coterie known as national and international American society."

Still, the Reverend Nichols' book was full of inaccuracies, reporting, for example, that J. P. Morgan was a descendant of Welsh royalty, and so the ladies whom he firmly classified as mere "viceregal leaders" might have disclaimed his ability to select at all. Certainly during the late 1890's and early 1900's a battle for social power second to none in history was going on. Mrs. O. H. P. Belmont, the former Mrs. Vanderbilt, was ruling as much of society and her family as possible with an iron hand. She succeeded in upstaging the other society dowagers by making her daughter, Consuelo Vanderbilt, marry the Ninth Duke of Marlborough, and received the sanction of Mrs. Astor, who marched in the wedding procession directly behind the British Ambassador and sat beside Mrs. Belmont at the wedding breakfast. Mrs. Ogden Mills, though, was not really impressed. Being a descendant of the Livingstons, she felt able to declare decisively, "There are really only twenty families in New York." It was not clear whether she included her rivals, Mrs. Stuyvesant Fish, who continued to attract the livelier set, or Theresa (Tessie) Oelrichs, who cut quite a swathe through New York and Newport before her mental collapse. But for all their efforts, they really proved Reverend Nichols right for once; no member of Mrs. Astor's generation succeeded in obtaining unique possession of her crown, and it went ultimately to Orme Wilson's sister Grace, who married Cornelius Vanderbilt III.

Mrs. Astor, for her part, remained confident of her position throughout her life, and seldom referred to the struggles of her fellow matrons, objecting only when they stooped to what she termed "entertainments that belong under a circus tent rather than in a gentlewoman's house." Her own last great party was exclusive enough to suit anyone (except possibly Mrs. Mills). She invited but seventy-nine guests, described in the papers as "Mrs. Astor's elect," to a banquet in honor of Prince Louis of Battenberg. The guest list was as rigorously screened as in the earliest days of the Patriarchs; even the Vanderbilts were left off.

And then in 1906, January came and went, and the expected invitations in Miss de Barril's hand did not go out. The report was that Mrs. Astor had slipped and fallen on the marble stairs of her home, and this may or may not have been so. From then until her death at seventy-seven two years later, innumerable rumors were passed through society in New York, Newport, and the rest of the nation. Her mind, and this at least is true, was affected, possibly by a stroke, or senility, or by the accumulated pressures of her tragic personal life. These could well have broken as unbending a nature as hers. People said that she wandered about the house (though other reports had her confined to a wheelchair) talking to the ghosts of her past—William, whose love she had not possessed and whose wandering spirit she had not been able to tame . . . Charlotte Augusta, whose stormy, passionate life had blemished her own record of rectitude . . . Emily, dead of childbirth after but five years of the marriage William had so vigorously opposed . . . Helen, too, lying dead when her mother arrived to visit her in England.

A legend sprang up that during these last years, regal in posture still, she would dress in her finest purple velvet and station herself beneath her portrait by Carolus Duran, bowing to imaginary guests, though this last strains credulity. The doctor, two nurses, three maids, and butler who cared for her to the end held their tongues. After her death the curious attended her funeral, betting with macabre humor that the casket would identify her only as Mrs. Astor. (It did not.)

Shortly before she withdrew from the world of society, Mrs. Astor had granted one of the few interviews she ever gave. "I am not vain enough to believe that New York will not be able to get along without me," she declared with dignity. "Many women will rise up to fill my place."

Caroline was wrong. Imitators and successors, yes, but no one then or in the years since has ever been able to replace *the* Mrs. Astor.

6

The Richest Man on the Titanic

"They lived a cat and dog life up there and we all knew it." With these words a surviving neighbor sums up the marriage of John Jacob Astor IV and his Ava.

Theirs was a marriage to fill the heart with compassion and horror, though it is a little hard at this distance—with John dead for half a century and even Ava claimed by death at eighty-nine in 1958—to say just who was deserving of which emotion.

"Ava [pronounced Ah-vah in the British style] was the most beautiful woman I have ever seen. It was an era of great beauties, but they all took a back seat to her. When she walked into a room every eye was on her." The sincerity of this tribute, coming from another woman, cannot be questioned. "But she was cold, hard, selfish and mean to her husband. I don't think she was capable of loving anyone."

And what of John Jacob? "He was a *most* unattractive man, too shy to talk well," the relentless recollections go on. "The only thing he really seemed to enjoy was working with his hands. If he had been poor, he would have been happier, because he could have been a mechanic."

The future mutual misery was certainly not foreseen by the parents, who were eagerly pushing the match. *The* Mrs. Astor, John's mother, wanted his happiness, but her narrow view of the world led her to assume that good family and good nature necessarily went hand in hand. Her vis-à-vis, Mrs. Willing, was not so well born as to scorn the Astor millions. As for the young couple—well, they were young, and Ava was so lovely, the belle of Newport each summer and Philadelphia each winter. The townspeople of Newport, who in those days lined up to watch the Casino Balls at a cost of one dollar a head—looked for Ava first, to see who she was dancing with and to admire her elegance. Her face, with its Roman nose and dark flashing eyes, and her figure, narrow-waisted and full-bosomed, were incomparably beautiful. Those who knew her still wax eloquent in the memory of her flawless back revealed in ballgowns; even her ankles, feet, and hands were of surpassing loveliness. Hers was the kind of ego that required her to bring off a brilliant marriage, and *Town Topics* had informed the world of society that John was "one of the richest catches of the day." She overlooked, at least at first, his strangely shaped receding forehead, concentrating her attention instead on the slender, narrow-shouldered figure that possessed a certain elegance. Accustomed to a domineering mother, young Astor was not put off by Ava's sharp tongue. "We do not converse in Newport, we eat," she squelched him in a sibilant whisper as he tried to make small talk at one of the interminable dinners. He did not realize until too late that living with an unkind assertive woman is quite another matter from being with a doting one.

Ava married him, but she did not feel she needed to be nice to him. She did, after all, risk her perfect figure in the first year of their marriage to bear the required son and heir, who was named William Vincent. The William was inevitable, since John Jacob V had been pre-empted by William Waldorf for his first born, and no other names could be considered by an Astor; Vincent (the name by which the child was to be known) was in memory of Count von Rumpf, husband of the long-dead, pure Eliza. Motherhood did not have the same softening effect on Ava that it had produced in her mother-in-law. She treated her son with the same unkindness that characterized her relationship with her husband, irritated beyond endurance by the little boy's clumsiness. Cursed from babyhood with huge hands and feet, Vincent was always knocking things over. His mother did not hesitate to raise her cultured voice in a shout of "Stupid!" at him in front of a roomful of people. She removed herself from all blame in his heredity, attributing his failings to what she, with characteristic tactlessness, referred to as "bad Astor blood." Her guests found this more amusing than the family did.

And there were always guests, whether the family was wintering at the mansion on Fifth Avenue, summering at Beechwood in Newport, or spending between-season periods at Ferncliff, the estate William Astor had loved. Following his father's bent as a gentleman farmer, John operated a model dairy, an activity Ava never commented on at all; perhaps she was unaware of it. The aspect of Ferncliff that she knew much better was its private country club atmosphere. Stanford White, architect to the Four Hundred, was called in to create an athletic complex of a tennis court, two squash courts, a 65-foot-long marble swimming pool, a rifle range, a bowling alley, and a billiard room, along with the requisite dressing rooms. Ava most enjoyed tennis or bridge, and weekend guests were selected for their abilities. Of the two activities, the host enjoyed the former only, a fact that was of no concern at all to his wife. A strangely revealing snapshot has survived to show the prevailing spirit of those long-ago weekends. John Jacob is on the tennis court stretching his long thin arm up to serve the ball, while Ava is seated on the sidelines, her back carefully turned to the tennis game. She began to devote most of her time at Ferncliff to bridge, a game that John Jacob abhorred. He was a pathetic figure, as the more perceptive of the guests realized.

"He shambled from room to room, tall, loosely built, and ungraceful, rather like a great overgrown colt, in a vain search for someone to talk to," recalled Elizabeth Lehr, who, with her prankish husband, was a regular guest at the Astors.

Ava was completely indifferent to his boredom, and if anything, was irritated by it. Although fascinated by the mechanical principle of the player piano, he was not allowed to pass the time by amusing himself with the instrument. He would start a roll playing, and Ava would promptly dispatch a servant to tell him that the noise was disturbing the bridge players.

The Germanic trait of punctuality had been drilled into John, and he saw it as a part of a gentleman's code of behavior, but Ava could not be bothered to leave the bridge table until it was too late for her and the other players to appear at dinner on time. Sundays were perhaps the worst days for him; he would go to church alone, correct in his cutaway coat and top hat, leaving his wife and her friends at the bridge table. Rather than fight the battle of getting them to lunch on time, he took to having his meal served to him alone on a tray in the study.

When not playing bridge, Ava indulged herself in a series of escapades, staggering when one considers the era and milieu she lived in. Ruled only by the desire to do what she wanted when she wanted to, Ava thought it a great lark to slip away from the Fifth Avenue mansion to go down to Chinatown to a chess parlor and match wits with a Chinese mandarin. His flamboyant gesture of sweeping all the pieces off the board when he won delighted her sense of drama; not that as loser she would even consider bending down to pick them up. There was always someone else to do the picking up for Ava. If she felt like slipping into a saloon in a poor neighborhood to drink a glass of beer, she would, and again, her presence was such that a "no ladies invited" sign simply meant no other ladies. In Newport she held court on Bailey's Beach—though not in the style of her mother-in-law. It was her way rather to take stage center by performing the czardas in short skirts and tights that revealed her exceptionally shapely legs. (A daring *World* photographer succeeded in sneaking onto the sacrosanct beach, no doubt disguised as a member of society, and obtaining a picture of Ava en déshabille.)

There was never any question, though, of a desire to lead the simple life. However she felt about her husband, she was perfectly satisfied with his bank account. In her element at balls, she spent as much of his money on them as she possibly could. When it came time to hand out favors at one party, she appeared driving a gilded sleigh banked with flowers and drawn by servants in livery. Within were the fans and knickknacks that she handed out with the manner of a Roman empress.

London was her favorite of European capitals, and her visits there took British society by storm. If there was any prejudice against rich Americans, Ava certainly did not meet it, as everyone up to and including Edward VII expressed nothing but eagerness for an invitation to her magnificent balls.

Such international acclaim enhanced her reputation in America, and there were those who thought she might rival her mother-in-law as arbiter of New York society. Nothing could have been more foreign to her personality; she could never put up with the boredom of organized society. Dull or ugly people were to be avoided at all cost. She preferred to shock, startle, and stun society than to run it. When her wayward cousin Augusta was being ostracized, Ava gave a reception for her—and her motive was probably more to flaunt society than to support the position taken by *the* Mrs. Astor. In Newport she gravitated toward the set of bachelors who formed the Gooseberry Island Club, devoted to drinking, fishing, and nude bathing (they insisted that they always dressed before the ladies arrived for lunch). In New York she was as one with her relatives, the Kane boys, and others of the Knickerbocker Dudes, the "in" group of the city's young bachelor set who made all the rules and broke them whenever the mood struck. One night they would attend a ball in black satin knickers and the next would appear garbed in the most severe and proper British style. Whatever they did was done so well that one visiting Englishman seeing Lewis and Winthrop Rutherfurd, two prominent Dudes, on one of their British nights immediately pointed them out to Edith Wharton as fellow countrymen of his; no Americans, he said, could be so well dressed. The Dudes could make any woman a social success—or failure. Beautiful Ava never needed anyone to help her on her way and conquered the Dudes as she conquered all men.

In fact, the persistent whisper went, Ava was not one to overlook the most exciting way for a society matron to retain an interest in life—the attention of young men. Ava rather encouraged these rumors, enjoying her thoroughly deserved reputation of femme fatale. Although not really an intelligent woman, she had early in life learned a sophisticated manner of making small talk, which she enlivened with the outrageous or insolent remark. Some, of course, were repelled by her arrogance, but far more fell hopelessly under her spell. She believed that no man she desired could possibly resist, and this confidence was nourished by a succession of prominent and brilliant men. And so when in her unwearied sixties she left a dull dinner party pretending to have a headache, she expressed surprise when the hostess thoughtfully sent the host after her. "Does she think I'm so safe?" she drawled, and she was only half joking. There was nothing safe about the young Ava, and the women in her social set kept their husbands or lovers away from her when they could. One of her most notable conquests was dashing Winthrop Rutherfurd, who figured in one of the best-known and most tragic stories of thwarted young love in the Gilded Age. Young Rutherfurd and Consuelo Vanderbilt fell madly in love, but her mother, the redoubtable Mrs. O. H. P. Belmont, tore her from his arms, intercepted his letters, and forced her to marry the Duke of Marlborough. One can only assume that the devastating Ava came into his life at a later date; otherwise it is clear that even if Mrs. Belmont had smiled on the match, Ava would never have permitted him to think of it.

Her flirtations notwithstanding, Ava continued to enjoy her position as Mrs. John Jacob Astor IV. But though John appeared to be Ava's henpecked mate and maladjusted shadow at home and at their parties, this is hardly a complete picture of the man. He had a life of his own—and a fairly full one. No two accounts of the period agree as to the extent of his participation in the family business, some reporting that he directed it personally, and others insisting that the trustees were dominant. The truth probably lies somewhere between the two positions, and it is evident that John exhibited more interest in the property than his father did and was fairly often seen behind the heavily barred windows of the two-story red brick Astor Estate office on Twenty-sixth Street, west of Broadway. Although William Waldorf considered the world of commerce unworthy of a gentleman and spent as little time in the office as possible, common interest demanded that the two cousins work together at least occasionally. It was never a truly harmonious relationship, because William Waldorf was impossible to get along with, and John Jacob IV was not a man to brook opposition, except, to be sure, when it came from his wife. The younger cousin can have felt nothing but profound relief when his unpleasant relative packed up and took off for England, retaining his real-estate interests in absentia. The Astor Estate office remained partitioned, with one half occupied by the seven clerks and managers running William Waldorf's half of the real estate, while the other housed John when he was there, his three managers when they were there, and twenty-two clerks who were always there.

John Jacob IV, ostensibly left as monarch of all he surveyed,

William Waldorf Astor, first Baron Astor, first Viscount Astor, founded the prominent and powerful British line.

Mrs. William Waldorf Astor, the former Mary Paul. Her husband wanted to make her *the* Mrs. Astor.

John Jacob Astor IV, his son Vincent, a friend, and Constance Warren, enjoy an afternoon at Newport, favorite resort for generations of Astors.

One of the last photographs ever taken of John Jacob Astor IV. He is at Waterloo Station, London, waiting for the train that was to carry him to the *Titanic* and his death.

Mrs. John Jacob Astor IV, the former Ava Willing, one of the great society beauties of an era.

RIGHT: Cartoon of Lord Ribblesdale, who, in his youth, was lord-in-waiting to Queen Victoria, and in later life, second husband of Ava Astor.

Ava Astor in a rare mood of sentimentality with her little daughter Alice.

LEFT: A view looking down Fifth Avenue to the old Waldorf-Astoria Hotel. The Empire State Building stands on that site today.

Lewis Stuyvesant Chanler, elected Lieutenant-Governor of New York in 1906, was the best known of "Maddie's" eleven children.

Widowed in 1912, Madeleine Force Astor asked the police to protect her from cameramen who followed her even when she walked her terriers.

Vincent Astor who left much of his vast fortune
to charity instead of to Astor heirs.

Nourmahal, Vincent Astor's palatial yacht at anchor, just before President-elect Franklin Delano Roosevelt came on board for a pre-inaugu-
ration cruise.

moved modestly into a plebeian office that was in striking contrast to the grandeur of his home. He sat behind a rolltop desk, moving to a table when he needed to open his ledgers. A few plainly framed pictures and a red carpet were the only concessions to décor. There were two windows, but the outlook was not calculated to encourage window gazing and dreaming; opening onto a narrow court, they faced a blank white wall. John could truly say that he was asking no tenement dweller to put up with what he would not endure himself—in terms of view only, of course.

Still, the man did dream, as his science-fiction novel about the future, *A Journey in Other Worlds*, was to show. This is not a book to be judged in terms of literary merit; only the Astor name and money could conceivably explain its publication and the gentle reviews accorded it by the critics. It shows that Ava's stiff, awkward husband did have a lively imagination, which he was too inhibited to reveal in conversation. His knowledge of science and engineering was considerable, however, and the science-fiction portions of the book hold up better than might have been expected. Global weather control, a subject that is still occupying leading meteorologists, is managed in the book by the Terrestrial Axis Straightening Company. Rain making has become an exact science, and the Aleutian Islands have been blown up to allow the Japanese currents to warm the arctic. Space travel, as Astor saw it, is made possible by utilization of the force of "apergy," the opposite of gravity. All transportation on the face of the earth is driven by electricity instead of the horse. War, characterized by airplane bombing, has become so appalling that the world is united—well, his description of war has come true anyway. Germs are employed to destroy poisonous or harmful animals. The Astor eye for profit is not completely closed either. The hero, Colonel Bearwarden, approaches the planet Jupiter with excitement: "How I should like to mine those hills for copper!" The love story is handled with far less skill than the sections dealing with science or business—true in the author's life as well as in his writing. The heroine is a beautiful socialite—but she attends Vassar, where her average is ninety. Passion is hardly a factor in her life. Perhaps John missed having something to talk about with Ava more than he missed tenderness in her embrace.

147

It was fortunate for him that he was able to find outlets for his energies that did not depend on her. While Ava was sparkling in the ballroom or at the bridge table, John spent hours of his spare time working on mechanisms, models, and blueprints for a series of inventions of varying degrees of merit. He developed a brake suitable for use on bicycles with solid tires, and had the common-sense idea of attaching vacuum cups to the legs of steamship chairs so that they would stay in one place on a rolling deck. His Pneumatic Road Improver, capable of blowing dirt off roads, won first prize at the World's Columbian Exposition in Chicago in 1893. Another imaginatively named mechanism, the Vibratory Disintegrator, was designed to obtain gas from peat. Perhaps his most ambitious invention was a type of marine turbine engine. At least where his inventions were concerned, John did not go along with his ancestor's view that giving something for nothing weakens the giver, and presented them to the public as a gift.

Considering his mechanical bent and his wealth, he was naturally one of the very first men in the country to own the newly invented automobile. And he was not unaware of its attracting power. While Ava played bridge or flirted, John Jacob would invite one of the local belles at Rhinebeck to go for a ride with him—and some old ladies still remember how they lacked the will power to resist the lure of that car, despite his reputation with women. ("He pawed every girl in sight.") In the summertime John and a few other millionaires—William K. Vanderbilt, O. H. P. Belmont, and Harry Payne Whitney—took to racing on the beach at Newport to the cheers of their gloriously gowned wives.

One of the great events in the annals of the resort's history was the Newport obstacle race, in which the cars careened wildly around dummies of horses, dogs, children, and policemen. Ava rode with Harry Lehr and John's companion was a neighbor, Mrs. Adolph Ladenburg. Most of the other competing cars were fantastically and imaginatively decorated with stuffed eagles, arbors of hydrangeas, and the like, but it was John Jacob IV who won.

With this triumph behind him, Ava consented to accompany him down Fifth Avenue in a surrey with a steam-driven engine under the seat. Little Vincent, to whom his father was much attached, was taken along for the ride. Ava was accustomed to excited comments from onlookers, and John Jacob was filled with the pride of ownership, and so neither saw anything but admiration and envy in the shouts and gestures of the crowds on the sidewalks. They remained blissfully unaware of the fact that the engine had caught fire, until the heat became so intense that they were forced to jump from the burning vehicle.

This mishap did not dampen John's enthusiasm, and he soon became the owner of eighteen cars, among them a European racing car with a seventy-horsepower engine. By 1903 he was boasting that he could drive the 115 miles from New York to Newport in a mere four hours and twenty minutes. To encourage others to follow his example, John made one of his mansions near Ferncliff into an automobile club. Drivers could stop there to break the exhausting journey between the city and upper New York State. Such demonstrated devotion to the road was rewarded with an appointment to a national highway commission.

Railroads held similar appeal for him, and trains were ordered to make special stops at Rhinebeck to pick up or deposit Astor and his guests. It was indeed delightful to be a tycoon in those days. If John was in the mood, he would take the throttle from the engineer and run the train for a while.

Like his father, he enjoyed yachting, and partly for the same reason—escape from an unhappy home life. But John Jacob was not a natural commodore, and the number of collisions into which he steered his *Nourmahal* were a source of many sly society jokes. Astor had little sense of humor to begin with, and the whole subject appeared considerably less than funny to him when the Vanderbilts sued him for $15,000 damages for running into their *North Star*. He rallied from this blow to redecorate the *Nourmahal*, and expanded the dining room so that it could seat sixty fearless guests. For reasons not clear to anyone else, he was extremely worried about pirates and had four guns mounted on the deck. But John Jacob had guessed wrong; no pirates attacked, and the renovated *Nourmahal* only met disaster in the form of some rocks that were clearly behaving in an aggressive way.

There was no lack of money with which to indulge the *Nourmahal* and his other costly tastes. As the Astors continued in their time-honored policy of reticence, the exact amount of the fortune at any given time was a matter of conjecture. The combined estate of John Jacob Astor IV and William Waldorf had been estimated at $250 million in a widely read article published in *Forum* magazine in 1889. This figure was used for many decades as a base on which to calculate the growth of the estate due to appreciation of property values. No one but the Astors could say whether the *Forum* article was accurate, and, of course, they would not. There is, in fact, only one public utterance on the subject made by anyone actually involved in the business. In 1890 Charles F. Southmayd stated that the joint estate of the cousins amounted to a little under $200 million—and cautious Southmayd was never noted for exaggeration.

Hanging on to what they possessed remained the Astor formula for financial success, a legacy from John Jacob I. The personality of the founder of the family fortune retained its force long after his death. Were the date not known, one might assume that the following piece of testimony taken from a hearing before a State Senate Committee studying tax assessments was made in 1840 rather than 1890:

"You have just said that Mr. Astor never sold?" asked the counsel for the committee.

"Once in a while he sells, yes," replied the president of the Board of Assessments and Taxes, who was trying to explain why the Astor property was assessed at a rate so far below its real value.

"Isn't it almost a saying in this community that the Astors buy and never sell?" persisted the counsel.

"They are not looked upon as people who dispose of real estate after they once get possession of it."

The rents poured in, and though William Waldorf, heir to the massive real-estate holdings of John Jacob III, got a lion's share of anywhere from six to nine million dollars, John Jacob IV was hardly pressed for ready cash with receipts topping three million dollars. The population and naturally the worth of the tenements increased steadily. "The more wretched the immigrants, the more valuable the land becomes," wrote an observer of the period, adding that one hundred people were being jammed into space that fifty years earlier had been occupied by a single family.

Astor's reputation for great wealth was such that he received between thirty and forty begging letters a day—and this was a period when most poor people could not write. Nor were appeals limited to Americans, as this letter sent from Stockholm to John Jacob Astor IV, "Richest Man in All the World," reveals: "Honored Sir—I would like you to send me at once 30,000 thalers; a mere bagatelle to you, but a fortune to me." Another, more modest, requested $25 so that an invalid wife could be sent to the country. A sophisticated clerk in the estate office, however, recognized the return address as that of a downtown saloon.

The Astors were not good marks for individual requests for charity of any kind, as John Garvey, described in the papers of the time as the "Astor tramp," was to learn. This vagrant stumbled into John Jacob's mansion one winter's night and slept in the laundress' bed. She was apparently elsewhere that night; in any event, the complaint did not come from her. When Garvey was found the following morning, Astor was outraged. Times might be bad, but a man's home is sacrosanct after all. He insisted on having Garvey indicted for burglary. As the tramp was pitiable and clearly feeble-minded, Astor's uncharitable action was vigorously attacked in the press. John Jacob was quite unable to understand why this should be. Although imaginative in some ways, he held a view of the poor that was remarkably similar to that of his grandfather, William Backhouse. Poverty was beyond his comprehension.

The tramp, it is likely, had wandered into Astor's mansion drawn by the lights and activity of the hotel next door. It was just another indication, thought John, of the way a hotel, however luxurious, changes a neighborhood. When his cousin, William Waldorf left for England, he had repeated almost verbatim the avowed ambition of John Jacob I to create "the largest most elegant hotel in the world." William was not present during the years of the Waldorf's gestation and birth, and the fact that he achieved his ambition was due largely to his manager, George Boldt, a German immigrant with the soul and outlook of a hotelkeeping Ward Mc-Allister: "I should prefer to see Mrs. Astor drinking an unprofitable cup of water in the Palm Garden than to serve a rich newcomer the most expensive dinner."

William did not come to New York for the opening, and it was his cousin who had to look on enviously from the sidelines. The

Waldorf opened on a stormy night in March of 1893, with a benefit concert and dinner for St. Mary's Free Hospital for Children.
The guest list numbered 1,500 socialites. Even then, it can be seen,
charity balls were seldom small or select, a fact rarely realized by
those moaning how times have changed as they struggle through
the magnificently-gowned mob at a modern benefit party. Oddly
enough, the beneficiary on the Waldorf's opening night was not
one of those favored by the Astor ladies, but "belonged" to Mrs.
William K. Vanderbilt. Still, as the Vanderbilts and the Astors
were speaking by then, it was not the *gaffe* it would have been a
mere ten years earlier. The Lowells and Sargents from Boston, the
Drexels and Biddles from Philadelphia, and Mrs. Potter Palmer of
Chicago joined New York's inner circle in paying five dollars
apiece for charity.

The dinner, which featured *côtelettes de riz de veau*, was over-
seen by Oscar Tschirsky, who was soon to lose his last name and
become known simply as "Oscar of the Waldorf." He had gotten
his start as an eighteen-dollar-a-month busboy at Hoffman House,
noted for its paintings of nudes at the bar and for the fact that its
proprietor had shot Jim Fisk. Oscar was far better attuned to the
greater refinement of the Waldorf. It was his fate to gain the un-
merited reputation of chef, whereas he was really greeter and dining room manager. The true chef, Noillard, has slipped into oblivion, losing his first name instead of his last, and his great creation,
that ubiquitous salad with cut-up apples and walnuts, is known as
Waldorf not Noillard salad. Inside rumors had it that Oscar never
split tips with him or anyone else for that matter, considering gift
boxes of cigars at Christmas as quite sufficient for cooks and waiters. Guests were far more enchanted with Oscar's winning personality than were his fellow workers; he dominated the hotel's dining
room and boldly revised dinner and supper menus. The nation's
hostesses owe him the chafing dish, filled preferably with chicken à
la king or lobster Newburg (even in the early days of the Waldorf, at least eight hundred portions of the latter were consumed at
midnight suppers), plus such lesser items as deviled eggs and an-
chovies, preferably served at small tables, each lighted with a rose-
shaded candle.

Boldt checked every detail carefully, insisting that candlesticks be placed in every room, because a failure of electricity would be a disaster too terrible to contemplate. With Victorian niceness, he had ordered pretty china cuspidors instead of the crude brass ones usually found in hotels and public rooms. In each room intended for a foreign dignitary, a large canopied bed stood upon a dais, adding a regal touch to the décor. Room service, customary in Europe but new to the United States, was instituted, as was the Parisian breakfast in bed. Really important guests (by Boldt's standards) received boxes of cigars and bottles of old wine as gifts of the house. When they left for Europe, champagne and baskets of flowers preceded them to the staterooms. The guests were not always appreciative of Boldt's efforts. On one occasion when Li Hung-chang, a Chinese statesman, was due to arrive, Boldt and Oscar journeyed to Chinatown, copied banners and signs, and had replicas made and hung in his suite. Special Oriental delicacies were purchased for him. The two hotelmen were cut to the quick by the Chinese official's response. Smiling courteously all the while, Li Hung-chang insisted on having his own cooks prepare all his meals on stoves brought along for the purpose from China.

Other guests responded better to the graciousness of the Boldt regime, and stimulated him to even greater efforts. He was so convinced of the perfection of the hotel that when a guest dared to complain that the bill was too high, Boldt tore it up: "Don't pay it and don't come back." A rulemaker par excellence, Boldt decided that refinement demanded the entire staff be clean-shaven. All beards had to go, with a single exception, his own sleek spade-shaped beard. He went so far as to insist that the cab drivers who stationed themselves at the Thirty-third Street entrance of the hotel comply with the regulation. The outcry from drivers, waiters, cooks, porters, and handymen was instant and violent; attacks on the edict appeared in the columns of the New York *Sun*, and frantic meetings were called by the Association of Hack Drivers. Objections meant nothing to Boldt, and the beards soon disappeared.

One cannot say if the absence of beards had anything to do with the success of the Waldorf, which was swift and great. Everyone of the rooms that had been allocated for permanent guests was quickly occupied. Oscar claimed that on an ordinary day twenty-five thousand people walked down the red-carpeted corridor between the Palm Room and the Empire Room, which the society editor of the *Tribune* had named Peacock Alley. When someone important was staying at the hotel, Oscar continued, the number mounted to thirty-five thousand—well, maybe he was exaggerating a little. Even William Waldorf on a rare visit to New York walked down Peacock Alley—once. He stayed in the hotel on but a single occasion. That time he saw as little as possible. Staff members reported that he never raised his eyes from the carpet and dashed down the hall as if pursued, entered the elevator, head still down, and was taken to his room.

His cousin, John Jacob IV, was discovering that he could hardly ignore the teeming activity and excitement of the Waldorf. His mother and he had been forced to realize that homelife in the immediate vicinity of the hotel was hopeless, and a château was constructed for them thirty blocks uptown at 840 Fifth Avenue. Everyone was asking what they planned to do with their old home. For a while Astor threatened to build a stable there. He had a rather macabre sense of humor and figured this was a sure way of infuriating his cousin. The stable ploy was one he had already used to anger the managers of the Temple B'nai Jeshuran, which was located at Sixty-fifth Street and Madison Avenue, adjacent to his property. His threat then had been so convincing that the temple directors had appealed to the state legislature to stop him. A bill was duly passed decreeing that no stable could be constructed within one hundred feet of any religious building. The governor, possibly thinking to please Astor, vetoed the bill, but John, who had undoubtedly never intended to do anything but cause a stir, dropped the whole plan and never mentioned it again. When it came to the hotel, the stable idea threw Boldt into a frenzy, and he rushed to one of the Astor Estate's business advisers, Abner Bartlett, pleading with him to do something. Bartlett had little trouble in convincing John Jacob IV to do what came naturally—build a hotel that would be even grander than the Waldorf.

All his life John ran a never-ending race with his cousin, seemingly directed by the anything-you-can-do-I-can-do-better concept. William Waldorf had married a beautiful woman; John countered by marrying the most beautiful woman of the era. William turned his hand to the writing of historical fiction; John tried to top him with a novel about the future. Now came the Waldorf Hotel, with its 450 bedrooms and 350 baths, its Empire Room, which was a replica of the grand salon in King Ludwig's palace in Munich, its Palm Gardens, where guests were required to wear full evening dress, its bar, where Diamond Jim Brady held forth nightly, and its guest list, made up of royalty, diplomats, socialites, and celebrities in the arts and politics. Could John Jacob IV top that with a hotel of his own? He could certainly try.

Although the projected hotel was next door to the Waldorf and logically had to be connected, a clause was inserted in the contract that the building could be sealed off if the worst in family relations came to the worst. It was hard to imagine their being any more unpleasant. Only two years before these negotiations, William Waldorf had given a big dinner in London on the night when John's sister, Mrs. James Roosevelt Roosevelt lay dead in that city. Perhaps in retaliation the following year, when Mrs. William Waldorf's body was being returned to this country for burial, Ava and *the* Mrs. Astor appeared at the opera together. Society was shocked at the impropriety, but John raised no objections. Continuing to flout decorum, Ava led the cotillion at the Assembly Ball in New York and then departed for Philadelphia to attend the Assembly held on the night of the very day when Mary was buried in that very city. Still, the Astors were not the first family to place business considerations above personal ones, and clearly, two hotels were better than one.

Because, like all of her children, John was devoted to his mother, he wanted to name the hotel the Schermerhorn, in her honor. That was too much for William Waldorf to swallow; Mrs. Astor's recent behavior had added the final insult to the injury she had done his Mary by defeating her in the *the* Mrs. Astor competition. A compromise was worked out, and the second hotel was named after that long-ago seat of empire, Astoria. Ward McAllister's daughter Louise suggested brightly that the names be combined and hyphenated, and for years it was a slightly precious inside society joke to say, "Meet me at the hyphen."

Linked by more than a hyphen, the combined hotel flourished as no hotel had ever flourished before, boasting one thousand bedrooms and a grand ballroom that could seat 1,500 for a dinner dance. Arnold Constable's decorators and buyers, armed with a budget of $300,000, scoured Europe for furnishings to add to those taken from the Astor mansions. John Jacob IV did have his little triumph over William, because the Astoria was made taller than the Waldorf and cast a shadow on the older hotel.

By the time the Astoria opened in November of 1897, Boldt and Oscar had succeeded in making the hotel an elegant clubhouse instead of merely a place to sleep. The idea, commonplace now, was revolutionary then. The gentlemen of New York flocked to the four-sided bar presided over by eight bartenders capable of making five hundred different drinks. The *Literary Digest* magazine some years later, in a study of the early days of the Waldorf-Astoria, wrote that profits from the bar had paid the overhead of the entire hotel. A popular cartoon of the period showed a policeman bringing two drunks in formal clothes into the police station. "What's that you've got, O'Hara?" asks the captain. "Society as oi have found it, sorr!" returns the policeman in the words, if not the accent, of Ward McAllister. The effects of alcohol were withstood better by those who sampled freely of the ample free lunch featuring platters of cold Virginia baked ham and roast Vermont turkey, as well as hot beef, chicken, or seafood casseroles.

But the income from the bar did not satisfy Boldt, who, as we know, wanted Mrs. Astor with her unprofitable cup of water. The question was how to get her. He stationed a trio of Tyrolean yodelers in the Palm Gardens and had Turkish coffee served in the lobby, where a string orchestra played. Ladies remained uncertain that hotels were socially correct. Although members of the inner circle deny it now, the social seal of acceptance was placed on the hotel by one of the most notorious dances in social history, the Bradley Martin Ball, held in the Waldorf a few months before the opening of the Astoria. Although a bit on the nouveau side, the Martins had won the approval of McAllister some time before, had married off a daughter to an English lord, and were on the invitations lists of the Astors, both *the* Mrs. and the John Jacob IV's. Hearing that there was a business recession in the winter of 1896–97, Cornelia Sherman Martin naïvely observed that a costume ball for nine hundred guests would be a philanthropic act, because it would "give an impetus to trade." Society members did their best to oblige, and Mr. Belmont, to take one example, handed his costumer ten thousand dollars to create a suit of gold-inlaid armor for him to wear. *The* Mrs. Astor—she did not mean to go, but could not resist Harry Lehr's blandishments—gave impetus to Worth's trade by having him copy a black satin dress with a lace collar and cuffs from a portrait by Van Dyke. And hairdressers' business was certainly improved when Mrs. Martin hired them to do the coiffures of her guests at fifteen dollars an hour. The *quadrille d'honneur*, to be danced to the music of Victor Herbert, successor to John Lander, was rehearsed at the Astors' home. John Jacob was selected by Mrs. Martin to be her ball partner, an honor that won him the title *King* of the ball. It is the only social occasion on record in which John shone more brightly than his wife.

But Cornelia's economic innocence was not shared by the general public or by the press, and objections were vehemently expressed as to the poor taste of such extravagance at a time when thousands were starving. Although Mrs. Martin paid but $4,550 for the ballroom and supper and $658 for the band, published estimates of the total outlay ran as high as $369,200, a figure explained by purchases of costumes and jewels. Attacks on them were so virulent that the Martins fled the country and went to England to live.

But although social consciousness may have been aroused in the poor and the middle-income groups, it remained quiescent in the very rich. Although some social historians cite the Bradley Martin ball as a turning point for members of society, they can only be reporting what they think should have resulted, not what actually did. Only recently, as if following the dubious example of Mrs. Martin, the parents of a Midwestern debutante imported a New York hairdresser for considerably more than fifteen dollars an hour to set or comb out the hairdos of several hundred lady guests. Returning to the 1890's, only two years after the Bradley Martin so-called fiasco, Rudolph Guggenheim, Borough President of Manhattan, gave a dinner at the Waldorf-Astoria. Guests plucked and ate grapes from arbors planted at the entrance to the ballroom and then settled down to a banquet of oyster cocktail, green turtle soup, lobster, columbine of chicken, roast mountain sheep with purée of chestnuts and brussels sprouts and asparagus, sherbet, diamond-back terrapin, duck with orange and grapefruit salad, fresh strawberries and blue raspberries that had been hothouse-bred for the occasion, vanilla mousse, bonbons, and coffee. Sherry, white wine, champagne, burgundy, port wine, and liqueurs whet-ted the palates for the one-hundred-year-old brandy uncorked as a grand finale. Those who had not fallen into a dazed stupor as a re-sult of the food and drink were charmed by the song of nightin-gales perched on the branches of a grove of trees lining the walls.

More subdued and elegant affairs were given at the Waldorf-Astoria by members of the inner circle, and even *the* Mrs. Astor held a few small parties there. Well, it was all in the family. None-theless, a hotel was no place for an unescorted woman, and not one had ever appeared in the lobby until the night when Ava, leaving a party late and alone because she was bored, decided to stay at her husband's hotel. As she disdained to give her name, the desk clerk refused to give her a room. Luckily at that critical moment, one of the other men in the office recognized her, or the Waldorf-Astoria and its entire staff would surely have found itself put up for auc-tion in the morning. As it was, her reaction was so violent that the staff held a hurried meeting and decided to relax the rule about women.

Men remained dominant in the hotel life anyway, with J. P. Morgan, Henry Clay Frick, Charles Schwab, and other tycoons settling in the Men's Café after the Stock Exchange closed. On one such afternoon, the U.S. Steel Corporation was conceived. The Waldorf-Astoria took some business away from Caulfield's, the city's leading gambling establishment, on Forty-fourth Street, and from the House of the Bronze Doors, which was just down the block. Poker games with a thousand-dollar limit were played regu-larly in the $20,000-a-year apartment at the hotel maintained by "Bet-a-Million" Gates. That famous gambler would bet on any-thing, and one rainy day found him and his millionaire cronies bet-ting on the speed of the raindrops running down the window at one hundred dollars a drop. John Jacob Astor IV, while enjoying the reputation and income of New York's leading hotel owner, did not join in these games; perhaps they appeared too similar to Ava's never-ending bridge.

It is human nature to undervalue what one has, and so Astor took his tremendous wealth and importance in the business community for granted and longed instead for a military career. He was influenced, no doubt, by his uncle's romantic reminiscences of the Civil War and his father's regrets at not having been allowed to serve. In 1895 John joined Governor Levi P. Morton's military staff, but peacetime military service is nothing very much to satisfy a bored millionaire. The Spanish-American War, beginning three years later, gave him his great opportunity, and he rushed to offer both his yacht and himself to the government. An introduction was quickly arranged to Theodore Roosevelt, then Assistant Secretary of the Navy, and this resulted in an appointment as inspector-general, with the rank of lieutenant colonel. Astor inspected army camps first in this country and then in Cuba, where he observed the battle of Santiago. An untimely bout of malaria cut short his military career, but he had done enough to be promoted to colonel for "faithful and meritorious service," and he enjoyed hearing the title of his rank for the rest of his life.

Because Colonel Astor, like all rich men, longed to be loved for himself not his money, he was dismayed to realize that his chief contribution to the war effort was not to be his services but rather his gift of an entire battery of artillery. Even for that time the idea was daring in conception. One can only wonder what would happen today if some individual offered to buy a nice new long-range missile. In 1898, however, the government accepted with alacrity, and Peyton C. March, later a general, was dispatched by the army to New York to become the leader of the battery. Unable to find any trace of it, he went to the Astor Estate office, where he was told with a smile that "the Astor Light Battery is simply a checkbook." But a checkbook has power, and soon March was drilling recruits on Astor land in the Bronx. Uniforms for the men were made to measure in four days by Wanamaker's, with the tailors receiving a bonus for working so fast, and guns were smuggled in from France. Upon discovering that there was no army manual covering such weapons, Astor had one written to order and printed. The battery fought in the Philippines and suffered casualties of two dead and eight wounded. The surviving soldiers were permitted to keep their well-tailored uniforms afterward, and the army received the leftover guns and ammunition.

War's end was celebrated at Newport with a ball at which Harry

Lehr made one of his skillful accidental-on-purpose mistakes. *The Mrs. Astor,* who had turned over the arrangements to Harry, told him to be sure to have the band come in uniform. She was, she declared later, astounded when they climbed onto the bandstand dressed in army, not band, uniforms. Harry replied blandly that the musicians had all served with Colonel John Jacob Astor, and, of course, these were their only uniforms at the moment.

John Jacob had returned home by then to his lovely but cold wife; to his warm but aging mother; to the temperamental little son he loved; to his homes in New York, Rhinebeck, and Newport; to his yacht the *Nourmahal;* to his clubs—the Union, Metropolitan, Knickerbocker, Brook, Tuxedo, City, City Midday, Downtown, Authors', Racquet and Tennis, Country, Turf and Field (of which he had been one of the founders), New York Yacht, New York Riding, Auto Club of America, Cocoa Tree (London), and Travelers (London and Paris); to his directorships—Astor Trust Co., Central Railroad Co., Mercantile Trust Co., Morton Trust Co., National Park Bank, Niagara Falls Power Co., Plaza Bank, Western Union Telegraph Co., and Delaware and Hudson Co.; to his trusteeships—New York Life Insurance and Trust Co. and Title Guarantee and Trust Co.; and to his memberships—Hudson-Fulton Commission, New York Chamber of Commerce, Academy of Science, American Geographical Society, Zoological Society, New York Botanical Gardens, Society of Colonial Wars, Military Order of Foreign Wars, Metropolitan Museum of Art, American Museum of Natural History, National Guard of New York, and Delta Phi fraternity.

It would have been a never-ending grind for any man who tried to keep up with all the social and business enterprises involved, and John Jacob IV, for the most part, did not. It was his practice, particularly as he grew older, to send proxies to the stockholders' meetings and to leave corporate decisions to the managements involved. (This was so generally recognized that Astor was not much affected personally by the insurance scandals of the early 1900's, despite his financial association with companies charged with misuse of funds. Only a few reporters commented pointedly on the Astor policy of contributing heavily to campaign funds of influential politicians.) When it came to the Astor bread-and-butter holdings, the real estate, economists are struck by the way in which both John Jacob IV and William Waldorf failed to take advantage of the immense increases in property valuation in the years immediately after the Spanish-American War. William had the disadvantage of being absentee landlord, but John was on the spot.

"A man of daring and foresight could have multiplied the $200-odd million fortune into a billion" is the view of one real-estate expert, "but they continued to rent property on long-term leases, with rents based on valuation at the time of signing. As much of the property increased in value by 50 or 100 percent during the term of the lease, the sublandlords repeatedly raised rents without benefitting the Astors at all."

With Fifth Avenue becoming the fashionable shopping center, the Gorham Manufacturing Company was delighted to pay the Astor Estate $36,000 a year in rent for the corner of Fifth Avenue and Thirty-sixth Street. The terms of the lease required the firm to erect its own store, but even with that expense to be amortized, Gorham got a real bargain when rents for comparable locations were soon lifted to far higher levels. Altman's, which had put up its own building on Astor land on Sixth Avenue in the 1870's, had learned the advantage of such a lease, whereas the landlord had not. It was, therefore, able to repeat the experience on Astor land on Fifth Avenue when the original lease ran out. The rapid appreciation of property values can easily be seen by following George Boldt outside business hours. Boldt, who had been a poor man when he came to the Waldorf, became a millionaire himself in a mere seven years as a result of hints dropped by the Astors. In 1900 he bought the southeast corner of Thirty-seventh Street and Fifth Avenue for $1.2 million, and in 1901, ignoring the Astor "do not sell" rule, disposed of it for two million dollars. At that, he might have done better had he emulated his employers and held onto it for a few more years.

On October 27, 1904, an event took place that was to increase values of all New York City real estate in general and Astor land in particular. Handsome Mayor George B. McClellan, son of John Jacob Astor III's favorite general, turned the sterling silver handle of the throttle of the city's first subway, and the train left City Hall station, ran along under Fourth Avenue to Grand Central Station, then west to Times Square and up Broadway, until it finally reached its northernmost point at 145th Street. During the course of that historic afternoon, the Astors and fifteen thousand other important personages took their first subway rides by invitation. The subway was opened to an eager and excited public that evening, and the first rush hour was underway. "Men fought, kicked, and pummeled one another in their mad desire to ride on the trains," reported the New York *World*. "Women were dragged out, either screaming in hysterics, or in a swooning condition."

The Astors, who had vigorously fought the coming of the subway for two generations, had no need to swoon or scream. Every piece of midtown property overnight became more valuable. As the subway was extended mile by mile, the Astor fortune grew proportionately. Once again, as had happened in the great days of John Jacob I and William B., the Astors could sit back and let the city work for them. The subway was soon afterward extended to the Bronx, and the route selected went right through Astor land, a fact hardly surprising to any aware of the family's political power. Far from paying for the advantage of having the subway there at all, the Astors insisted on being paid for it. Offered $12,000 for a right of way, John Jacob IV insisted on $129,000 and got it.

Although his conservatism kept him from making the most of some of his land holdings, Colonel Astor was enough in tune with the times to see what the development of steel construction could do for buildings. Skyscrapers, twenty or twenty-five stories high, a truly magnificent source of income, could be erected, and Astor was quick to invest in apartment houses and commercial buildings. A single office building, the Schermerhorn, brought in $75,000 in annual rent from the American Surety Co. Even so, the Astor tenements continued as a major source of rents and of misery. For a twenty-five-foot lot, valued at $18,000, John Jacob IV received $4,260 in rent from the sublandlord, who seldom allowed his expenses to mount above $450 a year. The sweatshops continued to flourish, despite social agitation and the rise of the first labor unions. Astor himself, his intimates insisted, knew very little about the conditions in the tenements; the sublandlord stood between him and his tenants, and nothing in his background encouraged him to delve more deeply. His father, living for what pleasure he could find, and his mother, living for her children and society, never discussed the unpleasant source of their wealth. John was probably unaware that forty years after the passage of fireproofing laws, many of his tenements were fire traps, lacking even fire escapes. The harsh facts of business life were responsible: The sublandlords could put up an unsafe tenement for $17,812, whereas it cost them $20,342 to construct one with moderate (not the best) safety measures. The danger of fire increased in direct proportion to the multiplying population; in the early 1900's, five hundred families were packed in the single Astor-owned block between Avenue A and First Avenue. The deathrate of 23 per 1,000 matched that of Calcutta.

As the new century began, John Jacob decided to depart from the no-sale policy and get rid of some of the worst of the old tenements put up by William B. Astor. Although no Astor would sell anything that he believed had any value at all, he had no trouble in finding buyers. Henry Morgenthau picked up some of the ones around Avenue A, and moneyed German immigrants purchased fifty tenements in the First Avenue district for $850,000, more than the land was valued at. The Astors, it can be seen, had not lost their ability to bargain.

The Astor Estate office was still partitioned; the rivalry between the cousins continued despite the distance separating them. Not content with the Waldorf, William had built the Netherland Hotel for the "discriminating elite," and then the Astor, aimed somewhat more at the mass market. John, determined to outdo him, constructed the St. Regis to counter the former and the Knickerbocker to counter the latter. Of all his hotels, the St. Regis became the one that was closest to his heart, an enthusiasm he imparted to his son, Vincent. Colonel Astor applied his mechanical gifts to its construction and designed a system of heating and air conditioning notable for the period in that each guest was able to control the temperature of his own room.

The aim of the management, employees were told, was "to remember that we are not dealing with a type of ordinary hotel, but with the solution of a social problem forced on us by the conditions of the present day. . . . In these days, a hotel must reckon with people to whom the thought of dispensing with home comforts, good service and cuisine and the atmosphere of taste and refinement has ever been a hardship." With the hotel kept up to the mark by John Jacob IV, the guests included the Cornelius and William K. Vanderbilts, the Daniel Guggenheims, the Ogden Mills, and of course, gravitating to wherever the living was easy, the Harry Lehrs. The Knickerbocker, on the other hand, with its avowed aim of offering "Fifth Avenue luxuries at Broadway prices," was profitable, but not appealing to Astor. His financial successes did not lead to comparable successes at home. Colonel Astor accompanied Ava to all major society events, but although both were accomplished dancers, it was clear that he would have preferred to be alone and that she would have preferred to be with someone else. Her friends declared that with such a husband, they could not blame her, whereas his, naturally, felt sorry for him. Always reticent, he became almost taciturn, brooding silently. Ava was graying prematurely, but it only enhanced her style and beauty. The passage of time did not slow her at all in her breakneck dash through society.

In an effort to enliven her social set, she was one of the moving spirits in creating an organization startling for its day—a women's social and athletic club, similar to those patronized by the gentlemen. Unable to withstand an appeal by Ava and her cohorts, J. P. Morgan put up $10,000 for the building of the clubhouse, a figure matched by August Belmont, Jr., and William C. Whitney made all other male benefactors look small with $25,000. No one but Stanford White would do as architect, and Elsie de Wolfe, first of the great interior designers, worked on the furnishings. Elsie had been a frequent guest at the Patriarchs Balls during their heydey; otherwise she would never have been asked to display her talents. Four years in the building, the Colony Club opened in 1907 with facilities for both social and sports enthusiasts. The athletic complex included a gym, running track, squash courts, and Turkish bath. Best of all was the sunken swimming pool of white marble surrounded by mirrored walls to reflect the still lovely shape of Ava and the less lovely forms of some of the other swimmers.

Ava was a magnificent sportswoman and on one of her visits to St. Moritz set a record for the Cresta run on a toboggan driven by a single person. But such exploits and the Colony Club at its liveliest were not enough to satisfy Ava, who ran from New York to Ferncliff to Newport to Europe and back again, seeking escape from the uncongenial atmosphere at home. The birth of a daughter, Alice Muriel, to the not-so-loving couple in 1902 did nothing to cement their relationship. By 1905 neither could continue the dissimulation required of them by the society of the period. Colonel Astor went to Europe alone, and Ava visited a sister in Washington, D. C. After this separation they again lived under one roof for a while, separated in spirit, though, as they had always been. The collapse of *the* Mrs. Astor in 1906 made it possible for them to avoid the tension of a summer in the glass bowl of Newport society. John Jacob stayed home, attended to business, and tinkered around with his cars, and his wife made her invariably spectacular appearance at Aix-les-Bains.

A permanent breakup was inevitable, but still they dallied as the months went by. John, it was generally believed, could not bear to hurt his mother, who was slowly deteriorating. She had already lived through one scandalous divorce, how could he—her youngest and the one who shared her home—add to her misery? Rumors and gossip must have reached her while her mind was capable of absorbing them, but she was used to rumors; her own William had been the subject of many. It was appearances that she, as a social leader, valued. And then in 1908, Caroline died at last. The ignorant speculated that Ava might assume the throne vacated by "the Queen," not realizing that, even had her temperament permitted, the moment for that had passed forever. Ava went to London alone, and the cumbersome divorce proceedings got underway. In 1909 she returned to New York for a secret hearing before Supreme Court Justice Mills. The grounds for divorce? There is only one in New York—adultery. At that time and for years afterward, members of society displayed more interest in the probable size of the divorce settlement than in the name of the corespondent (never revealed, because the papers were sealed). Figures ranging from $50,000 a year to a lump sum of $10 million were bandied about, but contemporaries in a position to know put it at $787,000, which was in addition to Ava's prenuptial settlement of $1,738,000.

The divorce became final a year later in 1910, and Colonel Astor received the news while he was cruising on the *Nourmahal* with

Vincent, a boy of eighteen and his father's favorite companion—of the male sex, that is. John was sensitive enough to realize that no matter what their legal positions, he had come out of the divorce as the discarded husband of a desirable wife. Determined to look anything but pathetic, he returned to New York City and gave a party for 150 guests, spending $25,000 for flowers, decorations, favors, food, wines, and music. Ava's friends met the challenge with a party of their own at Sherry's. Harry Lehr, caught between the two sets of socialites, tied in with John Jacob IV and led the cotillion at 840 Fifth Avenue—whether out of loyalty to the late *the* Mrs. Astor or out of the shrewd realization that Ava, who announced plans of settling in London, was out of the picture.

With neither mother nor wife to object, Colonel Astor renovated the fifteen-year-old mansion to suit himself. He ripped out the grand center staircase adored by the women and put a large central reception room in its place. The old reception room became a dining room, and a portrait of John Jacob I was hung prominently over the fireplace. What had been the dining room became a room known as the library, but it was such in name only, because no books lined the walls, which were covered instead by a tapestry with an intricate design of cupids. John's colleagues in the Authors' Club must have been shocked.

Colonel Astor, by then in his mid-forties, was certainly through with women like Ava, but he was by no means through with women. It would be impossible to find anyone more unlike his first wife than the girl with whom he fell in love in Bar Harbor, Maine. In age, Madeleine Talmadge Force might have been Ava's daughter; she was slightly younger than Vincent Astor. In appearance, she was blonde and slender, pretty rather than beautiful, appealing rather than queenly. In character, she was uncertain rather than domineering, and in emotions she was passionate, often recklessly so, rather than cold. As to family background, hers was rather average; her father ran a forwarding firm in Brooklyn.

The infatuated Astor squired Madeleine to many balls and dinner parties. New York society, thus made aware of the romance, refused to take it seriously. Even when an engagement was announced, most people believed that the whole affair would still blow over. On September 9, 1911, Colonel Astor landed his yacht at Newport, handed his dainty fiancée ashore, and set out in search of a minister to perform the ceremony. Under the divorce decree from Ava, he could not marry again in New York. Getting married proved to be far more difficult than living in sin would have been, because a number of ministers, although offered $1,000 by the bridegroom, refused to perform the ceremony. At last one was found, and the wedding took place in *the* Mrs. Astor's huge ballroom at Beechwood. The groom was forty-seven years old, and the bride was eighteen—and society frowned. In keeping with the Astor tradition, she gave up her dower rights in return for a handsome marriage settlement of $1,695,000.

"She only married him for his money," said one socialite. "She was common."

But Alida Chanler Emmet, John Jacob's cousin, still persists stoutly, "He was her great love."

Unsuitable though Madeleine may have been in age, it is hard to see how anyone could have begrudged John the peace of possessing an admiring and loving little bride after the stormy years with Ava. But the criticism was so unpleasant that soon after the wedding the couple set off on a trip to Egypt and then to England. The following spring, with Madeleine pregnant, they decided to return home so that she could have their child in the United States. Accustomed to the best, John followed the example of other notables and booked passage on a new luxury liner scheduled to make its first trip across the Atlantic: the *Titanic*.

When the great ill-fated ship struck an iceberg on the night of April 15, 1912, Captain Edward J. Smith, aware of social differences, hastened to inform the important Colonel Astor before allowing the general alarm to be given. John accepted the news with his customary quiet dignity. Madeleine, always emotional and loving, wanted to stay on board and go down with him.

"Get into the lifeboat," he told her gently, "to please me."

To please me was an expression he had often used with her.

As the lifeboat pulled away, leaving behind her doomed husband and hundreds of others, tenderhearted Madeleine heard a child crying from cold. She immediately took off her shawl and gave it to the little one, accepting the mother's thanks, in Swedish and incomprehensible to her, with her sweet smile.

The following morning, when the news reached a stunned world, readers of the New York *American* were given the distinct impression that the tragedy lay in the loss of Colonel Astor. The main part of the story was devoted to an account of this man and his career and history. At the bottom, as a sort of afterthought, came the mention of the 1,500 other men and women who had also been lost on the "unsinkable" liner.

When the survivors landed in New York, the pregnant widow was met by her contemporary and stepson, Vincent Astor, who had brought two doctors, a trained nurse, and a secretary. The body of John Jacob IV was recovered, with $2,500 in sodden bills in his pockets. He had needed spending money of this kind, because his expenditures ran to such items as an $800 lace jacket bought on impulse for Madeleine when a salesman boarded the *Titanic* during a short stop.

Her much older husband, it was soon learned, had endeavored to restrain his young bride from remarrying in the event of his death, with the proviso that remarriage would lose her the income of a five-million-dollar life trust as well as the use of 840 Fifth Avenue. As Madeleine's passionate nature, New York society to the contrary, was swayed far more by love than by money, she did not hold her trust fund for long.

The most startling revelation in Astor's will was that he had dared to defy the decree of John Jacob Astor I. For the first time since it was accumulated, the wealth was not to be guarded by the leapfrog method. Outside of a five-million-dollar trust fund for Alice and a three-million-dollar trust fund for the unborn child Madeleine was carrying, the entire estate was left to Vincent in fee simple. As John Jacob Astor I had feared, with this change the American portion of the Astor fortune went out of the family within a generation.

Ava did not know what the provisions of the will would be when she awakened in England on that morning of April 16, but she was galvanized into instant action. She rushed back to the United States to be with her usually neglected son Vincent and to see to it that Alice was not overlooked in any legal negotiations. The next four years were extremely hectic for her as she shuttled from Newport to London to Fifth Avenue, entertaining in lavish style everywhere. In 1916 she decided that nothing more was to be gained by remaining and returned to England. There, as she had once captured the greatest catch in New York, she succeeded in capturing the greatest catch in London—Lord Ribblesdale, a widower and former lord-in-waiting to Queen Victoria. The apparent benefits of this marriage were such that Ava decided it was worth giving up her divorce settlement, which was forfeit to remarriage. Lord Ribblesdale was known to lead a very fast life, and the parties he gave were among the gayest and wildest in London society. Clearly a man after her own heart, thought Ava, and she was sure he would be a delightful contrast to earnest John Jacob.

"She married him only to find that he was tired of the gay life, had sown his wild oats and wanted to marry a beautiful woman and carry her off to his old Tudor horror of a home and read the classics to her in the evenings with his magnificent bass voice," says Ava's grandson, brought up on her memories of the marriage. "She fumed and must have killed him with her invective."

It took him, however, until 1925 to die. Restored to London society, Lady Ribblesdale was as notable a figure as ever she had been as Ava Astor. Accompanied everywhere by four or five yapping cairn dogs, trailing clouds of perfume, she was very much the grande dame in her own and everyone else's drawing room.

"Her lovers were legendary," says a member of the family admiringly. Ava was by no means averse to the buzz of gossip linking her name romantically to one or another of the noted political, literary, or artistic figures of the era.

Her fondness for the outrageous remark increased as she grew older, and her comments ranged from the merely unkind "Everyone I want to talk to is always at the other side of the tea table" to her cutting description of a young author (in his presence, of course) as a "rhinestone in the rough." One night she was seated at dinner next to a titled lady, a position that obviously did not suit Ava, who wished to be surrounded by men only. She ignored her companion throughout the meal and then left, saying to the group in an audible whisper, "I wonder where I heard that Lady ——— can be amusing." Besides men, Ava's enthusiasm for bridge never left her, although she took to complaining, "There's no one left to play with; they won't play for high enough stakes." And she developed a greater interest in art; famed dealer Duveen, who was a friend, was naturally delighted to aid her in building a collection.

Although many people considered her more sinning than sinned against, she took a rather somber view of the world. There was a strain of melancholy in her nature that she would not trouble to conceal. "How can I believe in heaven with what I've seen here?" she used to ask her young cousin, now Viscount Astor.

In 1940, Ava went back to America and regained the citizenship she had lost when she had remarried. Although she renounced her title publicly and said that she was henceforth to be known simply as Mrs. Ava Willing Ribblesdale, she had herself listed in the telephone book as Lady Ribblesdale.

Some of her old friends say that they were shocked to see her again after her return: "Her face had been lifted too many times." "Her hair was dyed every which way." "She developed a speech impediment in her old age and stammered slightly."

But these are women. Men continued to fall under her spell. One, a noted writer, insists that she was still "bright and charming" when in her eighties.

Although she proclaimed toward the end that she was desperately poor, she left an estate of three million dollars when she died.

"In later years she never spoke of her first husband," says an intimate. "She felt that she had somehow been cheated by his dying so soon after the divorce and leaving his second wife that big trust fund. Ava liked money."

7

The Ultimate Triumph of "the" Mr. Astor

A notorious actress recently became so enraged by the belittling comments of one of New York's widely read society columnists that she declared her intention of renouncing her United States citizenship and making England her base of operations. Although she later changed her mind and decided to give another chance to the country where she had found fame, love and money, the threat was one that others had carried out before her. Perhaps the most conspicuous of these was William Waldorf Astor, whose reasons for leaving the United States seemed quite as trivial to his contemporaries as the actress' did to hers. Most of his countrymen felt that "Wealthy Willie," with eighty million dollars or better, in United States property, had little cause for complaint. Those who knew him well, however, saw how little by little his dissatisfaction mounted until expatriation appeared the only possible solution for his problems.

William Waldorf did not die until 1919 and one can still find many people who remember him vividly, but their recollections are of the extraordinary, overpowering personality he became rather than the soulful young man he once was. His grandson, the present Viscount Astor, recalls him in a cutaway coat, top hat, flannel trousers, and sneakers, no longer caring how he looked. Yet in his youth, he had been strikingly handsome, with brilliant blue eyes, blond hair and mustache, and ruddy complexion. Well over six feet tall, his build was powerful and muscular and his bearing military.

"In the end he seemed an almost inaccessible person," wrote a friend after his death, "an imprisoned soul immured within walls of his own making." Yes, it is hard to imagine this forbidding presence as ever having been young and in love, but his family to this day believes that his character was changed by an early disappointment in love. There was a dash of wild, romantic emotionalism in his nature, unconquered by the puritanical severity of his upbringing.

"He had been madly in love, but his parents discovered that there was tuberculosis in the girl's family and they did not let him marry her," says Lord Astor. "I think this affected him all his life with a sort of nostalgia and longing."

Even his mother, tenderhearted Augusta, could not be moved to accept such a bride for her only son. And in truth, for all her kindliness to others, she did rather little to give William a happy life as child or youth.

As in Victorian novels, a more suitable marriage was arranged for William with Mary Dahlgreen Paul, the charming Philadelphia girl who was to prove so unequal to her struggle with her aunt-in-law. Mamie, as she was called, with her liquid dark eyes and long gleaming black hair, was much sought after by the young bachelors of Newport and Philadelphia. But Mamie was never lucky. Her beauty, shyness, and perfect manners would surely have won any man whose heart was not engaged elsewhere. The match, so delightful to both sets of parents, was considerably less than that to the couple involved. "It was not a happy marriage," says an old lady who knew them. She lowers her voice: "He was not nice to live with." Even before her inevitable social defeat at the hands of *the* Mrs. Astor, Mamie was sadly aware of the fact that her husband was disappointed in the marriage.

Finding a way to burn up his limitless energy was a lifelong problem for this ambitious, discontented, and imaginative man. He had never gone to college but had been tutored privately at home and in Europe. This method left him well grounded in academic courses, informed about the arts, and adept at the sports considered necessary for a gentleman, but it also encouraged his egocentricity, and he remained permanently unable to get along with others. He rejoined his contemporaries at Columbia Law School and graduated in 1875, when he was already twenty-seven years old. The

Astor Estate office beckoned, and William did what was expected of him—for a little while, chafing every minute. Luckily his father, who similarly found that money brought him "nothing but a certain dull anxiety," understood his son's boredom and did not object when William Waldorf expressed interest in a career in politics.

The young man's mind was not as closed to suggestions then as it later became, and he had the good sense to accept professional advice that he become active in the Union League Club and make substantial contributions to the campaign funds of prominent Republican politicians. Despite their involvement (viewed by them as strictly business) with Tammany's Boss Tweed, the Astors had been Republicans since the Civil War and had been active supporters of Ulysses S. Grant. This proved helpful to William's budding political career, because the New York State Republican machine was dominated by Grant's good friend, Roscoe Conkling.

With such guidance and kindly assistance, Astor, aged twenty-nine, found himself duly nominated and elected to the New York State Assembly. "I do not go in the interests of any class, but for the city's good," he declared piously.

Nonetheless, he spent his term of office conservatively voting with his party on all issues. Having thus made no enemies, William had no problem in being nominated and elected to the New York State Senate two years later. By this time his dominating nature was beginning to make itself felt. His fellow millionaires, August Belmont, Russell Sage, and Jay Gould, were appalled when in 1879 he introduced a bill to halve the ten-cent fare for the New York elevated, which they controlled. There was considerable speculation as to his motives, with some observers convinced that he was trying to injure the rival tycoons personally and others maintaining that he thought a lower fare would increase travel to the Annexed District (the Bronx), where the Astors owned considerable property. It is interesting to note that nowhere is there any suggestion that he might have been considering the benefit of the people he was representing. In any event, the bill did not pass.

William then became a vigorous proponent of a measure to remove the ugly Croton Reservoir from its location at Fifth Avenue and Forty-Second Street, which was altogether too close to Astor homes and property. To his chagrin, the bill, after passing the Senate, was defeated in the Assembly. A story became current shortly thereafter that Astor kept a list of all the Assemblymen who voted against his bill and that he subsequently made it a point to vote against any measures they presented. This nasty tale may well be untrue, but taking the unbending character of the man into account, it is by no means improbable. Thus early in his career did a cloud of unfavorable publicity begin to hover around his head.

Driven by ambition, the following year he ran for Congress. Both Conkling and Grant made personal appearances for him, but unfortunately for Astor, the power of these men had passed its zenith. In a deadlocked presidential convention, Grant's nomination was blocked by the supporters of James A. Garfield, and the sop thrown to Conkling was a mere vice-presidential nomination for his lieutenant, Chester A. Arthur.

Caught on the wrong side of the civil war within the Republican Party, William was not helped by the undeniable fact that he did not even live in the part of the city he was to represent. "I have as great an interest in the Seventh Congressional District as I have in the part of the city in which I live," he protested vainly. Unpleasant remarks were passed on his neglecting to campaign personally in the Avenue A district, where many of his tenements were located. Newspapers published reports that he had tried to buy votes and that he was ruled by the party machine. His victorious opponent cried jubilantly, "We have no landlord aristocracy here, thank God!" Although the New York *Tribune* wrote kindly, "It is always dangerous for men of great wealth to expose themselves to the suffrage," William Waldorf damned the press as a whole and from then on was hostile to all efforts to write about him. His anti-Americanism dates from this period, and he suggested to his father that the family as a whole move to England. John Jacob III would not hear of it, and William, so domineering to others, never opposed his father.

Back in the New York State Senate, after his national defeat, he had the pleasure of seeing the bill to remove the reservoir passed. It was to be his last political satisfaction. In 1881, in his bid for re-election, he came up against Roswell Pettibone Flower, a securities broker who was a favorite of the Tammany party machine. For once Astor's fortune was not really suitable as a campaign issue, because Flower himself was extremely rich—not as rich as Astor, to be sure, but then, nobody was. *The New York Times* commented gloomily on the poor caliber of both candidates and allowed that Astor was probably the lesser of the two evils. The *Sun* disagreed, with a report that William Waldorf was never to forgive or forget: "Apart from his money, Mr. Astor is one of the weakest aspirants who ever stood the suffrages of a New York constituency."

The campaign expenditures of both candidates were high enough to incur the wrath of social reformer Jacob Riis. In what is generally conceded to have been a most corrupt election, Flower was the victor. He ultimately went on, with similar tactics, to become the governor of New York. As for Astor, his career as an elected representative of the people was over—but the memory lingered on, painful and embittering. His father counseled, "Take the trick whenever you can, and go on with the game." But proud William Waldorf could not bear to lose a trick.

His political friends did not forget him, though. When the assassination of Garfield put Vice-President Arthur into the White House, Astor gained an appointment as Minister to Italy. His father, John Jacob III, had found his greatest happiness in military service in the Civil War; William Waldorf found his in Rome. The warmth and imaginativeness of the Italian people appealed to the frustrated romantic within him. The other, autocratic, side of his nature was satisfied by the pomp and formality of Italian court life. Both as an Astor and as the representative of his government, William Waldorf was welcomed by King Humbert and his Queen Margherita and accepted in the highest circles. This was his first taste of how the European aristocracy lives, and it was to have a profound effect on his career thereafter. Housed in the Palazzo Rospigliosi, with seven reception rooms and an enormous ballroom, the Astors entertained the Italian inner circle. Even shy Mamie flowered in the kindly warmth and for the first time in her life became a ranking hostess. Her charm made her a favorite at court. When a visiting dignitary one day asked Margherita about her, the queen replied warmly, "Mrs. Astor is the most beautiful woman in Italy."

Impressed by the art treasures around him, William Waldorf began what was to become a magnificent collection, starting with some notable paintings by Holbein, Clouet, and Murillo. Like thousands of other visitors to Italy, he was enchanted with the beauty of the Villa Borghese. "How much would it cost to buy the entire balustrade?" he asked coolly. "Including fountains and statuary?" returned the stunned Italian owner. "Of course." A price was agreed on, and it was his.

For all his conviction that he was really an aristocrat, Astor was at times guilty of the most incredible coarseness. It is sometimes said that each man is the sum total of his ancestors, and William had inherited his great-grandfather's crude commercialism. It never occurred to him that a gentleman should not presume on his position at court to introduce a salesman from Tiffany's to the king. As he refused to listen to criticism, he apparently remained unaware of the storm this stirred up in diplomatic circles.

Far less was said about the disinterested kindness he was also capable of showing. When his high church connections in Rome gave him the opportunity of asking for a favor, he immediately remembered an old priest whose church was on Astor land. The priest had been removed from the church on account of drunkenness. William asked that the cleric be given another chance, and it was done. When Astor later returned to America, the priest, completely rehabilitated, met him at the boat. It gave Astor satisfaction to recall this for years thereafter.

Still, the life of a diplomat and art collector did not occupy all his time, and Astor, ever restless, decided to try his hand at writing a historical romance about the infamous Borgia family. Always at odds with the views of the world, William Waldorf made a hero of the character modeled after cruel, treacherous Cesare Borgia. The novel, *Valentino*, was submitted to Scribner's, which—if there be any credulous enough to swallow the statement solemnly reported by the Astors—accepted the book without knowing who the author was. Awkward in construction and unnatural in dialogue, the book, surprisingly, does display the type of facile writing still common in pulp-magazine fiction. The plot, wildly imaginative and romantic, is totally lacking in sophistication, which seems odd coming from an author who was highly educated, widely traveled, and well read. For all that, intimates recall that his favorite writer was

Alexandre Dumas, whose books today are read by children.

The happy years in Italy drew inexorably to their end, along with the presidential term of Astor's backer, President Arthur. Grover Cleveland was elected in 1884, and the following year William and Mamie moved back to 4 East Thirty-third Street, the house that his father had given him when he married. The readjustment to the mundane facts of life in America proved to be completely impossible for Astor. The only career he had really wanted, a political one, was closed to him. He was a member of the board of such enterprises as the Lackawanna, Delaware & Hudson Railroad, Illinois Central Railroad, United States Trust Company, and Farmers Loan & Trust, but he was never encouraged to, nor did he ever attempt to, run any of the companies. The Astor Estate administration was, of course, of greater interest to him, and he did join his father in the office. But any pleasure he derived from managing the highly profitable real estate was marred for him by the steadily mounting wave of public criticism. Where his grandfather, William Backhouse Astor, landlord of New York and builder of tenements, was utterly oblivious of any hostile murmurs, William was cut to the quick.

"Always sure he was right, he despised all adverse criticism, yet was too sensitive to cease to resent it," said a friend.

The outcry against conditions in the deteriorating tenements simply would not be stilled. As had been done repeatedly in the past, the mayor responded once again by appointing an investigating committee. And true to political practice, a place for William was found on the committee. Convinced that he was capable of disinterested impartiality, Astor was infuriated by the objections to his serving. Possibly influenced by these complaints, he did sell about a million dollars' worth of the worst tenements.

He took what satisfaction he could from the trivia of life, and these began to occupy a disproportionate amount of his time. He was certainly not alone among rich men in this, as Pierre Lorillard V, a well-to-do sportsman, was shrewd enough to realize. Lorillard was owner of thirteen thousand acres of land around Tuxedo Lake, a tract that had been in his family since 1814, when his father had taken it over for debt. It struck him that many of his society friends were at a loss for something to do between the New York and Newport seasons. Some of the time could, of course, be spent in Europe and some at strictly private country estates—William Waldorf, for example, owned a home at Hempstead, Long Island —but still there was a gap. And Lorillard set out to fill it. He decided to establish a private club at Tuxedo Park, with a clubhouse surrounded by cottages to be sold to a select and selected group of members. And although the club was incorporated in 1886, six years before McAllister's publication of his famous list, the magic number of four hundred was already in use, and socialites (particularly those who were on it) liked to call the membership list "a guide to who is especially who in the 400."

With considerable imagination and expenditure of money, Lorillard created what a debutante of the period described as "a country-club community enclosed by a high fence; the entrance strictly guarded against intruders." Because the distance from New York City was forty miles, not at all inconsiderable in the 1880's, the need for such protection was imaginary rather than real and was designed to feed the snobbism of members. Surely no one would set off on such a journey without a clear understanding that a welcome awaited him.

The clubhouse itself held one hundred bedrooms and but one bathroom, if accounts of the time can be believed in this regard. The staff was uniformed in club colors—green with gold-striped vests. Members liked to appear in these colors, too, and haberdashers to the elite hastily stocked up on green and gold ties and socks. In addition, all members possessed as a badge, a solid gold pin in the shape of an oakleaf. In the vast circular ballroom, eighty feet in diameter, separated from the rest of the club by a long hall, a series of balls and parties were given. The annual Autumn Ball, first held there in 1886, is still one of society's favorites, retaining most, although not quite all, of its early exclusivity. Entertaining was almost continuous in the beginning, and, said one of the few who wearied of the life quickly, "it was considered unfriendly not to attend all the balls."

William Waldorf was one of the first and most active members. The club suited his social need by establishing an aristocracy to which he could belong. He soon found a way of putting his interest in history to work and became head of a committee—surely he thought it up himself—to "Examine into the Original Names of the Tuxedo Region." After considerable research, he proclaimed his success. Tuxedo was an Anglicized version of the Algonquin Indian name *p'tauk-see-tough*, meaning "home of the bear." Ever the writer, William made a full report on his research and had it printed and nicely bound. A copy can still be found in the New York Public Library, though there is rather little call for it.

This small book, if such it can be called, was hardly enough to occupy the novelist he considered himself, and Astor passed some of the other hours of those somewhat sterile (for him) 1880's by writing another historical romance about the Italy for which he already felt nostalgic. In *Sforza, A Story of Milan*, the imaginative Astor made use of the timeworn device of having the heroine masquerade as a boy. She was so successful in her disguise that neither the hero, Sforza, nor the reader suspects her sex until she is unmasked on page 256. The story ends dramatically with Sforza, freed after ten years of solitary confinement, dying of the ecstasy of freedom. Scribner's once again was the publisher, and the reviewers were only mildly unkind. The *Atlantic Monthly*, for example, praised individual scenes, but pointed out, "The joints of the story are loose."

The book is dedicated to "my dear wife," a small tribute to a woman doing her very best to please her difficult husband. During those years, she became the mother of two boys—need one ask their names?—William Waldorf, Jr., later known simply as Waldorf, and John Jacob Astor V, and two daughters, Pauline and Gwendolyn. (In one of life's most bitter ironies, Gwendolyn died of tuberculosis in childhood, making her father's long-ago loss of his first love completely meaningless.) Although largely absorbed in her children, Mary was not totally uninterested in leading the high society life of the period. Her beauty and, of course, her family's wealth and position, virtually guaranteed her social success. *Harper's Weekly*, in a nineteenth-century "profile" of Astor, insisted that he left social duties almost entirely to his very beautiful wife. But the writer missed the distinction that was so clear in William's mind: the balls and parties were not of themselves interesting to him; recognition of their importance by others was.

There is no question that William's insistence that Mary become *the* Mrs. Astor was for him rather than her. Everyone who knew her agrees that a desire for social leadership was hardly in keeping with her retiring nature. It is not that he wanted her to be *the* Mrs. Astor so much as that he wanted to be *the* Mr. Astor. Seen from the vantage point of seventy-five years, the power struggle between Caroline Astor and her nephew seems a tempest in a teapot. Most people today laugh a bit unkindly at Caroline's pretensions, and yet, put into perspective, they are much easier to understand and sympathize with than are William's. The nineteenth century offered a driving woman few ways, outside of the social, for satisfying ambition. In the totally male-oriented culture, however, it appears that William Waldorf could have achieved his ends in a higher-minded way.

How is one to explain why any man, however autocratic, should stoop to such childish maneuvers as that of ordering postmen to give his wife all mail addressed to "Mrs. Astor"? The extreme importance he placed on outranking his aunt must be explained in part on the man's boredom. He simply could not find enough to do, and frivolous and important things became equal in his mind. William never saw his social ambitions in perspective and allowed them to dominate his life. And if he had won over Caroline? With what we know of the man, it is clear that would not have been enough. The defeat at her hands was only one of many defeats. It followed the loss of the great love of his youth, the political fiascos, the end of his diplomatic career, the public objections to the tenements that made him rich, the discovery that wealth and property brought him criticism instead of unquestioning admiration, the realization that his novels made people think him odd rather than artistic.

That is how matters stood with him when his father died in 1890, and William became the richest man in America. That he was richer by far than *the* Mrs. Astor's husband William or her son John Jacob IV was a result of his grandfather's having left the most valuable real estate to his father rather than his uncle. Showing the touch of sentimentality that was an integral part of his nature, William Waldorf kept his father's desk exactly as it had been on the last day it was used. On William's orders a vase of fresh roses was replenished each day. He had no wish to sit at that desk in the small back room that the heads of the Astor family traditionally used as their office. Business, even when it was his own, continued to bore him. What is more, William had little desire to be brought into closer contact with his cousin John Jacob Astor IV, his junior by sixteen years and a young man whom he simply could not abide. And so he turned over the management of the estate to others.

Even aside from business, the responsibilities attendant on being head of the house of Astor held little appeal for him. Although, like most Astors, John Jacob III had not been particularly philanthropic, he had supported the family's major benefaction, the Astor Library. Serving as trustee and treasurer for more than thirty years, his cash gifts during his lifetime had amounted to roughly seventy thousand dollars, and he had donated three plots of adjacent land for a second addition to the Library. Although the family fortune had doubled and redoubled since the time of John Jacob I, the donations to charity had not, and John Jacob III left the Library the same amount, $400,000, that his grandfather had bequeathed. Upon his father's death, the Board of the Library hopefully asked William to fill the vacancy. Libraries for the public held no appeal at all for this proponent of aristocracy, and he was, if anything, annoyed by the suggestion.

The newspapers criticized Astor roundly, which only irritated him further. Any opposition automatically convinced him of the rightness of his position, and so a few years later when the suggestion was made that the Astor Library be merged with the Tilden and Lenox Libraries, he gave his approval in a somewhat contentious letter: "For many years that institution [the Astor Library] has been censured by the American Press sometimes along comprehensible and occasionally upon unintelligent grounds. One particular of these complaints always remains the same—that it was an appendage of the Astor family which controlled it for purposes of self-glorification to the detriment of public interest."

Such "incomprehensible" attacks on his position in regard to the library and real estate made him increasingly dissatisfied with life. In the summer of 1890 he reported receiving threats that his children would be kidnapped. This was, he announced, the last straw, and he determined to quit this country forever and go to England. His estate could be managed by a distant relative, Charles

A. Peabody, Jr., and his Thirty-third Street mansion, as we have seen, could serve as the site for a hotel. John Jacob I had proved with his Astor House that a hotel was a profitable venture, and his thinking was still being followed three generations later, even by so rebellious a personality as William Waldorf. The fact that the proximity of a hotel was annoying to William's aunt gave an added fillip to his pleasure. *The* Mrs. Astor snapped that she would not visit William on her trips to London, a deprivation that he would clearly be quite able to bear with equanimity. She added more sharply that he was simply being ostentatious and implied that he was a social climber who wanted to be accepted by the British aristocracy.

If the American press had been hostile to William Waldorf before, it was utterly enraged by his decision to move. Before leaving he was quoted in one of the most insufferable statements ever made: "America is not a fit place for a gentleman to live."

This quotation has never been forgotten and is considered rather a curse by William's English descendants. The present Lord Astor makes a point of insisting that it is legendary and that he, for one, is convinced that his grandfather never said it.

True or false, the damage to his image in America was irreparable, and accounts of his activities in England were written in so unkind a style that in July of 1892, exhibiting a streak of childishness, William had a report of his death sent to the American newspapers. Except for the *Herald,* which wisely waited for confirmation, the major papers carried obituaries. If William Waldorf had been indulging in the sophomoric fantasy "They'll be sorry when I'm dead," the news stories must have come as a terrible disappointment. Said the New York *Tribune:* "The death of William Waldorf Astor, though not an event of great and lasting significance either in the world of action or the world of thought, will be generally deplored." The discovery that his death notice was a hoax brought forth reflections on the soundness of his mental condition.

Blandly putting this notable failure behind him, William Waldorf began to work his way into British high society. It was much less fluid than the American, even American society of the Patriarchs and the Four Hundred, because a gentleman became such at birth or never. The manner of speech marked a man for life, and there was little possibility of changing pronunciation by means of schooling; the few top public (private) schools were bound by their own class consciousness to accept children of the upper classes only.

These problems, of course, were not faced by Astor, whose grandfather had been made a gentleman in the more mobile United States. Arriving in London then as a member of the upper class and also the possessor of a beautiful, refined wife and millions of dollars, he was in no danger of not being accepted into society. His older son went to Eton at once and then to Oxford, and the younger one followed in his turn. William Waldorf rented a town-house for $25,000 a year and then, deciding that it was not grand enough for entertaining in the style he intended to maintain, purchased a mansion on Carlton House Terrace. Such notables as Prince Alexander of Teck, Grand Duke Michael, the Earl of Cadogan, and the Lord Mayor of London joined him and Mamie at immense dinner parties served on a forty-foot-long banquet table. But Astor, as we have seen, was never satisfied with just being in high society; he had to be at the top. His carriages, for example, were a chocolate-brown color, which may have seemed modest to anyone who did not know that this was the shade of the royal coaches.

William Waldorf had quickly realized that the difference between society in America and in Britain lay in the existence of royalty and the nobility. As one of the Astors, brought up on family legend, puts it: "England then was like France in the time of Marie Antoinette. The nobility was really admired and looked up to." An exaggeration certainly, but William clearly believed that. It seemed to him that he could not possibly emerge as *the* Mr. Astor unless he were Lord Astor—Baron Astor—Viscount Astor.

Aware that the ennobling of a butcher's grandson would take some doing, he determined to find aristocratic ancestors in the hazy background of John Jacob I. The vague possibility that the mother of John Jacob was a von Berg was not enough for him; he wished to find a nobleman in the male line. A family tree that met his specifications was tortuously traced by a genealogist hired for the task. The point of departure selected was the arrival in Walldorf in the 1660's of one Jean Jacques d'Astorg, a Huguenot, fleeing from persecution in France. D'Astorg's antecedents were pursued relentlessly for five hundred years through Joseph d'Astorg, Marquis de Roquepin, back to Antoine d'Astorg, Baron de Monbartier, and at last to Pedro d'Astorga, who obtained a title from the Queen of Spain before falling at Jerusalem in 1100. But the press, at least in America, remained unmoved by these revelations, and the New York *Sun* went so far as to employ an expert genealogist, Lothrop Withington, to prove the family tree a fabrication. The paper added the sly and, to Astor, intolerable hint that possibly the family should be traced to a Jewish doctor, Isaac Astorg, who lived in the early fourteenth century.

Noble or not, William could at least live like an aristocrat, and he soon observed a key fact about British society: the country estate was far more important to gentlemen of means and title than the city mansion, however palatial. An Englishman could become almost maudlin when describing the rolling acres possessed by his family. Passed down from one generation to the next, the land gave the English a sense of permanence, endurance, and stability that became an integral part of the national character. William Waldorf, unluckily, had no castle to inherit, but he was not a man to be halted by such a minor obstacle.

Located outside of London on the banks of the Thames, near Maidenhead, stood Cliveden (pronounced *Cliv-den*), an estate with a genealogy that could top even William Waldorf's fanciful one. Old documents tell that in 1666 a mansion was built in "Cliefden's proud alcove" for George Villiers, the "witty and wicked" second Duke of Buckinghamshire, a favorite of King Charles II. In the eighteenth century the estate came into the hands of the Earl of Orkney, and he rented it for a summer residence to Frederick, Prince of Wales, father of King George III. It became the scene during those glamorous years of boat races, concerts, and plays, among them the *Masque of Alfred,* forgotten save for an ode set to music and known by every Englishman—"Rule Britannia." Fire destroyed the magnificent mansion in 1795. Rebuilt and bought by the Duke of Sutherland, it was again gutted by flames in 1848. The house that was erected then and that stands to this day was designed by Sir Charles Barry, architect of the Houses of Parliament. And he made Cliveden into an Italian-style villa, with terraces extending the length of the front to a spacious four hundred feet.

In 1893, when William Waldorf decided that Cliveden was destined to be the ancestral seat for generations of lordly Astors born and unborn, it was in the possession of the Duke of Westminster. Upon payment of a sum rumored to be $1.25 million, Cliveden changed hands, and a new chapter in its history began. Barry's work, good enough for Parliament, did not quite suit William Waldorf. He brought in artisans and artists to lay a mosaic floor in the hall and to paint a fresco showing a banquet of the gods on the ceiling of the dining room. Wood paneling was taken from a hunting lodge at Asnière that had belonged to Mme de Pompadour. Recalling his happy days in Italy, Astor had marble statues placed everywhere, indoors and out, and on the grounds was erected a fountain, probably the largest privately owned in the world, made of pieces of perfectly matched Siena marble.

As dukes, princes, Astors, and their guests of both high and not so high birth have observed, Cliveden is one of the most beautiful of English estates. A description published in London many years ago waxes lyrical on the subject: "Situated on high ground and bordered below by the Thames that threads its way through the woody slopes of this exquisite estate, like a silver riband linking the various shades of green, the ideal landscape thus presented lingers long in the memory."

William Waldorf, however, did not care to have it linger long in the minds of anyone whom he had not specifically invited. He ordered the woods closed to picnickers, and expressed horror at the very idea of any boating party daring to land on the river banks near Cliveden. The Duke of Westminster had allowed the public to enjoy the clear cool water of a spring on the grounds; his successor had it closed off. To discourage curious people from coming to stare at him, he surrounded as much of the estate as possible with a wall and, it was said, had broken glass put on top. This last sounds like, and probably is, an exaggeration; William invariably got a bad press, and many of the charges against him are not convincingly documented.

For all his eagerness to be Lord Astor, he was not British enough to understand that the aristocrats felt a sense of responsibility to the people on their land and in the nearby villages. The lord-of-the-manor concept is, after all, lacking in America. It is hard to find a small town in the United States where the citizens look up to the wealthy owner of the largest nearby estate not only as an influence on their lives but also as a protector. But in England, particularly before World War I, a modern version of feudalism had evolved, and there was a lord of the manor who felt that the townspeople were his people and the village was his village. The tremendous disparity between rich and poor—phenomenal in both countries in the late nineteenth and the early twentieth century—was accepted as a condition of life in England whereas it never was in the United States. The wealthiest of the landed gentry had incomes of possibly five thousand dollars a day; vast numbers of workingmen drew five dollars a week, and both groups took this as a matter of course. The lord and lady of the manor were expected to take an important part in the village life, holding flower shows, attending church functions, judging Morris Dance competitions, caring for the sick and indigent. It was not in Astor's character to do any of this, but it all came naturally—thanks to his providing them with the means—to the next generation. For William Waldorf, both city and country homes were to be used to entertain as many of the right people as possible.

Through the background of all this moves the shadowy figure of his wife, like an unhappy wraith. Still lovely, still charming, Mary did her part as well as she could, caring for her children and acting as hostess for her husband.

"They had a lovely home in London and they gave big parties, but it meant nothing to her. She was beautiful, but miserable," says Alida Chanler Emmet. William Waldorf had succeeded his father as trustee for the Chanler children, and they dutifully visited the Astors in England. "Whenever she saw me, she got so homesick. Oh, how she used to envy me going home when she had to stay!"

In her own quiet way, though, Mary was popular in the court set around Queen Victoria. The Duchess of Buccleugh, known far and wide for her dislike of Americans and Jews (whom she rejected equally), went so far as to have Mrs. Astor named to the honorary position of Mistress of the Robes. For once William was completely satisfied with his wife.

But despite his preoccupation with society, the old desire to be a power in the political life of a nation, thwarted in America, reasserted itself. As he quite obviously could not run for elective office in a country of which he was not a citizen, he did the next best thing and bought a newspaper. This provided him not only with a powerful tool of influence but also an opportunity to get even with the press that had always been so harsh to him. The newspaper he purchased, the *Pall Mall Gazette,* was Liberal; no matter, Astor could impose his will on it and he did. Henceforth it was to be Conservative and, as he put it, a paper "by gentlemen for gentlemen." A number of staff members walked out, but Astor was indifferent; he could, and would, hire new ones. The editor he selected, Henry Cust, was not only a member of Parliament but also the heir to the Earl of Brownlow and a gentleman indeed. Cust was installed in a magnificently furnished office and, along with the other editors, treated as few journalists have ever been. At the dinner parties regularly held for the staff in the Grand Hotel, Astor insisted on such touches of gentility as having the light softly diffused over the tables from tiny light bulbs concealed within the artfully worked centerpieces of roses. An orchestra, hidden behind a veritable forest of potted palms, provided a musical accompaniment to the shop talk. It was a far cry from the typical noisy city room.

Cust soon found, however, that editorial life was not all a bed of lighted roses. Astor did not take kindly to objections to anything he suggested. "Pray, Sir, who pays the bill?" demanded Astor one day when Cust was particularly intractable.

But Astor did not win all their encounters. Cust was no rubber stamp and showed considerable skill in managing his employer. He even succeeded in dealing with one of the trickiest problems to beset an editor—the suggestion by the publisher that he write for the newspaper himself. "What you need for your work is a literary magazine," said Cust tactfully, sidestepping the issue.

Astor could find nothing to object to in that idea, and because no suitable publication existed, he founded one, the *Pall Mall Magazine* and prepared an article for the first issue. The editor did not refuse to publish this. Once started on the career of press lord, William's appetite increased, and he soon added a weekly magazine, the *Pall Mall Budget.* By this time he had broadened his publishing scope sufficiently to be playing a part in the cultural as well as the political life of England. Rudyard Kipling and James Barrie contributed to his magazines. Mrs. Astor revealed a surprising taste for science fiction, and the books of the Astor publications show that H. G. Wells received five pounds apiece for such stories. Like many other writers, Astor was unhappy about the brief lifespan of magazine stories, doomed to be thrown out with the waste paper, and so he had his collected and published in book form. A reading of these stories indicates that his imagination did not become more sober with the onset of middle-age. The hero of "Brabantio's Love," one Almodoro, falls in love with a mermaid, and "Mme Récamier's Secret" is that she is really her husband's daughter.

The literary magazine brought William the most pleasure, but it was the newspaper that gave him hopes of rising to the British nobility. Could such a position then be bought? The British, of course, denied it categorically, but observers across the Atlantic were not so sure.

"Are we to argue from Mr. Astor's apparent migration that the opportunity of the very rich lingers in England?" queried *Harper's Weekly* as early as 1893, only three years after William's expatriation. The answer, it appeared to the writer, was affirmative. "In England they take their millionaires more seriously than we do and are much readier to give them a chance and fit them out with a suitable rank and proper employment."

The British, in any event, move slowly, and William Waldorf was still far from obtaining a peerage when, three days before Christmas in 1894, Mary died. Yielding to her wish when it could no longer matter to her, William sent her body home to America for burial. With the same touch of sentiment that led him to keep roses on his father's desk in an office he hardly ever saw, he ordered that a blanket of fresh lilies of the valley cover her grave for years to come. Whether he had loved her, he felt her loss. Though he outlived her by a quarter of a century, he never married again. When he was seventy, there were rumors that he was thinking of it, but they were never confirmed, and certainly, nothing came of them. And yet, he was a man who found it hard to get along without a wife socially. As to the other, sexual, aspects of marriage, much less is known about this exceptionally reticent man. After his early doomed romance, he remained silent on the subject.

Without Mary's gently restraining hand, William became increasingly nervous. He built a house on the Victoria Embankment to serve both as home and Astor Estate office, and fearing assassins, devised an arrangement whereby he could, if startled by an unexpected sound, touch an invisible spring and instantaneously fasten every door in every room in the house. Any intruder would thus be locked in the room he had entered until the spring was released. It is interesting to speculate how many times tradespeople and innocent visitors were trapped by this maneuver. One gentleman who was so entrapped observed to his horror that there were no handles on the doors. After he was rescued, William gruffly showed him the secret that could have released him—a button mechanism hidden behind a sliding panel. This information was a compliment, he was told, given only to those whom Astor trusted. The ground floor windows were kept heavily barred, and there was only one door from the outside. Not secure in this security, William Waldorf kept two revolvers, which he was quite capable of using, by his bed.

His fears seemed funny to most people then. It was a period when psychological interpretations of difficult personalities was uncommon. Astor's anxieties were in fact tragic for him. "I die many deaths every day," he admitted in one of the rare moments when he revealed himself to another.

Those friends not frightened off by his truly terrifying precautions against such deaths found the house as luxurious as a royal palace. This was not surprising, considering that Astor had spent close to $1.5 million on building and decorating, putting in floors of marble and jasper and having frescoes painted on the ceilings. Mounting the staircase, the visitor was amazed to come face to face with statues modeled to represent the characters in William Waldorf's novels. The most sentimental of the Astors, he prominently displayed portraits of John Jacob I, William B. and John Jacob III, and, the most egotistical, William Waldorf himself.

The completion of this mansion was celebrated with a lavish party at which Astor immeasurably increased his reputation for unconventional behavior. Most social affairs in London got under way late, and it was eleven o'clock before most of the guests had removed their coats or furs and begun to dance. On the stroke of the hour, William Waldorf ordered the orchestra to stop playing and called for attention in his peremptory way. The dancers stopped short, and the gentlemen at the buffet put down their champagne glasses, wondering if, as in the days when Mamie was hostess, the announcement would come that the incomparable Nellie Melba was to sing or Ignace Paderewski to play. Not at all. "It's late and I'm going to bed. The party is over," decreed Astor. "You will find your carriages waiting for you at the door."

Nonetheless, since many members of society fear boredom above all else, his outrageous behavior, if anything, increased the number of his social contacts. His next invitation, to a tea party, was accepted by three duchesses, and before long William Waldorf was presented to the Prince of Wales (soon to become Edward VII). Edward took a liking to the rather strange American and arranged for William to be taken in at the Prince's own club, the Carlton. Astor went on to make this friendship an extremely uncomfortable one for Edward and the other aristocratic club members. One evening a guest brought Captain Sir Berkeley Milne to a concert at William's home. Sir Berkeley was commander of the Royal Yacht and a gentleman to the core, but Astor viewed anyone whom he had not specifically invited as an intruder and made his opinion known. Sir Berkeley left in a huff, but his annoyance was as nothing to what he felt a few days later when he read this statement in the newspaper: "We are desired to make known that the presence of Captain Sir Berkeley Milne of the Naval and Military Club, Piccadilly, at Mr. Astor's concert last Thursday evening was uninvited."

London society was aghast. The Prince of Wales unaccountably stood by William, but other members of the Carlton Club demanded that an apology to Sir Berkeley be given. Astor did not wish to be dropped from the Club, and so he yielded.

By this time, as with many converts, he was becoming more English than the English. The moment had clearly come for him to be an Englishman in fact as well as heart and mind, and in 1899 he became a citizen.

Astor's former countrymen had not gotten over their annoyance at his expatriation, possibly because the newspapers would not let them (headlines with the Astor name have always been remarkably helpful in selling newspapers). William was quoted, no one can say whether with accuracy: "America is good enough for any man who has to make a livelihood, though why travelled people of independent means should remain there more than a week is not readily to be comprehended."

William Waldorf was told that an effigy labeled "Astor the Traitor" had been burned in Times Square. Responding to this in the worst possible way, Astor had the execrable taste to purchase the flags of the United States frigate *Chesapeake*, captured by the British in the War of 1812, and to present them as a gift to the Royal United Service Museum. He never lived down this *gaffe*; in fact, a few years later the American magazine *Cosmopolitan* pointed to William as the "one blot on the escutcheon" of the Astor family. The Astors were alone among possessors of great wealth in having a "clean fortune" untainted by scandal (the writer conveniently overlooked the tenements and the Tweed Ring whitewash). Only William fell below their high standards, as witness that unfortunate battle flags incident.

The boards of the Gallatin and Astor National banks and the Lackawanna Railroad asked him to resign on the grounds of nonattendance. Astor was seldom in New York, and indeed on one occasion when he came he was subjected to one of the most staggering snubs of all time. He invited Theodore Roosevelt, then a rising national figure, to dinner, and Roosevelt first accepted and later sent his regrets. The story given out was that Roosevelt had believed that the Astor invitation came from John Jacob IV, and his aboutface occurred when he learned his error.

The Waldorf Hotel had by this time been linked with the Astoria of John Jacob IV, so William considered it an impossible place for him to use during his rare visits. For that matter, he wondered if it were really suitable for any gentleman. He therefore had the Netherland Hotel built for those too refined for the Waldorf-Astoria, a group in which he included himself. Not all guests lived up to Astor's standard of refinement, however. In 1900 Marcus Daly, founder of Anaconda Copper Mining Company, lay dying in the Netherland Hotel. By a strange coincidence his arch rival for control of the copper mines, United States Senator William A.

Clark of Montana, was also staying there. Each morning Clark would ask the desk clerk, "Well, is that old son of a bitch upstairs dead yet?" One can only hope that Astor was in England at the time and missed hearing such ungentlemanly talk.

Despite his poor showing with the Library, William was not an ungenerous man. He simply did not approve of American charities, he wrote in an odd article in his *Pall Mall Magazine*. Why German or British charities were better was apparently so obvious that he declined to explain. He responded to a request for funds from his great-grandfather's Astor Haus in Walldorf, gave $100,000 to Oxford, the same amount to the University of London, and $50,000 to Cambridge. With true British patriotism, he donated $100,000 to the cause of fighting the Boer War.

Queen Victoria died in 1901, and Edward VII, William's friend for a number of years, succeeded to the throne. Astor was now as close to the nobility as he could ever have wished; all that was lacking was personal participation. But friendship was not enough, and Edward's reign from 1901 to 1910 brought Astor no closer to realization of his dream.

During those years the interest in history that had found one outlet in the writing of historical fiction found another in the acquisition of a truly historic castle. In the early 1900's, William Waldorf first heard about Hever, a small and simply designed castle built in the thirteenth century and bought by the Boleyn family in the 1500's. Doomed young Anne Boleyn had lived there before her marriage, and after her execution, her father, avoided by his fearful neighbors, remained until his death. Henry VIII then took it over and gave it as a present to ugly Anne of Cleves, the fourth wife, whom he was divorcing. The castle later passed from hand to hand, achieving a certain notoriety in the late seventeenth century, when it was occupied by the illegitimate daughter of King James II and her husband, the first Baron Waldegrave, comptroller of her father's household. By the turn of the twentieth century, Hever stood neglected and in disrepair, waiting for the hand, interest, and fortune of an Astor. William Waldorf, attracted by its romantic past as well as by the undeniable charm of its setting, made it his in 1903.

William threw his energies into the restoration and re-creation of

Hever. Cliveden had been lovely already (maybe lovelier before he got it; William's irrepressible daughter-in-law Nancy took one look at the décor and exclaimed, "The Astors have no taste") and his town houses were matched by many others in the luxurious residential sections of London. Then out of what was little more than a neglected fortified farmhouse, he created a perfect jewel of a small castle surrounded by a Tudor village. To this end, he spent a sum estimated by stunned observers at ten million dollars. On the walls were hung the world-renowned Holbein portraits of Henry VIII and Anne Boleyn; the Titian masterpiece depicting Philip II of Spain; the François Clouet paintings of Edward VI of England, Eleanor and Elizabeth of Austria, and Charles IX of France; and the small priceless Lucas Cranach likeness of Martin Luther. In the dining hall the suits of armor worn by Francis I and Henry II of France were displayed beneath Flemish and Burgundian tapestries contemporary with those rulers. The toilet articles of Queen Elizabeth I, among them clothes brushes and satin bedroom slippers, were placed in a long gallery on the second floor. The headboard and posts from Anne Boleyn's bed, the Bible owned by Martin Luther, even the sedan chair of Cardinal Richelieu, were bought for the castle. When William took over, the castle grounds had deteriorated into marshes and ill-kept orchards and meadows. He poured money without stint into the reclamation. On his orders workmen struggled for four years to clear thirty-five acres of the land. The small river Eden was then diverted to flow over this area, forming a lake large enough to sail boats on. Behind the lake were created gardens like those of the Roman villas that were Astor's ideal of beauty, with statues, grottos, cascades, and a "gallery of fountains."

William Waldorf's imaginative and rather highstrung personality included a strong streak of mysticism. Surely, he felt, the unquiet spirit of Anne Boleyn must inhabit the home from which she had gone as an ill-fated bride. Members of the Psychical Research Society were called in to watch for Anne each night during Christmas week, when Astor felt she was most likely to appear. But to his disappointment, and possibly relief, her shade was never seen.

Astor was probably the first owner in several hundred years to make use of the drawbridge over the moat. His fear of earthly intruders was far greater than his concern about spirits, and the bridge was pulled up at night as a security measure just as it had been in medieval times. Guests were not lodged in the castle with William, but were accommodated in the houses of the Tudor village. Once they retired, the drawbridge effectively kept them from rejoining their host.

Most of his entertaining, however, was done at Cliveden. For all its luxury and the fact that one could be sure of meeting the bearers of noble names, a weekend at Cliveden was not unalloyed joy for the guest. The meals, to be fair, were superb, because Astor loved good food, and plenty of it. (As a prebreakfast snack, for example, he consumed artichokes and prawns; clearly the man had a truly royal digestive system.) Still, a visit does not consist of food alone. A careful schedule was worked out by the host, allotting just so many hours for eating, horseback riding, walking, driving, resting, dressing, and dancing. No deviation was allowed. One lady guest returned home in a rage with a tale that was to enliven tea-table conversation for years thereafter. It was letter-writing time at Cliveden, but she had no letters she wished to write, and so she strolled out into the garden instead. After a few moments she noticed that she was being followed by a nervous servant. He approached her timidly and asked if she had perhaps forgotten that this was letter-writing time. Mr. Astor would be annoyed were he to look out and see that she was not following the schedule. Hardly able to believe her ears, she said she would leave rather than remain in any place where she could not do as she liked. Please to call her carriage. The footman, red in the face, stammered that he would not dare to call for a carriage before the time appointed by his employer for leaving.

His schedules were particularly rigid, because of his obsessive punctuality. It is an Astor family trait, as we have seen, but in William Waldorf's case, it was carried to an extreme. Should anyone be a minute late, William would fix him with what the family describes as a "cold and fishlike stare." This was his reaction to any other behavior that annoyed him, too. It was all a bit hard on his motherless children. The eldest boy, Waldorf, would sometimes remonstrate with his father. Astor would listen in silence, without ever changing expression. "Thank you," he would say, and make no further comment. Poor Pauline, as the only girl, really had her troubles. Except when guests were present, she was required to read aloud to him at all meals. He sat there giving no expression of pleasure, an odd-looking figure in his stiff-bosomed dress shirt, linen jacket, and rubber-soled tennis shoes. The selections of reading matter were his alone, of course, and most often consisted of accounts of Napoleon's campaigns or the lives of the Borgias. It is perhaps surprising that Pauline's nature was not warped by the cold, autocratic rule of her father, but all who know her are agreed that it was not. "My aunt," says the Honorable Gavin Astor, publisher of the London *Times,* "is an angel."

Hard as he may have been to live with, Astor did want to do the right thing for his children, and when Pauline came of age he decided that she must make a proper debut. Having no confidence in any female relatives or friends, he felt that he could handle the affair just as well as his aunt in America would have done. With male logic he came straight to the point: a debut was intended to introduce a girl to eligible young men, was it not? And so he wrote to the secretary of the Bachelors Club and asked for a list of fifty bachelors to invite. Pauline survived the rigors of this introduction to society and married Lieutenant Colonel Herbert Henry Spender-Clay, graduate of Eton and Sandhurst and holder of the medal with six clasps for the Boer War. It is sad that her father did not live to see how close this marriage was to bring his family to the throne. Pauline's daughter Rachel grew up to marry the Honorable David Bowes-Lyon, youngest son of the Earl of Strathmore and Kinghorne, and brother to the lady who is now Queen Mother Elizabeth.

Two years after Pauline's wedding, her older brother Waldorf made the most spectacular of the Astor marriages, to Nancy Langhorne of Virginia. Like the true Englishman he had become, the groom's father gave them the ancestral home, Cliveden. He had owned it, after all, for thirteen years by then. They would, he knew, in time pass it on to their eldest son, and the Astors would become the landed gentry of William's dreams. Although he still had Hever and two London houses, he was always looking for something new and spent one million dollars for a villa in Sorrento that he used during the winter months.

William could well afford such expenditures by then, although financial experts maintain that with better management and less personal extravagance (that ten million dollars for Hever is hard for businessmen to swallow), he could have had far more to invest and/or bequeathe. He had shifted some of his investments to England, but much of his fortune still consisted of the land and buildings of Manhattan. With the Waldorf and Netherland hotels operating profitably, William put eight million dollars into building the Astor Hotel on Broadway. This hotel—unlike the others, we are asked to believe—was not his idea, but was brought to the managers of his estate in America. Opening in 1904, the Astor Hotel was a success, particularly with members of the group that was in time to become known as café society. With a grand ballroom capable of seating five thousand guests at one time, the Astor was much in use for conventions and banquets.

At one business affair where the dinner was priced at five dollars, a guest declared in stage whisper, "Three dollars goes for the food, one dollar to the hotel and one dollar to the greatest absentee landlord in the world."

The guest might have been interested in learning that stores along the Broadway side of the hotel brought that landlord an additional $240,000 in rent money a year. Upon hearing complaints that the hotel was too narrow, William bought up the brownstones behind it and had the Astor enlarged piece by piece.

Even though the width of an ocean separated him from the bulk of his real estate, he observed the coming in America of a new type of housing and hastened to invest in the construction of the enormous apartment houses that were to dominate Manhattan in the twentieth century. These were in a sense descendants of Rutherford Stuyvesant's daring venture of the 1870's, when he adapted the tenement principle of housing for higher class people. At the time Commodore Cornelius Vanderbilt had sneered, "Gentlemen will never consent to live on mere shelves under a common roof" —a view with which young Astor had heartily concurred. But many socialites settled into the Stuyvesant apartments, and as the decades passed the concept had become acceptable to thousands, if not to Astor personally. Under his orders two huge dwellings, the Apthorp and the Belnord, were put up on Broadway. They still survive, looking like Neanderthal structures among modern stream-lined buildings. Constructed on land bought for a few thousand dollars by William B. Astor in 1860, they are massive and embellished with ornate stonework. An air of privacy is given by the heavy wrought-iron gates that swing open to allow entry into an inner court protected by a uniformed guard.

Successful from the start, these American ventures made possible the purchase of another British newspaper, an investment that was to increase Astor's influence in his adopted country immeasurably. The publication he selected was the Sunday *Observer*, a paper founded in 1781 and still priding itself on its greatest news scoop, the outbreak of the Crimean War. The *Observer* took its place in the Astor newspaper empire in 1911.

While everyone was asking "Will he or won't he?"—become a lord, that is—Astor was investing his money in places where it would do him the most good.

"He must be either very vulgar or too ill-known who cannot buy his way into a certain recognition in London," *Cosmopolitan* magazine had written in 1905. Certainly, neither descriptive term could have been applied to William.

Prominent politicians had learned that his heart was extremely soft when appeals for campaign fund donations were made. Collectors for British charities were not turned away with the John Jacob I retort that wealth does not increase the "disposition to do good." During World War I, William Waldorf's contributions, for the first time in Astor history, approached what might be expected from a man of his wealth. More than $200,000 went to the Red Cross; $125,000 was donated to the fund sponsored by the Prince of Wales (by then the other Edward who was so briefly to be Edward VIII); another $125,000 was offered for the support of families of officers, $25,000 was allocated to Queen Mary's fund for women, and the same amount was contributed to the *Daily Telegraph*'s fund for bonds for the Army.

In the last days of 1915 the High Court of Justice handed down a most interesting decision: the judges found that an act passed back in 1870 and not observed heretofore had given naturalized citizens of England all the same rights under the constitution that were guaranteed to the native-born. Its meaning for William Waldorf Astor was clear. All of a sudden the obstacles were swept away; the years of waiting were over, the moment was there: on King George's New Year's List in 1916 it appeared that William had been granted a barony. On April 16, his tall figure garbed in traditional red velvet robes trimmed with ermine, William heard the clerk in the House of Lords announce in ringing voice the preferment of "our trusty cousin, William Waldorf Astor to . . . Baron Astor of Hever Castle." His impassive face concealing his emotion as always, he followed the Garter King of Arms and took his place on the barons' bench.

A listing in Burke's *Peerage, Baronetage & Knightage* was his, which meant infinitely more to him than the appearance of his name in America's *Social Register,* where it had been included from the very first issue. A magnificent coat of arms was designed for the new lord with "a falcon resting on a dexter hand couped at the wrist . . . in chief two fleurs-de-lis. . . ." Although Astor ignored the impertinent suggestion of his irrepressible cousin and ward, John Armstrong Chanler-Chaloner, that a butcher's cleaver be depicted, John Jacob Astor I was not overlooked. As supporters of the coat of arms were placed "on the dexter a North American Indian and on the sinister, a North American Fur Trapper."

"There does not seem to be much enthusiasm displayed in English papers on the new peer's behalf," wrote the *Literary Digest,* in a report on the event.

But what cared Astor? The opinions of others meant nothing to him. He had what he wanted, and there was more to come. In June of the following year, in the King's Birthday Honors, he was made a Viscount. He had achieved his life's ambition to be *the* Mr. Astor, and he had secured his family's position in British high society.

No one could have been more British thereafter than the Astors. Less than forty years later, William's grandson, the Honorable Michael Astor, told *Vogue* readers, "Although I enormously enjoy my visits to the United States, while I am there, I can never escape the feeling of being in a completely foreign country." William would have been delighted.

The second title was of particular importance to him, because it was hereditary; the family was in the nobility to stay. But as many fathers have learned to their sorrow, sons are not always pleased by the efforts made on their behalf. Waldorf was enraged at the prospect of having to succeed to the title and accused his father of destroying a promising political career in the House of Commons, which was exactly what happened. Although the barony was not hereditary, it might as well have been, because John Jacob V, William's favorite son, in time won the right to bear that title himself.

John might indeed have been the scion of an old titled family, naturally good at the things Britons admire. A sportsman of the highest caliber, he was national singles champion at racquets and was noted for his abilities at cricket, golf, polo, hunting, and even tiger shooting. Not only did he serve as an officer in the First Life Guards, along with his brother-in-law, Lieutenant Colonel Spender-Clay, he was in the bodyguard to King Edward VII. John Jacob V also followed English tradition so far as to be aide-de-camp to Lord Hardinge of Penshurst, viceroy of India between 1911 and 1914. His military career in World War I was outstanding, capped by his winning the French Legion of Honor but marred by the loss of a leg. His marriage, which—surprising for a modern-day Astor—was to endure for half a century, was to Lady Violet Mary Elliot Mercer-Nairne, daughter of the Earl of Minto, Governor General of Canada from 1888 to 1904 and viceroy of India from 1905 to 1910. Lady Violet's first husband, Lord Charles Mercer-Nairne, had been killed early in World War I. Her second husband's father did not make the newly-weds wait to inherit Hever, but gave it to John Jacob V as a gift and moved out. His financial arrangements for this couple, however, were ultimately to blight their old age.

Like all the Astors from John Jacob I on, William was most interested in planning for his fortune to live on after his death. The Waldorf Hotel and the *Observer* were given to Waldorf, and huge trust funds were set up, based on American real estate valued at $46,421,000. Similar arrangements were soon made for his Astor Hotel, valued at $4 million, the Astor Theater at $1 million, his Broadway apartment houses, valued at $1.5 million, and finally the balance of his New York property. Much was divided equally between the two sons, with a lesser amount going to Pauline, in keeping with the family policy of giving most of the money to those who carry on the Astor name. William's relations with Waldorf were soured by the young man's disapproval of his father's peerage, and he was disinherited in a very modest sort of way. Some property was divided between John Jacob V, Pauline, and Waldorf's sons, instead of Waldorf. Living up to the traditions of the Astor family, William set out to insure his grandchildren's future by allowing his children life interests in the trusts, with the entire capital left to his grandchildren.

Aside from his activities for post-mortem, he found little to occupy him in his last years. He could have sat in the House of Lords, but as often happens, the opportunity to take part in public life came when he no longer wanted it. Astor appeared in the House of Lords but twice in his life, on each of the occasions when he was granted a title.

Ever restless, and with Hever and Cliveden occupied by his sons, he bought yet another house at Brighton. Unable to conquer his fears of death, despite all his preparations for it, he immediately hired workmen to construct a high fence around it. Now that he had all he desired, he no longer needed to entertain, and he virtually retired from the world, seeing no one but his family and the very few people he liked. He would invite his oldest grandson to visit him, an experience that was overpowering for the child, who found himself seated at meals with only his grandfather at the opposite end of a long banquet table. William's interest in food and drink reached new proportions, and he kept a special book on hand in which he jotted down the menus for several days in advance. Special events were celebrated, usually in solitude with special meals. He wrote a letter to a grandson that is pathetic in its implication of loneliness. He was celebrating the boy's birthday, he wrote, "by drinking a glass of the very best brandy."

The last two years of his life were an anticlimax, ending in a manner far removed from the noble. On October 18, 1919, he went into the bathroom after a dinner of roast mutton and macaroni and did not reappear. When at last his valet broke in, it was to find Baron Astor of Hever, the First Viscount Astor, dead.

8

Our Nancy and the Cliveden Set

The most overpowering personality the English Astor family ever had was neither English nor an Astor. But Nancy Witcher Langhorne Shaw of Virginia, who married Waldorf Astor, was what one of her sons described "as much a household word as later became—though for different reasons—Mrs. Roosevelt, Greta Garbo, and Marilyn Monroe."

Had his late wife possessed a fraction of Nancy's vitality, William Waldorf Astor might never have left America. Always daring, his daughter-in-law called him "Old Moneybags." Nancy could, of course, get away with anything, as her fiancé should have realized. Instead he spent weeks worrying how to tell his autocratic, unreasonable father about his engagement to an American divorcée. Although twenty-seven years old by then, Waldorf knew that no Astor father relinquishes his power until death. Unpredictable William Waldorf took the news with aplomb: "If she's good enough for you, Waldorf, she's good enough for me." And he gave Nancy a $75,000 tiara in which was set the famous Sanci diamond, and blessed the match with several million dollars and, even more important, Cliveden. Nancy's gratitude for this gift was expressed by ripping out his "improvements" to Cliveden as quickly as possible. Out came the mosaic floor, off went the frescoes on the ceilings, and away with many statues. Nancy had found her place in the world, and from then on there was no holding her back.

Millions of words have been written about this most amazing Astor, and yet, as is often true in accounts of people whose lives are public property, they make her both more and less than she was. Her wit and charm are mistaken for intellectual brilliance, and the naïveté and sincerity of her desire to do good are misunderstood or overlooked.

"My mother had two strains in her character," says her eldest son, Lord William Astor, "a worldly and wild strain which came from her father and a deeply religious one. Both could be seen in her throughout her life."

Her father, Chiswell Dabney Langhorne, was a Virginia planter who was ruined—temporarily—by the Civil War. Sure that something would turn up, he was not too proud to put in a brief stint as night porter in a hotel and then as auctioneer of tobacco and horses, playing poker the while to augment his income. That something he had been waiting for turned up in the person of a northerner who had just obtained a railroad concession in Virginia. Undeterred by any lack of experience, Langhorne talked his way into becoming the contractor. It was easy then, he pointed out, "to find some damn-fool, who likes hard work, to build the railroad." Contracting railroads made him a rich man, and he built an estate, Mirador, near Charlottesville.

Nancy and her sisters and brothers grew up there; it was a pleasant childhood, not much occupied with education. This sketchy schooling, quite sufficient for the young lady of fashion she was expected to be, was to prove a major handicap to Nancy, whose career was to make demands on her that she was not prepared to meet. Still, she had read the Bible from cover to cover by the time she was fourteen, influenced by a six-foot-three-inch tall parson from Kent doing missionary work in America. This, she always maintained, made up for her other educational failings.

From girlhood on, she became accustomed to being known as one of the "five beautiful Langhorne sisters"—not by any means the most beautiful, however. That accolade went to her older sister Irene. Society is a very small world, after all, and so, long before there was any thought of a union with the Astor family, Ward McAllister, *the* Mrs. Astor's prime minister, had come into the lives of the Langhorne girls. Seeing Irene at a dance, he was dazzled, as was everyone else, and invited her to the Patriarch Ball of 1893. Thus launched, Irene married an artist and moved to New York. Everyone then and still today knows what Irene looked like with her proud lovely face, long curved neck, full bosom, and wasp waist. For a generation at least, she stood as the model for American beauty, much as Jacqueline Kennedy did when she was First Lady. Irene, too, was known by her married name. Her husband, Charles Dana Gibson, made hers the face and form of his Gibson Girl.

Nancy, at seventeen, was sent to New York for a year at Miss Brown's finishing school and then decided to stay on for another year with her sister. Although she could not compete in looks with Irene, her personality and spirited slangy way of talking proved attractive to men. At the big society balls the floor was bordered by rows of little gilt chairs. Nannie, as she was then called, would invariably pick two right in the center of the front row and issue an order to her frequently dazed beau: "If anybody takes these while we're dancing, punch him in the nose."

An accomplished horsewoman, she attended the horse show and polo matches, and it was in this way that she had the ill fortune to meet and fall in love with Robert Gould Shaw II, an excellent rider himself. Scion of a prominent Boston family, Robert was justly proud of his father, an abolitionist who had died leading a Negro regiment in the Civil War. Shaw was good-looking, and most people found him very easy to get along with. This was not the case for Nancy. Marriage to him, or for that matter, to any man, came as a terrible shock to Nancy, who was the most innocent of girls, even for that Victorian era. The second night after they were married, feeling that she could not endure it, she left Shaw and somehow managed to make her way home to Mirador. Her father convinced her that it was her duty to return and she did. But her fears about sex were never completely conquered, and years later she was still to make remarks more suitable for the naïve girl she had been than for the sophisticated-appearing woman she had become: "To wish to attract attention to your figure is just a desire to attract the male sex through its most vulnerable point. Is that really worth doing? Don't we women have to pay for these methods in the long-run?"

She never spoke of the sexual aspect of her marriage, which was a disaster in every way; she insisted all her life that it was ruined simply because Shaw was a drinker. Still, she bore him a son, who was named Robert after him. The only other thing Nancy and Shaw had in common was their love of riding and hunting, and both were active in the Myopia Chase and Country Club. Their stables were large, and they entertained the horsy set at their home in the fashionable Boston suburb of Prides Crossing. It was not enough for a marriage, of course. Once again Nancy left her husband, this time for a period of six months, hoping he would give up drinking. It was a vain hope, and the situation deteriorated steadily. In the early summer of 1902 Nancy returned to Mirador and Robert went to Louisville. It was the final separation and their social set, newspapers of the day reveal, waited for word of the inevitable divorce. Though Nancy was not as much concerned as most women would have been by the social connotations of divorce in an era when such action was uncommon, it offended her deeply religious, idealistic nature. She really had no choice, however, particularly as she had to consider the effects of her husband's behavior on their child. And so in 1903 after six years of marriage, they were divorced and Robert was "enjoined and restrained from interfering with Mrs. Shaw"; Nancy was given custody of little Bobby. That Shaw had been as unhappy with Nannie as she had been with him was made evident when two days after the divorce he was married to Mrs. Mary Converse, a widow. Nancy never fully recovered from the effects of her years with Shaw and retained a life-long aversion to drink.

It was a great relief to her to be free, and she went to England to hunt and to meet some new people. Nancy was then as beautiful as she was ever to be (though not quite the great beauty she appears in the famous and flattering portrait by John Singer Sargent). What she had was a kind of bright, lively good looks. Her features were clean-cut and aquiline, her blue-gray eyes were always dancing, and her figure was small and trim, brisk in its movements. Her personality was both challenging and appealing. An aging society matron greeted her with the words "I suppose you've come over to England to take one of our husbands away from us." Nancy snapped right back, "If you knew what difficulty I had getting rid of my first one, you wouldn't say that."

Because the Astors were already as prominent in London society as in America, Nancy soon came in contact with them. The first Astor she met was the one she was least able to get along with—Mrs. John Jacob Astor IV. The two women were alike in their desire to charm, startle, and shock those around them, and both had the ability to take the center of the stage. If one must compare weapons, Ava was the more beautiful, and Nancy the wittier.

Her second Astor was the man she married, who by coincidence had been born on the same day as she, May 19, 1879. Completely different in character from her ex-husband, Waldorf Astor was quiet, reticent, serious, responsible, and conscientious, a man whom Nancy could admire. He was neither handsome nor homely, with his big nose, large brown eyes, dark mustache, and curly hair. His tall thin figure had the elegance characteristic of the Astor men of a generation or two ago.

For all his quiet unassuming ways Waldorf was not a cold man. When Nancy met him he was involved in a Graustarkian romance with Queen Marie of Rumania. Queen Marie was a great beauty, and to have her favor was a dizzying distinction for a shy young commoner (William Waldorf had not yet achieved his peerage). Aside from the difference in their respective positions, one must add that Marie was married to King Ferdinand, and there was never any question of her leaving him for Waldorf. Still, she visited Astor at Cliveden, and he visited her at court in Bucharest, and the aftermath of the romance lingered for a time. Even after Nancy Shaw had banished Marie from Waldorf's affections, they continued to write to one another. Nancy soon put a stop to that with her characteristic forthright vigor.

Her second marriage offered Nancy both the one husband ideally suited to her and the way of life that was most congenial to her. With her as its mistress, Cliveden fulfilled each of William Waldorf's ambitions. One would have to look far to find a more perfect example of the great landed estate of prewar England. Forty gardeners tended the parks, gardens, and fruit and vegetable farms. Nancy ran the house with the aid of twenty indoor servants—eight maids plus four scullery maids, a groom of the chambers, an odd-job man, a chef, a valet, a butler, and three footmen. Until World War I the last four named powdered their hair and wore knee breeches. William Waldorf had not been able to make Cliveden achieve its potential, because of his antisocial nature, but Nancy did so with ease. Cliveden was the center of the world for everyone who lived there, worked in the house or grounds, or cared for White Place, the farm. One building on the estate was a social club containing a billiard room and a hall with a stage for performances. A fancy-dress ball for all employees was held there each winter. On Saturdays a Cliveden team played cricket or football matches against residents and employees of the neighboring estates. The August Bank Holiday was the occasion for races and competitions, the high point being a tug of war between Cliveden and White Place Farm. Waldorf did the judging, and Nancy handed out the prizes, embarrassing and delighting one and all with her witticisms.

The stables, under Waldorf's supervision, became among the finest in England. He founded the Cliveden stud, which soon gained world renown. "He was," declares his son, "an absolute genius at breeding racehorses." Seventy-five percent of his horses placed in the money in races; they won the Oaks six times and came in second in the Derby five times.

The social reputation of Cliveden soared; guests were, of course, an integral part of life for people like the Astors. It was customary for the landed gentry to invite large numbers of relatives and friends for a weekend or longer, since there was ample space and a sufficiency of servants to minister to their needs. These were considerable at a time when it simply would not occur to the average daughter of the rich that she might unpack her "Noah's ark" of a trunk, holding for a typical three-day visit three evening gowns, three teagowns, two tweed jackets and skirts, a riding habit, boots, indoor and outdoor shoes, and hats to go with everything. Help with dressing and coiffures was desperately needed. Nancy was considered exceptional in her ability to dress herself with just a little assistance from her maid Rose Harrison, who remained with her for thirty years. "I was three years getting to understand Lady Astor," Rose liked to say. "Rose, I have never understood you," Nancy would reply, displaying her customary gift for the charming and unexpected remark.

With forty-six bedrooms at Cliveden, most of them occupied on a weekend, the maids arose at five in the morning to clean the main rooms before the breakfast onslaught. The organization of the household was a staggering task; yet Nancy, for all her seeming nonchalance, was a martinet and missed no detail. Each morning, invigorated by a cold bath and setting up exercises, she would call in Monsieur Gilbert, the chef, appropriately dressed in white jacket—servants were elaborately costumed in the Astor house—to discuss the menus. Then Lady Astor would go over all other essentials with the butler and the housekeeper. The gardener had the additional task of arranging all the cut flowers in the house in such a way as to suit Nancy, which was far from easy to do. No matter how much she demanded of them, members of her staff adored her and struggled mightily to please.

The behind-the-scenes planning was never obvious to the visitors. A natural hostess, Nancy laughed at the rigid schedule enforced by her father-in-law and encouraged her guests to do whatever they wanted. Her only problem as a hostess was her inability to limit the guest list. She would tell the chef to make lunch for eight and then at noon throw him into a frenzy of preparation with the casual remark that a dozen or so extra guests were arriving momentarily. At dinner the number often swelled to such proportions that there were not enough places to seat everyone. Nancy had one of her brainstorms. Each person was taking up too much room, she decided. Taking out her tape measure she calculated that eighteen inches of table space was adequate for plates and cutlery. With this in mind, she ordered dozens of the smallest-sized dining chairs anyone had ever seen, and the new spacing went into effect. Her guests soon found that everything was fine so long as they did not eat but that they could neither help themselves from serving dishes nor lift forks to mouths. The butler was the first to rebel. At Buckingham Palace, he stated firmly, each guest was allotted two feet six inches. Presented with this information, Nancy yielded.

The guests had been prepared to put up with the discomfort, being completely captivated by Nancy's charm and wit. In an anti-American social set, she made her Americanism a positive asset. No one even objected to her habit of chewing gum, but then, they pointed out that she hardly moved her jaw. Her gaiety was contagious, and people could never tell whether she was joking or being serious. She would pretend one guest was another and pick on yet a third to introduce to new arrivals as her husband. At dinner she liked to startle her partner by surreptitiously popping a huge set of celluloid false teeth into her mouth and going right on talking without a break. Turning on a southern dialect, she would hold the table enthralled with her stories about the Negroes of her native Virginia. If she was in the mood to perform more elaborately, she would invite her guests into the library after dinner, arrange the chairs as in a theater, and begin to act. She might be a refined lady with an affected accent and the deep conviction that Americans were boorish, or a horsy Englishwoman who swore lustily, or a horrible old shrew with no teeth and a dark view of humanity. Sometimes the other guests, inspired by her example, would join in. Her husband, of course, never did; nothing could have been more unsuited to his modest, retiring nature.

Waldorf's quiet ways may have been the result of the ill health that troubled him throughout his life. His heart was weak, and at the age of twenty-six he had been stricken with tuberculosis, the curse of his generation of English Astors. This condition improved, but by 1908 his doctors insisted that he abandon all strenuous exercise because his heart showed strain. This was a terrible blow to him, because the hearty fellowship of the men's clubs bored him, and he had few intellectual interests, caring neither for literature, art, music, or the theater. Some activity had to be found to occupy him, and incredible as it sounds, according to Nancy's biography by Maurice Collis, he decided to go into politics for something to do. In 1910 he was elected to the House of Commons as the Conservative representative of Plymouth.

Whatever his original reasons for launching his political career, he was both interested and able, and was re-elected several times. Conscious of the dangers of tuberculosis, he became chairman of a committee to combat this disease on a national level. He was an ardent supporter of temperance measures, indicating, if proof were needed, that he was far more under the influence of his wife than his father. William Waldorf stoutly declared that he had drunk wine since he was seven: "I should not have my excellent health today had I not used stimulants freely all my life." Nancy, on the other hand, refused to have liquor served to visitors at Cliveden; knowledgeable thirsty guests learned the wisdom of making friends with the butler.

During those years when Waldorf was enjoying his brief political flowering, Nancy was undergoing the only decline of her life. She had become the mother of William Waldorf, who had been born in 1907, (Nancy) Phyllis Louise in 1909, and (Francis) David Langhorne in 1912. Repeated childbearing, whether because of physiological or psychological problems, left her physically weakened. The vitality that had seemed to be a basic part of her character deserted her, and she turned into a semi-invalid. Her doctors with singular lack of understanding, ordered a rest cure, and she spent much of each day in bed, fuming and miserable. She tried to keep herself amused by inviting guests to dinner parties served in her bedroom, but eating in bed is not really so amusing as all that. Her health under this regime showed no improvement.

Her father-in-law liked to say: "One of my rules for long life is to kill my doctor. It is usually the doctor who kills the patient." Although she never listened to William Waldorf, Nancy's salvation, when it came, was remarkably similar. In 1913 she discovered and embraced Christian Science, and from then on it was a dominating force in her life. Its tenets were particularly compatible with her natural self-sufficiency and her unconquerable spirit. With her reliance in herself strengthened by this religion, she rose from her bed. Nor did she relapse later when Michael was born in 1916 and John Jacob VII in 1918. In fact, from the day of her conversion, she declared, she was never tired or ill again.

She was fully restored to health when, upon the outbreak of World War I, the tennis court building at Cliveden was turned into a two-hundred-bed hospital for Canadian soldiers, with Astor paying for the services of ten medical officers, twenty nurses, and a number of orderlies. None other than Sir William Osler, Canada's most noted physician, came to the hospital once a week to supervise. The patients found Nancy's onslaughts far more startling. She was never the quiet, soothing angel of mercy, but no angel ever had such an effect on injured men. On entering the hospital one day, she overheard a nurse saying that two soldiers who had been severely burned had lost the will to live. Nancy bent over them: "You're going to die and I would, too, rather than go back to Canada." They instantly defended their country against this foul slur, and by the time she was through with them, they both wanted to live. "You have to insult men to rouse them up," she remarked airily to the stunned nursing staff.

She was less successful in assisting her husband in his battles with a succession of ailments. Not long able to withstand his persuasive wife, Waldorf was converted to Christian Science. It seems to have been conspicuously less effective in his case than in hers; in addition to a weak heart and questionable lungs, he was virtually crippled by sciatica. Nancy maintained firmly that Christian Science had done wonders for his condition.

His health, nonetheless, had been too poor for him to enter active service in World War I. The closest he came to it was as an inspector in the quartermaster corps, with the rank of major. He remained in Parliament and was named a member of several government commissions dealing with wartime medical research. When Lloyd George became Prime Minister in 1916, Astor was made a Parliamentary Secretary, along with Philip Kerr, founder and editor of the political quarterly *Round Table*. The long and fateful friendship between the Astors and Kerr, who is far better known as Lord Lothian, the title he inherited in 1930, dates from that time. Kerr was a regular visitor to Cliveden through the years. Falling completely under Nancy's spell, he was the most prominent of her converts to Christian Science. He remained an ardent follower to the end of his life and refused to call a doctor in his final illness. Many people said that he was in love with Nancy, although she, with the innate good sense common to wives, always insisted that he was really Waldorf's friend.

When William Waldorf achieved his life's ambition at the cost of his son's, Waldorf knew that his days in Parliament were numbered. Banishment to the all-but-powerless House of Lords awaited him as soon as his father died, and he succeeded to a title he did not want and could not legally renounce. (That privilege was not extended to the privileged classes until the summer of 1963, when Anthony Wedgwood Benn won the right to refuse to be Lord Stansgate and thus retain his seat as Labor Party representative of southeast Bristol in the House of Commons.) For two years Waldorf upbraided and argued with his father, behavior foreign to his moderate nature, to no avail. William Waldorf died in 1919, and his son became the second viscount. "Some people find it hard to get titles," murmured Nancy, "Lord Astor is finding it even harder to get rid of his."

Hope of salvaging his career did not die all at once; resource-fully, he introduced a bill to allow peers to be elected to Commons. The problem, as he saw it, was one of time only. While the meas-ure was being debated, the Conservatives would find and back an-other candidate for his constituency, the Sutton division of Ply-mouth. Should this successor be elected, it was hardly likely that he would later agree to step aside in favor of his predecessor. It was then that what seemed like a suitable interim candidate was sug-gested—Waldorf's wife. In 1918 women had been given suffrage and the right to sit in Commons. Nancy, as anyone who knew her should have realized, would have been no readier to step aside for Waldorf than any other politician, but because his bill never passed, the matter was luckily never put to the test.

Some sober spirits wondered why anyone would vote for inex-perienced Lady Astor. "Will she win on popularity?" asked the London *Times* (not yet an Astor property) dubiously. Of course she would and did by three thousand votes. She liked to point out that she was physically responsible for one of them. On election day in Plymouth she heard a woman holding a baby complain loudly, "What good is the suffrage when I can't vote anyway, as I have no one to leave the baby with!" Nancy took the infant forth-with, and the woman went in to vote. When she returned to Clive-den after her victory, the gardeners and tenants harnessed them-selves to a carriage and pulled her down the drive, a tribute to their lady of the manor.

Nancy's first major decision as an M.P. was woman's eternal one—what to wear in Parliament. She made up her mind that it should be simple and sober, a black dress with a white fichu and cuffs and a tricorne hat. Once decided, she had enough copies made so as to be able to wear the identical outfit daily. When the first group wore out, she ordered some more and appeared in Par-liament in that conservative dress for nearly twenty years.

Thus attired, on December 2, 1919, Lady Astor became the first woman to be seated in the House of Commons. (She was not—one must, in the interest of accuracy, explain—the first woman elected, but Constance Countess Markievicz, who had that honor, belonged to the Irish Revolutionary Sinn Fein, and in order to annoy the British refused to take her seat.)

"Parliament was like a men's club," Nancy said later. "No one wanted me there."

On the occasion of her first appearance, she seemed possessed, whereas "the Prime Minister and Mr. Balfour had all the ingenuous shyness of boys at their first dance."

The late Winston Churchill ignored her presence completely, the type of treatment she was least able to endure. She asked him why, and their exchange has become one of the many classic anecdotes associated with both great names. "When you took your seat I felt as if a woman had come into my bathroom and I had only a sponge with which to defend myself," he told her coolly.

"You are not handsome enough to have worries of that kind," she retorted.

Nancy was off to a running start, and the public and the press loved it. "I have been in it [Commons] a week, and I never saw a house where women were more needed." She exhorted one audience of women: "Don't blame men. They are just what we have made them and the mistake we have made is to tell them that they are the stronger sex, knowing in our hearts that they are not. They are the nicer sex, but not the stronger."

Never one to be inconspicuous, she practiced her golf swing on the terrace of the House during the tea break.

Once the conservative members of Commons had gotten somewhat accustomed to her presence, she settled down to fighting for the things she believed in. And when Nancy fought, she used every weapon. For all her good breeding, Lady Astor was never one to observe Parliamentary propriety and maddened speakers by making running comments throughout their speeches. The moment was to come when Labor's Aneurin Bevan exclaimed in exasperation, "It really is intolerable when this old gas bag gets up and gabbles away!" The two main principles for which she did battle were temperance and the improvement of the position of women. To speak of drink, which automatically meant drunkenness to her, was like waving the proverbial red flag in front of a bull. During one parliamentary session an opposing M.P. rose to speak against Nancy's proposal to prevent the sale of alcoholic drinks to persons under eighteen. She soon saw that he intended a British version of the American filibuster, talking so long that there could be no vote. Infuriated, she jumped up, went over, and started pulling on his coattails so as to make him sit down. Her effort at physical intimidation failed, not altogether surprisingly, because she was such a lightweight. The bill was talked out, but only for the moment; two weeks later it passed. Still, subsequent efforts to effect at least partial prohibition in England failed.

Very conscious of her position as a representative of her sex, she considered much legislation from the woman's viewpoint. When a bill was introduced to make divorce easier, everyone expected her to support it in view of her own past. Instead, she opposed it on the grounds that only men would take advantage of the change. On the question of equal rights for women, she was vociferous.

"We are not asking for superiority, for we have always had that," she declared to the delight of all female listeners. "All we ask is equality."

Lady Astor's ability to make the world take notice of her was significant in and of itself in elevating women from their traditionally second-place status. This public relations aspect of her parliamentary career did far more for the woman's rights movement than any legislation she supported. Parliamentary law was beyond her; she lacked the background to understand major issues and the patience to study them. Except for the Bible and *Science and Health,* read for emotional rather than intellectual reasons, Nancy was seldom to be found with a book.

Her breezy, confident manner infuriated Churchill, just as his opposition infuriated her. "If I were your wife I'd put poison in your coffee," she burst out. And he topped that with, "And if I were your husband, I'd drink it." This exchange has been quoted so frequently that it has become a classic in insult lore.

But neither Winston Churchill nor anyone else could intimidate her. "I am always a nuisance," she remarked. "You have to be if you have strong convictions."

On a trip to the United States in the early 1920's she was asked not to discuss the League of Nations, because the Americans had refused to join, and feeling ran high. Well, of course, Nancy talked about the League, saying first in ringing tones that since she had been told not to mention the League of Nations, she would call it the "League of Peace."

Despite her American birth, relations between British and American Astors remained tenuous. They saw one another on transcontinental visits but remained on rather formal terms. A rare exhibition of family solidarity was seen when young Vincent Astor led her to the platform to address the Convention of the League of Women Voters in the United States.

He can hardly have been delighted by her remarks when she visited the Astor Estate office in New York. The view of tenements she expressed was remarkably similar to that of many social reformers attacking her husband and his family on their American holdings: "It is bad business to tolerate slums," she asserted, pointing out that bad housing wrecks the health of its tenants—a fact proven repeatedly in the Astor tenements. "The community cannot afford to have consumptives."

In England, too, she was an ardent proponent of better housing, answering those who said she was too rich to know what she was talking about: "One did not need to be born in a slum to have a heart."

Those were Lady Astor's great years in public life, and everyone loved "Our Nancy," as she was called. Campaigning was a positive delight to her. She would appear on the street or in a courtyard in Plymouth and shout, "Hey, you there!" Heads would bob out of windows and she would begin to speak. Hecklers only stimulated her to do her best and to produce the quips that had been dubbed "Astorisms."

"Come on, I'm ready for you," she would cry, and she was.

"You have enough brass to make a kettle," yelled one.

"You have enough water in your head to fill it," she retorted.

A farmer wanting to show that she was incapable of representing rural districts cried, "How many toes are there on a pig's foot?"

"Take off your shoe, man, and count for yourself."

A woman in the crowd rushed for Nancy to kiss her baby. The infant, frightened by the noise, was crying, but when Lady Astor picked him up, he began to play with her necklace and quieted down. "The way to keep children happy," she remarked cheerfully, "is to let them play with a rope of pearls."

Although every one of these words was quoted and requoted as if spoken by Socrates, Nancy was not satisfied. "The press doesn't give women enough publicity. They've got to murder their husbands to get into the papers."

"Your husband's a millionaire, ain't he?" asked a hostile workman.

Waldorf Astor, who was standing there, looked pained, but Nancy replied blithely, "That's one of the reasons I married him. And don't you wish you were rich?"

Although in the background then and forever after, as far as the outside world was concerned, Waldorf was no nonentity, his family insists. "My father made the decisions," says the present Lord Astor, "and when he put his foot down, my mother yielded, even when she didn't like it."

A younger son, Michael, avers that Waldorf's will prevailed in major issues and that he restrained Nancy's impulsiveness. The London *Times* gave what is probably the most accurate appraisal of the situation: "He set aside his own political ambitions in order to further the political career of his wife. Thereafter the limelight fell almost exclusively on her, but her husband's judgement and public spirit were always of much influence behind the political scene."

"He did not resent my mother's success," asserts Lord Astor. "He wanted her to be successful and popular."

Of this, at least, there can be little doubt. Everyone who knew Waldorf speaks of his fair-minded attitude, greatness of spirit, and rectitude of character. A brother-in-law goes so far as to describe him as a saint. But his goodness was such as to render him almost as inaccessible as his far from saintly father had been. He lacked a real understanding of others less perfect than he. His standards for his children were virtually impossible for them or indeed any human beings to live up to. As for his personal life, he was moderate in his expenditures, neither smoked nor drank, used no expression stronger than "Drat!" and after the Queen of Rumania, was never linked romantically with any woman but his wife.

One of his few eccentricities was a fear of tuberculosis, natural enough under the circumstances, but in his case touched with a degree of hysteria. When he traveled with the children, for example, a cow from the Cliveden farm went right along on the train, together with a farmer to milk it. How else, he asked, could one be certain that the children might not drink milk from a tubercular cow? His fear, to be fair, did have some scientific basis.

Waldorf had considerable knowledge of animal husbandry and farming; scientific agriculture was one of his major interests, and he wrote a number of books on the subject. It is typical of the man that, although Cliveden had a large farm on the grounds, his interest, according to his son William, was academic rather than practical.

He was similarly remote in his handling of the enormous estate that was supporting him and his family. Distance and estate managers succeeded in removing him from the day-to-day problems of business, much as his wife kept him out of the hurly-burly of politics. The British portion of the Astor Estate consisted not only of the fifty million dollars of American real estate on which the trust funds had been based, but also of a considerable fortune in stocks and bonds: 4,000 shares of Delaware, Lackawanna & Western Railroad, 3,024 of Pittsburgh, Fort Wayne & Chicago Railroad, 2,732 of Illinois Central Railroad, 2,300 of Pullman Co.—to cite a mere fraction of the whole.

Living in one country and deriving a good portion of income from another may be enjoyable, but it is hardly economical, taking double taxation into account. In 1919, for example, Waldorf and his brother, John Jacob V paid $1,134,000 in taxes to the United States and $1,680,000 to Britain, a combined figure that equaled or even slightly exceeded the rents they were receiving. The orders went out to their New York managers to sell the least profitable of their holdings. These were judged to be rows of tenements along West 15th Street, West 129th Street, West 130th Street, upper Broadway, and Avenue A. Within six years many of these dilapidated buildings had been put on the block and sold, a move very much in keeping with Nancy's anti-slum policy. After this went the Exchange Court Building and some of the Wall Street property. The great Astor empire in the Bronx, a legacy of John Jacob III, was diminished by the disposal of 1,669 lots. The only one of the hotels that had suited William Waldorf, the Netherland, was sold, as was the northern half of the old Astor House put up so long before by John Jacob Astor I. In England there were some sales, too, with the heavily fortressed Estate office purchased by the British Society of Incorporated Accountants and Auditors. It would be quite a mistake to assume that these sales marked the beginning of the end of the Astor fortune. If anything, the disposal of the least profitable of their holdings improved their financial position. What was left was the best, and by 1929 the value of the American property had climbed to one hundred million dollars. By this time Nancy and Waldorf had for their personal use a mansion at 4 St. James Square in London, with a large ballroom and two dining rooms, a fifteen-bedroom cottage near a golf course at Sandwich, a house in Plymouth, and, of course, Cliveden.

In addition to the real estate and securities, the first viscount had left his sons the foundation for a press empire. The cornerstone of this was the Sunday *Observer*, which had been turned over to Waldorf in 1916. Self-effacing as usual, Astor left the running of the paper to the editor, J. L. Garvin, a hawk-nosed man whose eyes looked as if they were about to pop out of his head. Garvin was so violent in his opinions that the paper was described as a "weekly thunderstorm." Waldorf was hardly the man to battle his way to possession of a press empire, but his younger brother, Major John Jacob Astor V, was ideally suited to such activity.

"He has the direct manner of a typical army man," said a friend, "not easily swayed from a settled objective."

In the early 1920's his objective became the powerful and influential *Times* of London. This newspaper had been in the family of its founder, John Walter, for four generations, and then in 1908 had been sold to Lord Northcliffe, one of the first of the great press lords. Lord Northcliffe became mentally ill, and a struggle for control of the paper was well under way when he died in 1922. The terms of Lord Northcliffe's will gave John Walter IV an option to buy, but there was a catch: the sale was to be made only at the best price obtainable. This proviso virtually canceled out the option, because Walter was by no means wealthy enough to match the five million dollars being offered by Lord Rothermere, another powerful press lord. To the surprise of all but a small circle of insiders, Walter countered with an offer of $6,547,500. Those insiders knew of the existence of a silent backer, a man so rich that he had instructed Walter to pay any price needed to outbid Rothermere. When the smoke cleared, it became apparent that the backer, John Jacob Astor V, owned nine tenths of the *Times* and Walter the remainder.

The *Spectator* magazine consoled Englishmen with the observation that the paper "could not be in better hands." After all, it added, both owners were "old Etonians."

The editor selected by Astor for his new newspaper was Geoffrey Dawson, who had been associated with Philip Kerr in the *Round Table*. John Jacob was a much easier man for an editor to deal with than his father had been, because he subscribed to the belief that you hire the right man for the job and then leave him to it. Regardless of method, the son found, as his father had before him, that control of a newspaper is extremely helpful to anyone seeking advancement in a career. In 1920 John Jacob V had run for the House of Commons and had lost; the London *Times* had opposed his candidacy. In 1922, as publisher of that influential paper, he was elected as Tory representative of the Dover division of Kent and succeeded in holding this office for the next twenty-three years.

Although fellow publishers, the two brothers were not on intimate terms. They visited one another often, but on a somewhat formal basis. Nancy had the faculty of putting her stiff brother-in-law's back up. "It's the press that's always causing the trouble," this wife of one and sister-in-law of another press lord stated one day. "I can't tell you what contempt I have for the press." Waldorf took this sort of utterance with a grain of salt, but his brother was annoyed. Aside from his natural reaction to such Astorisms, John Jacob was old-fashioned and never gave his wholehearted approval to Nancy's parliamentary career. He was certainly not alone in this, because acceptance of women in politics was slow in coming.

One cannot doubt, however, that Nancy's influence on British affairs would have been major, even if she had never set foot in the House of Commons. She combined her social genius with a sense of destiny, a predilection for people of importance, a fabulously wealthy husband with a famous name, and Cliveden. Nancy ranks among the most brilliant hostesses in her own or any other generation, and she made her home a center of influence long before the words *Cliveden Set* were coined.

To name the guests at Cliveden is to give a who's who of half a century. In Cliveden's first, and happiest, period, royal guests included King Edward VII and, after his death, King George V and Queen Mary, the Archduke Franz Ferdinand of Austria (before June 28, 1914, of course), and his consort the Duchess of Hohenberg. Crown Prince Gustav (now King Gustav VI) of Sweden was such a favored guest that the Astors lent their house in Sandwich for his honeymoon when he married Lady Louise Mountbatten (later the aunt of Britain's Prince Philip). Nancy subsequently became friends with the Prince of Wales (Edward VIII) and liked to play golf with him. (Their most publicized match took place in 1933, and Nancy implied that it took all her ability to manage to lose to him, despite the fact that her daughter Phyllis had telephoned to announce her engagement to Lord Willoughby de Eresby just before they teed off.) Among the noted statesmen who sat down to dinner with Nancy were Lord George Curzon, viceroy of India, and (on a different weekend) his enemy, Lord Horatio Herbert Kitchener, who had commanded the British forces in India. Long before the unhappy poisoned coffee or bathroom encounters, Winston Churchill visited Cliveden. The meeting with Nancy was not a success—it was repulsion at first sight for both. Although Lady Astor was not much of a reader, she liked to have famous authors around. Her opinions on them depended on their social behavior rather than their talent. She declared that James Barrie had been spoiled by success; as for Rudyard Kipling, he was a bore, because he sat quietly on the sofa and turned to his wife for moral support whenever he was asked a question.

It is easy to see why any shy man would blanch when asked to live up to Nancy's standards, which demanded that a man be prominent and also amusing and bright. Mealtimes were a running competition between conversationalists, and it was observed that Garvin of the *Observer* often abandoned his roast beef altogether in his efforts to hold the floor. At any time guests might find themselves expected to perform cleverly at charades.

George Bernard Shaw was the one writer who completely satisfied her demands for fame coupled with wit. What is more, Shaw, like Nancy, was somewhat repelled or frightened by sex. Nonetheless, the friendship was so deep and long-lasting that Nancy sometimes feared it might be misunderstood. Questioned about it at one point, she stated firmly, if illogically, that they became friends because "I adored his wife, Charlotte, and he did, too." When Hesketh Pearson was writing his biography of Shaw, he asked for permission to include letters to Nancy. She insisted that he cut off the "My dearest Nancy" salutation; after all, her son by her first marriage was Robert Shaw, and people might think George Bernard was the father. In one of the letters that has been revealed to the public, he calls her "Loveliest Nan" and says that he hopes she has not been devoured by wolves, "though you would be if I were a wolf." Shaw's admiration of her was so celebrated that both were asked repeatedly if she was the model for *Candida* or *St. Joan*, despite the fact that the former was written years before they met. The playwright's attachment to Lady Astor never faltered; decades later when he lay dying, she was the only friend he wanted to see.

Shaw introduced Nancy to another strange personality to whom she was also naturally drawn—Lawrence of Arabia, then hiding from the world in the Royal Air Force under the name of T. E. Shaw. Lawrence often left his barracks of an evening to make a swift run on his motorcycle to St. James Place or Cliveden. Stopped when returning late to quarters one night, Lawrence gave as excuse—so the possibly legendary story goes—that he had been detained at dinner with Lord and Lady Astor and George Bernard Shaw; his fellow soldiers only laughed at him. Sometimes Lawrence would take Nancy riding on his motorcycle, a rare mark of favor for this embittered misogynist. He liked it, she realized, because she would balance on the seat without so much as touching his body. Neither of them liked to be touched.

The only people allowed to fall short of Nancy's high social requirements for guests were those whom she felt were "good"—in what is almost a child's interpretation of that word. A Christian Science practitioner, automatically "good," was included in virtually every group. Even wit would not serve, if she felt an individual to be "bad." No invitation was issued to anyone who had been the guilty party in a divorce suit or who was living a "sinful" life (if Nancy knew it).

Gandhi's unassailable goodness attracted Nancy as strongly as the sex appeal of a movie star attracts another kind of woman. He convinced her rather easily of the rectitude of the nationalist aims of the Indians and was, thereafter, very much at home with her. Lady Astor's imperialistic friends were astounded one day to enter her drawing room and find Gandhi sitting on the floor, turning his spinning wheel.

Throughout her parliamentary career, Nancy harbored the pleasant delusion that bringing together people of different political parties and opposing convictions would lead to better understanding between them. Her reputation was such that they came to her parties, but the hoped-for results seldom followed.

Private life for the family at Cliveden was irretrievably mixed in with the public, as a result of the excitement and glamor of Nancy's parliamentary career and the celebrated guests who clustered about her. The five Astor children plus their half-brother Robert Shaw reeled under the impact of their mother's personality. She took a voracious, though, perforce, sporadic, interest in their lives. Each morning when she and they were at home, they were called into her room to join her in "doing the lesson," which consisted of reading passages of the Bible and *Science and Health*. And although Nancy was completely in earnest about her religion, even the "lesson" had to be light in tone. Switching into the Negro dialect she assumed so well, she would declare: "Yassir, I'se gonna help yew. Me and Mistah Jesus is gonna help yew." The rest of the children's day, typical of the British upper class practice of the time, was spent in the care of servants. At five o'clock, bathed and neatly dressed, they joined the grownups once again for the "Children's Hour." Sometimes Waldorf would read to them or Nancy would tell them plantation stories from her Virginia childhood.

Although it sounds idyllic, life was not easy for the Astor children because of the character of their parents. Nancy expected and demanded such a high degree of attention and demonstrated affection that her children found it hard to live up to her. She wanted, and felt it her right, to control their very minds. Her husband, on the other hand, was remote but firm. Trained in the Astor tradition, he felt that the word of the father was the ultimate law and that any difference of opinion was insupportable. And yet, despite the demands and requirements, neither was at all child-centered. The children were but one of many responsibilities, interests, and enthusiasms. Their eldest son William speaks most pleasantly of both his parents, but the real warmth in his voice is reserved for Nannie Gibbons. Pausing before the portrait of her he had ordered an artist to paint, he muses: "So kind, so gentle. She was a real influence on us, you see, as Mother and Father were so busy."

As they grew a little older and went away to school—Eton remained the public school for the Astors—Nancy would descend on them periodically, scattering chaos in her path. Her sons were agonizingly embarrassed by her way of stopping any boy of any age and asking him personal questions—"Have you cleaned your teeth?" Teachers were subjected to equally painful inquisitions. On the day after one of her visits, Michael Astor's tutor admitted that he had heard Lady Astor's voice in the hall and had hidden in a closet until she left. Luckily she was too busy to come very often.

She took the problems of her constituency, Plymouth, to heart and, with Waldorf's cooperation, gave many gifts to the city. Astor contributions went to the building of Virginia House and Astor House as social centers for youngsters, the founding of maternity centers, and the construction of housing for workmen.

In spite of her lack of comprehension of basic issues, she was not content to remain occupied with the relatively safe problems of Plymouth, women's rights, and temperance. She wanted to be a positive world power, and the presence of leading statesmen and politicians at Cliveden encouraged her to believe that she could. Gradually signs appeared that Nancy might be getting in over her head when it came to world politics. Her opposition to the Russians was expressed in an incredibly sophomoric manner. In 1925 she blithely offered to pay all expenses for any family deluded enough to want to spend two years in Russia. It is hard to know what Waldorf can have been thinking of to let her go so far. But she had said it, and the Astors lived up to it and duly sent a Britisher to Russia. He returned, perversely saying everything was wonderful.

In 1931 George Bernard Shaw was asked to visit Moscow and wangled invitations for Lord and Lady Astor and their son David.

Shaw was tremendously popular in Russia and had entree everywhere up to and including the Kremlin, and the Astors followed along in his wake, Waldorf, as was his way, kept his mouth shut, but Nancy got off a series of inappropriate clever remarks that she was never able to live down, even though she later claimed that some of them were apocryphal.

"Now tell me honestly, wouldn't you rather not have had a revolution at all?" she is supposed to have asked Maxim Litvinoff, foreign commissar.

Litvinoff replied solemnly, "My whole life was spent in preparing for one."

When introduced to Stalin, her question was even more tactless. "When will you stop killing people?" (This is one remark she later admitted having made; the fact is that she was rather proud of it.)

Stalin was annoyed and argued with her. "We are living in a state of war. When peace comes we shall stop it."

In her own descriptions of their interview she reported that Stalin had asked how England had built such a magnificent empire. Nancy had informed him that the English character was formed by the Bible and that Russia might be just as great if the people returned to religion. Shaw unkindly said that she had made up this entire colloquy.

Despite having been a goad to the Revolutionaries, Nancy returned to find herself under attack for pro-Russian sympathies. Shaw was making pro-Russian speeches, and in press reports the Astors were lumped in with him. It was Lady Astor's first taste of generally unfavorable publicity.

Far worse publicity was to follow. It was unfortunate for Nancy that her public career lasted so long that it took her into an era she was not equipped to understand. One might think that Lady Astor, with her Bible and her devotion to the good, would have unerringly cast her vote against Hitler and Mussolini. But the choice did not appear clear-cut to her at all. "The worst thing a human being can do is hate," she said many times, and this, the cornerstone of her philosophy, meant opposition to the mass hatred that is war. No one can quarrel with that lofty view, but in Europe of the 1930's it led to encouragement of much that was base in human beings. Any measures that could prevent war automatically

appeared good to Nancy, even though they required that she con-
done the practices of the Nazis and Fascists. Somehow the hatred,
aggressiveness, and brutality displayed by the Germans and Ital-
ians toward weaker peoples and minority groups passed over her
head. Nancy was, for one thing, an American southerner, brought
up to think that people of a different race were inferior. In the
plantation stories that so delighted her set, she invariably portrayed
the Negroes in kindly fashion, but as childlike underlings nonetheless. The Italian take-over of Ethiopia was, therefore, no real tragedy for anyone who counted. In addition, Nancy possessed all the
prejudices of her class, just as did her formidable great-aunt, *the*
Mrs. Astor. But the effect of Caroline Astor's prejudices, unpleasant though they were, was relatively harmless. Nothing but the
feelings were hurt by a snub, a blackball at the club, a refusal by
the invitations committee of the Patriarchs' Ball. But the same prejudices in Nancy's strife-filled world of the 1930's meant giving
tacit approval to the imprisonment, torture, and murder of those
socially unacceptable Jews and Catholics. Lady Astor had nothing
against Jews—why, her afterdinner performances included a perfectly hilarious bit about a Jewish businessman who giggled and
became hysterical when faced with trouble—but their problems
and those of other minorities did not move her deeply. They really
should have the good taste to keep quiet; she went so far as to say
that anti-Nazi feeling in the United States was whipped up by Jews
and Communists. Her dislike of the Catholics was never concealed
at all.

When it came to national sympathies, the French struck her as
being unprincipled (they drank more than the British or Germans
and were more openly interested in sex). The personality of the
Germans, on the other hand, appealed to her. And she heard her
husband and Lord Philip (Kerr) Lothian, both of whom she considered good, as well as Geoffrey Dawson, whom she considered
intelligent, declare that the terms of the Treaty of Versailles had
been too hard on the Germans. It was Lady Astor's stated conviction that the Germans were being goaded into aggressive behavior
by being treated as inferiors, a statement that might have come
right out of the Nazi propaganda mill. In 1933 Germany withdrew
from the League of Nations; Nancy felt that they must be brought

back, no matter what. She went on to urge Britain to disarm, on the principle that Germany would then follow the example and abandon the arms race, too. Many government officials concurred.

The guest list at Cliveden became top-heavy with Conservative statesmen. The spacious house was visited regularly by Sir Samuel Hoare, who agreed to the Italian take-over of Ethiopia in 1935; Sir John Simon, who in the positions of Foreign Secretary, Home Secretary, and Chancellor of the Exchequer, advocated a policy of appeasement toward Germany; Lord Edward Halifax, who long held the same views and as Foreign Secretary had the opportunity to put them into execution; and Neville Chamberlain, whose name was to become a synonym for appeasement. An even less savory element of the British Fascist movement, headed by Sir Oswald Mosely, also sipped tea in the beautiful drawing rooms of Cliveden. And, if that were not enough, Hitler's ambassador, Joachim von Ribbentrop, was considered an acceptable dinner guest at Cliveden and at the Astors' townhouse, 4 St. James Place. Nancy, completely missing the point, felt that she had done all that could possibly have been expected of her as a representative of virtue when von Ribbentrop greeted her with the Nazi salute and she tossed back, "Stop that nonsense with me."

She fully agreed with Lord Lothian that Hitler's demands were "reasonable" and that they should be met in order to avoid war. Lothian went to Germany as late as 1937 to talk with Hitler and Goebbels. Although he declared that Hitler "left me cold," he was not sufficiently repelled to refuse to become a member of the Anglo-German Fellowship group.

During the 1930's the Astor eldest son, William, entered politics, serving first on Sir John Simon's staff and then becoming Parliamentary Private Secretary to Sir Samuel Hoare. The sole dissenter to the views held by the Astor family was young David, who had traveled in Germany in 1931 before entering college and happened to come upon a Nazi parade in Heidelberg. To his horror he observed that the side streets were lined with truckloads of police armed with truncheons to use on anyone who objected to the marchers. From then on he was unequivocally opposed to the Nazis. His elders, however, did not listen to him.

As owners of both the *Times* and the *Observer*, the Astors had two tremendously influential outlets in which to express their opinions. These newspapers held to the line that Hitler must and could be appeased. "It was a crude blunder in the peace treaties to forbid the union of German Austria with the German Republic. It will be safer policy to expect and allow for the expansion of German interests along lines which it is patently destined to follow." Not only Dawson but subeditor Robert Barrington Ward of the *Times* and J. L. Garvin of the *Observer* were regular visitors to Cliveden and influenced and were influenced by the Astors. *Time* magazine in America remarked that the pro-German propaganda in the London *Times* was "a great deal better than Dr. Paul Joseph Goebbels and the Ministry of Propaganda could turn out."

In 1937 a journalist named Claud Cockburn, in a small news bulletin, *This Week,* shot the sobriquet heard around the world. In a bitter and vigorous attack on appeasement policies, he coined the term *the Cliveden Set.* Cockburn accused Lady Astor, together with the editors of the *Times* and the *Observer* and the Conservative statesmen who were their friends, of plotting appeasement. They were in effect ruling the country, he wrote; as Britain's "Second Foreign Office," they were responsible for a pro-German policy. *This Week* was one of the least important or influential of newspapers, if such it could even be called, but major newspapers all over the world picked up its story. The label *Cliveden Set* was fastened onto the Astors and their friends and could not be removed no matter how its bearers struggled.

Waldorf wrote a letter to the *Times:* "It is absurd to associate Cliveden with conspiracies for any particular set of views."

Nancy wrote in similar vein to the *Herald.* Both continued to deny throughout their lives that there was ever such a thing as a Cliveden Set.

And yet, of course, there *was* a Cliveden Set. It did not have quite the degree of power attributed to it by Cockburn and his supporters ("I am supposed to have more power than had Queen Elizabeth, Marie Antoinette, and Cleopatra combined," commented Nancy wryly), but its members unquestionably influenced the thinking of the government. They did not plot; they did not need to plot. They were the Establishment, bound by background and schooling to the highest government officials. And if the

Profumo Scandal of 1963 showed nothing else, it served as a reminder of the tremendous power of the Establishment. That power was certainly greater twenty-five or thirty years earlier. The Astors were not behind-the-scenes operators only; in 1935 five members of the family were sitting in the House of Commons —Lady Astor and her son William, her son-in-law Lord Willoughby de Eresby, John Jacob Astor V, and a nephew, Ronald Tree, in addition to Lord Astor in the House of Lords.

Nancy, by personality a leader of this Cliveden clique, had the opportunity to do the good she so constantly sought through Christian Science, and she bungled it—without ever knowing that she had. When her old enemy Winston Churchill described Munich as a defeat, she remarked, "Nonsense." She visited the United States that year, and declared fiercely, "I abhor Hitler and Hitlerism," but still urged that war be avoided by coming to terms with him.

The declaration of war with Germany brought all such talk and thinking to an abrupt end, and Lady Astor, whose patriotism had never been questioned, threw herself with characteristic energy into the war effort, as did the entire Astor family. A Canadian war hospital was again set up on the Cliveden estate. The Astor sons entered the armed forces and served with valor. In his fifties and with but one sound leg, John Jacob V staunchly took his place as lieutenant colonel with the Fifth Battalion of the City of London Home Guards. Nancy and Waldorf devoted themselves principally to her constituency of Plymouth, where they had been elected mayoress and mayor in 1939. Nancy remained in Plymouth in the war years, setting a magnificent example for the inhabitants throughout the bombings. Danger, excitement, and stress brought out the best in her. Oblivious to danger from the air, she went from shelter to shelter during air raids, cheering and encouraging the people huddled there waiting for the all-clear. With large sections of the city bombed out and morale sinking, Lady Astor had the bright idea of starting public open-air dances on the Hoe. And she, in her sixties, but still light on her feet, attended and danced with the sailors and townspeople. To them, she became a symbol of indomitable spirit and courage.

Toward the end of 1944, with a new parliamentary election

coming up, Lady Astor announced that she would not run again, in deference to her husband's wishes. He had always assisted her in her career, and at sixty-five no longer felt able to do so. The outside world knew little of what this simple announcement had cost her, but her immediate family was shaken by it.

"She was as mad as can be," recalls her son, William. "She kicked like————, but in the end she had to yield to him."

Nancy, like an aging glamor girl who cannot recognize the changes brought by time, could not see what was so apparent to her husband. Her political reputation had been damaged beyond repair by her prewar appeasement policies. She was not likely to win an election and would only dim the luster of her name by trying and failing.

Never easily discouraged, she suggested that she be elevated to the House of Lords. "I believe I have something to give the House of Lords. I'm not certain they want what I've got." Winston Churchill and the government most certainly did not want what she had, and she was turned down flat.

The return to private life was hard for her to endure. "I am an extinct volcano," she lamented. But it was not really true. Her sparkle, irrepressible wit, and unconquerable independence continued to place her at the center of the stage wherever she went. When she came to America in 1946, *The New York Times* reported her arrival: "Then Lady Astor followed by the almost unnoticed Viscount went to the less-cold waiting room of an adjoining pier where the newsreel men had set up their cameras."

Six years later, as quietly as he had lived, Waldorf died. What was perhaps the perfect epitaph for him was spoken by Sir Clement Jones, chairman of the Royal Institute of International Affairs which Waldorf had headed for many years: "He was always anxious for others to receive credit for his own ideas."

With Waldorf gone, the Cliveden period of Nancy's life was over. Lord Astor had given Cliveden to the National Trust in 1942, opening house and grounds to the public on special days, a practice that his father would thoroughly have abhorred. He left an endowment to pay for its upkeep on the proviso that he and his heirs could continue to live there. But Lady Astor did not wish to remain at Cliveden as a widow. Her son William, who had inherited the title, moved in, and Nancy moved out and bought a new house in London.

Even then it was impossible for her to stay out of the limelight. She visited the United States in 1953 and again made news. At one of the parties she attended, her keen eye spotted the late Senator Joseph R. McCarthy lifting a cocktail glass to his lips. "Too bad it isn't poison," said Our Nancy. Unlike Winston Churchill, McCarthy was quite unable to top that.

Physically she had changed rather little from the slim, trim, pretty young woman who had traded insults with Churchill. Her looks, of the type that wear well, were not dependent on artifice. She had never been a woman to seek glamor in beauty parlors and the only makeup she ever used consisted of foundation cream and powder. As had been true of her since her conversion to Christian Science, she remained in excellent physical condition. On her eightieth birthday she was still able to play golf. "It's wonderful to be so aged and yet so agile," she told an astonished reporter. But an unaccustomed mood of sadness took over: "Years ago I thought that old age would be dreadful because I would not be able to do the things I want to do. Now I find there is nothing I want to do after all."

Still, she remained so confident of retaining the public's interest that she wrote instructions into her will for her executors to appoint an official biographer. He was to be paid up to $14,000 plus research expenses, plus royalties on sales, to present her to the world as she wished to be remembered.

She died only days before her eighty-fifth birthday in May 1964. A few months earlier she was interviewed on a television show and was still able to summon her old spirit and scorn for an answer to the question "Do you believe in God?"

"I think that question's an insult," replied Lady Astor with considerable heat. "Do you think I'm a half-wit?"

9

The Man Who Gave the Money Away

"This was the finest friendship I ever had in my life. I knew that if I ever needed anything, Vincent would give me the shirt off his back."

"Difficult . . . that's the first word that comes to mind when I think of Vincent."

"The first year I worked for Captain Astor was the happiest of my life."

"He was not very bright."

"He was a most intelligent man. Make no mistake about that."

"He was a vicious, evil man."

"I was very fond of Vincent. He had a nice side, a kindly side."

"What can I tell you about Vincent? He got married, divorced, and he sometimes drank too much."

"When he wanted to, he could be as attractive as any man I ever knew."

"A weekend with Vincent was like staying with a dinosaur."

Which of the Vincent Astors described in these conflicting statements, each made by an individual who knew him well, was the real Vincent Astor? He presented a different face to every person. For each kind action reported by one friend, there is a slight described by someone else.

Vincent is dead now, and the true measure of the man must be taken out of the mass of contradictory evidence. One fact emerges: the true Vincent had a personality larger than life, with both the good and the bad in him exaggerated to an extent beyond the normal. It was a difficult character to begin with—the heritage of an Astor father and a temperamental Willing mother—and the possession of so great a fortune intensified every unreasonable trait.

"It is hard to be rich," remarks an intimate of his late years. "His friends were wealthy, but not on the same level. People tended to want something from him. No matter how wealthy, they welcomed a free six-month trip on his yacht or an investment in their business enterprises or political campaigns. It makes a man suspicious. What could his relatives do right? If they ignored him, that was wrong. If they were nice to him, were they after something in his will?"

Vincent's dark view of humanity was deepened by the unhappiness and coldness that marred his early life. Son of the loveless marriage of Ava and John Jacob Astor IV, Vincent realized early in life that his mother could hardly bear the sight of him. Possibly as a result of this rejection, Vincent worshiped his similarly rejected father. Colonel Astor loved the boy in his inarticulate way but really had no idea how to bring up a child. Until he was twelve, Vincent was left primarily in the care of first an Irish nurse and then a German governess, and a male tutor. It was indeed the "poor little rich boy" story down to the detail of his parents considering very few children well bred enough to be acceptable as playmates. He was to all intents and purposes an only child, because his sister Alice was not born until he was ten and was whisked off to Europe by their mother a few years later. His father, despite the warmth shown him by *the* Mrs. Astor in his own childhood, frequently assumed the role of rigid disciplinarian. When Vincent did not live up to his strict code of behavior, he hit the boy with a shoe or a strap or sent him to bed with a glass of milk instead of dinner. Such severity was alternated with excessive leniency. The boy was sickly, and tuberculosis was feared, so Colonel Astor several times put aside his business responsibilities and accompanied Vincent to St. Moritz in Switzerland. On Vincent's eleventh birthday, his father gave him the present for the boy who has everything: permission to drive a car alone around the estate at Rhinebeck. When Vincent entered St. George's School in Newport, the other side of John Jacob's nature took over, and the boy was given the miserly allowance of fifty cents a week, to be cut to thirty-five cents if his marks were low or his behavior poor. To assist him in maintaining suitable grades, the late news commentator H. V. Kaltenborn, then a young newspaperman, was employed as tutor.

When he was eighteen his parents were finally divorced, and he stood beside his father on the receiving line at the ball at which John made his second debut into society. By then Vincent, as his mother had foreseen, had grown up to look like an "elongated Neanderthal man," according to the unkind comment of a contemporary. The thin, hollow-chested six-foot-four-inch body was topped by a head with the same strangely receding forehead that spoiled his father's appearance, and he had a protruding upper lip. He walked with his large feet turned out, which, he used to joke, gave him a feeling of kinship with penguins, and he adopted them as his mascot and trademark. His speech was rapid, but rather indistinct, sounding as if he had not quite swallowed something.

While his father went on to make his second marriage to a contemporary of Vincent's, the son entered Harvard. Already fascinated by the sea, as he was to be all his life, he wanted to go to Annapolis, but dictatorial John Jacob IV would not hear of it. At Harvard he studied physics and had his first taste of the life that was waiting for a rich young heir, even one whose father kept him on a very tight budget string. During his Christmas vacation he came to New York and, like thousands of other young men of his generation, fell madly in love with beautiful, blonde Ina Claire, then starring in *The Quaker Girl*. But, of course, he was not like thousands of others of his contemporaries. Miss Claire, although she said he was a mere boy and could not be taken seriously, nonetheless went out with him several times.

The gay undergraduate life came to an abrupt end on the April night in 1912 when his father died on the *Titanic*. The avid reporters gathering at the White Star Line office the following morning watched Vincent come out weeping. The loss of his father was a terrible blow to Vincent, and he never quite got over it. When the dead John Jacob was recovered from the sea, Vincent took the gold watch from the body and wore it all his life. But to an Astor, a father's death was more than just a personal matter. It catapulted Vincent into a position with responsibilities that were far too great for a young man of twenty. The strain did much to mold his character. His mother rushed to his side, but their relations had never been such as to allow him to fall under her sway. There was too much bitterness on his part. Even years later, when she was old, he could not always bring himself to spend Christmas with her. As for his stepmother, she was no older than he and a rather giddy girl at that.

"He has an income of $10,000 a day and can't afford to go to college," wrote *Current Opinion*. But the magazine and almost everyone else had scant sympathy for the inheritor of $69 million. His plight was hardly one to rend the heart.

As the first of the Astors to come into his father's fortune outright, Vincent's youth was cut short. He reacted to this by retaining a childish streak all his life. Twenty years later a friend who was asked how Vincent spent his spare time replied in perfect seriousness: "He liked to play with his model trains. He spent hours and hours with them." A perfect model of a steam train, three feet long and running on a quarter mile of tracks, was built to his specifications at Ferncliff. Each car was large and solid enough to hold his weight. His pleasure in this childlike hobby never deserted him. Regardless of his age, immature antics were alternated with sober, considered statements and actions. After having inherited thirty cars from his father, he promptly bought a $6,000 racer that could go one hundred miles per hour. (The memory of this extravagant purchase did not temper his scorn twenty-one years later when his half-brother, John Jacob VI, celebrated the coming of age by buying ten cars.) A poor and reckless driver, Vincent was arrested for speeding any number of times and was in several accidents. In Newport he crashed into Mrs. Ogden Goelet's car, which caused quite a stir in his social set. Yet, he had an earnest, almost sophomoric desire to "do good" with his money, saying and believing, "It is my duty to show my gratitude now by taking an interest in great public movements and in every way to attempt to aid mankind."

His efforts to do so swung wildly between the worthwhile and the naïve. He ordered a playground built on a Harlem block valued at one million dollars, invited slum mothers and children to go on boatrides, founded a home for emotionally disturbed underprivileged children at Rhinebeck as a memorial to his father, raised the salaries of the employees at Ferncliff, urged a group fighting anti-Semitism in Rumania to use his name, and established agencies to help immigrants. His anti-vice crusade, though, was almost simple-minded, conducted by means of ringing doorbells in his dilapidated West Side tenements to determine whether brothels were being run there. He declared virtuously that he could not accept tainted rent money. The net result, as anyone with more experience of the world might have told him, was zero. He drew an almost complete blank when it came to uncovering vice, and honest tenants complained mightily about the invasion of their privacy.

The example of marital lack of bliss that he had seen as a child did not discourage Vincent from marrying as quickly as possible. Helen Dinsmore Huntington lived near the Astor estate, Ferncliff, and Vincent had known her all his life. As has been true of most Astor wives, she has a long and distinguished American heritage, being descended from Samuel Huntington, a signer of the Declaration of Independence, and Alvin Adams, founder of the Adams Express Company. Helen was a tall, statuesque ash blonde with cool good looks, perfect grooming, and great poise. Intensely interested in music—an interest Vincent did not share—she played the piano well. Her manner was a trifle stiff, concealing a great deal of warmth and kindness.

Typical of the mixed feelings Vincent always aroused in those around him is a brief exchange held recently with a relative. "I always rather liked Vincent." That was a pleasant enough statement, but it was followed a moment or two later with the inconsistent: "I wonder why those nice women married him."

At the time of his first marriage to nice Helen in 1914, he was ill; indeed, this big, gangling man was far from robust in his youth and found it hard to throw off the aftereffects of injuries incurred in a motorcycle accident. Always happiest at sea, he recovered sufficiently to enjoy a honeymoon trip aboard his yacht.

During World War I he offered the yacht to the government and, encouraged by his friend, neighbor, and distant relative, Assistant Secretary of the Navy Franklin Delano Roosevelt, tried to persuade other yacht owners to do the same. Financially he contributed two million dollars to the Liberty Loan and personally joined the navy and served first in France and then, to his joy, at sea, rising from ensign to the rank of lieutenant. Helen, never one to sit at home, followed him to France and became the YMCA's woman chief for the Bordeaux district.

With all this war effort, it later came as quite a shock to Vincent when Senator Gerald Nye's munitions committee accused him of having profited financially from the war. He denied furiously having had any connection with companies making war supplies. But the charge itself embittered him and increased his feeling that money was a burden. In time he was to become a strange, moody man who carried his millions as if they were a heavy weight on his back, while—and here is the contradiction in the man—demanding the obeisance and admiration that they brought him.

Even in his young days, Astor took his position as head of the family with great seriousness and was intensely irritated by his stepmother's behavior. One day Madeleine went shopping for her infant son and came home with an ermine wrapper and muff that cost her $230. John Jacob VI was an adorable baby, according to the evidence of old photographs and his mother was so taken with his appearance in his furs that she ran out and bought him a matching little ermine robe for $185. As he grew a little bigger, she added a larger mink coverlet for $580. By the time he was three, Madeleine had run through nearly $6,000 on just his clothes and toys. The result was that she went to court to ask for an increase in her income; she simply could not manage on $25,000 a year. The judge was unsympathetic and refused; her stepson, in charge of the trust funds left by his father, was unsympathetic and annoyed. An older man might have been better able to understand her silly extravagance, but Vincent only found it infuriating. He was also too young to think that his baby half-brother was cute. Both mother and son were unwelcome reminders to him of his dignified and respected father's rather undignified second marriage to someone more suited in age to be Vincent's bride. Vincent, of course, would never have married so frivolous a girl.

It was particularly irksome to him to have any question raised as to the justice of his having received his father's fortune, while his half-brother, every bit as much an Astor, had but a three-million-dollar trust fund. Madeleine and in time John Jacob VI and their friends insisted that John Jacob IV had intended to alter the will upon his return to the United States and to give the expected child a larger share. Any plans, if such there were, went down on the *Titanic*, and Vincent took violent exception, as was certainly natural, to any suggestion that he give his half-brother more than the will required. It was just as natural for John Jacob VI to take violent exception to his not doing so. "He had the legal, but not the moral right to keep all the money," says John. Madeleine soon lost interest in the problem. Extravagant she may have been, but never money-mad, and Madeleine soon renounced her five-million-dollar Astor life trust and the magnificent house at 840 Fifth Avenue in order to marry William L. Dick.

Restored to the possession of Vincent and Helen, whom lady magazine writers were describing in gushing terms as "America's Number One Family," *the* Mrs. Astor's old home again became a center for New York society. Each January, on the anniversary of her famous ball, the art gallery–ballroom was filled with the children and grandchildren of those debutantes and dowagers of the 1890's who had looked so hopefully toward the throne. *The* Mrs. Astor's throne was gone, but the house was basically the same. Its vastness and old-fashioned magnificence were such that they had quite swallowed up the alterations made by John Jacob IV. The enormous rooms were still crammed with a museum's worth of paintings, marble sculptures, tapestries, ornaments, gilt, marble, and paneling, all in the spirit of *the* Mrs. Astor's ponderous formal era. Thomas Hade, who had been in charge of Caroline's menage, was still much in evidence, white-haired now, but the keen eyes behind his sparkling pince-nez missed no household lapse. Of a breed already then almost extinct, Hade could handle the Vincent Astors' regular house staff of twenty domestics as well as the extras brought in for parties. Inexperienced servants were transformed into impeccable maids under his training. The food at the balls was as superb as it had ever been, the service faultless, the music delightful, but everything was different. Hade was well aware of this; the only slip he ever permitted himself was an occasional regretful murmur about the way *the* Mrs. Astor used to do things. It was the people who had changed, of course. This was a period of revolt against the rigidity of Victorian social life. Why, Helen and Vincent went so far as to run the January ball as a charity benefit. Their guest lists regularly included celebrities, actors, Catholics—any number of people who would never have passed McAllister's scrutiny. And they had far less of a sense of formality than their grandparents. There was actually to come a day when flamboyant, imaginative, fun-loving Elsa Maxwell was to arrange some parties for the Astors. Vincent really took little pleasure in parties, however lively.

"It is pretty hard now to get me to many formal functions," said Helen as early as 1920, "but it is infinitely harder to get my husband. In the evenings he wants to hear real talk and see real people."

At that period she told a reporter firmly that she did not think a woman should devote much time to her clothes. Refusing *the* Mrs. Astor's diamond-studded splendor, she remarked that she would not spend several hundred dollars for any dress. She had far more pleasure from a little suit made for her by workers at the Women's Exchange in Rhinebeck.

For all her husband's theoretical dislike of formality, he was virtually dependent upon servants. As a boy he had been unconditionally forbidden to make any demands on servants. Human nature being what it is, this had produced a man who could hardly make a move unaided. If he wanted a highball, he had to call for help. One day when his valet Jepson was sick, Vincent found it impossible to get dressed until nearly noon. He had not the slightest idea of where to find his socks, high collars, white shirts, dark conservative business suits, or ties. At one weekend house party where he had been asked not to bring a valet, Vincent appeared at breakfast without his shoes. He had not been able to get the trees out of them, he remarked sourly. As Vincent's early-morning bad temper was legendary, none of his fellow guests had the courage to laugh.

Luckily Jepson usually went with him as he traversed the typical timeworn Astor circuit of New York, Ferncliff, and Newport. Ferncliff, where he is now buried, is the place he loved best, and he came as close to being lord of the manor there as it is possible for an American to be. Determined to be an influence for good in the community, he was horrified one night to look through the windows and see in the distance the ghostlike figures of Klansmen lighting a fiery cross. Without hesitation he ran into the midst of the hysterical group, stamped out the fire, and told everyone to go home. His dignity was such that they did.

In Newport, Vincent and Helen had inherited Beechwood and the social reputation of his doughty grandmother. Despite the passing of *the* Mrs. Astor and Ward McAllister, Newport remained the personal preserve of the very, very rich. Each morning the Astors, Vanderbilts, Goelets, Van Alens, and Bruguières gathered on Bailey's Beach to swim and talk, almost secure from the glittering eyes of the *nouveaux riches*. Ladies lunching at the Casino still furnished a fashion show, and the dowagers continued to go driving in the afternoons. Vincent and Helen joined the younger set at golf or tennis. In the late afternoon, instead of the cocktails popular elsewhere—Newport has never recognized the cocktail hour officially—bridge was the relaxation of choice. Easily bored, Vincent refused to join in the games. Almost every night the elite met at parties in the cottages or in marquees set up on the grounds. In a number of homes dinner was served by servants in livery (for that matter, these costumes are worn in the homes of some of the older ladies to this day). Vincent, along with many of the other Newport gentlemen, kept his yacht anchored and ready to carry him off to New York or on a cruise any time business or boredom demanded. In this he was following the example of his grandfather, that seagoing fugitive from *the* Mrs. Astor.

But if the pattern of life was in its broad aspects the same as it had always been for the Astors, the estate itself was changing. At long last the Astor motto that had survived a century—"Never sell land"—was relegated to the grave of its originator, as Vincent sold, sold, and sold again. In just about a decade, he disposed of roughly half of the sixty-three million dollars' worth of real estate he had inherited, realizing some forty million dollars.

His sales philosophy was expressed in a new Astor motto, an early business associate recalls: "By the time the public thinks a thing is good, it isn't good any more." In an effort to stay ahead of the public, he sold the Schermerhorn Building for $1.5 million, the Longacre Building on Times Square for $2.4 million, and the land where the Paramount Building was to be built for nearly $4 million. And at last, one hundred years after the site came into the family, Vincent and his English cousins agreed to sell the Waldorf-Astoria Hotel, to Boldt's successor, Lucius Boomer, and Coleman du Pont. Each branch of the family received $7,560,000 in payment for land that had seemed overpriced when William B. Astor had bought it for $25,000. The new owners operated the Waldorf-Astoria for a mere four years and then resold it at a tidy profit, so that the Empire State Building could be erected in its place. The wreckers moved in and demolished the splendid old hotel. An auction of furnishings was held, and sandwiches were sold for twenty cents apiece in the Palm Garden where Boldt had once dreamed of serving *the* Mrs. Astor an "unprofitable cup of water." It was the end of an era, though some said the handwriting had been on the wall for twenty years, ever since "Bet-a-Million" Gates had switched his all-night poker games to the Plaza. The Astor connection with the hotel was broken, but the name lived on, sold to shrewd, foresighted Lucius Boomer for one dollar. He used it to the advantage of the hotel that now stands on Park Avenue.

Doing his best to break with family tradition, Vincent tried, and almost succeeded, in getting out of the hotel business altogether. Prohibition was reducing the profits of the Knickerbocker Hotel's bar, known to drinkers as the "42nd Street Country Club." This was one of the factors leading Vincent to decide to have the hotel made into an office building. Astor, who was a great worrier when it came to details, was faced with the knotty problem of what to do with the Maxfield Parrish painting of "Old King Cole," which had hung over the bar. Many drinkers were sentimentally attached to it. The picture was ultimately to find a home at the St. Regis, but at that time Vincent was arranging to sell the St. Regis, too, so he dispatched the painting to the Racquet and Tennis Club.

Despite the sell policy, the Astor hold on New York real estate, though dwindling, was not yet at an end. Vincent added to as well as subtracted from the total. He built the Astor Court apartments on Broadway between Eighty-ninth and Ninetieth Streets, near the Belnord and Apthorp apartments put up by his English relatives —all three on land bought by the aging William B. Astor in 1860 for less than $17,000. Swinging way over to what was then still the unfashionable part of the East Side, he purchased land along

Eighty-sixth Street between Avenues A and B (later York and East End Avenues). In the Bronx he owned the Astor Concourse of low-priced apartment houses and on Long Island purchased some three hundred acres and put up beach houses, tennis courts, and bridle paths.

Vincent, at twenty-eight, was already a director of such leviathans as Western Union, American Express, Illinois Central and Great Northern Railroads. It was quite enough to give a man a touch of megalomania. He invested in a great many companies, but confessed that his favorite was the Roosevelt Steamship Company, which became the basis of the International Mercantile Marine. (This was the company in which he made his single attempt to get his half-brother, John, a job.) "Shipping is about the only business that's still got romance in it," declared Vincent boyishly.

Particularly when young, he was able to leave his business worries in the office, never discussing them with Helen in the evenings. He sought change and relaxation, and like millions of less wealthy Americans, he was a devoted listener to the "Amos 'n Andy" radio show. A friend telephoned a few minutes after seven o'clock one evening and was told by the butler that Vincent was out but would be back at seven-fifteen. After the same thing had happened to him on several occasions, he asked Astor just where it was that he went at that time each night. Vincent laughed and admitted that he was really at home—he even changed business appointments in order to be there—listening to Amos 'n Andy. Once the program was over, dinner could be served. The balance of the evening was spent drinking, talking, and playing chess with his few close friends. Unlike the generations of taciturn male Astors who preceded him, he was a good conversationalist. A heavy smoker, he went through one cigar after another all day long and then shifted to a corncob pipe in the evening. The arts and music had little place in his leisure, despite the fact that they were his wife's consuming interest. A vital force in the musical life of New York City, she was one of the founders and is to this day a chief supporter of the Musicians' Emergency Fund. Helen also served as director of the New York Philharmonic Symphony Society and Metropolitan Opera Association. When the New York City Center of Music and Drama was established some years afterwards, she was one of the incorporators. "She devotes almost all her time to music," one of her friends was to say of her later. Her husband, some averred, was tone-deaf.

Still, they respected one another's interests and were careful not to destroy pleasure. Theirs was a live-and-let-live marriage. Helen for some years had a house in Paris where Vincent was seldom seen. He, on the other hand, loved his yacht and often slept aboard while she remained ashore. Because the pitiless light of publicity was always shining on them, as on all Astors, divorce rumors were circulated before they had been married for a decade. Nothing was more calculated to enrage Vincent, who disapproved of divorce as an indication of weak character.

By the mid-1920's, Vincent decided that their Fifth Avenue townhouse, built for his grandmother, was cumbersome and out of date, and so it followed other Astor properties onto the block. Descendants of the first Four Hundred gathered in the ballroom for a farewell ball. As was the way at Astor parties from the earliest days on, the Mayor of New York, this time Jimmy Walker, attended. Vincent's sister Alice was there, too, with the first of her husbands. Prince Serge Obolensky, an old-world charmer whose hold on Vincent's affection outlasted his hold on Alice's. In another city or country, the building would have survived as a landmark, but in New York a building is used and destroyed. *The* Mrs. Astor's last house followed her previous ones into oblivion. The building and land went for $3.5 million to Benjamin Winter, a one-time immigrant peddler, who passed it on to the Temple Emanu-El. This is a fact about which members of Old Guard society, which has not quite outgrown *the* Mrs. Astor's prejudices, shake their meticulously-styled heads.

To replace this home a six-story house in the Georgian style was erected at 130 East Eightieth Street. Although Vincent parted with his grandmother's possessions without a pang, his attachment to his father was sentimental. He ordered that the bedroom of John Jacob IV be reproduced in the new house and that even the fixtures from the old bathroom be transferred. Although modern heating rendered it quite superfluous, the little fireplace that used to warm John Jacob IV in his bath on chilly mornings was reconstructed there, too. Only the bathtub, an oversized marble creation was different. The decorator, who clearly refused to imagine this huge, homely ungainly man in the tub, added the incongruous touch of a little cherub sitting on a shell. Years later when the house was being renovated for the Junior League of New York, workmen were baffled in their attempts to move this enormous tub. Installed before the building had been completed, it was too large to go out through any of the doors. In the end it was simply destroyed, chopped to bits and sold for marble dust. Only the cherub remains, standing in the Junior League garden.

The ultimate fate of this home as a clubhouse is curiously fitting, because Vincent was one of the last of the great clubmen. A diligent reporter in the 1930's ferreted out the fact that he belonged to thirty-eight clubs. They included the Holland Lodge of Masons (which had proved so useful to John Jacob Astor I), Pilgrims, New York Yacht Club (he was its commodore for a time), Knickerbocker, Union, Brook, Tuxedo, Clambake (of Newport), and Travellers (of London). Along with Marshall Field, Clarence H. Mackay, and Harry Payne Whitney, he was a founder of the exclusive Creek Club on Long Island and joined his fellow socialites in allocating more than one million dollars to lay a golf course. The only one of the social clubs that he really liked was the Brook, and for many years he made a practice of dropping in there in the late afternoon. Knowledgeable New Yorkers observed that he often wore the club tie. The Brook had been founded in a tradition of practical joking, which appealed to Vincent. The legend has it that the Brook was begun by two young men-about-town who had been expelled from the Union Club for having cracked an egg on the bald head of a distinguished clubman seated in a big leather armchair reading *The New York Times*. When questioned, the unregenerate pair had remarked ingenuously that they were trying to fry the egg.

It was the sort of thing Vincent might have done himself. The childish streak in his nature found an outlet in practical jokes, and a visit to one of his luxurious homes was as often an ordeal as a delight. Some of his pranks were of the prep school toad-in-the-bed genre, based on such tired routines as the waiter who has been instructed to spill coffee all over a guest or to call him names when asked for service. But being rich, Vincent did not need to limit

Alice Astor, at various times Obolensky, Von Hofmannsthal, Harding, and Pleydell-Bouverie, and always a patroness of the arts.

John Jacob Astor VI and his first wife, the former Ellen Tuck French, after their wedding. Crowds lined the Newport streets to catch a glimpse of the attractive couple; he was 21 and she 18.

Young William Astor plays a duet with Charlotte Fisk shortly before their 1956 marriage.

Cliveden, a social and political center for three generations of Englishmen, today the home of Lord William Waldorf Astor.

John Jacob Astor V, later Baron Astor of Hever. In his old age he had to move to France in order to save his heirs a fortune in death duties.

Lady Nancy Astor takes time off from Parliamentary duties to visit her son Michael at school.

Lady Nancy Langhorne Shaw Astor, whose wit and charm took the Astors, England, and Parliament by storm. (Drawing by W. E. Tittle)

Lord Waldorf Astor, second Viscount, photographed Nov. 28, 1933.

An Astor family group. (Standing, left to right), William Waldorf, Viscount Waldorf Astor, Robert Gould Shaw III (Lady Astor's son by her first marriage); (seated), David, Michael, Lady Nancy Astor, John Jacob VII, and Phyllis. BELOW: Gavin Astor, Publisher of the London *Times*, with his mother, wife and five children.

Lord William Waldorf Astor, the present Viscount, proudly leads his winning horse, Ambiguity, after the Oaks Race at Epsom Downs.

himself to such rudimentary humor, nor did he do so. His elaborate preparations for a joke often began long before the scheduled visit. He would write a scurrilous and suggestive news story, linking the guest's name with a scandalous affair, and would have it printed and inserted into a newspaper as part of the feature section. The guest would then get this special paper on his or her (it got more of a reaction from lady visitors) breakfast tray. On one occasion, when he was told that the intended victim was on her guard, he had a number of false papers printed and circulated among all the neighbors. As a final touch, he asked the nearby newsdealer to put a stack prominently on the stand.

A cruise on Vincent's yacht could be harrowing even for the best of sailors. One well-to-do businessman returned home from such a trip shaken. When the yacht was three days out, a stock market report came through on Vincent's wireless set: the businessman's stocks were collapsing. He tried frantically to reach his broker, but was unsuccessful. He spent the next few days in black despair as each report, worse than the one before, revealed that he was utterly ruined. Back on dry land, he discovered that he had been a victim of one of his host's favorite jokes. Astor had prepared by getting an exact list of his friend's holdings.

Vincent's sense of humor did not extend to his little half-brother, who spent a weekend or two with him each year and always succeeded in annoying him. John Jacob VI remembers those visits as having been rather unpleasant, although Helen did her best to be kind to him. The problem was that Vincent was childless and had lived through a thoroughly unnatural childhood, so he had little idea of how a youngster should behave. His sister Alice had responded to the difficult family situation in her early years by outward obedience that concealed her inner turbulence. ("Oh, Alice always does everything you tell her to," her strict English nannie told one of the other nurses during one of the periods when Alice and Ava were in Ferncliff.) But John simply would not behave in the manner that Vincent considered suitable for an Astor.

For all his intolerance of his half-brother's foibles, he was invariably kind to his strange, disinherited great-uncle Henry.

"Vincent was one of the only relatives to come to visit Henry in his late years," says a cousin. "Henry was so anxious for visitors then; it meant a great deal to him."

Vincent's friendship once given, was both warm and enduring, and it was to the swimming pool at Ferncliff that Franklin Delano Roosevelt came for exercise after his paralyzing attack of poliomyelitis. The two men, with neighboring estates, were firm friends for many years. Coming from the same background—Roosevelt was a great-nephew of the Franklin Delano who had married Laura Astor—they understood one another. Both took for granted wealth and the power that goes with it, and both had a sense of mission. Although Vincent lacked the brilliance, direction, drive, and charm that propelled Roosevelt into the White House, he shared the desire to do something worthwhile with his life.

"It is unreasonable to suppose that because a man is rich, he is also useless," Vincent declared, perhaps a little wistfully.

Vincent, like the rest of the American Astors, lacked the personality for a career in politics and, unlike several of them, had the good judgment not to try for one. He was influenced in this decision by the stage fright that affected him whenever he had to make a speech. One day when Edward Barrett, now head of the Columbia School of Journalism, mentioned that he was on his way to give a talk, Vincent remarked with heartfelt sincerity: "I envy you your calm. There is nothing I dread more than making a speech."

Of course, no Astor could ever be ignored by politicians, and first one political party and then the other tried to convince him that the most useful thing he could do was to devote at least a bit of his riches to them. As a young man, he had been a Republican, following a family allegiance that dated back to the prosperity brought by the Civil War. Vincent contributed to Harding's campaign fund in 1920 and to Coolidge's in 1924. Shortly thereafter he became acquainted with Democratic bigwigs Herbert Lehmann and William H. Woodin, later Secretary of the Treasury, and influenced by their ardor, switched to that party. In 1928 Vincent contributed to Al Smith's campaign for the presidency and his friend Roosevelt's campaign for the New York governorship. By the time Roosevelt was elected President in 1932, Vincent was in that small coterie of intimate friends who supported him and his policies both financially and intellectually.

Roosevelt often joined Vincent on the *Nourmahal*. Showing his "kindly side," Astor had a special ramp built so that Roosevelt's wheelchair could be taken directly on board. The *Nourmahal* was the size of a small ocean liner and could cross the Atlantic in nine days. It had been built in Germany in the late 1920's for about one million dollars, taken in part from profits on an investment in the movie *Ben Hur* and in part from the sale of the previous yacht. Like his father and grandfather before him, Astor always had one. The asking price for the old yacht was $200,000. A potential buyer offered a strange bargain that no one but Vincent would have accepted. This man agreed to take the yacht if Vincent would pay him $5,000 for his orangutan Freda, which he loved but could not care for. This was just the kind of eccentricity that Vincent appreciated, and he took the ape. Its former owner then decided that he did not want a yacht anyway. Vincent kept Freda and she remained at Rhinebeck where she soon became known as "Mrs. Astor's pet orangutan." After four years the delight of having such a pet wore thin and Freda was presented to the Bronx Zoo, where she promptly relieved her keeper of his broom and then turned his hose on him. The new yacht that had indirectly brought her into Vincent's life had three decks, a pine-paneled library, a number of lounges, a walnut-paneled dining room where eighteen people could sit comfortably at table, and an emergency operating room. In order to accommodate his friends, it had eight guest cabins, with private baths, in addition to the master cabin, decorated in beige and scarlet, and Helen's cabin done in Alice blue. With what some described as foresight and others as pessimism, he had gun emplacements put on deck in case of war. Each officer of the forty-two-man crew had his own cabin. Maintenance bills ran to $125,000 a year, because Astor insisted that the crew remain on board and the ship be kept ready for use all year round.

In early February 1932, a month before the inauguration, President-elect Roosevelt took a ten-day vacation trip with Astor aboard the *Nourmahal*. Having Vincent's up-to-date wireless equipment at his disposal, he was not completely cut off from Washington. He kept in constant touch with Raymond Moley, a member of his first Brain Trust, who was forming the Cabinet. Vincent felt himself to be in on the making of history.

On February 15, the *Nourmahal* landed at Miami, Florida, where Roosevelt was to address a political rally. Moley joined them at the yacht and for the first time met Astor. It was the beginning of a lifelong friendship, perhaps the deepest of both their lives. As the procession of cars set off for Bayfront Park, Moley sat with Vincent two cars behind Roosevelt's. When the President-elect, who had been helped to the top of the rear seat of his car, began to address the crowd, Vincent had a sudden premonition of disaster. Many members of the Astor family have considered themselves psychic, and any such feelings have always been taken with great seriousness.

"Why, anyone in the crowd could stand back and shoot Roosevelt!" he exclaimed to Moley.

And at that very moment Giuseppe Zangara, a bricklayer and stonemason who hated all Presidents and had refrained from attacking Herbert Hoover only because he believed the Washington climate would aggravate his stomach trouble, was taking aim at the President-elect. The shots rang out, but Roosevelt had dropped down to his seat at the conclusion of his speech and escaped injury. The scene was bloody, nonetheless, as the bullets fatally wounded Mayor Anton Cermak of Chicago and struck four of the bystanders. Zangara, who never had a chance of escaping, was seized and placed on the trunk rack of the car in which Astor was riding. A policeman held the assassin while another perched on the running board. One of the injured men was put inside the car. Vincent held his head, put a cigarette in his mouth, and tried to soothe him. The wounded man responded to the crisis in very human fashion by muttering over and over that his wife would not be able to get home, because the keys to the car were in his pocket. When they finally arrived at the hospital, they met Roosevelt coming out. Vincent thought that the future President appeared shaken and suggested that he and Moley come back to spend the night quietly on the *Nourmahal*.

After Roosevelt's inauguration, his bold and far-reaching program was swiftly put into effect. In dizzying succession came the Bank Holiday, the gold embargo, the creation of the Civilian Conservation Corps, the beginnings of public works programs and farm relief, the creation of the Tennessee Valley Authority, passage of the National Recovery Act, and the abandonment of the gold standard. And Vincent was there on the inside, close to the President, a trusted friend. He was an intimate of the leaders of his country, just as on the other side of the Atlantic, his English relatives were close to the policy makers of Europe.

Vincent, as was his nature, wanted to take a more active part in the national life and thought to emulate the British Astors and purchase a newspaper. At that time W. Averill Harriman and his sister, Mrs. Mary Rumsey, were also in the market for a news property and had asked Raymond Moley, then Assistant Secretary of State, if he would edit whatever publication they bought. Although Harriman was also a member of the Astor-Roosevelt social set and came from the same background of wealth and privilege, he and Astor never liked one another. And once Vincent took a dislike to anyone, he became impossible to deal with. "No one could be more charming if he liked you," remembers another member of that set, "or more unattractive if he did not." Still it seemed the wise move for them to consolidate their efforts, and the Harrimans' choice of Moley as editor was the very thing to win Vincent over. Moley was the type of person whom Astor admired—a gentleman, urbane, well-spoken, intellectual, intelligent, hard-working, and the intimate of great men. He was also intransigent and unwilling to make any compromise with principle. Being fond of Moley, Vincent showed only his charming side.

"I heard other people complain that Vincent was a tough man," says Moley, "but never to me."

In fact, Moley had the distinction of being the only person whom Astor could endure seeing in the early morning, a time of day when he hated the whole world.

After failing in a bid for the Washington *Post*, the prospective publishers decided to create a news medium instead of buying one. They would start a weekly news magazine to compete with Henry Luce's ten-year-old *Time* and Thomas J. C. Martyn's newborn *News-Week*. When they told Roosevelt about their plans, he said he would be their first subscriber and gave them one dollar on the spot. The Harrimans agreed to put up $125,000 apiece, Vincent matched them with $250,000, and the first issue of *Today* appeared in October 1933. The publishing triumverate was not to rule for long. On a cold December day of the following year dynamic Mary Rumsey went riding. Her horse threw her and she was killed. Vincent, who had never liked being only co-equal owner, took over Mary's share in the enterprise and became the dominant partner.

Although Roosevelt was its first subscriber, *Today* was not for long a supporter of his policies. Moley broke with Roosevelt early, resigning from the Cabinet and leaving the Brain Trust, and he criticized the Administration vigorously in the magazine. Vincent was one of Roosevelt's close friends, but true to the tradition of his British cousin, John Jacob V, he never meddled with the policies of his editors. In 1935 Astor urged Roosevelt to take a vacation on his yacht, pointing out that the *Nourmahal* was always in condition to take off at a moment's notice. Roosevelt then came back with the famous pronouncement that if the rich could afford such unnecessary extravagance, perhaps it was time to "soak the rich." Although the "Soak the Rich" tax program offended Vincent financially, contrary to most reports, the two men remained on good terms personally. Vincent was always intensely loyal to the few people he really liked.

"People say that I broke up Vincent's friendship with Roosevelt," remarks Moley, "but it's not true. They remained friends until Roosevelt's death, although they disagreed on most things. Whatever their differences, Vincent voted for Roosevelt all four times, though I voted against him three times."

The magazine reflected Moley's, rather than Vincent's, view, in any event. In 1937 *News-Week*, in serious financial trouble, was bought and merged with *Today*. The name of the latter was thereupon scrapped, and the former lost its hyphen. To handle the new combined magazine, Malcolm Muir, president of the McGraw-Hill Company, was asked to come in as editor, and Moley was named as contributing editor. Muir had his doubts about getting involved in a magazine that might just be a rich man's plaything, but Moley reassured him about Astor's sincerity and intentions. It was fortunate for the publication that Vincent was both rich and interested. Never one to accept failure, he funneled hundreds of thousands upon hundreds of thousands of dollars into the magazine as it struggled to survive the economic pressures of the depression. In the nine years that it took *Newsweek* to break out of the red, Vincent put five million dollars into it.

Moley, friend as well as editor, was drawn into the second of Astor's pet possessions, the St. Regis. The hotel had been sold to Benjamin N. Duke in 1929, but Vincent had retained a five-million-dollar mortgage. The new owner was unable to carry the St. Regis through the black years of the depression, and in 1934 it went into receivership. A judge appointed Moley as the receiver; Astor foreclosed the mortgage, and, after a celebrated court fight over the furnishings, the hotel was his again. Moley lived there for fourteen years, at which point Astor arranged for a rent-free apartment in one of his luxury buildings.

Vincent could not do enough for those people he really liked. Serge Obolensky, by then divorced from Alice, never forfeited Astor's good opinion—Vincent blamed Alice for the breakup—and was called in to serve as what Obolensky himself described as "sort of general consultant, promotion man, and trouble-shooter" for the St. Regis. Serge did a superlative job, and a long and brilliant career in the hotel business was launched.

Still, where Vincent left the editors of *Newsweek* free, he supervised every detail of the management of the St. Regis himself. He threw himself into the planning with boyish enthusiasm, as if it were a new toy to add to his model trains. Vincent's friends were buttonholed and earnestly asked what kind of mustard they liked and how thick should a slice of roast beef be. Members of the staff were sent to the great hotels of Europe—the Claridge in London, the Ritz in Paris—to learn from their example. Those hotels, it was found, excel in the receiving and handling of each guest as an individual and learning his tastes. The St. Regis version of this led to the O.G. (Old Guest) cards kept on file with facts about each guest carefully listed.

Astor went to the St. Regis almost every day when he was in New York. The bartender knew his preference for martinis, with an occasional switch to rum or scotch. The chef was most often asked to prepare fish *sauté meunière* or in a white wine sauce for this lover of the sea. Vincent appreciated good food, although he never ate heavily. The same table was reserved for him in the Oak Room every day, but he was far too practical to let it stay empty if he was not going to be there. He would telephone the headwaiter before the lunchtime rush and tell him to give the place to someone else.

And as always, when involved with something or someone he liked, he displayed his best side at the St. Regis. "He was a great gentleman, treating every bellboy as an equal, every maid as a lady," says Pierre Bultinck, who managed the hotel for him for seventeen years. "Captain Astor had no children. The St. Regis was his baby; he loved it."

During the 1930's Vincent gave almost the same kind of loving care to the luxury apartments he owned. "He worried about the garbage disposal and the elevator service," recalls a business associate. "Even the doorman had to be just right. If the tenants of a building were settled and dignified, he would insist that an elderly, distinguished-looking man be hired. If the tenants were young and gay, he felt a man-of-the-world type was needed."

He kept an apartment and office for himself at 120 East End Avenue, which was close to the original site of the Hellgate estate of John Jacob I (taking changes in topography into consideration). Rents in this building ranged from $4,000 a year for a small apartment to $25,000 for twenty-three rooms. And even in the depths of the depression, it was four fifths rented, with vacancies in the cheaper apartments only. In order to improve the neighborhood, Vincent bought up those nearby tenements that he did not already own. They were renovated under the supervision of Serge Obolensky, who named one group of these "Poverty Row" and the other "Busted Row." Apartments rented for $40 to $100 a month, and tenants were carefully screened. For one year, they included Obolensky himself.

The era when the name Astor was synonymous with physical neglect of property was over. The watchword of his forebears, "Let others improve," was anathema to Vincent, and he tried to improve his holdings. Along with this change came another and more basic one: the tenements that had brought wealth to his father, grandfather, and great-grandfather at last passed out of Astor hands. During the administration of New York's battling mayor Fiorello H. La Guardia, slum clearance became more than an election slogan, and a Tenement House Department was established in the New York Housing Authority. There were fires in the slums as always, of course, and attacks in the press, this time led by Ernest Gruening, editor of the New York *Evening Post*. Vincent was not impervious to public opinion, as some of his ancestors had been, and was not planning to quit the country as William Waldorf had done. Possessed of a desire to do good, he had objected to "tainted" rent money when he was little more than a boy. And so Astor decided to offer the bulk of his remaining tenements to the Housing Authority, telling the Commissioner to "write his own ticket as to the price to be paid." The ticket was written at $189,281, which was considerably less than the assessed valuation of the land alone. The buildings were in such terrible condition, though, that a third of them had to be torn down, and the rest were rebuilt, and a municipal housing project constructed. Astor sold some of his property, improved other parts of it, and as his forebears might have warned him, he was "landlord of New York" no more.

This was not so important to him as it had been to his ancestors, for it was becoming clear that one branch of the Astor dynasty was coming to an end with Vincent. He had no children, nor was he to have any. When his sister had divorced Obolensky, Astor had asked if he could adopt their son Ivan, but they refused. He seldom thereafter spoke of his own childlessness. His half-brother believes that Vincent was sensitive on the subject and that their relationship, always bad, to be sure, grew even worse when at the age of twenty-two John Jacob VI became a father. The son, who is grown up now, reports that not once in his life did he ever meet his uncle.

The lack of an heir did not lead Astor to treat his business responsibilities in a cavalier way, but they were never his whole life, as they had been for earlier generations of Astors. He was not happy as a businessman, believing that he could have had a fuller life as a scientist, continuing the studies begun at Harvard, or as a marine engineer. His business manager, Hoyt Ammidon, once wrote him about a new kind of helicopter developed by a company he was thinking of acquiring. Astor sent back a ten-page letter in longhand discussing the scientific principles involved in the invention of this type of aircraft; he completely ignored the question of whether it would be a good investment. Business was a duty, not a pleasure. The only thing that brought him lasting joy was his yacht.

"The sea was the great love of his life," according to one of the people who knew him best. "Whatever else is said about Vincent, that cannot be left out. The only books he really liked were sea stories or naval histories. He knew the name and the size and the build of every ship afloat in the Navy anywhere and could describe any vessel listed in Jane's *Fighting Ships*."

Several months of every year were spent cruising the waters of the world on the *Nourmahal*. He often combined his greatest pleasure, the life at sea, with his dream of making at least a small mark as a scientist. Many of the cruises became scientific expeditions, and the staterooms of his huge yacht housed some of the country's leading botanists, ornithologists, and marine experts. With their guidance, he collected specimens of rare fish off the Galápagos Islands and presented them to the government aquarium at Bermuda, found rare spineless cactus, which were planted in Panama, and gathered unusual forms of sea plants and animals in the Fiji Islands. Switching from the serious to the absurd, he had a typical rich man's fancy of stocking the waters off Bermuda, where he had a large vacation home, with Newport lobsters. Thirty-six parent lobsters were installed in special tanks, and the *Nourmahal* set off on its journey; unfortunately, the creatures died in the heat while the yacht was cruising through the Gulf Stream.

With Helen an unenthusiastic yachtswoman—she found it hard, she said, to stay away from New York and the music that meant so much to her—Vincent often invited not only scientists but also large parties of friends to cruise with him. Serge Obolensky was asked to come along on the second of the voyages to the Galápagos, a mark of favor calculated to show Vincent's extreme disapproval of the divorce his sister had insisted upon. His own future was not yet apparent to him, even though another guest on that cruise was gay, high-spirited Mary Benedict "Minnie" Cushing. She was the oldest of the extremely marriageable and marrying Cushing sisters, daughters of famous brain surgeon Harvey Cushing. Betsey, the first married, to James Roosevelt, was also the first divorced, and went on to marry John Hay Whitney. Barbara, after nearly bringing romantic Serge Obolensky to the altar, married first Stanley G. Mortimer, Jr., and then William S. Paley. Vincent met Minnie at a dinner party at the Roosevelts during the period of Betsey's reign as Mrs. James Roosevelt. Minnie, a nice-looking young woman in her mid-twenties, was bright, alert, and possessed of a driving energy. Vincent was impressed with her and offered her the supreme compliment of a trip on the *Nourmahal*.

The expedition, in addition to collecting wild life, had the wholly superfluous (for Astor) additional goal of searching for buried treasure. Although it is hard to conceive of what Vincent might have done with any more money, he was, like any school- boy excited by the idea of finding a pirate treasure that was ru- mored to lie beneath the sands of Cocos Island. The *Nourmahal* arrived there, and the Astor party found itself in competition with a poor and far more desperate group of treasure hunters. Tempers became so explosive that the Costa Rican government sent soldiers to the island to prevent bloodshed—and obtain a share of the booty—if anyone found the buried hoard. Astor, always sure that he was right, was convinced he had located the general area of the cache, but neither he, nor Obolensky, nor Minnie, nor any of the other treasure-seeking yachtsmen or women was able to uncover the pirates' gold.

Over the next few years Minnie was often a guest aboard the *Nourmahal*. And in time Vincent realized that he had fallen in love with her. The problem of what to do about it was particularly difficult for him. He did not want to hurt Helen, to whom he had been married for more than a quarter of a century. Their rela- tionship had always puzzled outside observers, who made much of their frequent separations, totally different interests, and, above all, childlessness. And yet, in their own way, Vincent and Helen were very attached to one another. The durability of their rela- tionship was such that it had stiffened Vincent in his opposition to divorce as a matter of principle. In this he was every bit as unyield- ing as his ancient relative, Margaret Chanler Aldrich, whom he used to visit regularly.

But he was only human, and although he still considered divorce reprehensible for other people, he believed that the force of his emotion made him a logical exception to his rule. He asked Helen for a divorce. She went to Wyoming, where she spent the requisite amount of time on a dude ranch, and sued for divorce on the polite grounds of "mental cruelty." Mrs. Aldrich, unmoved by Vincent's passion, saw no reason for changing her opinion and refused to see him any more.

Because Astor hated publicity, the marriage was kept a secret from the press until after the ceremony. Minnie, revealing that streak of practicality observed only in the very rich, wore the same dress for the wedding that had seen service a year earlier at the marriage of her youngest sister Barbara. It was a woollen dress of American Beauty red, and with it she wore prune-colored shoes and a prune-colored Lily Daché hat with a wine-red veil (if *The New York Times* society page of September 28, 1940, can be believed about these implausible color combinations). Minnie, at thirty-four, was fourteen years younger than her husband. The surprise guest at the wedding was the groom's mother, Ava Ribblesdale, still able to dominate the room and make all the other women clutch their husbands nervously. After the ceremony the newlyweds retired to the *Nourmahal*, enjoying the fact that the crew did not yet know that they were married.

When Helen married again, it was to a longtime member of Vincent's set, real-estate broker Lytle Hull. To the surprise of those who knew them only slightly they all remained friends. And when Hull years later became ill, Astor came to see him every day, always bringing some little gift that would amuse him. Vincent's feeling for Helen was curiously unchanged by their legal parting, and he never got out of the habit of sharing his life with her.

"Whenever anything important or exciting happened to him," says a friend, "he would rush to call her or see her."

She was in a sense his family, because he could not get along with his mother, and with typical unreasonableness, he had never forgiven his sister for her divorce. As for John Jacob VI, the complete break between the half-brothers took place in 1940. In later years, when they would see one another on the street, they would walk on without speaking.

World War II took him from the side of his second wife only a year after their marriage. The outbreak of hostilities did not surprise him; he had been expecting it since 1928, when he had ordered the gun emplacements for the deck of his new yacht. He immediately offered the *Nourmahal* to the government. Although Astor was by then close to fifty, he was always a great patriot (his vote for Roosevelt during the last presidential campaign had been, he said, based on his belief that a strong leader was needed in a war-torn world) and sought active service. A captain in the Naval Reserve, he was made a convoy commodore and assigned to bring war material to Europe and wounded men back. Minnie, sharing his life as best she could, joined in the work of the Navy Relief Society and a variety of other wartime organizations. Her natural gaiety and energy were put to good use in organizing parties for ships' crews on leave in New York.

Vincent's rank of captain in the navy remained his greatest source of pride long after the war, and all business associates were careful to address him as "Captain." At one time, when spending a few days in Maine, Astor was enraged that the doorman at the hotel persisted in greeting him as "Colonel." He was not at all soothed when old New England hands told him that the doorman had meant to be flattering. In Maine, anyone who owns a dinghy is a captain; colonels, on the other hand, are rare.

He never asked for or got the *Nourmahal* back after the War. His friends, noting his increasing gloominess as he grew older, urged him to buy another yacht, perhaps a smaller one, but he never did. The *Nourmahal* and his happiness with it belonged to another period of his life; it was over and there was no going back. He bought himself an airplane, but clearly never considered it a substitute.

While Vincent was away in the navy, the old office on West Twenty-sixth Street that had been the home away from home for generations of Astors was purchased by Frederick Vanderbilt Field for $30,000. Sold again in 1957, the office was then rented to the Communist Party. Commented the Party's administrative secretary, "It's considerably less than we paid for our old offices at 101 West 16 Street." Had John Jacob I been alive, he would have been relieved to learn that at least it was not in Astor hands; to be accused of charging a lower rent than some other landlord would have been unendurable.

As he grew older, Vincent was so atypical an Astor that he took to thinking deeply about charity. The Astor Home for Children in

Rhinebeck, founded thirty years earlier in memory of John Jacob IV, was not doing well. It occurred to Astor that perhaps a church could better handle its administration. When at the Brook Club one day he remarked that he would like to meet Cardinal Francis Spellman. If there is one thing that Brook Club members have, in addition to money, it is contacts, and so it was the work of a minute for a fellow member to arrange a lunch date for the very next day. Astor arrived at the Archdiocese of New York and asked an unassuming little man standing in the front hall to take him to Cardinal Spellman. "I'm Spellman," said the little man. This type of unaffected approach pleased Vincent, and the two became great friends. And what about the Astor Home? "I'll take it tomorrow," said the Cardinal, and did.

Continuing to break out of the Astor stereotype of a money-making machine, in 1948 he founded the Vincent Astor Foundation, dedicated to the "alleviation of human misery."

It was an effort to disprove the rueful despairing words he had spoken in one of his rare interviews nearly a quarter of a century earlier: "If you label a man as a scientist, he is instantly accepted by the public mind as a more than ordinarily useful person. If you label a man as a lawyer or give him any professional tag, the public mind associates him with worth-while achievement. But if you say of a man that he is merely rich, he is immediately docketed as a wealthy wastrel and whatever he attempts to do to show that he is a sincere well-wisher of his fellow men is either discounted or misinterpreted on account of his wealth."

And, to be sure, there were those who talked of tax benefits and others who thought he was trying to protect himself from personal demands for charity. During the Foundation's early years the Astor Home for Children, which was being administered by the Catholics, and the New York Hospital, of which Vincent was governor, were the chief beneficiaries of the grants. Astor was often surprisingly amenable to odd requests for funds. The Mackinac Island Medical Center asked for a contribution because John Jacob I had once had a trading post there. His business advisers considered this "the silliest reason to give a grant," but Vincent gave one anyway. And although William Waldorf had peremptorily freed the Astors from responsibility for the New York Public Library, less vehement Astors, including Vincent, had continued to make donations. He even became a trustee, a position that had been angrily rejected by his uncle. Minnie served on the Library's Women's Council and on some of the committees.

Vincent liked his wife to take an interest in his pet project, the St. Regis, and she decorated some of the suites. The Astor name was so closely connected with the hotel that the Duchess of Windsor held Minnie responsible when a table reservation at the St. Regis was not held for her. Minnie had replied, according to the gospel of Walter Winchell, "My good woman, why don't you act your age?" The press made the most of every trifling incident in the lives of the Astors, looking for news, because Vincent shunned both formal social affairs and the café society circuit. Most of their entertaining was done at home, and their circle of friends included such diverse personalities as Cardinal Spellman, Moss Hart, Rex Harrison, and members of the artistic set that Minnie liked.

Although they were even more different in personality and taste than he and Helen had been, Vincent remained deeply in love with Minnie. In fact, there are those who insist that she was the great love of his life and that he actually talked of shooting himself when she left him. The man who still violently disapproved of divorce was divorced for the second time in 1953. That same year Minnie married the artist James Whitney Fosburgh.

Luckily for Vincent he met and fell in love with (Mary) Brooke Russell Marshall, granddaughter of an admiral and daughter of a Marine Corps general. Like Vincent, Brooke had been married before, but unlike him had a married son and twin grandsons. She, too, had refused to be useless and had worked for eight years as feature editor of *House and Garden*.

"Vincent's marriage to Brooke was wonderful for him," says a friend. "She interested and stimulated him."

A mature and intelligent woman, she possessed the rare gift of being able to get along with Vincent, who became even more moody and temperamental as he grew older. The gift, it appears, was basically the tried-and-true wifely gambit of humoring him. If he wanted to watch a silly Western on television, the sort of nonintellectual activity that his previous wives had found boring, she would cheerfully sit down and watch it with him.

The various responsibilities of an Astor wife passed from one to the next. Brooke replaced Minnie on the New York Public Library committees and tried her hand at decorating the St. Regis. This pleased Vincent more than it did the St. Regis management, which had to find some way of reconciling the extremely different tastes of the two women. The second Mrs. Astor liked bright colors and chintzes, whereas the third Mrs. Astor preferred a more subtle style.

The Astor Estate underwent changes quite as drastic as those in Vincent's personal life during those years. Under the management, first of Hoyt Ammidon, now president of the United States Trust Company, and then of Allan W. Betts, the investments were completely reorganized. Astor's stockholdings, in their view, were "all the wrong kind," and so a broad buying program in common stocks was instituted with one objective—capital appreciation over a long period. As this plan was started in 1953, just about everything purchased went up.

As for the real estate, Betts reports that he looked over the list one day and "was shocked." The holdings were not of the type a man like Astor should have had, considering the tax structure. The return on many of the holdings amounted to less than 1 percent after taxes. Most of the properties had been held so long that depreciation had run out. The luxury apartments on East Eighty-sixth Street and East End Avenue had been made cooperatives or sold before them. What remained included some extremely small and unprofitable properties, such as a building in Flushing with a Nedicks and Regal shoestore on the ground floor and a second floor that was condemned for use. Nonetheless, all of his associates, possibly due to years of catering to Vincent, insist that he had "good real estate sense."

Astor and his managers began to sell and to make new plans. Vincent came to the office every morning and discussed the suggested sales and purchases. His business manager considered the St. Regis a "lusterless" investment.

"Captain Astor would not sell it. He went there for lunch every day."

At one time Betts suggested that they invest in a real-estate development in Venezuela, but Astor refused unequivocally. When pressed, he told how once years earlier he had been cruising in

Latin-American waters on the *Nourmahal*. One of the dictators then in power invited Vincent to go shark fishing. At dawn the following day, just as the party was about to set out, two soldiers led a horse onto the deck. Astor was puzzled, but remained silent. The sadistic intent became evident only when the boat entered shark-infested waters. The horse was then thrown overboard, and the dictator and his minister riddled it with machine gun bullets. The sharks, attracted by the blood, swam in, and the "fishermen," roaring with glee, shot at them. The return trip turned into a drunken brawl, and when the shore was in sight, the intoxicated dictator insisted that one of the cabinet ministers strip to his underwear and swim to shore. The dictator fired in circles around the man as he swam.

"What better example do you need of a lack of morality and stability?" asked Vincent, and of course, he had his way, and the investment was not made.

Two great real-estate ventures occupied his declining years: the building of a seventeen-million-dollar office building in Cleveland's Public Square and the far more ambitious Astor Plaza at Park Avenue and 53rd Street that was intended to be his Rockefeller Center. He announced plans to put up a forty-six-story office building with a heliport on the roof, at a cost of seventy-five million dollars. But a new era of Astor real estate was not to dawn. Everything, both foreseeable and unforeseeable, went wrong. The land beneath the projected building was owned by the William Waldorf Astor Estate, a coincidence that turned out to be of no advantage at all. Vincent asked for a mortgage on the land to provide him with the capital he needed for the Plaza. It is not customary for mortgages to be given on land under office buildings, and although Vincent and his English cousins were good friends and entertained one another regularly on transcontinental visits, business was business, and they were not inclined to make an exception in his case. Then came the 1957–58 business recession to render it all but impossible for Astor to obtain financing. He tried to find a bank to act as backer, but none approved of his list of prospective tenants. A great number of rescue plans of varying degrees of merit were offered him, among them Ivan Obolensky's suggestion of merging the St. Regis with the Ambassador and moving the combined hotel into the building. Vincent would not listen to any ideas of his nephew at that time. Ivan, the father of three, had recently been divorced, and Vincent disapproved of such a procedure on the part of anyone (besides himself). Astor Plaza was nicknamed "Disaster Plaza," though no one even dreamed of mentioning this to Vincent. Finally in 1958 he was forced to admit defeat, and the First National City Bank took over the site and put up its own building there. It was the fall of the House of Astor real estate.

Although the recession was undoubtedly the key factor in this failure, Astor's friends and associates attributed his poor judgment in getting himself into such a predicament on one of two factors— the choice depended, it would seem, on how fond they were of him: his drinking or his failing health. In point of fact, in his late years, the latter condition forced him to curtail the former activity.

The succession of illnesses that troubled his last years intensified his natural irascibility, impatience, and pessimism. His circulatory difficulties were such that it was hard for him to walk. Nonetheless, he managed to get around a bit, as a statement by his English cousin, Lord William Astor, indicates: "His latter passion was for prolonged and serious games of croquet."

It was, of course, the only sport in which he could still participate, and all avocations were invariably pursued in deadly earnest.

Despite the Astor Plaza fiasco, Vincent's fortune had mounted, largely as a result of the common stock holdings. For all his mistakes, he had nearly repeated William B. Astor's accomplishment of doubling his inheritance. He had worked it up from $69 million to better than $127 million. But times had changed, and other millionaires had outpaced him. In 1957 a *Fortune* magazine study of wealth revealed that at least sixteen people were ahead of him in the race to be "richest man in America." Oilman Jean Paul Getty clearly won with his $700 million to $1 billion fortune; then came the names of seven Americans possessed of $500 to $700 million, among them, H. L. Hunt, J. D. Rockefeller, Jr., and Paul Mellon; the third grouping found eight more with fortunes in the $200 to $400 million bracket—including Irenée and William du Pont, Howard Hughes, J. P. Kennedy, and Sid Richardson; Vincent's name appeared with thirty-eight others in the $100–$200 million group. With him were Doris Duke, Mrs. Edsel Ford, and Nelson Rockefeller. Still, he was classified as richer than Averill Harriman, J. Howard Pew, Mrs. Marjorie Merriwether Post, and Robert Kleberg, Jr., all in the $75–$100 million bracket. Vincent's renowned ancestor, John Jacob I, would have found scant comfort in that.

And so Vincent died at sixty-seven, neither the richest man in America nor landlord of New York. His relatives had been convinced for several years that he was writing and rewriting his will, cutting them in or out, depending on his mood. After his death, it turned out that, except for some relatively small bequests, he had cut them all out. There had been some speculation that he would select his nephew Ivan as his heir or at least leave him the St. Regis Hotel; he did neither. Few believed that he would bequeath much money to the half-brother he hated, but some thought he would remember John's children in order to keep the fortune in the Astor dynasty. But Vincent saw himself as the last of the American Astors. His third wife was remembered with a generosity unparalleled in Astor history: she received two million dollars outright, plus a life interest in half of the estate, with permission to do what she would with it after her death. As for the other half? He gave the money away—to the Vincent Astor Foundation.

After his death, many fine-sounding words were spoken about him. Moley described him as "an extraordinary figure, a man of great capacity and character." Lord William Astor added warmly: "His ungainly, plain but lovable figure, his individual and highly specialized sense of humor, his fund of unexpected knowledge, the real kindness of his heart—his friends will miss them all." But the saddest epitaph was spoken in private by one of his cousins: "I was sorry he didn't have more of a life. Vincent had a lot of money, but he had no fun with it."

10

The Two Worlds of Alice Astor

She believed that she was the reincarnation of an Egyptian princess, that in another life she had been a disciple of Ikhnaton, founder of the world's first monotheistic religion. In order to follow Ikhnaton, she had run away from her father, a high priest of the old Egyptian god Amon. When Ikhnaton died her father had taken her back, forced her to abandon the new hopeful religion of light and life and return to the traditional mysteries of death and darkness. On many nights as Alice Astor lay halfway between sleep and wakefulness she would have a vision, more real than any dream. A large, decorated mummy case would appear in the shadows of her room, and its top would open to reveal the body of a lovely, dark-haired girl who looked just like Alice. This double was dressed in rags, but her neck and arms were circled with jewelry bearing the ram's head design that was a symbol of high birth. Just as she was about to rise from the mummy case, a hand would reach out and push her back into the darkness.

When the tomb of Tutankhamen, in the Valley of the Tombs near Luxor, was opened, Alice, then a girl of twenty, was one of the first four people to dare the famous curse by setting foot inside. The death-centered religion of Egypt appealed to the mystic in her nature. She obtained from this tomb a strange and magnificent necklace—indeed, an Astor could have anything. Around a large circle made of semiprecious stones were ranged hundreds upon hundreds of tiny rams' heads formed out of bitumen covered with soft gold. The necklace, at least when worn by Alice, seemed to possess an unusual unworldly power that made some of those who saw it uneasy.

Although the visit to the tomb of Tutankhamen had been made possible through Ava's friendship with the Earl of Carnarvon, one of the men who discovered it, Alice's belief in mysticism took her into another world where her worldly mother could not follow. Domineering, dominating Ava was no more loving as a mother than as a wife. Alice's childhood was, if anything, harder than Vincent's had been. Her father's death on the *Titanic* deprived her of any hope she might have harbored of someday developing a relationship with him. Ava did not remarry until Alice was seventeen, and Lord Ribblesdale did little at that date to provide his stepdaughter with the warmth and security she longed for. Shifted from America to England and back again, as mood or remarriage suited Ava, Alice was not able to put down roots anywhere. Yet the one word invariably used to describe Alice by those who knew her as a child and young girl is *spoiled*. And she was spoiled in the true sense of the word—by getting too much of everything except the one thing she needed, love. Like many spoiled children, she grew into an adult who was willful and capricious. Unlike many, however, she was able to be a good mother herself when in time she had children of her own.

Ava, who had succeeded in obtaining for herself in marriage the possessors of two great fortunes (even if she had not liked either of them very much), was determined to do no less for her daughter. And Alice would have been easy to marry off, even without the five-million-dollar trust fund settled on her by her father. Although not the great beauty that Ava had been, she was a lovely-looking girl. Slightly above the average in height, she had beautiful black hair with blue highlights, brooding eyes, and a soft mouth, with a slightly discontented droop that added to its attractiveness. There was a look of rare distinction about her; she did in truth resemble the Egyptian princess she imagined herself to have been in an earlier life. Like her mother, her hands and feet were graceful and shapely. A man, middle-aged now, but once a dancing school partner of the young Alice, still recalls how beautiful her slender legs were, even in the black stockings she wore in the year after her father's death. In addition to these external attributes, she was an intelligent girl, a serious and dedicated student of art, literature, music, and Hindu and Egyptian religions. Unlike her temperamental brother, she was charming to everyone, regardless of whether she liked him. Her voice had a little lilt in it that was particularly winning.

Lady Ribblesdale had every hope of marrying Alice to a fabulously rich man and was furious when the girl fell in love with Prince Serge Obolensky-Neledinsky-Meletzky. One might imagine that any title-hungry American would have been delighted with Prince Serge who could trace his lineage back eleven hundred years to Rurik, Grand Duke of Novgorod and Kiev. The catch, as far as Ava was concerned, was that his family's wealth was gone with the Bolshevik wind that had swept over Russia. He also happened to be married, but that appeared less of an obstacle to Ava than his poverty; after all, it was much easier to correct that fault. Practical Ava was not won over by Obolensky's aristocratic good looks and the charm that has overpowered several generations of women, but Alice, although she seemed quiet and almost shy to strangers, was one of the few people able to withstand her mother's fury, plotting, and determination. This revealed incredible strength of mind, because Ava's sharp tongue and biting criticism were destructive and undermining.

Criticism failing, Ava tried cunning and sought to distract Alice with a series of dashing and eligible bachelors, among them Helen Astor's brother. Despite her brother's candidacy, Helen favored the romantic match with Obolensky, and the infatuated couple often met at her house in Paris. The idyl was cut short by the suspicious Ava, who first swept Alice off to Spain to the estate of a wealthy sherry-maker and then, with Alice still intractable, took her to America. All Ava's efforts were in vain. As soon as Alice was twenty-one and as free of her mother legally as she had been for years psychologically, she returned to London to wait for divorce to free Serge for her. They then became the most thoroughly married of husbands and wives, going through three ceremonies on the same day, July 24, 1924: a civil ceremony, with Paul of Serbia as best man; an Episcopal service, at which the Second Viscount Waldorf Astor gave the bride away; and a Russian Orthodox service, attended by Russian, Greek, and English nobility, along with members of the British Astor family. Ava, accepting fate at last, gave the wedding breakfast with her customary aplomb.

Handsome Serge and beautiful young Alice then settled down to face the problem of the very rich—how to fill their days. And they did this in the way that has been found successful by members of society for generations: constant movement. They went to Canada to buy a ranch, but Alice did not like the bleak loneliness of the region, so they gave up that idea. Instead they visited Vincent and Helen in New York and at Ferncliff, attended one party after the other, and played tennis and golf. Alice was a fiercely competitive golfer. Back in London, which both the American wife and the Russian husband accepted as home base, they bought a luxurious house, Hanover Lodge, in Regent's Park, from Admiral and Lady Beatty. After making the sale, the Beattys had second thoughts and offered to buy the house back at a higher price. Alice, the only Astor to feel every bit as rich as she was, suggested that Serge accept the offer and keep the profit as a gift. This was not consistent with the dignity of a Russian nobleman, and the upshot was that they refused the offer and kept Hanover Lodge.

They quickly staffed it with a chef, maid, chauffeur, and butler-valet, and filled it with antiques. In 1925 Alice gave birth to a son, Ivan, and Waldorf Astor was asked to be a godfather; it was the last really close tie between the English and American Astors. When Alice had recovered from the birth, the Obolenskys returned to their truly king-sized social life. During the London season they entertained or were entertained nightly by fellow members of society and royalty. In the daytime many aristocratic friends came to play tennis on the spacious grounds of the Lodge. And into their storybook lives came the storybook figures of the queen of a country, which must be kept nameless, and an English duke, also nameless. The two, hopelessly in love but kept apart by the responsibilities of their respective positions, were able to snatch a few hours together unromantically playing tennis on the Obolensky courts.

On weekends the couple visited her cousins at Cliveden or went to the castles of rich and titled families, where they rode to hounds and shot grouse. In midwinter, of course, there was St. Moritz for the skiing, Paris for fun, and vacations from vacationing on the Riviera. Some years they toured Europe, stopping in Venice, where Elsa Maxwell was reviving the jaded palates of the international set with treasure hunts and fabulous fancy dress balls.

Bridge was almost as essential a part of the lives of their social set as hunting, golf, tennis, and dancing. Alice, who had too often been forced to be Ava's partner, hated to play, but found it impossible to avoid the game altogether. One evening when playing bridge at the home of a collector of rare books, the smiling hostess handed Alice a volume taken from the library of the Marquis de Sade, who has given his name to one of psychology's best-recognized aberrations. The binding was made of human skin from the body of one of the mistresses of the imaginative marquis. The equally imaginative, but far more sensitive Alice was horrorstruck and departed quickly, leaving Serge trapped at the bridge table, playing hand after hand until he felt it would be polite to follow.

Luckily this type of sophisticated torture was not to be found at Newport, where many summers were spent with Vincent, whose humor ran along far homelier lines. Vincent, who at that time was getting on well with Alice, gave her ninety-nine acres of his property in Rhinebeck, and she built a thirty-room stone house upon it. The Obolenskys moved in, according to the manner of those accustomed to living like birds of passage, without ever having thought to buy linens or kitchen utensils. Alice, who possessed the blithe certainty of the rich that somehow someone would take care of her, had invited weekend guests. And as always, someone was found to send in everything that was needed and in time. The price made little difference to Alice, who was the least stingy of Astors. In fact, Serge was hard-pressed to prevent her from showering him with such showy gifts as a string of polo ponies. Because he realized she could not be induced to just save the money, he suggested that she use it to start a foundation to help impoverished White Russian exiles.

For all her spirit, determination, and the firm hand of nurses and governesses throughout her childhood, Alice remained poorly disciplined. The product of generations of Germanic Astors who made punctuality a virtue, Alice was invariably late. She had the clocks in her homes set ahead forty minutes, but then, she knew that they were wrong and never looked at them. A poor sense of time was compounded by her inability to decide what to wear. Her clothes were striking, and she was extremely fussy. One dress after the other would be discarded while the minutes ticked by. One day she had a brainstorm: she would keep a large mirrored makeup box in her Rolls Royce and thus be able to put on her cosmetics while on the way to a party. This made the drives a bit more interesting for her but quite failed to solve the problem. As an Astor living in England, she was often invited to parties attended by members of the British royal family. Protocol, never broken by anyone else, had it that all nonroyal guests be ready and waiting five minutes early. On several occasions Alice slipped in late, hoping that no one would notice.

These minor excitements were not enough to keep her happy. "She was by nature easily bored," says an old friend. "She was bored with her life; she was bored with everyone."

And if she was less bored with her dashing husband than with most other people, she nonetheless became discontented with her marriage rather quickly. The way of life typical of their social group has never been conducive to stability in marriage, even for people satisfied far more easily than Alice. The rounds of parties, the weekend visits, the caravans of chauffeur-driven cars carrying dozens of pleasure-seekers to one place after the other gave opportunities for husbands and wives to talk, play golf, or hunt with someone else's husband, wife, sister, or friend. Serge became jealous of Alice's companions and she of his. In his autobiography, written thirty years later, Obolensky recalls having been jealous, wrongly he is careful to point out, as early as two years after their marriage. Alice's suggestion that a bachelor friend join them for a month's golfing vacation in Holland was hardly one that a young husband might be expected to greet with enthusiasm, even though such practices were not uncommon among their fellow socialites. She in her turn took exception to the amount of attention that Serge, a magnificent ballroom dancer, paid to some of his dancing partners. With money so free, friends so prominent and gay, no business to attend to in the mornings, and a nurse to listen for Ivan's early cry, the quiet evening at home was virtually unknown. It was the type of existence that encourages selfishness; if either Serge or Alice was ill or not in the mood to go out, the other could see no reason to stay home.

Five years after having defied her mother and battled her way to a romantic marriage with her prince, Alice asked for a divorce. She found that it was no easier to get out of marriage than it had been to get into it. A period of three years of separations, attempted reconciliations, and mediation efforts by friends and relatives followed. Vincent was particularly insistent that they remain together. The brother and sister had reacted quite differently to the marital difficulties of their parents. Alice, who had never seen a happy relationship between a man and woman, had matured into a person without any confidence in marriage. Vincent, on the other hand, was—well, for a while—determined to show that his parents had been wrong and that a long and successful marriage was possible. He hastened to find a job for Serge, who had come to America to prove that he could be independent of Alice. She in time followed him, arriving with thirty trunkloads of possessions. These, it turned out, were not an indication of any desire to set up housekeeping with him again. Serge shared an apartment with a Russian friend, and Alice kept on insisting that she wanted a divorce and refusing to listen to her brother.

Though Vincent and Alice had always gotten along ("after a fashion," say their friends), they never really understood one another. Her whims and careless way with money irritated him beyond measure. When staying in New York, she would suddenly get the idea of visiting him at Ferncliff and would immediately set off in a taxi, a mode of conveyance that seemed more fun to her than a chauffeur-driven limousine. Her extravagance was so well known that a story went around that she had gone so far as to purchase a New York City taxi for her own use, allowing the driver to pick up other fares when she did not need him. It was quite useless to remonstrate with Alice, who simply would not listen. The years with her mother had developed this trait in her to a high degree.

Finally in the summer of 1932 she succeeded in overriding the opposition and went to Nevada to establish residence for a divorce, despite the fact that she had become pregnant in the interim. Vincent made the unbrotherly gesture of having his own lawyer, Cass Ledyard, represent Serge. The bone of contention during the proceedings was the education of their son Ivan, to whom they were both devoted. Although as members of British society, there had never been any question about the necessity of a "Nannie" for the child, Alice had always been jealous of this nurse. She would probably have been happier had she lived in a less wealthy milieu, where she could have taken sole charge of her little boy. By the time of the divorce, Ivan was seven—the same age Alice had been when her parents had instituted their year-long divorce proceedings— and Alice, the American, felt that the only proper education was English, whereas Serge held out for American schooling. In the end, the father won. He was given custody of Ivan and Alice of Sylvia, the little girl born while the divorce was underway. Because Serge did not want to deprive his son of a mother's love, Ivan spent summers in England with her. She attempted to make what she could of this short time to correct what she considered the shocking lapses in American education.

"Every summer she hired a Cambridge tutor to work with me. I learned a lot that stood me in good stead later," recalls Ivan, philosophical now that it is all over. "She also insisted on an early bedtime, seven-thirty, until I was about ten, and so I read the classics by the dozens at night, which was also helpful afterward."

It is hardly surprising that Ivan shares his uncle's view of the divorce. "They should have gone back together," he says. "They were crazy about each other."

To make his position clear, Vincent promptly offered his ex-brother-in-law a job in the Astor Estate office and then, as we have seen, let him handle the St. Regis Hotel, invited him on the cruises of the *Nourmahal*, and considered him an intimate friend. Particularly during the years immediately following the divorce, this was anything but agreeable to Alice. She, on the other hand, remained on pleasant, though certainly not intimate, terms with the half-brother whom Vincent could not stand.

Shortly after the divorce became final, Alice was married again, to Raimund von Hofmannsthal, an Austrian writer, who had worked with famed theatrical producer Max Reinhardt in Vienna. Raimund's father was the noted poet, Hugo von Hofmannsthal, composer of libretti for Richard Strauss. In sharp contrast to the enormous, well-publicized three-part wedding to Obolensky, a marriage was performed quietly, almost in secrecy, in Newark, New Jersey. The main reason for this concealment was that Vincent was not alone in opposing Alice's divorce, and the newspaper publicity had been rather nasty for months. News about the Astors, after all, has always been played to the hilt by editors and columnists. Eager to avoid headlines, the newly-weds planned to leave for Austria before some too-garrulous friend leaked the news to the tabloids. They booked passage on an ocean liner and hoped to slip away unnoticed, although Alice, with her dark, brooding beauty and her mounds of luggage, was the least inconspicuous of travelers.

As luck would have it, though, just when they were getting ready to leave for the ship, they learned than Ivan had become terribly ill. Although Serge had custody of the child, Alice, always the good mother, rushed to his side. She would not go until Ivan was quite well, and by then of course, the newspapers had their fill of her second marriage. Again, after having overcome the obstacles in the way of this union, Alice was not content in it for long. Despite the birth of a daughter, Romana, this marriage also ended in divorce.

Alice's passionate, discontented nature drove her ever on in search of love and happiness. Each failure left her crushed and disappointed, but then someone new would appear, and she would hope again that *this* time it would be different. She was to marry twice more during her lifetime. In 1940 she became the wife of Philip Harding, an English newspaperman then serving in the anti-aircraft battery in the British Army. A daughter, Emily, was born of this marriage before it, too, was terminated. Her final marriage, which also did not endure, was to David Pleydell-Bouverie, an architect.

But Alice's life added up to a great deal more than a mere catalogue of husbands. None of the Astors, as we have seen, was truly creative, but Alice came very close.

"She had many talents, but she never channelled them," says her son sadly. "She could have been a writer, but she only wrote thousands of letters."

But if she was not an artist or writer herself, she was always in the midst of a group of artistic people. Just as her cousin Nancy Astor made Cliveden a center for political figures, Alice's homes in London and New York were centers for artists, writers, and dancers.

"Her love of art was sincere," states a lifelong friend. "She knew just about everyone in the arts and they all liked her."

Her brother Vincent often visited her before her first divorce and played billiards with ballet dancer Vaslav Nijinsky. But an interest in the dance or the arts never really absorbed Vincent; it was the passion of Alice's life. The artists in her circle were fascinated by her somber chiseled face. In Pavel Tchelitchew's portrait, she looked every bit the mystic she was to become, and Cecil Beaton's photograph, one of his finest, reveals her external beauty at its height.

These famous names notwithstanding, Alice was far less of a celebrity hunter than either her cousin or her mother, being willing to listen to the yearnings of those who had not yet arrived. Art did not need to be fashionable for her to like it; she had complete and deserved confidence in her own good taste. And so she became the only one of the Astors to be a true patron of the arts. She expected no return for her money; in fact, she did not even want any. This descendant of generations of businessmen had no interest in the source of her wealth. Real estate, stocks or bonds, or art as an investment only bored her.

Alice supported the Sadler's Wells Ballet from its start, long before anyone else thought much of its potential. She sought out impresario Sol Hurok and asked him to take the ballet company to the United States. Hurok snorted: "It won't sell. The public is not interested in English ballet companies." Alice raised a carefully shaped eyebrow at such a trivial objection. She would guarantee all expenses—naturally. It never even occurred to her to ask for a cut of the profits should there be any, as indeed there were when the ballet achieved both critical and popular success.

Her relations with her mother during those years remained rather distant, although both were renowned hostesses in London. When World War II broke out, Ava returned to the United States, obtaining space on an ocean liner "at the command of the White House." This type of flight was not for Alice. As had once been said of her great-grandmother, "she could not be made to feel frightened." One night during the height of the bombing Alice invited Serge, a friend again after all those years, to dinner. When the alarm sounded, she refused to go to the cellar for shelter; she never went down during air raids, she told him. The best he could do was to talk her into sitting on the floor with him underneath the dining room table. And yet on the night when a bomb did hit the garden near the tennis courts where they had so often played, it was the chauffeur, not Alice, who was killed.

During the war Alice at last found full-time outlets for her driving energies, although even then she confided in Serge that she was not happy in her personal life. For a time she drove an ambulance; then she organized a canteen for the antiaircraft batteries in which her husband of the time, Philip Harding, was serving, and drove it herself from one area to the other. Another year found her working in a factory making electronic equipment. In the evenings she still had the energy to give dinner parties with much of her old dash and flair. Everything had to be of the best, and food rationing was a challenge to her. One night she announced proudly to her guests that Vassily, the Russian chef who had been with her since her marriage to Obolensky, had prepared sorrel soup, chicken, a salad, and a soufflé. She had even managed to obtain some scarce salad oil. But because she had inadvertently bought mineral oil instead of olive oil, the meal was rather memorable for her guests.

Although unconcerned for her own safety, she did send her two older daughters—Emily was just a baby—to New York with their Irish nurse. They lived in Obolensky's apartment, which was vacant during his overseas Army service, and attended Brearley, the school favored by intellectual socialites.

After the war Alice returned to New York and made it her home for the rest of her life, providing the New York City Ballet Company with the same type of support she had given the Sadler's Wells in England. In Serge's autobiography he writes that he had hoped to marry her again at this time and was disappointed when she turned to Pleydell-Bouverie. But even when that marriage ended, the two were not reunited. Perhaps as Obolensky has said, "It was in the cards and willed that way."

As Alice grew older, the mysticism that had always attracted her became the dominant force of her life. A friend of Aldous Huxley, she, like him, was fascinated by accounts of the mystic experiences resulting from the use of mescaline and hallucinogenic mushrooms. She probed ever more deeply into the studies of Hindu and Egyptian mystic practices. Every aspect of the world of the mind and spirit beckoned her. She investigated spiritualism through the use of a medium, but was really more interested in developing her own extrasensory perceptions. Thought transference was possible, she firmly believed. The brain, according to the school of thought to which she subscribed, is capable of both transmitting and receiving electrical waves; acting in a sense like a radio, it could, if used properly, serve as a means of communication between peoples separated by thousands of miles. To augment her abilities, Alice made an "antenna" similar to those worn thousands of years earlier by the high priests of Egypt. It was fashioned out of copper and had a sort of horn sticking out. Her son, who tried it on one day, reports that his perceptions seemed to become much keener. The force of Alice's belief and personality, of course, can hardly be eliminated as factors in his experience. She also placed her confidence in a device, the Copper Cage, created by telepathic practitioners of that time and based on the protective qualities of copper: the mystic enters the cage and, removed from all extraneous electricity around, is left free for mind reading.

Alice was not the first of her family to respond to the odd appeal of the mystic philosophy. The Chanlers, as we have seen, were often in receipt of messages from beyond the grave. Moody William Waldorf Astor felt the fascination of a strangely cut ruby. A jeweler once told him that it might bear a message from the past. Astor took the stone to Rome to an expert on such matters and was stunned when the gentleman died shortly after examining the ruby. William often studied the jewel thereafter, but feared that his powers were not great enough to unravel its mysteries.

"It is obviously unlikely that an unimaginative man of affairs could attune himself to mysteries so subtle and elusive," he mused, expressing a view of himself not borne out by his novels.

Alice, completely confident of her powers, devoted her last years to a search for these subtle and elusive mysteries. The mystical religions of the past obsessed her; she had learned to read hieroglyphics so as to gain a fuller understanding of the Egyptian mysteries. Unfortunately, as sometimes happens to those of extraordinary sensitivity, she in time became as much possessed by as she was possessed of mystical powers. The whole area of mysticism and spiritualism offers opportunities for fakery, and many people saw in this field a way to get close to Alice Astor and her millions. Particularly after her divorce from David Pleydell-Bouverie, she was unable to cope with these mystics and pseudo-mystics. Her judgment, sound where art was concerned, was completely unreliable when it came to anything to do with extrasensory perception. She was ready to believe any claim, however suspect or implausible. Her friends worried about the influences under which she found herself, but she would not listen. Still a passionate woman, she was in love, unhappily so, with one of the practitioners, a married man who would not get a divorce.

This personal problem coupled with the intense psychic life she was leading affected her greatly. Even those who shared some of her mystical beliefs were concerned about her. "She opened Pandora's box," says one, "and unleashed forces she could not control."

On the surface, though, she remained as charming and attractive as she had always been. She visited neighbors at Rhinebeck one evening in the summer of 1956, in her fifties by then, but lovely still. "She had aged well," according to her dinner partner of that evening. "The only changes were the lines around her eyes and, oh yes, the discontented droop of her mouth was more pronounced." She was excited about a planned trip to Boston to see a mystic who was using the Copper Cage.

A few nights later she was dead. By her bed—the Egyptian *Book of the Dead.*

Of Alice's three children, darkly handsome Ivan Obolensky reveals traces of his mother's interest in mysticism and extrasensory perception. It seems fitting, therefore, that he inherited the fabulous necklace of Tutankhamen taken from the cliff-tomb near the Nile so many years earlier and treasured by Alice Astor from then until her death.

This necklace has also appeared and may yet be appearing in the visionary life of a stranger. Shortly after Alice's death a man who knew her only slightly and had never heard of her other-worldly visions was talking with Ivan about the strange nature of dreams. In recent weeks, he said, he had begun to have a recurrent dream. An Eygptian mummy case stood in the shadows of his room. All at once the top would swing open to show a beautiful dark-haired girl within. Around her neck was fastened an unusual necklace made up of row upon row of tiny golden rams' heads surrounding a large central ornament. Just as the maiden would begin to rise from the mummy case, a hand would reach out and push her back into the darkness.

11

Of Trials and Troubles

The divorce case of John Jacob Astor VI versus Dolores Fullman cries out for the presence of a modern-day Portia. We are left with the uncomfortable feeling that the lawyers brilliantly sought to have justice done without mercy. By the time the arguments were concluded, Astor was declared legally married to two women.

It is certainly true that a grown man should know better than to marry a girl when he has only a questionable divorce from her predecessor in his affections. But then, men were losing their heads over women long before Mark Antony abandoned a kingdom for Cleopatra. Astor sums up the basis of his problems perfectly when he murmurs sadly, "I thought she was simply *adorable!*"

John's propensity for trouble has provided more than a generation of society columnists and tabloid newspapermen with copy of the most interesting and circulation-building variety. His life has been the stuff tragedy is made of. There are all the elements—the father dramatically killed before the son's birth, the older, harsh, unsympathetic half-brother, the unfair inheritance. But John is not and never could be a tragic figure. What he lacks is the physical appearance and manner of the tragic hero. Losing the slenderness of youth early, John became large and heavy, remarkably unphotogenic. He has followed the traditional path of the wronged heir, but not in silence; instead there has been a succession of suits by and against women, and unwise remarks to the eternally hovering reporters. Tragedy has been made to look like farce.

"Vincent spoke of Jack to me only once, and that was to launch into a diatribe against him," states a business associate of Vincent Astor's. "But who can say that another man would have reacted in a different way than Jack did? The situation was such that almost anyone would feel sorry for himself. If his father had lived just six months longer, he might have shared equally in the estate."

The fact that Alice, born considerably before the sinking of the *Titanic*, received only a fraction of the estate, does not appear significant to John or to any of the family. Everyone recognizes that it has been traditional for Astors to favor sons financially over daughters. "If a man has a fortune of $100 million, he should still leave $5 million to the daughter and $95 million to the sons," John expresses the family view. "I'd do it for my daughter, if I had such a fortune and I couldn't be fonder of her."

And so the injustice of having received but a three-million-dollar trust fund from the father who gave the other son nearly $70 million left John permanently embittered. His hatred of Vincent became a great and sustaining passion. "He robbed me of my birthright." The fact that everyone has always assumed that John was as rich as his half-brother has rubbed salt into the wounds. The common belief is that he, too, was left seventy million dollars. In fact, one writer of a recent book about the rich went so far as to castigate Astor for running through that sum, which, as we know, he never had. The key reference book on the lives of socialites and celebrities is slightly more moderate, settling the whole matter of the fortune by printing a "quote" by John in which he declares that he has but thirty-three million dollars. He has changed his name from John Jacob Astor VI to "plain John Astor," because the dynastic triple name "implies great wealth, which I don't have." But it does absolutely no good. To the world at large, he is still John Jacob Astor VI (sometimes called John Jacob Astor III by those who feel that long-dead ancestors do not belong in the count) and the inheritor of an immense fortune.

"Even the workmen I hire to do a job for me have heard that I have seventy million dollars," avers Astor. As a result, he is overcharged nearly as often as he thinks he is. It cost him one thousand dollars to have just the dining room of his New York apartment painted.

Well, of course, anyone living off the income of several million dollars, even if it might or should have been half of seventy million dollars, is anything but pathetic to the average person, and John's plight has won him little or no sympathy. Instead, while his half-brother invariably got a good press, John has been the recipient of utterly damning publicity. When not recounting his marital difficulties, the society columnists fill space with minor items about him written in a snide and sneering manner; he was seen sleeping in a nightclub or looking for a dropped dime in a telephone booth. Even the nickname, sometimes used in place of John Jacob Astor, "Jackims," is belittling. "I've given up struggling against the image in the press," he says. "Otherwise I'd be in a strait jacket. I just don't read the columns." Most of those who do read them would be surprised to learn that far from being adjudged an unfit father, he has shared custody of his son and daughter and that both love him, that he is on reasonably good terms with two former wives, and that he is neither a fool nor lacking in charm.

But none of this is good copy. John's side of the family had been predisposed, long before his day, to a type of love life that makes tabloid writers sit up and take notice. His beautiful mother had similarly provided fodder for those seeking to fatten their columns. John Jacob Astor IV may have been the great love of Madeleine Force's life—as her friend Alida Chanler Emmet insists—but he died when she was little more than a girl. There were so many years remaining to be filled, and she was a woman made to love and be loved. Her second marriage to William K. Dick, for whom she gave up her Astor widow's rights, was still society page rather than gossip column news. It was one of those nice romances that everyone likes to see, as the lovely heartbroken young widow finds happiness again in the arms of a rediscovered childhood friend who just happens to have inherited three million dollars from his grandfather.

Madeleine married William Dick in the socially approved resort of Bar Harbor, Maine, and John, who was then six, was present at the ceremony. The marriage, which endured for fifteen years, provided him with two half-brothers, named John and William (almost as if they were Astors). John Astor got along with these Dick half-brothers far better than with the Astor one, and they remained friends after the parents parted. John Dick, who became an ornithologist, never married; William, dead now of leukemia, was, in one of the innumerable examples of society's tight little world, at one time married to Virginia French, sister of John Astor's first wife. To return to Madeleine, her second marriage gradually deteriorated. The reporters were not privy to the intimate details of the couple's life right away, and outsiders believed that the Dicks were happy together long after it was untrue.

"Madeleine tried to make a go of it," declares one of her confidantes, "but he had a terrible temper."

"What really brought an end to the marriage and provided society with a new sensation, however, was the appearance on the scene of a virile middleweight prizefighter with whom Madeleine, turning forty, fell in love. It was an infatuation of the type that has produced countless movie scripts and popular magazine stories. The true annals of society, too, are filled with such misalliances. She was rich and aging; Enzo Fiermonte was twenty-six and strong and poor, handsome enough to have won a male beauty contest in California. He also happened to have a wife in Italy, who, hearing of his romance with the rich Mrs. Dick, was not prepared to make it easy for him to get a divorce. Still, after a property settlement had been worked out, the divorce took place, and Madeleine went to Reno in 1933 to obtain her freedom as well. The marriage was performed at Doctors Hospital in New York, where Madeleine was confined with a shoulder fracture. The sons of both her previous marriages, the society columns noted, were at her bedside. Society, while avidly reading all published details about the romance, did not clasp the newlyweds to its bosom. When a party in their honor was held at the Newport Casino, fully half of the resorters declined to attend. It is ironic that twenty-two years earlier, the Old Guard had stayed away from balls given for Madeleine and John Jacob Astor IV; at that time *she* was the one considered socially unacceptable.

The marriage, as everyone had predicted, was impossible from the start. For five years the Fiermontes quarreled and made up, only to quarrel and become reconciled again.

"In the end he left her when he saw that she was getting old and losing her looks," recalls a friend. "It was bound to happen. He was so much younger."

They were finally divorced in 1938. If Fiermonte should be charged as having been a fortune hunter, the fact was that there really was not very much of a fortune for him to hunt. Madeleine, who had given up the benefits of being the widow of a fabulously wealthy man so as to marry a merely very wealthy one, relinquished her claims on that money, too, in order to wed the young prizefighter. There are many ways, however, of earning money out of a sensation-producing marriage, and these were quickly learned by Fiermonte. He wrote six titillating articles about the details of their marriage for *True Story* magazine and then began to make a movie about their life together. It was interrupted by Madeleine's death in 1940, which reduced public interest in her sex life. Fiermonte then passed out of the family's ken; many years later one of the Dick brothers ran into him on a street in Rome. The former prizefighter said that he had become a movie producer. After having had millions of dollars at her disposal, Madeleine's estate amounted to twenty thousand dollars, which was left in trust for the sons of her second marriage. John Astor, as she was careful to note, had been provided for elsewhere.

His memories of her are rather distant. She passed through his life as a somewhat shadowy figure, more involved in her love life than in its living results. "She was a young soul all her life," says a friend. "It was never her way to talk about serious matters with her children." Then, too, she was always frail, suffering from heart trouble. In the summers, when the family went to Europe, Bar Harbor, or Newport, a doctor traveled or lived with them. Nonetheless, no one thought to give John innoculations against typhoid fever before a trip to Italy when he was thirteen, and he contracted a case that, he maintained in court later, had left him weakened for life. When it comes to the first of his stepfathers, John remembers him without affection, but without rancor, feeling that as those relationships go, it was better than most. It was, unfortunately, for a boy who needed direction badly, not better than having a father. John had little to do with Dick's successor, Fiermonte, because he was already grown-up by the time of that marriage.

The coming of age of an Astor and the control of great wealth has always been taken seriously by the family and followed with avid interest by the press, and John's was no exception. The fortune that was to support him amounted to about five million dollars, the three-million-dollar trust fund left him by his father having appreciated to that extent in tweny-one years. This was not much by Astor standards, but a fantastic sum to almost everyone else in the depression year of 1933. With no guiding hand to restrain him and a natural taste for the best things in life, he plunged into heavy expenditures immediately. Newspaper readers of the grim 1930's were painfully eager for the vicarious thrill provided by a look into the very different lives of the very rich, and so considerable space was devoted to John's private railroad car, as well as the purchase of ten new automobiles, including a yellow Rolls Royce. Home in New York was a town house at 7 East Ninety-first Street, which required the care of a staff of twenty-five servants. Newport had always been a favorite Astor stamping ground, and so John had to have a cottage of his own. He set his heart on possessing the fabulous Marble House, which was being offered for the merest fraction of the two million dollars that O. H. P. Belmont had spent on its construction during Newport's golden age. Unfortunately, Vincent, who was in charge of the trust, did not make the funds available to John for ten weeks, and by then someone else had snapped up the bargain. Chetwode, the cottage he purchased there instead, was the size of a small apartment house and needed a minimum of fourteen in help inside—the kitchen was so inconveniently located that smooth mealtimes depended on the services of a cook, a second cook, and kitchen maid—and six gardeners for the grounds. Looking back, it is not hard to see where that seventy-million dollar legend started. When asked why he needed so much, he told a reporter with awe-inspiring naïveté, "I am an Astor."

Although he denies deserving the playboy label, he admits, with a rueful smile, his fondness for girls. And it was with the girls that the expenses spiralled higher and higher. Astor was barely of age when he began to think of marriage to eighteen-year-old Eileen Gillespie, who traveled the same New York–Newport circuit as he. Their engagement was marked with the presentation of an Astor family heirloom, a ring that had once belonged to Empress Eugénie of France. This gift alone was valued at better than $100,000. As marriage settlement, a trust fund of $500,000 was arranged for Eileen. People close to the Astor family informed the press that

John, showing the streak of impetuousness that has proven troublesome to him emotionally and financially so many times since actually had to be talked out of making it a cool $1.5 million. Astor's romances were never calm, and the two quarreled violently and sometimes publicly—once in the lobby of the Savoy-Plaza Hotel. All this, of course, was observed and noted by the newspapers. A final bitter argument took place, and the engagement was broken, with hard feelings on both sides.

Once it was all over, Astor took a trip around the world, seeking, the newspapers declared, "relief from his shattered romance." A reporter in Shanghai cabled *The New York Times* the description of John "gazing morosely out of the window upon China's never-ending stream of humanity." The trip succeeded in its objective and Astor soon found love again in the person of Ellen Tuck "Tucky" French who was to have been a bridesmaid at the cancelled wedding. A few loose ends from the past remained to be tied up. Before giving back the ring and other gifts, the Gillespies insisted that John make a "written apology for his language to their daughter" during the heated period of the breakup. This done, everything was returned through Cartier's, the jewellers. On July 1, 1934, the marriage to Tucky took place in Newport and was one of the most widely heralded of the decade. The years of terrible publicity still lay ahead. Astor and his bride were presented as America's dream couple. The John of yesteryear was described in *The New York Times* as a "tall lean young man" with an "engaging smile." And Tucky was 18, a cousin of William T. Vanderbilt, and possessor of a slim figure and a fresh, wholesome pretty face.

Reporters and photographers climbed out onto the window ledges and rooftops of houses across the street from the church and perched precariously on the iron fence around a nearby graveyard. The New York *Herald Tribune* devoted the entire Sunday rotogravure section to photographs of the appealing young pair and the house they were to share at Newport. *The New York Times* considered the wedding worthy of front page coverage and gave almost a full page farther back to an exhaustively detailed account of the affair. It noted that the groom's mother attended without her controversial new husband. No mention was made of the conspicuous absence of the Astor half-brother, Vincent, nor was Alice present. Instead the Dicks were there in full force, and William Dick served as an usher for his half-brother. Tucky's father, Francis O. French, revealing early a penchant for embarrassing his son-in-law, had insisted on inviting Dr. Ernst F. S. Hanfstaengel, a personal aide to Adolf Hitler. The large crowd lining the Newport streets to catch a glimpse of the wedding party, gasped when this unpopular figure appeared.

As the young couple left the church, the onlookers murmured, as they invariably will, about the beauty of the bride. "But why doesn't she smile?" asked some. "And how solemn he looks!"

Seven months after the wedding John announced that he was going to work. The newspapers made much of this. At twenty-two, it was his first serious effort to make something of his life. His schooling, first at New York's Bovée (now defunct) and Buckley and then at St. George's prep school had failed to arouse his interest in any profession. John refused to go to college, and there was no one in his life then to influence him to change his mind. Many members of society at that time eschewed higher education; John maintains that fully one third of his class at St. George's did not go to college. Even Vincent, as we have seen, left Harvard after his sophomore year to look after his inheritance. And so John alternated the next few years between trips around the world and periods of doing what he admits was "nothing much" in New York.

It was unfortunate for John that the one place where an unskilled Astor could be sure of finding employment was with one of his half-brother's companies. And Vincent had him hired by the International Mercantile Marine Company for twenty-five dollars a week. John was shifted from job to job within the company in order to learn the business from the ground up. His first assignment was on the piers in the Chelsea district, and after that he was moved to the main office. John stuck it out for a year and a half and then quit. "I felt I wasn't getting anywhere," he explains. And considering Vincent's customary hostility, that is very likely.

Yet John was quoted—quite possibly apocryphally—as having quit for the most stupid of reasons: "Sometimes I didn't get through till five o'clock. It would be six o'clock before I reached home and I would have to get up very early the next morning." The staid *The New York Times*, to be sure, did not stoop to such snide reportage, but even there, in the major news story devoted to Astor's leaving his job, a non-sequitur paragraph was appended describing his purchase of a large yacht and his misadventures while cruising on it. Two boiler tubes had blown out during a cruise of Narragansett Bay, and Astor and his party had barely escaped serious injury.

The die was cast. From then on John Astor has been the prototype of the playboy of whom nothing good could be said or written. He has been criticized for having been unable to find constructive uses for his time and money. And yet, putting it into perspective, one cannot fail to see that his life has not been so different from that of any number of scions of well-to-do families, who are treated much more kindly by the press. In fact, a recent study of the tax returns of 398 Americans with incomes of more than one million dollars a year, revealed that 137 of them—just about a third—did not work at all, or to be exact, declared no income from salaries or wages, and most of the others derived an average of only 3 percent of their annual income from pay checks. (The bulk of the income, should anyone wonder, came from capital gains and dividends. Clubs, sports, travel, a tour of the art dealers, a stop at the broker's—it is easy to keep busy. Even among the Astor clan, there are many, bearing other names, who have never held a job or sat in an office. This one writes a never-finished biography of a little-known historical figure; that one collects ceramics. Not all members of this or other rich families are occupied with good works either, despite the tax benefits to be derived from philanthropy. And there are many well-to-do gentlemen whose marital difficulties and entanglements are every bit as numerous, though possibly not so involved, as John Astor's. Although no one would praise the lotus-eating, self-centered way of life led by some of the very rich, nonetheless, it seldom merits the degree of public censure accorded Astor.

The difference, of course, lies in the name. *Astor* is the symbol of society, and possessing the name has singled John out for criticism. Vincent was aware of the readiness of the public to damn him and fought vigorously against the idea that "just because a man is rich, he is also useless." John, bearing the dynastic name, even though he has tried to escape it, failed to understand this.

And yet, it was John, not Vincent, who fathered an heir, the only male Astor to carry on the name and tradition of the American Astors. The child was not given the John Jacob Astor appellation; his father hated the name and felt no emotional kinship with the founder of his family's fortune. He learned that June 17, 1963, was the two-hundredth anniversary of the birth of John Jacob I only when the elevator man in his building told him so. John's son was named William instead. There have been and are any number of Williams in the Astor family; it is the second traditional name used. But John specifically selected it in honor of his grandfather, husband of *the* Mrs. Astor.

"My aunt [Mrs. Orme Wilson] always said that I am more like my grandfather than my father," remarks John, "and I have always felt closer to him."

There is much in common between them—a fondness for women, an enjoyment of the pleasures of life, a dislike of routine work, a distaste for the ways of formal society—and both have known what it is to live in an atmosphere of disapproval expressed by others in the family and community.

The early harmful publicity that set a pattern to endure apparently for life was given additional material, if any were needed, by the unusual behavior of his father-in-law. Francis O. French had been unconventional long before his pretty daughter married John Astor, but prior to the Astor connection, not quite so much attention had been paid him. Only the fellow members of his social set knew of his taxicab driving venture in the 1920's, when his brokerage business failed. To draw the contrast plainly between his true station in life and his vocation, he told his friends to write him care of the Harvard Club or to meet him at the Knickerbocker, because, of course, he would maintain his memberships. He was not a success as a cab driver, and after netting only seventeen dollars in five days, he decided to abandon the whole idea. But he continued to enjoy pointing up the contrast between his lot and the great wealth of his friends and family. In 1938 he made the front page of *The New York Times* when he applied for relief on the grounds that he was down to his last fifteen dollars. The Newport *Daily News* reported that an "unimpeachable source" indicated that the Astors had been giving him money for several years, but all French would say was that he did not want assistance from his rich son-in-law. Instead, "I am willing, if necessary, to undertake even labor's task." A male escort service offered him employment, but he said that he was too old for such work. He finally obtained a job selling equipment and acting as assistant manager of a golf driving range. It was all a source of great embarrassment to John and Tucky; they had little luck in keeping French quiet.

Astor's first marriage came to an end in 1943 in what has turned out to be his only routine divorce. He made a settlement on Tucky that he will merely describe as "big," but that has been estimated in the newspapers as one million dollars. Custody of William was divided equally between them, and because, when in New York, they lived only six blocks apart, the arrangement was a pleasant one for the boy. Brought up in the tried-and-true style of members of society, William attended the Buckley School, joined the Knickerbocker Grays, and duly outfitted with white gloves, was dispatched to the De Rham dancing class favored by Whitneys, Rockefellers, Roosevelts, Paines, Dukes, Goulds, and others of the Old and not-quite-so Old Guard of society. Like boys with not quite such illustrious names, William hated the refining influence of dancing class and often had to be dragged off to it screaming in a taxicab. His father, never wholly convinced of the importance of following the rules of formal society, sometimes weakened and let him off. John decided not to send his son to St. George's for prep school; the memories of his days there were not beautified by the softening haze of distance. Instead William was entered in St. Paul's.

By this time the susceptible John was a husband again. In 1946 he married Gertrude Gretsch, a marriage that was to prove his legal undoing. On the positive side, it produced a daughter, Mary Jacqueline, in 1949; on the negative, it laid the groundwork for one of the weirdest marital messes of the century, culminating in the moment when John found himself to be possessed of two wives at one and the same time, without being a bigamist. Stepping into the trap himself, John watched it being snapped shut by some of the greatest legal minds in the country.

The Supreme Court of Florida estimated his lawyer's fees in one year at $105,000. "That figure is conservative," says Astor. "In fact, it is much too low."

This particular set of troubles began for John in July 1954 in Miami, Florida, when he first saw Dolores "Dolly" Fullman. Then in her mid-twenties, Dolly was tall and had a beautiful figure, large blue eyes, and pretty blonde curls.

"In those days I thought she looked something like Kim Novak —you know, that vacuous charming look. I've always found it very appealing," murmurs John, his heavy face softening at the memory. "She had taken elocution lessons and that gives a girl's voice a special quality."

John fell passionately and blindly in love with her, and he had to marry her. Because he was separated from Gertrude, it seemed perfectly obvious to him that the next move was to get a divorce as quickly as possible and marry Dolly. It may have been the obvious move, but, at least as put into operation by John, not the wise one. Forty-one years of his life had passed without Dolly; he could not endure the thought of wasting any more of it. And so he obtained a divorce in Juarez, Mexico. Unfortunately, Gertrude had not consented to the jurisdiction of the Mexican court. Nonetheless, the divorce was granted, and John went on to woo and win Dolly.

"I would never want you to work after we marry," cooed Dolly, "because I wouldn't want to be parted from you for eight hours a day."

She fussed about his having enough reading matter on the airplane between Miami and New York as he shuttled back and forth to see her. John was not the kind of man who customarily gets such tender little attentions from a woman and concluded that she was "not only pretty, but thoughtful and practical as well."

Astor was as if besotted with her. On August 6, 1954, barely three weeks after their meeting, in keeping with his policy of excessive speed, he whisked her off to Gretna Green in Arlington, Virginia, one of the few places where a couple can be married on the same day the license is obtained. He placed a wedding ring on the finger that was already adorned with his engagement gift of a seven-and-a-half-carat diamond. Marriage brought a number of unpleasant revelations to both. He learned for the first time that Dolly was not quite the young innocent he had believed her to be but that she had been married before. She discovered that he was hardly the ideal husband she had hoped he might be. In any event,

John soon got the feeling that he was trapped.

Nonetheless, he speaks of those early days of his marriage rather tolerantly, feeling that for all their difficulties, there was a basic compatibility.

No one reading the published accounts that revealed the startling nature of the testimony about their ill-fated shipboard honeymoon could possibly have suspected that fact. The couple parted after only six weeks, and the legal battle was joined. John had not one but two adversaries to combat, because Gertrude Astor was not relinquishing her position either. She filed suit in New York to the effect that she was still married to John: the Mexican divorce was not valid, and therefore, the marriage to Dolly was not legal. But Dolly, for all her big blue eyes and Kim Novak look, was just as determined to reap the benefits of her six weeks with Astor—and looked for legal counsel.

"Her lawyer was just too good," says John's son William, giving deserved credit to the man who handled Dolly's case all the way up to the United States Supreme Court.

His first move was to have Dolly ask for a legal separation and demand that Astor support her as his wife. John countered by agreeing with Gertrude that his Mexican divorce was invalid and that Dolly was not and never had been his wife. He went on to ask first for an annulment of the marriage and, should that fail, for a divorce on the ground of extreme cruelty. It would seem that all that was involved here was a purely legal situation, devoid of drama, requiring simply the decision on whether that divorce was binding. What ensued instead was a series of emotional courtroom scenes with "revelations," purple prose, accusations, and counteraccusations. She accused him of misconduct, saying that the details were "so intimate in nature" that she did not want to tell them—though of course, she did—and he replied that these were scurrilous charges and innuendoes. She had married him, he declared with "greed in her heart," after representing herself as a "white flower of purity," to which she replied, "I have always had everything I wanted . . . I am not interested in his money."

But despite all the lurid testimony, her lawyer never forgot for an instant that the case really hinged on that document obtained so easily in Mexico, and he invoked the legal doctrine of "estoppel." According to this, no one may benefit from an illegal act that he himself had performed. John had not been forced to obtain that speedy divorce; he had been driven to it by his own passion. And so he had no right to expect the invalidity of that decree to save him from Dolly and her demands. This line of reasoning convinced the late Circuit Judge Vincent C. Giblin, who was presiding over the hearing, and he declared Dolly to be John's wife. He was not, however, as convinced of the utter purity of Dolly's motive in marrying John and granted her maintenance of only $75 a week, plus $12,500 in legal fees for Astor to add to his burgeoning legal budget. Before her marriage, Dolly's income had been $65 a week, but this could hardly be considered much of an improvement for her. And to have been criticized for her motives as well! She appealed to the Supreme Court of Florida, and the figure was raised to $250 a week.

John's other wife was similarly occupied during this period with plans to make him wish that he had never gotten into any marital bed at all. Her first move had been to attach his real estate, including his cooperative apartment at 998 Fifth Avenue and his interest in a building on the northwest corner of Fifth Avenue and Thirty-fifth Street. In a court hearing the judge vacated the attachment, whereupon she asked for $1,000 a week for her support, plus $50,000 in legal fees. This was whittled down to the still considerable $2,500 a month for her and $1,000 for Mary Jacqueline, plus $7,000 in counsel fees. Worse yet for John was the fact that the New York Supreme Court took a diametrically opposed view to that of Florida: the Mexican divorce was invalid, and Gertrude, not Dolly, was his wife.

There was John, whose sin had been to fall in love too often and too well, with one wife in Florida and another in New York, neither of them offering him the solace of her love, body, and company—and both requiring his financial support. It was the sort of situation for the theater of the absurd, not real life. Unable to think of a solution, Astor took the problem to the Supreme Court of New York with the sorry plaint: Would they please tell him "which . . . is the lawful wife of the plaintiff?" "Both," found the court coldly. And Dolly was even granted additional counsel fees for the cost of having had to defend herself against him in New York.

Discouraged, but not utterly defeated, John made a last attempt to throw himself upon the mercy of the Florida court. He filed for an annulment of the marriage to Dolly, pleading that the previous finding be reconsidered in the light of the New York decision. Straining out the quality of mercy, Florida declined to reopen the case, and the Florida Supreme Court turned down the petition that followed. By now there was only one last court of appeal, and Astor went there: the United States Supreme Court. And here, too, he was turned down.

Most outside observers found it all rather amusing. As John has found all his life, nobody weeps for a rich man. Still, Astor was not to remain the man with two wives forever. Gertrude came to his rescue at last and obtained a legal American divorce, recognized in every state of the union.

The situation remains unique, even without Gertrude, John is single in some states and a married man in others. In some, his designs on women could be classed as honorable and in others as disreputable. The distinction depends on the law, not behavior. The deadlock between John and Dolly has entered its second decade, with agreement, at least of this writing, no closer than it has ever been. The two have given up attempts to arrive at a settlement and have not been in contact (even through lawyers) for some years. His hope that Dolly might want to marry again dwindles as she grows older; her life apparently is to be committed to the maintenance of the bond tied so swiftly in Florida. Despite the long record of failures to obtain relief, Astor has almost but not quite given up hope that the lawyers will yet solve the legal conundrum.

One of John's cousins does not consider the present situation as being altogether without merit: "He can't get married, which is very likely lucky."

So accustomed are the gossip columnists to marriage rumors that even though he is not free, the speculation as to what the writers like to call "possible mergers" still appear in the press. Although John insists that he is not interested in any more "mergers," his half-married state is irksome to a man of property. In those states that recognize Dolly as his wife, she has dower rights and must agree on the disposal of his holdings. New York does not consider him a married man, but the only New York property remaining consists of a couple of islands in Lake Champlain; in New Jersey, on the other hand, where Dolly is Mrs. Astor, he has land that he would very much like to sell. For some years he maintained a farm there and was so interested in it that he gave individual names to each of the 101 cows, but a regular loss of five thousand dollars a month made it too great a luxury, so it has been closed down, and may soon be abandoned.

John remains on relatively pleasant terms with those wives from whom he is properly divorced. Drinks at his home are still served on the beautiful silver tray inscribed with the names of the ushers at his first wedding in 1934. Tucky was at one time married to Raymond Guest, but has been divorced, and Gertrude is married to Count Sonio Coletti-Perucca. She shares the custody of Mary Jacqueline with John. When Gertrude was living abroad in the early 1960's, John kept "M.J." with him for two years, not even traveling, so as not to leave her alone. He is extremely proud of her and pleased that she is a "contented" girl, doing well in school. M.J.'s main addition to his large, beautifully furnished apartment has been an enormous ping-pong table in her bedroom. A tall, attractive teen-ager educated at a fashionable private girls' school, M.J. spends some weekends with her father and some with her mother.

The externals of Astor's life have not changed markedly over the years. Although lawyers' fees have been eating away at his inheritance, he lives up to his income, as has ever been his way. And the income, though not derived from a capital of seventy million dollars, is nonetheless substantial. At the time of Dolly's separation suit, the Supreme Court of Florida put Astor's net worth at $4.75 million, a figure that, like the estimate of his legal fees, is probably on the low side. It is based more on what he paid for investments than their actual value today. His income before taxes was found to be in the neighborhood of $250,000 a year.

This has not been sufficient to keep him in traditional Astor style. His New York apartment, although luxurious, can be kept clean and sparkling by two sleep-in maids and one day worker. And the Newport days are long since over. John, along with many other descendants of the gilded era's inner circle, found it too hard to keep up his cottage, Chetwode. "The last summer I used it, I ran it on a shoestring, with four gardeners and six in help inside. For a house of that size, this was just impossible, and so in 1948, it was sold." John regrets the loss of the house of which he was very proud, though the old Astor enthusiasm for Newport had died in him. "They were nice to me in Newport, but I hate the summer resort life, just social life and golf. I hate the summer."

A house in Miami has just about replaced Chetwode in his affections; for all his restlessness, his homes and their furnishings are very important to him. Always interested in construction, he supervised the building of the house himself. It was done in such a complicated way that the smallest repair requires going back to the men who put in the wiring. An office and secretary are maintained there, and Astor spends at least half an hour a day conferring on the long-distance telephone when he is anywhere else. The house is kept open all year round, so that he can fly there on a moment's notice. He called his son one day to say goodbye. "Where are you going?" "Florida." "When did you decide to go?" "Half an hour ago." "When are you leaving?" "In an hour." Well, his time is his own. And how does he spend it?

His day is considerably shortened by his chronic insomnia; he is awake until four or five in the morning. As a result he does not get up until noon. Then he goes out to lunch, and the afternoons fly by. After trying a succession of counselors, he has taken over the management of his own business interests and oversees his investments personally. A great reader, Sinclair Lewis is his favorite author. He collects art, particularly nineteenth-century landscape paintings, of which he would like to have more if he "could afford them." The pride of his collection is the possession of "four good and one not-so-good" works by George Inness. "I have no pictures of people," he says, "only of things." Nor has he ever kept a photograph album. This is a reflection, he is only too ready to concede, of his black view of the human race. If one asks him for pictures of his family, he offers photographs of the interior of 840 Fifth Avenue instead. It is a little sad that the one time sentimentality got the better of him and he tried to obtain the photographs used in the rotogravure section at the time of his first marriage, the *Tribune* told him that the files had been destroyed.

His greatest pleasure is in traveling, despite the memory of that harrowing bout of typhoid fever suffered in Italy when he was a boy. He has made close to thirty trips to Europe alone; in a single year he shuttled back and forth three times. In Spain not long ago he was surprised to find large numbers of Astors living in Barcelona. They are not relatives, as far as he knows, unless one gives credence to William Waldorf's family tree, which traced the ancestry back to the Spanish Pedro d'Astorga. Perhaps that questionable genealogy was inspired by some similar observation in the last century. When in Paris, John stays at the Hotel Meurice, commenting that it is just across the street from the hotel where his favorite grandfather died seventy-odd years ago during the trip to rescue Charlotte Augusta's reputation. But Astor is not altogether pleased by hotel life ("The first thing they ask when you check in is 'When are you leaving?' ") and is happier visiting with friends. Although he covers much of the same territory, John is not a member of the jet or any other international set. "Does this look like the kind of place where a member of the jet set would live?" he asks. And indeed, his apartment, with its solid, old-fashioned, well-constructed furniture does not.

Refusing placement in the jet set, he is even less inclined toward café society. The society columns notwithstanding, Astor declares that during the past year he has not spent more than a total of ten hours in all of the night clubs put together—and the headwaiters in the leading nightspots will, he says, bear him out.

This is ten hours more than his son William has devoted to New York's glamorous afterdark life. The younger Astor maintains that he has not been in any night club for two years. The society columnists have just about given up on him, and his name seldom appears in the newspapers at all. A tall, blond, all-American type, William has managed to stay in the *Social Register* and out of the divorce court. He has, in fact, done most of the things his uncle Vincent had wanted his father to do. He went to college, married a nice girl while still a student, and after graduation got a job as a security analyst with Bache and Company. Living quietly on three acres in New Jersey, he has fathered an heir suitably named William Backhouse and a daughter. Wearying of Bache, he did not retire to clipping coupons—there are not really enough to clip—but went into business on his own. Lacking the limitless resources of his forebears, he hopes to make his fortune by assisting others to make theirs. If a businessman plans to start a real-estate development or industry or introduce a new product, William helps him to raise the capital for it.

Although far from impoverished, William is the first of the Astors who does not live at all like an Astor. Of course, he does belong to the Metropolitan and Union clubs, but more to please his father than himself. He has thus far only been to the former a couple of times and has not yet entered the somber rooms of the latter. At home his wife does all the cooking, takes care of the two children and makes do with only a part-time cleaning woman; at his office he answers the telephone himself. Does this trouble him? Not at all. "The Astors do not worry," he declares, speaking more of himself than of his moody, brooding relatives.

The past sits lightly on his shoulders; he has but the haziest knowledge of family history. One day he did sit down with his grandfather's novel, but gave up on page eight.

"The Astors have been staid and stuffy except for Dad, who has added a bit of color," comments William. "All they did was hold on to money."

The fact that rather little of it has passed into William's hands enrages the father far more than it does the son. "There was a real feud between Dad and Vincent," says William. "It was like the Hatfields and the McCoys, or I guess you'd have to say like the Hatfields and the Hatfields."

So great is the power of self-delusion, however, that John never fully believed that Vincent really meant to cut him out of the will altogether. Imbued with the Astor tradition of money passed from generation to generation, he simply could not accept the idea that the fortune might just go out of the family. The farthest his imagination could take him was that Vincent would bypass him and leave the millions to William so that the dynasty could go on. He completely overlooked the fact that Vincent had never devoted so much as an instant's attention to William, possibly because of envy that his hated half-brother had the heir he lacked.

The discovery that Vincent left them not a penny came as a stunning blow to John. If he was to go down, however, it would not be without a fight, and he hired a documents expert to study the twenty-page will for erasures or insertions. None showed up. He then attempted to break the will by charging, first, undue influence on the part of the executors, and second, that Vincent was mentally incompetent to draw a will at the time of the signing. The pretrial hearing dragged on for months until it became as clear to John as it had been to everyone else from the start that his chances of overthrowing the will were virtually nil. He asked for a settlement of $2.5 million, but agreed to $250,000, to be taken out of the share left to the Vincent Astor Foundation. As usual, John was to pay the legal expenses. The gossip columns naturally kept their readers abreast of the situation throughout.

John had insisted from the beginning that he did not want the money for himself but only for his children, and after paying the lawyers, divided what was left between William and Mary Jacqueline.

"There have been three important Astors—one in the eighteenth century, one in the nineteenth century and one in the twentieth," states John somberly. "John Jacob Astor I, who made the fortune, William B. Astor, who increased it tremendously, and Vincent Astor, who destroyed it. People say that the British Astors are a branch of the family. That is no longer true. Today they are the trunk and we the branch."

William, however, does not take such a dark view of the situation. He hopes to become a millionaire himself. How does he plan to achieve this end? "I mean to earn it." The American Astors are thus coming full circle.

12

The Flowering of the English Astors

And in England the Astors continue to flourish like the green bay tree. John Jacob V has become the second Astor in a row to receive a barony; Gavin rules the powerful London *Times* and is so completely "in" the Queen's set that the Duke of Edinburgh is godfather to his youngest son; David runs the intellectuals' favorite, *Observer;* the third viscount * in luxury at Cliveden has married once, twice, and thrice; the John Jacobs have reached the count of eight; the William Waldorfs four, and the rents from more than one hundred million dollars in United States real estate keep on pouring in to sustain them all.

While the Astor family in America has been contracting, the English Astors have been growing ever more numerous. The relationships between all these Astors have by now begun to confuse people, leading to any number of whoppers of mistakes. The Honorable Gavin Astor is not and never has been Nancy Astor's son. He is the child of John Jacob V, Baron Astor of Hever, and the late Lady Violet Elliot Mercer-Nairne, a gentlewoman so quiet that her name appeared in the newspapers only on such suitable occasions as when she was made a Dame in the Order of St. John. In order to keep the English Astors straight, it is best to fix in one's mind the two main lines, one stemming from John Jacob V and the other from the late second Viscount Waldorf. They were brothers, children of William Waldorf Astor, founder of the English line. There is also a sister, Pauline, but because her children do not bear

* William Waldorf Astor, Third Viscount, died on March 7, 1966, after this book had gone to press.

the Astor name (being respectively Bowes-Lyon and Nichols) there is no confusion about them. The same can be said for Lady Violet's child by her first marriage, who is the eighth Marquis of Lansdowne, and his eldest son is the Earl of Shelburne. Her second marriage to John Jacob Astor V produced three sons, the afore-mentioned Gavin, Hugh Waldorf, and John—just plain John in this case, the John Jacob having been pre-empted by a cousin. These gentlemen are first cousins to the five children of Waldorf Astor and the effervescent Nancy. Again, of these five, one, (Nancy) Phyllis, is not at all confusing, because she married Lord Willoughby de Eresby, who became the Earl of Ancaster, and their children, of course, are not Astors. The eldest of Waldorf's sons is Lord William Waldorf Astor, the third viscount, then comes David (the two Astors in the publishing world are cousins, not brothers), Michael and John Jacob VII. The issue is further clouded by the way in which members of this generation have named their issue: Young David Astor, for example, is Michael's son, not David's, and John Jacob VIII is the eldest child of Gavin, not of John Jacob VII, who has given his firstborn the name of Michael. Well, at least Lord Astor has held to William Waldorf for his heir, and his cousin, just plain John, has used John Richard for his.

The children of John Jacob V are hard-working and conservative. Each of them is still married to his first wife, and has provided little fodder for the British tabloids which are rather more sensational than the American. Their way of life is probably a result of the influence of their father's strong character.

"He is the finest example of a British gentleman," declares his son, Gavin, with affection. "Although he was born in America, he became totally British."

Throughout his life he has appeared to be the prototype of the English aristocrat. This was so generally recognized that when *Life* magazine ran a story on English society in 1947, it was illustrated with a large photograph of John Jacob V taken at the famed Hurlingham Club, of which he was chairman. (He also, of course, is a member of the Carlton, Marlborough, Turf, Beefsteak, Marylebone, Cricket, and other clubs). And the following month the London *Times*, describing the preparations for the wedding of

Princess (now Queen) Elizabeth to Philip, singled out but a few of the one thousand wedding gifts for special mention, among them the antique James Rigby bracket clock from John Jacob and Violet.

In appearance and character, too, this man lives up to the popular stereotype of the upper-class Englishman. He is tall and spare, with a military bearing, despite the limp caused by the World War I loss of his right leg. His features are strong, with a straight firm mouth and jaw. There is nothing small about the man; even his mustache is a good size. Despite his wealth and prominence, he is shy and so reticent that people who meet him instinctively want to help him.

Far less conspicuous than his brother and sister-in-law at Cliveden, he received less censure than they during the 1930's, when the "Cliveden Set" was at its powerful peak. This was so, even though many attacks were centered on the appeasement policies of the newspaper that he, not they, owned. Excuses were found for him then and later. It has been repeatedly said that he made it his rule never to interfere with the policies of the professional editors of his newspapers. His own views did not take him as far on the pro-appeasement road as it did his editor, Geoffrey Dawson.

"I did my utmost," said Dawson subsequently, "to keep out of the paper anything that might hurt their [Hitler and his colleagues] susceptibilities."

John Walter, owner of one tenth of the *Times*, lodged an objection to the policy; not so John Jacob V. He had the power to fire Dawson, but did not use it. His failure to do so was the result of his having been convinced by his friends in the government that appeasement was the prevailing view and that it would be frivolous for him to intrude his personal opinion in so powerful a paper. As he always considered himself a military man, it must have been a blow to find himself blamed for inaction rather than action.

With that single exception, John Jacob V has received a uniformly good press in both England and America. His son Gavin attributes this largely to the fact that "he has never acted like a wealthy man; he does not just throw it around."

There has always been plenty to throw around, if he wished. The American trust, curse of Astor's old age, is based on real estate conservatively estimated by realty experts as worth "well over $100 million." Most of it is in land, rather than buildings, and the bulk is in Manhattan, of course. The Estate owns such incredibly valuable property as the land beneath the New York Hilton Hotel on the Avenue of the Americas between Fifty-third and Fifty-fourth Streets, rented for half a million dollars a year, and the Park Avenue lots occupied by the headquarters of the First National City Bank. To get an idea of the worth of Astor holdings, one need only look at the records of a recent sale: in September 1963, Tiffany & Company agreed to pay the estate $2.8 million for the plot of ground beneath its building—a mere 85 feet on Fifth Avenue and 125 feet on Fifty-seventh Street. ("Well, the family has contributed a lot to New York," one of the prominent English Astors reminds us.) Although little is left of the Astors' old hotel dominion, the English estate still owns the fashionable seventeen-story Carlton House on Madison Avenue between Sixty-first and Sixty-second Streets. Outside of New York City, there are substantial holdings in Rochester, Syracuse, and Fort Worth, Texas. Leaving the United States, but remaining on this continent, are possessions of land and buildings in Vancouver, B.C., and other parts of Canada.

As his son has said, John Jacob V has been no mere *rentier* living on the proceeds of the labors of his forebears, but has held many important positions, both during and after his twenty-three-year-long term in the House of Commons as Conservative M.P. for the Dover division of Kent. His is a good solid record of achievement, including twenty-five years as chairman of the Phoenix Assurance Company and nearly thirty years as director of Hambros Bank. In keeping with his character, John Jacob has been a public-spirited man, remarkably so, for one of his heritage. His interest in the press has gone beyond the mere reading of balance sheets for his newspapers and he was a key figure in the formation of a council to consider recruitment, ethics, and pensions. For a quarter of a century he served as president of the fund-raising Newspaper Press Fund and also headed the Commonwealth Press Union. Among his many charities, the Middlesex Hospital is his favorite, and one gift of nearly two million dollars made possible the establishment of a medical school and nursing home.

It came as small surprise to anyone when Colonel the Honorable John Jacob Astor's name appeared on the Prime Minister's List of New Year Honors for 1956 as Baron Astor of Hever, of Hever Castle in the County of Kent, "in return for public services." Exactly forty years had passed since his father had received the same honor. For the second time an American-born commoner donned the traditional red velvet and ermine and, preceded by two sponsoring lords, marched toward the Garter King of Arms, heard the clerk announce his preferment, and then went to the barons' bench. Three times he took his seat and three times he rose, doffed his three-cornered beaver hat, and bowed to the Lord Chancellor, who in return took off his own. The ceremony was over, and another Astor had joined the peerage.

"The average peer is a man whose great-grandfather was a moderately successful grocer," wrote J. D. Scott in his book *Life in Britain*, published in that same year. The aptness of the quote is a trifle close for comfort.

If ever a man's castle was his home, Hever, the seat of his barony, was that to John Jacob V. He never really enjoyed the glittering celebrity-packed parties that meant so much to his brother's family, and the luxurious London house at 18 Carlton House Terrace, inherited from William Waldorf, could not in his mind compare with Hever. There, surrounded by the art masterpieces of the past, he took up landscape painting as a hobby, turning out works given the limited but not altogether unflattering description of "highly competent." Of greater importance to him, as to many gentlemen of his class, were his dogs and his rifles. Long hours of each day were spent walking through the grounds of Hever. "There is not an inch of the gardens and fields that he does not know," said one of his friends. "He could recognize each stone, stick, or blade of grass." Astor and Lady Violet, generous to local charities and active in village affairs, were immensely popular in the tiny country towns of Hever and neighboring Edenbridge.

But this happy life was brought to an abrupt end in 1962 by the passage of a new Finance Act. The aim of this act was to end investment abroad by Englishmen seeking to avoid the English estate duty. This had certainly not been the intent of the Astor trust, based on property that had been in the family long before the discontented William Waldorf had decided on expatriation. Nonetheless, under the terms of the act, should John Jacob V die in England, death duties on the trust would be calculated at the top rate of 80 percent. Because the baron was seventy-six in 1962, he could hardly be so irresponsible as to avoid contemplating this eventuality. When passage of the act was first made public, most people assumed that Astor could easily avoid the ruinous death duties by selling the American property and reinvesting in British real estate. But Astor testamentary practice made this impossible for him to do. His father, William Waldorf, true to the policy laid down by the founder of the fortune, had merely given life interests in the trust to John Jacob V, his late brother Waldorf, and his sister, Pauline. As a result, none of them could touch the property, which was to go to their children. Renouncing the life interest might have been a solution, but the American law forbade that. John Jacob and his sister were truly caught.

"It would be very difficult for those concerned to meet the death duties both on the United States trust fund and on my property in England," John Jacob V explained, "and it would certainly mean that Hever Castle and much else would have to be sold."

The loss of Hever alone was unthinkable. On September 21, 1962, Baron Astor of Hever, therefore, announced that he was leaving England and moving to the south of France. "It is my firm hope that as a result my descendants will be enabled to continue to uphold the family traditions and responsibilities as I have always tried to do."

His sister, the Honorable Mrs. Spender-Clay, was similarly faced with the necessity of exile from England. This is particularly ironic when one considers that Pauline is the great-aunt of the Queen. Nonetheless, she did not wish her daughters, both widows, of Sir David Bowes-Lyon and Sir Philip Bouverie Bowyer Nichols respectively, to be impoverished by her death. Displaying the same fortitude as her brother, eighty-two-year-old Pauline departed for the Channel Island of Guernsey, which has an independent government under the British crown. And Pauline, a widow, had to make the break alone. As has been the way throughout her life, the newspapers gave her action in a mere postscript to front-page stories about her brother.

With the light of public attention focused upon him, John Jacob V behaved with British stoicism. Still, his voice broke a little as, leaving Hever, he murmured: "My home is called Mass Notre Dame. Mass means Farm. I had to ask what that means."

His homes in England went to his sons—Hever to Gavin and the magnificent Carlton Terrace house to John.

Whatever the British government may gain from the passage of the Finance Act, it is losing money on John Jacob V today. Prior to his departure he paid taxes on the income from the trust in England as well as the United States. Now France, with an infinitely lower rate, is the European recipient of his tax payments.

And what of his sons, Gavin, Hugh, and John? Will they, too, in their turn be forced to leave the country of their birth to face a lonely old age in a foreign land? Luckily for them, the hand of the dead will not reach down to blight them. They will inherit the trust fund outright and will be able to do as they wish with it. Reluctant to reveal anything concerning the fortune, they decline to say whether they will sell out their American investments to reinvest in British. It does, however, seem to be the obvious solution for them. Because Vincent had disposed of his property before his death, the end of the Astor hold on Manhattan real estate is coming into view at last after a century and a half.

Of the three brothers, John, the youngest, keeps the closest American ties. He spends considerable time in this country looking after his family's interests. John is the only one of his generation who still plays an active part in the British government.

"There was a time when the cry of 'Astor' would bring several M.P.'s to their feet," recalls an English newspaperman whose memory goes back more than a quarter of a century.

Today, despite their tremendous behind-the-scenes power, only John takes his seat in the House of Commons as Conservative M.P. for Newbury in Berkshire County, outside of London. His wife, Diana Drummond, whom he married in 1950, has allied him at least indirectly with another parliamentary house. Her father was a member of the House of Keys, the ancient legislative assembly of the Isle of Man.

The Astors' American heritage is shared by the wife of his brother Hugh. The former Emily Kinloch, daughter of the twelfth Baronet of Gilmerton, is the granddaughter of Frederick Y. Dalziel of New York. At their wedding, which took place just three months after John's, she was attended by three pages, including Hugh's four-year-old nephew John Jacob VIII, most charmingly turned out in burgundy trousers and white blouses. They might have stepped out of an old-fashioned novel, and perhaps that is what the bride had in mind. Some years later, when fulfilling one of the many social duties required of an Astor wife, Emily opened an exhibition of children's books dating from the year 1484. Books for children have changed, she remarked. "My favorite book was 'Little Lord Fauntleroy.'"

Hugh has always been the most adventurous of the three brothers. Obviously headed for big things—although not the top spot —on the *Times*, he started learning the business from not quite the bottom up as a writer and correspondent. In fact, he got some interesting and even hazardous foreign assignments and was sent to Palestine to observe at first hand the Arab-Jewish-British clashes and the terrorist activities that accompanied the establishment of Israel. Hugh, refusing to remain safely out of the line of danger, was shot by a sniper on the outskirts of Haifa. The bullet entered his left leg, fracturing his thigh. It was just the sort of thing his aunt, Lady Nancy Astor, would have expected; she became extremely heated whenever the subject of Jewish terrorism was raised.

In time Hugh abandoned such exciting activities and assumed the role for which he was destined by virtue of being the second son—deputy chairman of the *Times*, the position he holds today. He is also chairman of the board of the Times Book Company. As might be expected, he has inherited a goodly number of his father's multitudinous directorships and charity obligations. In 1960, for example, at the age of thirty-nine, he took over from his seventy-four-year-old father the directorship of Hambros Bank. In order to maintain the family's tradition of aiding the Middlesex Hospital, he serves on many committees there.

By far the most prominent of Baron Astor's children, and indeed one of the most prominent Britons today, is the Honorable Gavin Astor. He cannot inherit the titular lordship from his father, but by succeeding to the position of publisher of the *Times*, he has inherited a position as press lord. Very tall, erect, well and power-fully built, looking less than his age of forty-plus, Gavin has reddish-blond hair, small but twinkling eyes, the Astor ruddy complexion, and the Astor nose. A charming, outgoing man, he does not suffer from the Astor moody streak. "No one has ever called me melancholy," he declares with his ready laugh.

Still, Gavin takes his role in the family seriously and is most interested in its history. In 1961, together with his father and his eldest son, he traveled to America to attend the celebration of the sesquicentennial of the founding of Astoria. Neither John Jacob VI nor his son William, nor Alice's son Ivan Obolensky, nor any member of the closely related Wilsons, Chanlers, or Draytons was there. Gavin was so impressed that two years later when he went to Walldorf, Germany, to attend the two-hundredth anniversary of his great-great-great grandfather's birth, he delivered a speech in German in which he declared that if John Jacob Astor I had not opened the West by founding Astoria, the northern frontier of America might have been different and, what is more, California might have belonged to Canada.

Although as John Jacob VI points out logically, you have to go all the way back to William Backhouse to find a common ancestor for the British and American Astors, Gavin tries to keep up with his American relatives and remarks that they remain in contact and visit one another at least occasionally. ("Gavin is the only one of the British Astors I know," says John Astor, "and he couldn't be a nicer fellow!") Gavin is particularly delighted to point to the strangest of coincidences linking his wife, who is the former Lady Irene Haig, to the American Astors. She is related to that handsome George Ogilvie Haig who became the second husband of reckless Charlotte Augusta Astor Drayton, daughter of *the* Mrs. Astor. What is more, Lady Irene's middle name is Augusta. Times have so changed since the staid period when Mrs. Drayton's love life scandalized two continents that Gavin enjoys thinking of his connection with—"rather the black sheep of the family, wasn't she?"

There is certainly nothing in the least black sheep about Gavin, who is as established a member of the Establishment as one might find. In Anthony Sampson's *The Anatomy of Britain*, it is taken as a matter of course that Gavin is in the Queen's circle of friends, as well as that of the prominent government officials. Gavin serves as a director of more companies and corporations than one would care to name, but of course, his power derives mainly from his position as publisher of the distinguished old London *Times*—the paper that one "must write a letter to." In England where rich and usually titled gentlemen control the newspapers—Lord Beaverbrook, the second Lord Rothermere, Lord Thomson, Lord Camrose—the term *press lord* is particularly apt, and it is ironic that with all the lords in his family, Gavin is one of the few publishers to lack a title. His day may yet come, to be sure; his grandfather was sixty-eight when he won his title and his father seventy. In buying the newspaper, John Jacob V bought its 180-year history and prestige for himself and his family. They like to recall how Abraham Lincoln described the *Times*—"I don't know of anything which has more power, except perhaps the Mississippi"—and that Disraeli once remarked balefully that Britain sends two ambassadors to the key cities of the world, one from the diplomatic corps and the other from the *Times*.

If mass circulation were the sole criterion of success, the London *Times* today would be insignificant, with sales totaling a paltry 254,000 copies, a mere 2 percent of newspaper readership. Its style is hardly calculated to attract the bulk of the riders of the Underground. Instead of front-page headlines screaming of sex, rape, murder, politics, or cataclysms (although news of all of them appears on inside pages), there is column upon column of classified advertising. The *Times* has always done it that way, of course. But the paper's importance and influence is not dependent on the number of readers; "who" rather than "how many" is the key question, and the *Times* readers include everyone of note in the government and the nobility. In a recent survey, researchers found that 70 percent of those listed in *Who's Who* were *Times* readers, as opposed to 43 percent for the runner-up, the *Daily Telegraph*.

Even the newspaper offices in Printing House Square, off London's famed Fleet Street, are clearly intended for a newspaper run in the spirit of William Waldorf's *Pall Mall Gazette*—"by gentlemen for gentlemen." Reporters keep their jackets on to work in the new building that cost $13.5 million to erect. Their voices are well-modulated when they confer with one another, so as not to disturb others. Instead of the interruptions caused by high-spirited copy boys, copy is dispatched overhead in small tramcars. The library is referred to in grandiose fashion as the "Intelligence Room." Too gentlemanly to demand by-lines, the reporters are anonymous; perhaps the only name, aside from Astor's, known to the man in the street is that of Sir William John Haley, the editor.

But the newspaper, as some members of the Astor family have learned to their sorrow, is not filled with starchy, namby-pamby copy. The reporting of one scandalous affair was so explicit that a competitor complained loudly, "The *Times* gets away with legal pornography." Nonetheless, the newspaper, under Astor and the editors, presents such facts only if they are considered valid news, not for the sake of sensationalism or enticing readers. In opening a student journalism conference recently, Gavin Astor condemned any exploitation of sex or intrusion into private lives in order to satisfy mass morbidity or curiosity. His cousin Michael showed even greater sensitivity in a letter he sent to the *Times:* "A newspaper which carries an air of respectability prints a story that the executioner was a personal friend of the murdered man. A little macabre. A little shoddy, too."

The *Times* has on this and political grounds—Haley is seeking to remove the strictly Tory label from the *Times* and indicate that it is not the mouthpiece of any party—become more controversial during the last year or so. Nonetheless, in basic things it has not changed. One expert who claims that the best use for newspapers is to wrap fish 'n chips insists that he can recognize which paper was used: "I am such a great connoisseur that I can tell the difference between the tang of the Beaverbrook *Daily Express* and the mellow flavor of the *Times.*"

No such praise is given to the tea being served to sightseers at Hever Castle, home of the publisher of the *Times.*

"The only complaint I get is about the tea," worries Gavin, who is distracted from his duties at the *Times* by such housewifely concerns as sandwiches arriving after tea time, stale cake, and weak tea.

In 1963 the Astors, following the example of 750 other titled and almost-titled British families, opened their castle to the public on a given day each week. The admission charge helps to defray the truly phenomenal cost of keeping up the house and the Italian gardens. When the weather is good, about 1,200 visitors troop across the drawbridge to view the rooms lived in by Anne Boleyn, William Waldorf Astor, Baron Astor of Hever, and today by the Gavin Astors. They and their five children sleep in the Tudor cottages in back of the castle, but use Hever's living and dining rooms. In the living room stands a lovely old piano made nearly two hundred years ago by George Astor, brother of John Jacob I. Fame and success have passed over George's descendants, and none of the Astors today knows what has become of them. Only this piano at Hever and a barrel organ in the library of Lord William Astor's London home remain as reminders that, although William Waldorf gets all the credit, there have been English Astors for the better part of two centuries.

William Waldorf's great newspaper purchase, the *Observer*, has remained in the other side of the family, going to Gavin's cousin. The *Observer* is an old paper that has always prided itself on its independence in analyzing the importance of news events. The Battle of Trafalgar was dismissed with just a few lines. Independent thinking, luckily tempered by better judgment, has always been characteristic of David Astor.

"I was anti-Russian," he says, "even before it was fashionable to be anti-Russian."

David has invariably gone his own way intellectually, standing firm against the pressures of his persuasive family. In the 1930's he was the only one of the English Astors to be strongly anti-Nazi. In addition to the family opposition to this view, he had to withstand the opinions of others in the Establishment. David went on to revolt strongly for a time against the manner of thought of the social set dominated by his parents. Some of this revolt may have been due to emotional as well as intellectual factors, because all of Nancy's children reacted strongly to her desire to control them.

After such un-Astorlike activities as going to work first in a Glasgow factory and then in a London bank, he began his journalistic career as a junior reporter on the Yorkshire *Post*. In 1945 David joined the *Observer* as foreign editor, and three years later, in Astor style, became the editor. Serious and hard-working, he calls most staff members by their first names, which is far more unusual in formal England than in America. The reputation of the publication has improved under his leadership to the point where an American magazine rather enviously referred to it recently as an "intellectual citadel of the arts." The British magazine, the *Queen*, with a lighter touch, hailed the paper's stature: "In suburban society, it is more of a status symbol to say you work for the *Observer* or the *Sunday Times* [not owned by the Astors] than to be a crime reporter."

Among the Astors the lightest touch is most consistently maintained by the youngest of the brothers, John Jacob VII, usually known as "Jakie." His brother Michael recalls that years ago, when Jakie was asked how he would tell his father that he was doing poorly at Oxford, he remarked, "I may have to come clean and tell father the only thing I've passed this term is water, and not much of that."

Of all Nancy's children, Jakie is the closest to her in spirit, having the same kind of lively wit and love of fun. When he was a child, he took part in the afterdinner dramatics at Cliveden, and his performances as an elderly retired Indian army man or a ventriloquist's dummy showed a talent similar to his mother's. He shared the enthusiasm for horses common to both his parents and has always been an outstanding rider. The worst penalty his father could inflict on the youthful Jakie was to confiscate his horse.

Serving in the Royal Army in World War II, high-spirited Jakie displayed such conspicuous courage that he won both the Legion of Honour and the Croix de Guerre. In 1944, dressed in his khaki uniform with the blue wings of the airborne division on his tunic, Major Astor was married to Ana Iñez Carcano, daughter of the Argentine ambassador to Britain. Even in a family noted for its lovely wives, Ana's beauty stands out.

In postwar as in prewar years, politics was the obvious career for the Astor boys, and in 1950 three out of the four were standing for election. It fell to Jakie to inherit Nancy's constituency, the Sutton division of Plymouth. Nancy was ostensibly out of politics by then, but was rather wistful about it. With their father's kindly prodding, each of her candidate sons asked her to hold one big meeting in his constituency during the campaign. Feelings about her support were mixed, because it was impossible to control

Nancy, and she was capable of saying anything that came into her head.

For all his good nature, Jakie refused to go along with his mother on her favorite issue: "It is a man's own responsibility to decide whether he will drink or not."

Jakie lost the election of 1950 to the Labor candidate, Mrs. Lucy Middleton, by the narrow margin of 924 votes and then defeated her the following year by the even narrower margin of 710. He remained in the House of Commons until 1959, when he announced his determination to abandon politics. His decision is often attributed to his opposition to the government policy during the Suez crisis. It is just as likely, though, that the real reason is the one expressed by his older brother, Lord Astor: "Jakie hates an indoor life."

The third brother, Michael, also served in Parliament as M.P. for Surrey from 1945 to 1951, enduring the embarrassment of having his mother greet one of his speeches with a stage-whispered: "Where did you learn to do this? I feel like Balaam when the ass spoke." This was particularly hard on Michael, who was always extremely sensitive and troubled by his parents' attitude and way of life. Even as an adult, he has retained his bitterness about the British upper-class practice of sending boys away to boarding school at the age of eight. Although clearly admiring his mother in many ways, he was painfully aware of her shortcomings and struggled to resist her overpowering influence.

He did not take the pleasure in the parliamentary life that Nancy had and gave it up in favor of farming one thousand acres in Oxfordshire. Farming has, oddly enough, been an Astor avocation, if not vocation, both in America and in England since the days when *the* Mrs. Astor's husband escaped from the toils of society to his farm at Ferncliff. In the United States, John Jacob VI and his son William attempted for a long time to maintain a most unprofitable five hundred acres in New Jersey. In England, Hever is in the midst of a farm country, and Cliveden has White Place, a 250-acre farm. Michael's cousin John was prepared for the life of a gentleman farmer: he broke with Astor educational tradition so far as to attend the Royal Agricultural College at Cirencaster. The net result of this was that John has remained in politics, whereas Oxford-educated Michael has become the farmer.

He is, however, the most intellectual of farmers and has followed the example of his grandfather and great-uncle by turning his hand to writing, at which he shows considerably more skill than they. His recent book, *Tribal Feeling*, is a moving account of how difficult it was to grow up an Astor. As an art collector, he specializes in Impressionist works. Like his uncle, he dabbles with a paint brush himself, and a number of his pictures were shown a few years back in a London exhibition, with the theme "Painting Is a Pleasure." Michael's paintings hung alongside works by such other spare-time artists as Noel Coward, (the late) King Feisal II of Iraq, the Duchess of Gloucester, and John Jacob V.

Keen-eyed, gossip-minded Britons were rather surprised to find the news of Michael's divorce in 1961 buried on the bottom of page three of the London *Times*, well below a dull report on the appointment of the Queen's counselors. But Cousin Gavin's paper was right in its news analysis. As Michael stated in his book, the divorce was granted on the grounds of "an adultery I had not committed with a lady whose name I never discovered." (Had he read the *Times*, he would have learned that it was Sarah Jenkins.) He was married again a few months later to Patricia David Pandora Clifford Jones, daughter of the Honorable Sir Bede Edmund Clifford.

The doings of all Astor cousins, brothers, sisters, wives, aunts, and children are duly chronicled in the society listings of the British newspapers and women's magazines. The wives give birth, and titled gentlemen and ladies make haste to act as godparents to the new Astor infants. These are considerable in number, with four, five, and in David's case, even six children (at last count) fathered by members of this flourishing family. The husbands manage their business or press interests, attend board meetings, give talks, buy yachts, race horses, ride to hounds, and keep up estates. The Astors are to be found opening exhibitions, sponsoring charity affairs, attending debuts and balls, giving receptions and garden parties attended by members of royalty, and dining with Cabinet officers, the Prime Minister, and even the Queen.

The years of Labor governments, the increased opportunities for those born in modest circumstances, high taxation, and the opening of baronial mansions to sightseers have changed the lives of the aristocrats in many ways. And yet, as J. D. Scott insists in his book, England is still a "snob's Elysium." The class system, with the old-school-tie bit, is far from dead. The Labor government has not been able to wipe that out any more than it has abolished the House of Lords, which it at one time threatened to do.

A butler in a tailcoat opens the door to Lord Astor's luxurious home, and if high taxation has forced any privation upon him, it is hard to imagine what that might be. In terms of newspaper linage as well as lineage, William Waldorf Astor, the third viscount, wins over all the rest of his family. As eldest son, he inherited the title attained with such difficulty by his grandfather. His marriages, divorces, homes, social life, vacations, vocations, and avocations have been chronicled in the press of two continents. Today, in his late fifties, Lord Astor does not look the sort of man to have stirred up such a storm. Where his cousins and brothers have typical tweedy British good looks, he is rather undistinguished in appearance. Only slightly above the average in height, which is short for an Astor, he is slender and has thinning gray hair and a large nose. And yet, he does have something—the undefinable air, call it charm or flair—a ready smile and a pleasing manner. His friends say that he is kindly and generous, good qualities that have at times caused him as much trouble as faults.

As heir apparent to Cliveden and the title, his career got off to an early start. Appointments came quickly to him, not only because of his Astor connection, but also, as *Time* magazine once put it, because of his "energy and gumption." When but twenty-five years old, he was appointed private secretary to Lord Victor Alexander Lytton, chairman of the League of Nations commission on Manchuria. He accompanied the commission to the Far East where it studied the Japanese take-over at first hand and recommended that economic sanctions be imposed against Japan. William's opportunity to influence British policy increased considerably in 1935, when following in his mother's footsteps, he became a member of the House of Commons. His campaign was run in a casual direct style similar to Nancy's. He drove around his constituency in a little car with a sliding roof. Whenever he saw a group of people, he would slide the roof open, pop up through it, and make a speech. Although the manner was his mother's, the speech was not. Bill was never particularly witty, although he did develop a certain facility of expression.

Sitting in Parliament with his mother was hardly undiluted joy, because opponents found it all too easy to bedevil him. During one debate when he took an unpopular stand, one fellow M.P. nudged Nancy and said, "Spank him."

He remained in Parliament for ten years, with time off during the World War II period, which he spent in the Royal Navy. This interest in the sea gave him something in common with his American relative, Vincent, and they became great friends. Vincent, who was never noted for tact, persisted in teasing William about the fall from power of the British Navy. William who, on the other hand, is noted for his, recalls his efforts to restrain himself from counter-attacking with references to Pearl Harbor.

After the War, William, along with many other Conservatives, lost his seat in Commons in the Labor landslide, and was not successful in efforts to win it back until 1951. The following year the death of his father put an abrupt end to his political aspirations. As had happened to Waldorf thirty-three years earlier, he was kicked upstairs into the House of Lords.

His reaction was not the same, however: "I was really rather glad to leave Commons," he says. "As I have high blood pressure, I found that it was just too much."

He was more fortunate than his father, at least, in having no dynamic little wife to take his place in Commons and push him into the shade. In fact, at that time he was on the way to having no wife at all, because his marriage—his first—was foundering and was to end in the divorce court within the year. Bill had remained London's most eligible bachelor until he was thirty-eight years old. He had then married Sarah Norton, daughter of the sixth Baron Grantley, a descendant of the playwright Richard Sheridan, and more than a decade Astor's junior.

He brought suit for divorce on grounds of adultery, and the judge in giving William custody of their one-and-a-half-year-old son declared, "Lord Astor was devoted to his wife and did his utmost to preserve what was for a time a happy marriage."

The first Lady Astor was married to Thomas Michael Baring

shortly after the divorce became final.

Bill's second marriage took place in 1955 and his bride on that occasion was Philippa Hunloke, assistant stage manager at the Royal Academy and granddaughter of the ninth Duke of Devonshire. The groom was accompanied to the church by his appealing little three-year-old son, William Waldorf. Despite this charming touch of sentimentality, the marriage lasted for but five years, produced a daughter, and was terminated in 1960 on grounds of desertion.

A few months later Lord Astor was married to Bronwen Pugh, who as a high-fashion model, had been voted "woman of the year" for 1955 by a London fashion group. She is the daughter of Sir Alan Pugh, judge of Marylebone County Court, and she took up modelling because, like many well-born girls, she was not content with the empty life of the socialite. At the time of their marriage Bronwen was twenty-eight and William a lively, vigorous fifty-three. He refers to her proudly and quite accurately as "my beautiful wife," and his eyes light up when she enters the room. The present Lady Astor's beauty is of a somewhat different type from that of the typical American fashion model. Her lovely figure is rather full-blown, and she carries more of an air of radiant good health than is to be found on the pages of *Vogue*. She has high coloring and the clear, glowing skin that Englishwomen always attribute to the damp climate of their island. With her erect carriage and her high-piled russet-colored hair, she is quite as tall as her husband. Together they entertain at Cliveden and in their large expensively furnished London home on Upper Grosvenor Street. Bill remarks airily that he really should get rid of that house, because it is such an "extravagance." He bought it "for entertaining" in 1935, when he first sat in Parliament. New M.P.'s, who are not Astors, to be sure, have managed with somewhat less splendor.

Although he has put aside political ambition—there was no question of his taking advantage of the Peerage Bill in 1963, allowing lords to relinquish their titles and stand for Commons—he has always made a practice of attending the House of Lords when bills in which he is interested are to be considered. While the Lords has had no real power for the last half-century, some important legislation is initiated there.

"You can't just sit in the Lords when you want to speak, though," Astor points out. "You have to make a practice of going from time to time anyway."

Some of Lord Astor's speeches in the House have exhibited considerable independence of mind. He once made the valid and unpopular point that "if missionaries are going to be encouraged to take a bigger part in Kenya so that people could get the benefit of the Christian religion, it behooves the Europeans to give an example of that religion by abandoning practices, such as the color bar, which are wholly incompatible with Christianity."

On another occasion he lived up to what he called his "hereditary interest" in urging that women be admitted to the House of Lords. His father, he pointed out, had proposed this in the early 1920's. Bill did not mention his mother's vain attempt to talk her old adversary Winston Churchill into elevating her to the Lords after World War II.

"To oppose their admission to the Lords," declared Bill with fire, "would make the House absurd in the eyes of the country."

Women were admitted to the Lords in 1958; it was, unfortunately, a bit too late for Bill's mother, by then approaching eighty.

Lord Astor today is most interested in supporting bills that affect the fate of refugees. He has traveled all over the world, studying the plight of such peoples and offering assistance wherever he can.

"There are so many refugees everywhere," he says thoughtfully, "in Tibet, Hong Kong, the Arabs in the Middle East . . ."

Following the Hungarian uprising against the Communists in 1956, Lord Astor helped the defeated Revolutionaries to escape from that country and assisted them thereafter. His efforts were rewarded with the Grand Cross of Merit with the Star and Sash of the Sovereign Military Order of Malta, granted on the recommendation of the Grand Priory of Austria.

Invariably generous, Lord Astor continues to maintain the Canadian Red Cross Memorial Hospital, established at Cliveden during the war. He also set up a charitable foundation after his father's death, because, as he puts it with a smile, "I found I had too much money." The Foundation, which bears his father's name, gives fellowships to students. In its early years it concerned itself with science only, furnishing scientists with funds enabling them to study in the United States or in scientific centers in other parts of the world. By now it has been expanded to include those areas of study that are usually neglected, such as Chinese or Russian history. Young singers are also given grants to be used for their musical training.

"There's been little publicity about the Foundation," Lord Astor remarks. "We don't encourage it."

The "too much money" derives from the Astor Estate, and, upon his father's death, William gained control of the portion of the trust fund left to him by his grandfather. He comes to America periodically to check on the holdings. As cautious as all the Astors when it comes to talking about money, the most he will say is that he has disposed of much of the American property "for a variety of reasons."

The life of a lord today, we can see, is not all champagne and caviar. There is work to be done too. When not occupied with business, charities, or politics, Astor is happiest with the country life at Cliveden. True to the popular image of an aristocrat, he enjoys riding to hounds with fellow members of the English Establishment. This pursuit has risks not always apparent on the surface. It was back in 1950 that he was unlucky enough to take a rather bad fall from his horse while hunting. Such accidents are all too common in his set, and Britain's society leaders are often in the hands of osteopaths. The one recommended to Astor then was a most attractive young man, Stephen Ward. Although not yet established in practice, Ward was competent, and under his care, William was cured. A friendship developed between the two men, and Astor began to send some of his prominent and titled friends to Ward as patients. With all that came later, this appears ominous, although at the time, it could not have seemed less portentous.

Two years later, when William had inherited his fortune, Stephen Ward appealed to him for assistance in setting up a practice. No one could have been more openhanded than the new Lord Astor. Without hesitation, he lent Ward £1,250, telling the osteopath to pay it back in the form of treatments to be given whenever needed. A gentleman would have to fall from his horse many times indeed to work off such a loan, particularly because it was increased in the following year, when Ward opened a banking account, and Astor guaranteed an overdraft of up to £1,500. (To be sure, such sums are negligible in terms of the vast wealth at his disposal. Lord Astor speaks no less than the truth when he says that the Astors have always handled their fortune conservatively. "As a family, we have never gambled or done unwise things to squander it.")

Rich and titled gentlemen do not content themselves with riding other people's horses; they have their own, and William is no exception. Along with the old Astor money and the new Astor title, he inherited the famous Cliveden stud of racehorses and has managed this personally ever since. ("I'm not as good at it as my father was.") During the last years of Waldorf's life, while grooming his son to succeed him as viscount, he was also grooming Bill to succeed him as master of the stud. William's younger brother, John Jacob VII, was equally interested in horses, and the two acted as partners to their father. Waldorf had carefully arranged for the disposal of his horses upon his death. Bill was to get first pick of the filly foals and Jakie of the brood mares. The new Lord Astor selected Ambiguity, whose dam, Amber, had won the Jockey Club cup. It was a good choice, because the very next year Ambiguity won by a length the 175th Oaks at Epsom from Aga Khan's Kerdeb. It was a particularly pleasing victory for William, who was a good friend of the Aga's son, Aly, the never-replaced Prince Charming of the International Set.

The intense seriousness with which racing is taken comes as a surprise to most Americans who are not aware that love of the turf is deeply ingrained in members of the British upper class. Social climbers have learned long ago that although charitable affairs do not offer the road to social advancement, racing does.

"British aristocrats have a seemingly insatiable passion for horses," notes Charlotte Curtis, the acute and observant *New York Times* writer and editor. "One properly bred runner in the English Derby and several at Ascot . . . go a long way toward making one acceptable. . . . Britain has twenty-seven dukes at the moment and as a group, they are prominent in only one industry—horse racing."

It is at the race tracks where one will meet—or at least see—these dukes, the Astors, and sometimes even the Queen. The gentlemen are handsome in gray top hats, Oxford gray cutaway coats, with pockets in the tails for their programs, and light gray waistcoats and trousers. It is better if these outfits are not new, because in the best families, they are handed down from father to son. Lord Astor enlivens his with a carnation in his buttonhole. The ladies also abandon their tweeds to shiver in the cool British air in pastel silk dresses worn with formal long white gloves. Their hats are all too often the clubwoman type—flowers dyed to match the dress.

Although anyone, of course, can go to the races at Epsom Downs or Ascot, only the select can sit in the royal enclosure. This is not really as royal as all that, because the Queen's section at Ascot is separated from the rest by glass partitions, and the Prime Minister and other really important government officials are separated both from her and other members of the chosen by yet other partitions. As at American charity balls, the number invited to sit in the enclosure has steadily increased until it now stands at eight thousand. Even so they must meet the Queen's stringent requirements. Divorcées, though no longer banned, are by no means numerous.

The racing meets give yet another opportunity for entertaining on the grand scale, and huge parties are held at Cliveden and the other great homes. And indeed, it was from just such a party at Cliveden following the Ascot meet of 1963 that Lord Astor was called by the police to answer questions about the Profumo Affair.

13

Clouds over Cliveden

Although not quite the political and social center of Nancy Astor's day, Cliveden is Cliveden still—almost the romantic Manderley of Daphne du Maurier's *Rebecca*. And Lord William Astor might think himself a Maximilian de Winter, moving through a glittering and sophisticated world.

The rich and powerful members of Britain's ruling Establishment are regular visitors at Cliveden. They attend the parties at which Lord Astor, following his mother's social axiom, mingles writers, artists, and actors with members of the nobility, Cabinet ministers, diplomats, politicians, and world leaders. On weekends they occupy many of Cliveden's forty-six bedrooms and relax from world cares with tennis matches, refreshing swims in the pool, and delightful parties.

The fact that this is so is all the more remarkable, because Cliveden had shaken off the lingering shadows of the appeasement days of the 1930's only to find itself beneath a second cloud in the early 1960's. The Profumo Affair, with all its ramifications, is worth careful study to give some understanding of how it came about, whom it affected, and how Cliveden emerged virtually unscathed.

The Profumo Case has its beginnings in the way of life led by Britain's aristocracy. The Astors and others of the Establishment found, as many have before, that when you have the money and position to have or do everything, it becomes hard to think of things you really want. Anyone who represents a change from the familiar is welcome.

Lord Astor's glittering world touches at times the gay and

glamorous International Set. Some of Bill's friends believe that this is a result of his great admiration for Aly Khan, father of the present Moslem ruler, one-time husband of Rita Hayworth, and acknowledged leader of the wealthy pleasure-loving group. It is certainly true that even today, with Aly dead since 1960, Astor finds a way of bringing his name into conversations on completely unrelated subjects. It does not really take an Aly Khan, however, to induce the very rich to seek variety in their lives.

Now boredom has always been the curse of the upper classes. In America, during society's most formal days, this feeling found expression in the antics of Harry Lehr and Mamie Fish. In England it led to acceptance of the first William Waldorf Astor's behavior. But in that period, these people made up the smallest part of the inner circle, throwing the formality of the society ruled by *the* Mrs. Astor or Victoria into high relief. The majority of the Old Guard in the United States and the aristocratic set in England led measured stately lives of almost stultifying boredom and considered it right and good that this should be so. If one must compare, the English social life was by all odds the more staid, proper, and rigid of the two. There was little social mobility, and people stayed for the most part where they had started out in life. World War I began the process of change, and World War II shattered forever that dreamlike and dull aristocratic social life. Even those, like the Astors, secure at the top of the social pyramid and rich, despite increased socialism, were not immune to the pervasive spirit of restlessness.

Out of this background came the Profumo Affair to cast a blight on the Conservative government, to ruin the lives of its two leading figures, and to involve Lord Astor in the most unpleasant scandal his family ever faced.

Today his cousin Gavin sums up what happened: "William unluckily was in 'that set.' He is so nice that they took advantage of him."

It was indeed a gesture of kindness on his part that set the stage for the tragedy to come. In 1956 Lord Astor rented one of the cottages on the Cliveden estate grounds to his osteopath and friend, Stephen Ward. To Americans, this seems a most peculiar thing to do, but in England it is not at all uncommon for aristocrats to rent out cottages once needed for gamekeepers, gatekeepers, and extra guest houses but now fallen into disrepair. In Astor's case, his use of Cliveden was even more circumscribed than that of most of the landed gentry. His father gave the estate to the National Trust, and Lord Astor is technically a rent-paying tenant of the Trust. The agent of the Trust, therefore, must be informed whenever a cottage is sublet, and spokesmen concede that this was duly done in the case of Ward.

The famous cottage is situated on the banks of the Thames, about a quarter of a mile down a steep hill, or a mile by the road from the main house. It does not look like a setting for orgies, because it has the charm of many old-fashioned English country houses, with a high, sloping, turreted roof, elaborate chimneys, wooden pillars, a carved wooden balustrade, and half-timbered decoration. Lord Astor, a firm believer in the value of osteopathy, found it convenient to have Ward on the grounds and often had him come up to the main house to give treatments. Astor's prominent guests were also offered this service, courtesy of their host, and all bills were charged to him. This generosity had the side effect of increasing Ward's acquaintanceship with Astor's friends. In any event, the relationship was not simply that of doctor and patient or landlord and tenant. Ward was a frequent luncheon or cocktail guest, both at Cliveden and, when Lord Astor was in London, at the townhouse on Upper Grosvenor Street.

Stephen Ward was close enough to being a gentleman to get along with the snobbish set who became his clients and friends. His father, Arthur Evelyn Ward, was a canon of Rochester Cathedral, which just goes to prove the old saw about the minister's son being the wildest boy in town. In the 1930's Ward came to the United States to attend the Kirksville College of Osteopathy in Kirksville, Missouri. Back in England, after an interruption for wartime military service, he began his rapid professional and social rise. That other Ward, McAllister, had considerable to say about social climbing, but he hardly imagined that the profession of osteopath could lead a man into the highest social circles—and in a rigidly stratified country to boot. Ward, who resembled McAllister's successor, Harry Lehr, in his ability to amuse the rich, was charming, witty, and a skillful conversationalist (and, as was true of Lehr also, those not attracted were repelled by his quick and easy manner). "He was awfully good as an extra man at dinner," remarks a member of the society set that spans two continents. In addition to his exceptional gifts as an osteopath, he was a highly competent portrait artist, and his clients for the one vocation brought him sitters for the other. In both categories, these were people of great eminence in the aristocracy, politics, the arts, and business. Consider just a few of his osteopathic patients—the late Sir Winston Churchill, Jean Paul Getty, and Elizabeth Taylor. And then a few of those he sketched—Prince Philip, Princess Margaret, the Earl of Snowden, the Duke and Duchess of Kent, Princess Alexandra, and the Duke and Duchess of Gloucester.

"I must say that when I look at the list of Dr. Ward's patients, let alone his sitters, it seems to me absolutely providential that his name wasn't in the Birthday Honors," was the pungent comment of *Punch*, the British humor magazine.

Ward, however, was as well-known to the prostitutes, perverts, and drug addicts of London's half-world as to members of the Establishment. He would leave the drawing room of Lord and Lady Astor, where he was perfectly at home, to plunge into the dives of Soho, where he was equally at home. He could not do without both high and low life; each filled a need in his nature. Vice attracted him every bit as much as did the refined society life. Finding those among the aristocracy who similarly feel the strange drawing power of vice, Ward became the connection between that segment of the Establishment and the depraved. An amazing assortment of people passed through or came together at his cottage at Cliveden or his London flat at 17, Wimpole Mews.

English newspapermen considered it almost inevitable that a scandal would some day break around the pleasant and talented Mr. Ward. Indeed, they report that even in pre-Profumo days, he was involved in a somewhat nasty business concerning the sexual arrangements for notorious members of the International Set. That scandal, somehow, was kept comparatively quiet and Ward continued to please some friends with professional services, some with extraprofessional, and some with both. Although immoral and amoral, Ward like Dorian Gray, continued to look boyish rather than corrupt throughout his life. His personal inclination, like that of many of his influential friends, was for girls—very, very young, beautiful, willing and numerous. He married once, briefly, but monogamy clearly was not for him.

"I don't have any more sexual relationships than any other person of my age," Ward, then fifty years old, declared at his trial.

The courtroom exploded into laughter, but to Ward who was particularly popular with highly sexed, middle-aged gentlemen of the Establishment and International Set, his statement probably seemed only a slight exaggeration. He found the girls he desired by driving around the streets of London in a flashy white Jaguar and picked up others in night clubs with considerable ease. ("I am not handsome, I have never been rich," he said toward the end of his life, "but even today at fifty I can get most girls I want.") Those who became his mistresses, and some who did not, were introduced to a number of his powerful friends who also liked pretty girls, but were too aristocratic to make a pickup.

"He was a sort of perverted Professor Higgins," declaimed Jeremy Hutchinson, lawyer for Christine Keeler, most notorious of these Gelateas.

"I could have made Christine a duchess," Ward told one of his friends sadly while he was on trial. And the boast, to those who knew him in his heyday, did not appear utterly farfetched.

Ward had small hesitation about taking his pretty playmates around with him wherever he went, and the more conspicuous they were, the better. He thought it a particularly good joke to take Christine for a walk, leading her by a leash attached to a dog collar around her neck. Marilyn "Mandy" Rice-Davies, whose obvious charms had gained her a white Jaguar of her own by the age of seventeen, insisted that Stephen had taken her for cocktails to the Astors' London home and that she had met Lady Astor there. Mandy, Christine, and the other girls who had come to London to improve their lot had hardly imagined that good fortune would carry them to the fabled grounds of Cliveden. But Stephen Ward was only too happy to invite them to his cottage there.

And so it was that Christine Keeler, along with some others of her set, came to Cliveden on the fateful evening of July 8, 1961. What followed was the most famous swimming-pool party in history. Only a recluse can have missed the vividly written newspaper accounts of Christine swimming nude in the walled-in pool at Cliveden, while all unaware of the tragedy to come, John Profumo, Secretary of State for War, and his wife, actress Valerie Hobson, strolled through the gardens in the company of their hosts, Lord and Lady Astor. The inevitable encounter took place, and Ward, living up to his reputation as a prankster, threw Christine's bathing suit out of reach. The contrast between the naked Christine and the dinner-jacketed men—of course, they dressed for dinner—was particularly striking. They had but a glimpse of her tiny, slender but voluptuous body before she wrapped herself in a towel. She dressed hurriedly, but Christine is seductive with clothes on, too. Even her face, framed by dark auburn shoulder-length hair, is sensual, with its high prominent cheekbones, slanted eyes, chiseled nose, and full mouth. Just nineteen, her stormy life, which already included addiction to marihuana, an illegitimate child (dead in infancy), and a number of high-placed English and hot-tempered West Indian lovers, had added a touch of attractive world-weariness to her features.

On that night Ward and Christine were invited to the great house at Cliveden, where at least one of the art treasures was put to a use William Waldorf could hardly have anticipated: the gentlemen, full of fun, dressed Christine in a suit of medieval armor. Once that diversion palled, Profumo took her on a tour of the stately mansion, through the rooms where the Cliveden set had discussed the future of Europe.

It all seemed so harmless that the following day Lord Astor and his respectable guests joined the merry Stephen Ward and his merrier house guests at the swimming pool for more of same. By then Ward's party included Captain Eugene Ivanov, assistant naval attaché at the Russian Embassy. Lord Astor, Profumo, and Ivanov raced one another in the water, and the illustrious and the not-so-illustrious, the Conservative and the Communist, enjoyed the July sunshine. Although it was Ivanov who drove Christine back to London, the forty-six-year-old Profumo was equally, if not more, attracted by her. And of course, there was Ward ready to offer his friendly services to arrange the assignations between Christine and Profumo and Christine and Ivanov.

What followed would never have been a pleasant story at best, but the presence of the Russian added a sinister note that few of the actors in this sorry drama recognized. Only Profumo, warned by the British Secret Service of the danger of being one of the points in the Profumo-Keeler-Ivanov triangle, broke—a little slowly perhaps—with both Ward and Christine. Profumo had taken a photograph of Ward, Christine, and two other girls at the swimming pool and had labeled it "the *new* Cliveden set." He was joking, but Ward at least did want to play a part in history and use his influential friends. A Communist sympathizer, he hoped to improve relations between Britain and the U.S.S.R. Although Astor was by no stretch of the imagination in agreement with Ward's views, he could not say no to a friend. And so he wrote to the Foreign Office, introducing Ward and telling of the friendship with Captain Ivanov. Should the British wish to pass information to the Russian Embassy, either Ward or Ivanov might be of some assistance. On the strength of Astor's name, Ward was interviewed, and it took the experienced men of the Foreign Office but a moment to decide that they could do very nicely without his aid. The following year came the Cuban crisis, and Ward felt that the United Kingdom should call a summit conference. Ever persuasive, he talked Astor into telling Lord Arran, a most influential peer and journalist, that a Russian official (Ivanov) wanted to "pass information of an urgent nature to the British government." Arran quite naturally was interested, and Astor duly invited him, Ivanov, and Ward to dine at Cliveden. As in the interim, the Russians had agreed to withdraw from Cuba, this dinner lost its point altogether. It was, in any event, a far cry from the behind-the-scenes politics played by Astor's mother.

Everything might have ended painlessly had it not been for two related strokes of misfortune. Christine, who had never ceased alternating Establishment friends with members of London's West Indian set, was attacked in December 1962 by a rejected lover, John Edgecombe. He shot at her, missed, and brought the police down upon him, her, and ultimately John Profumo. While investigating the case, the police learned of some nationally known figures among Christine's following. A trial, with Christine as star witness, was in the offing. At this point appeared the not-so-innocent bystander—a young shirt manufacturer, who had been present at the Cliveden swimming pool party. Having newspaper contacts, he suggested to Christine that she had a story that could bring in far more money than her charm and beauty would ever win for her.

When Ward learned that Christine Keeler had sold her story to the Sunday *Pictorial,* he was appalled and turned to the closest of his influential friends at once. Lord Astor did not waste any time. Within hours of Ward's alarming disclosure, he visited Profumo and warned of the impending disaster. The three men, worrying what Christine might have felt like writing about them, tried to persuade the newspaper not to publish. Ward took the obvious approach and had his solicitor offer Christine £500. Always improvident, despite an annual income of some £4,000 ($11,200), Ward did not have the cash on hand, but that was never a problem for him. He applied, as he had so often in the past, to Bill Astor, glossing over the sordid use for the money and saying that it was needed for "legal proceedings." Lord Astor drew a check for that amount on the very day he was asked, adding a kind little note: "Pay me back when you can, or you can work some of it off in treatment, should I have any sprains, bruises, or hunting accidents." Christine refused the money anyway, and it went to pay Ward's rent and debts.

By this time rumors were flying, and it wanted only an incident to make the whole affair burst into the open. That incident occurred in March 1963, when Christine's passionate West Indian lover came to trial. Christine, the long-awaited key witness, was mysteriously absent; in fact, she was not in the country at all. Added to all the other rumors, therefore, were two new ones—that Profumo or Lord Astor had paid her to disappear. These were subsequently found to be false, but by then the damage to Profumo was done. In order to quiet these rumors, Profumo first assured a number of his fellow ministers that he had never slept with Christine—and as he was a gentleman they could not doubt his word—and then publicly declared his innocence on the floor of the House of Commons.

But, as we know, the affair did not end there. The unhappy shadow of Ivanov, returned to Russia by then, fell across Parliament, and questions about the danger to national security were raised. Had Ward asked Christine to play Mata Hari and to worm out of Profumo the date when the Americans were going to give the Germans the atomic bomb?

The police began to investigate Ward's activities. Clearly the weak link in the case, Ward got nervous and reacted as he always did by talking and writing too much. In an effort to induce the police to leave him alone, he wrote letters to everyone, from the Home Secretary to the leader of the Opposition, insisting that he was being persecuted and throwing Profumo to the wolves. These letters did neither man any good.

As the Labor members of Commons began to use the case as a weapon against the Conservative government in power, Profumo realized that the situation had gone further than he had ever dreamed it would, and no end was in sight. He found that he could no longer endure his crushing sense of guilt. After confiding the truth in his wife, who revealed great strength of character and stood by him throughout, he submitted his resignation to Prime Minister Harold Macmillan. It was June 4, not quite two years since the evening when Profumo had dined with the Astors and had first seen the woman who was to destroy his career and nearly topple the government. Four days after Profumo's resignation, Stephen Ward was arrested on the charge of living on the earnings of prostitutes.

The mass-circulation papers made the most of the case, with the *News of the World* capturing the prize of "The Confessions of Christine" (said to have netted her £23,000 or $64,000) in which she referred casually to Lord Astor as "Bill" and told about her torrid romances with the so gentlemanly Jack Profumo and the virile hairy chested Ivanov. Gavin Astor's *Times* was also not remaining silent in the face of the most dramatic news story of a decade. It had all the ingredients required to excite the public—sex, violence, beautiful girls, famous names, political repercussions, spies, national security—and the *Times* was to add one more—morals. While members of Parliament were insisting that the affair be judged on its security aspects only, the *Times* came forth with a leader (editorial) entitled "It Is a Moral Issue," in which it stated unequivocally: "Everyone has been so busy assuring the public that the affair is not one of morals that it is time to assert that it is. . . . Eleven years of Conservative rule have brought the nation psychologically and spiritually to a low ebb."

The editorial was widely reprinted and commented on, and the subsequent letters to the *Times* about it filled column after column, most of them approving the anti-vice, anti-Macmillan attitude. One Tory M.P. responded with a comment about *Times* editor Haley: "He is a man about whom it could have been predicted from his early youth that he was bound to end up sooner or later on the staff of one of the Astor papers." As this followed the statement that "this certainly has been one of the best field days that the self-righteous have had since Parnell was cited as co-respondent in O'Shea's divorce case," the implication was understood to be that the Astors are opposed to pleasure.

Gavin Astor's paper, ironically, was particularly effective in bringing news about the case to the attention of upper-class readers who would never buy the tabloids. Ironic, of course, because of the Astors' involvement. Cliveden, the pride of them all, was touched by the hot breath of scandal. The previous year a Cabinet Minister weekending with the Astors decided to rent a cottage on the grounds of Cliveden. Repairs and the addition of a kitchen and bathrooms, all arranged by the future tenant, took about a year. The furniture was already in the house and plans for moving in had been made when the rumblings of the scandal to come were heard. Realizing that the cottage was but four hundred yards away from Stephen Ward's, the Minister hurriedly withdrew. He had not acted quickly enough. This slight involvement with Cliveden was sufficient to give rise to rumors that the Minister was too well acquainted with Ward and, as one French newspaper put it, "sa troupe de girls."

Gavin Astor, publisher of the *Times*, although a friend of the beleaguered Macmillan, could not help but be proud of the role his paper and indeed the journalistic profession had played in the matter. And Macmillan at the height of the scandal, addressed the Commonwealth Press Union, which is headed by Gavin, in stiff-upper-lip fashion, urging freedom of the press and insisting on their right "to probe and criticize."

Only a few days earlier Gavin had received wide publicity for his speech praising the newspapers for their role in bringing the whole shoddy business to light and commenting on another point made editorially by his paper: "It is doubtful whether the truth would ever have emerged had the press not been seeking in the matter of Mr. Profumo and Miss Keeler, so far as the law of libel would permit, to do its job."

Criticizing the British libel laws, he stated firmly, "They can have the effect of imposing a silence and clamping a gag on the press and this has often prevented the newspapers from giving information which the public has a right to know."

Only two weeks later the information the public had a right to know was emblazoned in enormous headlines telling of the connection of his cousin, Lord William Astor, with the case.

"There was a gasp in the crowded courtroom when she named him," reported the *Daily Telegraph and Morning Post* on June 29.

And in America, the circumspect *The New York Times* gave front-page coverage beneath the headline: "Astor Is Mentioned at Ward's Hearing."

The public, titillated by the rumors of great names involved in the case, was by then ready for something specific. The London *Mirror*, doing its best to make freedom of the press look bad, had run a front-page photograph of Prince Philip beneath huge headlines, "Prince Philip and the Profumo Scandal," followed by the statement in small print that the rumor about him "is utterly unfounded." Harold Macmillan had already asked Lord Alfred Thompson Denning (Baron Denning of Whitechurch) to conduct a full-scale investigation of the affair, but no one could wait for his report. The something specific came when Mandy Rice-Davies, her blonde bangs almost touching her heavily made-up eyes, took the witness stand at the hearing being held to decide whether Ward should be held over for trial. When prosecutor Mervyn Griffith-Jones asked whether there had been any relationships with men while she was living at Ward's flat, she folded and unfolded her white gloves nervously and replied: "With Lord Astor." Though the embarrassed prosecutor sharply put in, "I don't want you to name names," and the court clerk paraphrased her testimony with the name left out, the newspapermen were writing away for all they were worth. They duly reported Astor's flat denial of her charge, but it most certainly did not make headlines.

Mandy then went on to describe Ward's proposal of marriage to her. When she had pointed out that he had no money, he had replied (or so she said), "We have always got Bill who can help us."

This statement gained significance as it followed earlier testimony by Christine, glamorous in a tight-fitting off-white wool suit, that Astor had once paid the rent for a flat on Comeragh Road that she was sharing with Mandy. Christine was careful to insist that "there was no ulterior motive behind the cheque that was handed to the landlord." The London *Daily Mirror* without comment ran that statement below Astor's picture.

By the time the hearing was ended on July 3, the revelations of Christine, Mandy, and a succession of beautiful girls had made Christine's published confessions look like no more than the appetizer to a ten-course meal. And the decision that Ward be held for trial gave promise of a veritable series of banquets. Ward, still seeming confident despite the damaging evidence, was released from prison on bail.

During the nineteen days that elapsed before the trial there was little any of the figures involved could do but wait and worry. Lord Astor retained a lawyer to observe the case and did his best to avoid the spotlight. Other illustrious gentlemen were in for greater trouble, as rumor linked them to the more depraved aspects of the scandal.

One Cabinet Minister was hard-pressed to refute the words, never spoken openly as an accusation, but believed by many, that he was the famous "man in the mask" described by Christine and Mandy. They told of attending a dinner party served by a man wearing nothing but a mask and a little lace apron about his waist. After dinner the guests, it was said, engaged in "perverted sex orgies."

Mandy, her pretty eighteen-year-old head quite turned by all the attention, was brazen in her desire to become one of the famous courtesans of history. "I am under contract to several newspapers at the moment," she said, apparently a bit envious of Christine's financial success. On another occasion she remarked happily: "I'm notorious. I shall go down in history as another Lady Hamilton."

The trial began on July 22 and continued for eight sensational days, described in lurid detail by an army of newspapermen from every civilized country in the world. Stories of sadism, perversion, voyeurism, drugs, and prostitution emerged. A procession of girls of varying degrees of beauty, but having youth in common, told of pickups and seductions, some taking place at the charming cottage at Cliveden. One girl was so overcome by her own testimony that she had to be given smelling salts. A slender, ash-blonde prostitute told of whipping elderly male clients with a cane at a charge of a pound ($2.80) a stroke. Her whipping costume consisted of flame-colored underwear and high-heeled shoes. Others told of bedrooms with two-way mirrors built into the door, so that some could perform and others watch the performance.

Still, one prostitute admitted that she had lied at the pretrial hearing, and the motives of others were sharply questioned by the defense attorney. Mandy, for instance, after repeating her electrifying testimony was asked whether she was not trying to bring in great names so as to increase the value of the story she was trying to sell to the newspapers. Christine, it appeared, had received more money from Ward than she had earned from her lovers. Ward left the court each day with a smile on his thin, sensitive face and made a thumbs-up gesture to the crowd. Free on bail, yet another friend was sharing a flat with him.

When Ward took the stand, he admitted openly that he was "a thoroughly immoral man," but insisted that his sex life, though varied, was normal and that money was not involved. He denied ever having told Mandy that he could count on Astor and other influential friends for financial support if they were married. As to the Astor check said to have been used to pay the girls' rent, a fact denied by Astor, Ward stated it was given him as just one of many loans.

As the conclusion of the trial approached, it became strikingly apparent that none of the illustrious gentlemen who had been his friends, patients, or portrait subjects was going to come forward on Ward's behalf. Not one of them appeared as a defense witness. Ward quite naturally was bitter about the failure of the people he considered his friends, notably Lord Astor, to speak up for him. "Their silence," he told a reporter for the London *Daily Express*, "crucified me."

In summing up, Sir Archie Marshall, the judge, commented on the desertion of Ward. "There may be reasons why he has been abandoned in his extremity," Marshall told the jury, "but you must not guess at them."

Those not required by jury oath to abstain from guesswork can hardly avoid selecting either of the two likeliest interpretations. Did these prominent gentlemen fear cross-examination and/or the effect on their reputations of further involvement in the whole sordid business? Or did they realize that their sworn testimony could only damage Ward's case more than their silence?

After hearing the summing up, Ward's usual confidence and cheerfulness deserted him. When he left the courtroom for the last time, he had accepted the fact that the case was lost. That night, Ward opened a bottle of Nembutal and deliberately swallowed one capsule after the other.

As he lay in a coma in the hospital, the judge sternly ordered the jury to determine the verdict. Ward was found guilty of the charges of living on immoral earnings. Sentence was never pronounced, because eighty hours after taking the pills, Ward achieved the peace he had longed for.

His death lifted the affair out of sordid case history into drama, restoring to Ward at least a modicum of the sympathy and compassion that had been so lacking during the trial, when an avid public had watched his downfall.

Lord Astor issued a statement to the press, which although undeniably true, was hardly a summation of the man's life: "Stephen Ward possessed remarkable gifts of healing which he exercised skillfully, conscientiously and generously. Those who were so fortunate as to have been treated by him will remember him with great gratitude. His readiness to help anyone in pain is the memory many will treasure."

But to some, Ward in death succeeded in making plausible a view that had seemed mere self-pity in him when alive. He had then told a reporter: "This has been a political revenge trial. Someone had to be sacrificed and that was me. When the Establishment wants blood, you can't wriggle out."

Britain's Angry Young Men felt a kinship with these bitter words. They entered the drama at last by finding in Stephen Ward an antihero, an example of the utter rottenness of the Establishment. Playwrights John Osborne and Arnold Wesker, critic Kenneth Tynan, and novelists Angus Wilson and Alan Sillitoe were the best known of the group that dispatched a wreath of two-hundred roses to the funeral parlor where Ward's body lay prior to cremation. They added a card: "To Stephen Ward, victim of British hypocrisy."

"British society created him, used him and ruthlessly destroyed him," declared Tynan dramatically. "The Establishment has closed its ranks around his body."

The implication remained that Ward, who had in truth faced a maximum sentence of fourteen years and could have been let off with a fine, had been on trial for his life.

The Conservative government was still reeling, but had not fallen, and everyone was waiting for the definitive study of the security aspects of the affair to be issued. Lord Denning put out his report in late September 1963 and found himself the author of a best seller. Within twenty-four hours, one-hundred thousand copies were sold. After taking the testimony of 160 witnesses, Lord Denning concluded that the British national security had not been damaged by the case. Denning went to considerable length to put to rest the rumors connecting this Minister and that one with orgies, perversions, and weird sexual tastes and performances.

Of the main characters involved in the Profumo Affair, only one, Christine Keeler, ended up with a jail sentence for perjuring herself in the assault trial of one of her West Indian lovers. Married the year following her release, she expressed the wistful hope that the public and the newspapers would forget her. All she wants is to live as a quiet, obscure housewife.

The leading figure in the tragedy, Profumo, is trying to remake his life with dignity as a volunteer social worker in a settlement house in the London slums.

The tragedy that destroyed Profumo's career and caused Ward's death missed Lord Astor. Aided by his own and his family's reputation and character, he was also fortunate in not being in the government at the time of the scandal. On August 21, just eighteen days after Ward's suicide, the Joseph Dever society column in the New York *World-Telegram and Sun* broke the news to the American public that Lord and Lady Astor were expecting a baby. "We are bubbling over with happiness," Lady Bronwen was quoted as saying. The impending baby made news once more in October, when the Denning report was making news in another genre. While vacationing on Jura Island in the Hebrides, Lady Astor was threatened with a miscarriage and had to be rushed to the mainland through heavy surf in a fishing boat. The baby, a girl, was saved and was born the following March.

"The Profumo Case has blown over," says Lord Astor. "I do all the things I did before. I was completely absolved by the Denning report."

And that is true. Denning found that Astor had not shared Ward's political views. His report states that Ward had not explained to Astor that he wanted the £500 loan in order to bribe Christine into stopping publication of her story. It declares unequivocally that Astor most certainly had not paid Christine to disappear during the Edgecombe trial, which took place while he was away in America.

In a newspaper story by Christine Keeler—never used, but revealed in the Denning report—she wrote of John Profumo with what was rare perceptiveness for her: "I believe now that a man in his position should not indulge in pastimes like me."

Those at Cliveden were luckier and were able to live down their "indulgence" in unfortunate tenants like Ward. At the end of the Profumo Affair, life at Cliveden resumed on its old basis with considerable dispatch.

14

Time Past and Time Present

The recent story about a prominent actress expressing her high spirits by breaking six-hundred dollars' worth of dishes in a restaurant in Athens brings to mind an old charity benefit stunt of Vincent Astor's. He set up a booth displaying crockery of all kinds and invited his socialite friends to shatter the dishes by throwing baseballs at them. It was a huge success, and a lot of money was raised.

As Astor grew older his charitable efforts took a more serious turn, and his death wish was to improve the lot of strangers, rather than his Astor relatives.

"John Jacob Astor I never amassed the fortune for it to be so dissipated," says disinherited John Astor.

His ancestor's vision of the dynasty he was founding was altered by a factor that no amount of careful will-planning could have controlled—Vincent's childless state. This was the one blow of fate that has changed the American Astor family irrevocably. As Vincent was the first of the Astors to be both childless and public-spirited, his death, expected though it was, caught his relatives unprepared.

His half-brother fought back as best he could and called in lawyers; a succession of these professionals have been the constant companions of his life. The only major result of the struggle was the holding up of the distribution of the assets for the better part of the year. At the end of that time, John was forced to face the fact that he was rich, but would never be commandingly so, and his children (unless William realizes his ambition) will be a little less rich, and so on down the line.

Vincent's nephew, Ivan Obolensky, was left with an original letter from John Jacob I on his hands. It had been intended as a gift for Vincent, the man who had everything else. Despite his disappointment in terms of a major inheritance, he—and, for that matter, his sister and half-sisters—were hardly left destitute. In addition to the money they inherited from Alice Astor, they shared equally in the three-million-dollar estate left by their grandmother, the dazzling Ava. Tall and slim, attractive in the continental style, Ivan lives with his second wife and their child on the fashionable East Side of Manhattan, surrounded by works of art inherited from his mother. Ivan, who wrote a novel in 1956 and founded a book publishing company in 1957, now spends most of his time as an investment banker. His sister Sylvia is the wife of Prince Azamat Guirey, who, according to Ivan, claims "jokingly" that he is descended from Genghis Khan. When asked to describe Sylvia, a friend of the family came up with the statement that she has become a marvelous cook and serves the best food in London. The child of Alice Astor's second marriage, Romana von Hofmannsthal, also living in London, is married to Roderick McEwen, a television producer and artist. In a strange coincidence, Emily Harding, Alice's youngest child, was married in 1963 to Michael Zimmer, nephew of von Hofmannsthal, her mother's second husband. The wedding reception was given by her aunt, Mrs. Vincent Astor, at Ferncliff. The society columnists who gathered for the event were fascinated to observe the appearance of Vincent Astor wives of time past and time present—namely Mrs. Lytle Hull and Mrs. James Fosburgh (numbers one and two respectively), as well as the widow.

Not only relatives but also friends and employees were stunned by the course of events that followed Vincent's death. The St. Regis Hotel and *Newsweek* magazine were in that portion of the estate left to the Vincent Astor Foundation. The staff of the St. Regis could not believe that it would ever be sold, not stopping to think that Vincent's sentimental attachment had to die with him. His business advisers did not view the hotel as their "baby"; they did not even go there for lunch every day. And so the St. Regis once more went out of Astor hands—this time, probably forever.

It has been sold three more times since then and is at present the proud possession of two real estate men from Brooklyn. Of course, it remains popular for debuts and fabulous charity benefit balls attended by Astors, Vanderbilts, Whitneys, Wetherills, Fords, Guests and Van Rensselaers, not to mention maharajahs, dukes, princes, and an occasional former king. The St. Regis benefits from the lingering glamor of the long Astor reign. In the publicity released on the occasion of the hotel's sixtieth anniversary in 1964, so many references to the Astors were made that it was a rare newspaper reader who could discover that the family was no longer in command. Cesar Balsa, enjoying his brief reign as owner, was there, seated it just so happens, at Serge Obolensky's table. Still handsome, this most colorful of Alice Astor's husbands, is now a public relations and hotel consultant. He makes his headquarters at the St. Regis, where Vincent gave him his start three decades ago.

As for *Newsweek*, Raymond Moley and the other editors were just as shocked as the St Regis managers by the Foundation's hard-headed decision to dispose of the magazine. "Vincent would never have sold it," insists Moley; "he loved *Newsweek* as his own creation." The employees went so far as to make an offer for it, but could not match the $8,985,000 put up by the Washington *Post*. Those with long memories recalled that thirty years earlier, Vincent and the Harrimans had sought to buy the Washington *Post*, but had been unable to wrest it from Eugene Meyer. In 1961 it was Philip Graham, Meyer's son-in-law and successor to his position as president of the *Post*, who gave his personal check for two million dollars as the down payment. Moley stayed on, but Muir, who had been editor since Vincent had merged *Today* with the old *Newsweek*, did not.

With the proceeds of the *Newsweek* and St. Regis sales added to the rest of the bequest—raising its assets to seventy-five million dollars or better—the Foundation began to expand its activities. Unsentimental though they were as regards the liquidating of Vincent's possessions, the Foundation trustees showed some signs of sentimentality in the spending of their funds. "It is better to have dead grass in the park than sick children in the tenements," Vincent had said many years earlier. And so it was decided that the first major project of the Foundation after his death should be to aid underprivileged children and combat juvenile delinquency.

"We are supporting a program to wipe out fighting gangs by working with the younger boys," explains Allan W. Betts, vice-president and treasurer.

Youth workers are assigned to seven-to-twelve-year-olds in sections dominated by teen-age gangs. Grants totaling $1 million dollars will be given over a three-year period to the New York neighborhood houses running the project.

Future grants will also concentrate on New York, states Foundation president Brooke Astor, because of "the association of the Astor name with the city for the past nearly two hundred years."

But the manner of this association had changed during Vincent's lifetime. "He had *no* real estate holdings at the time of his death, aside from *The New York Times* annex." It is hard to believe that this statement could possibly refer to an Astor, and yet it was made by his last business manager. Both the Astor Plaza and the Cleveland Electric building, the last of his great real-estate endeavors, were sold before he died. What American real estate remains to the family is in the absentee landlord hands of the English Astors.

If one is to look for the fulfillment of the dynastic dream of John Jacob I, it is, as John Astor has said, to be found in England. The sense of responsibility for the inheritance rests heavily on the shoulders of the older generation. When Lord Astor of Hever left England, he questioned sadly whether he and his wife would ever be able to return, even on a temporary basis. Well, visit they did—an Astor representative studied the tax law and reported that after one year's exile they could go back for as much as five months of any year—but hardly for pleasure. Lady Violet's failing health required medical treatment. It was to no avail and two years after the expatriation, Lady Violet died in the new home the aged couple had felt themselves forced to make in southern France. At least she was spared the knowledge of the sudden death, a few weeks after, of her son's wife, the American-born Marchioness of Lansdowne. An excellent shot who had won the British Women's clay pigeon championship in 1952, Lady Lansdowne was fatally wounded by a blast from a twelve-gauge shotgun in the gunroom of her Scottish home, Meikleour House. The tragedy was particularly poignant in that nine years earlier her seventeen-year-old daughter, Lady Caroline, had died in the same Scottish hospital of gunshot wounds.

For those who remain in England, life has been restored to its customary calm. Lord Astor alternates his time between Cliveden and London, delighted with his lovely wife, their fair-haired little girl, the new little baby, and the heir away at school, showing, his proud father boasts, a talent in art unusual for the Astors. William attends the House of Lords, supports his charities, manages his stud of horses, attends the races, and sometimes lunches with his impeccable cousin Gavin. While their mother's posthumous plans for a biography to assess her position in Britain's political life go forward, William and his brothers are arranging for another writer to bring their quiet father out of the shadows. As for politics, even when labor finally took over from the Conservative government, supported by most of the family, John, the only Astor to stand for election, retained his seat.

After three-quarters of a century in England and two centuries in America, it appears clear that wherever this family goes, "it's easy if you're an Astor." Open Burke's *Peerage* and the Astors are there; leaf through the pages of the New York *Social Register*, and the name appears again. (John Astor is the notable exception, eliminated by the arbitrary editorial board; he has been granted a place in the *Celebrity Register* instead.) The Astor relatives also still occupy many pages in the august black-covered book—the Chanlers, Draytons, Wilsons . . .

And if Newport is Astor territory no longer—Beaulieu has changed hands twice since the great days, moving from Astor to Vanderbilt to the Wiley T. Buchanan, Jrs., and *the* Mrs. Astor's fabled Beechwood went for a song ($49,500) in 1940—"cousin" James H. Van Alen is still much in evidence there. Descendant of *the* Mrs. Astor's daughter Emily, Van Alen is president of the Newport Casino and is in his element during Tennis Week, the high point of Newport's inner circle social season. So busy is he overseeing arrangements for the invitation tennis tournament that he seldom has time to take off his straw hat with its green, yellow, and white band, Casino colors, as any Newporter could tell you, and stop to watch the matches. His mother, Mrs. Louis S. Bruguière (it is also useless to expect children of members of society to bear the current names of the mothers), does watch, but only from the privacy of her large black Rolls Royce, which is parked close to the courts. Mrs. Bruguière still lives as if Caroline Astor were her neighbor on Bellevue Avenue. With hair colored, lavender, not black, in her case, she is heavily bejeweled, even at tea time, served in her cottage, Wakehurst, by footmen in black and yellow livery. Only those whom she considers socially acceptable are asked to join her at dinner. Although her style is similar, Mrs. Bruguière was a child during the era dominated by *the* Mrs. Astor.

Indeed almost all those who attended *the* Mrs. Astor's historic ball in 1892 are dead. In 1964 a New York society columnist could find but one survivor, Edith Wetmore, among his wide acquaintance; the Astor family supplies one more in Alida Chanler Emmet. There are several others, now in their eighties, who danced at some of the later balls and just missed inclusion in McAllister's famous list. But though the actual memories of her fade, *the* Mrs. Astor's stamp is still on society, influencing those who never knew the woman herself. Her dream of an elite inner circle, going through life in a manner as prescribed as any cotillion figure, lives on.

Nor has the stamp of John Jacob Astor I been lifted from the city of New York. Riding the New York subway that did so much to increase the value of Astor property half a century ago, one comes to Astor Place. It is no longer the fashionable residential neighborhood it was when John Jacob and his son William Backhouse stepped heavily out of their front doors to go to the Astor Estate office. This is just as John Jacob would have had it. The city, said Astor, will expand to the north, and houses and office buildings will rise on the cabbage farms of the poor and the country estates of the rich. And he put his fortune and energies into helping to make this happen.

The Astor name is still to be found in this and other cities the world over, lending its luster to countless enterprises. Wealth, power, and social acceptability—these are the connotations given to the name by John Jacob and his descendants. Even the U.S.S.R. has not been able to resist honoring this thoroughly capitalistic dynasty, and the Astoria is the leading hotel in Leningrad. The Astor Hotel in New York will soon be demolished, yet its name will survive in a host of other establishments. In how many cities, aside from New York, does one find an Astor hotel, club, theater, or—in the case of those attempting to add glamor to the mundane—garage, luncheonette, or small business? As for that little town in Germany where an inefficient butcher fathered a brilliant son, its name, too, has become world-renowned. The old Waldorf-Astoria Hotel was torn down, but when the new one arose, it bore the illustrious name again.

The original Astor Library building on Lafayette Street is being transformed into a theater. Shakespeare will be performed in the heavy brownstone building which once housed New York's first public library. The schoolboys of another century who alternately dismayed and gladdened old Joseph Cogswell's heart are dead. Only a drawing, believed by the family to be inaccurate, remains as a reminder of the Hellgate country estate of John Jacob Astor I. His Astor House was torn down more than a generation ago to make way for the subway. The stone house at Rhinebeck, built by Alice Astor when she was in love with Prince Serge Obolensky, has been sold for use as a home for unwed mothers. A good part of Ferncliff, sanctuary and pride of three generations of male Astors, is being given to the Roman Catholic Archdiocese of New York.

"It would be disastrous if the pattern of a dead customer got mixed up with the pattern of one still living," said C. Malcolm Johnstone, British custom tailor, after the death of T. S. Eliot. The brown paper pattern used to make Eliot's suits was, therefore, slowly and deliberately torn into small pieces.

In such ways all the physical evidences of human lives disappear or are altered beyond recognition. What remains, of course, is the most important. Eliot's poems are a part of the world's culture, and John Jacob Astor's vision of New York *is* New York.

Bibliography

Ainsworth, Brig. Gen. Fred C., and Kirkley, Joseph W., *The War of the Rebellion*, Series I, Vols. 1, 5, 51-Pt. 2; Series III, Vol. 3; Series III, Vols. 1, 4, published under the direction of the Hon. Elihu Root, Secretary of War, 1908.

Aldrich, Margaret Chanler, *Family Vista, the Memoirs of Margaret Chanler Aldrich*, New York, William-Frederick Press, 1958.

Amory, Cleveland, ed., *Celebrity Register*, New York, Harper & Row, 1963.

Amory, Cleveland, *The Last Resorts*, New York, Harper & Bros., 1948, 1952.

Amory, Cleveland, *Who Killed Society?*, Garden City, New York, Doubleday & Co., 1960.

Asquith, Cynthia, *Remember and Be Glad*, New York, Charles Scribner's Sons, 1952.

Astor, John Jacob, *A Journey in Other Worlds*, London, Longmans Green & Co., 1894.

Astor, Michael, *Tribal Feeling*, London, John Murray Ltd., 1963.

Astor, Lady Nancy, *My Two Countries*, Garden City, New York, Doubleday, Page & Co., 1923.

Astor, William Waldorf, *Pharaoh's Daughter and Other Stories*, London, Macmillan & Co., Ltd., 1900.

Astor, William Waldorf, *Sforza, a Story of Milan*, New York, Charles Scribner's Sons, 1889.

Baird, Robert, *Transplanted Flowers*, New York, John S. Taylor, 1839.

Balsan, Consuelo Vanderbilt, *The Glitter and the Gold*, New York, Harper & Bros., 1952.

Bristed, Charles Astor, *The Upper 10,000, Sketches of American Society*, New York, Stringer & Townsend, 1852.

Brown, Henry Collins, *Brownstone Fronts and Saratoga Trunks*, New York, E. P. Dutton & Co., 1935.

Burke, John Bernard, *Burke's Peerage, Baronetage & Knightage*, 1956, 1963.

Café Society Register, New York, C. S. R. Publishing Co., 1941.

Catton, Bruce, *Mr. Lincoln's Army*, Garden City, New York, Doubleday & Co., 1951.

Chanler, Mrs. Winthrop, *Roman Spring, Memoirs*, Boston, Little Brown & Co., 1934.

Collis, Maurice, *Nancy Astor*, New York, E. P. Dutton & Co., 1960.

Crawford, Iain, *The Profumo Affair*, London, White Lodge Books, 1963.

Crockett, Albert Stevens, *Peacocks on Parade*, New York, Sears Publishing Co., 1931.

Crowninshield, Frank, *The Unofficial Palace of New York, a Tribute to the Waldorf-Astoria*, privately published, 1939.

Current Biography, H. W. Wilson Co., Bronx, N.Y., May, 1954.

Denning, Lord Alfred, *Lord Denning's Report*, London, Her Majesty's

Stationery Office, Sept., 1963.

Eliot, Elizabeth, *Heiresses and Coronets*, N.Y., McDowell, Obolensky, 1959.

Fairfield, Francis Gerry, *The Clubs of New York*, New York, Henry L. Hinton, 1873.

Hamm, Margherita Arlina, *Famous Families of New York*, New York, G. P. Putnam's Sons, 1901.

Harriman, Mrs. J. Borden, *From Pinafores to Politics*, New York, Henry Holt & Co., 1923.

Harrison, Mrs. Burton, *Recollections Grave and Gay*, New York, Charles Scribner's Sons, 1911.

Hubbard, Elbert, *Little Journeys to the Homes of Great Businessmen*, East Aurora, N.Y., The Roycrofters, 1909.

Irving, Washington, *Astoria*, Portland, Ore., Binfords & Mort, 1951 (originally published by Carey, Lea & Blanchard, Philadelphia, Pa., 1836).

Johnson, Allen, ed., *Dictionary of American Biography*, New York, Charles Scribner's Sons, 1928.

Josephson, Matthew, *Robber Barons*, N.Y., Harcourt Brace & Co., 1934.

Kennedy, Ludovic, *The Trial of Stephen Ward*, New York, Simon & Schuster, 1965.

Lehr, Elizabeth Drexel, *"King Lehr" and the Gilded Age*, Philadelphia, J. B. Lippincott Co., 1935.

Lewis, Arthur H., *The Day They Shook the Plum Tree*, New York, Harcourt, Brace & World, 1963.

Lockwood, Sarah M., *New York, Not So Little and Not So Old*, Garden City, N.Y., Doubleday, Page & Co., 1926.

Lord, Walter, *A Night to Remember*, New York, Henry Holt & Co., 1955.

Lundberg, Ferdinand, *America's 60 Families*, New York, The Citadel Press, 1946 (originally published by Vanguard, New York, 1937).

Lydenberg, Harry Miller, *History of the New York Public Library*, privately printed, 1923.

McAllister, Ward, *Society as I Have Found it*, New York, Cassell Publishing Co., 1890.

Morris, Lloyd, *Incredible New York*, New York, Random House, 1951.

Myers, Gustavus, *History of the Great American Fortunes*, New York, Modern Library Inc., 1907, 1936.

National Social Directory, New York, National Social Directory, Inc., 1963, 1965.

New York Genealogical and Biographical Record, Jan., 1913.

Nizer, Louis, *My Life in Court*, Garden City, N.Y., Doubleday & Co., 1961.

Obolensky, Serge, *One Man in His Time*, New York, McDowell, Obolensky, 1958.

O'Connor, Harvey, *The Astors*, New York, Alfred A. Knopf, 1941.

Pearson, Hesketh, *The Marrying Americans*, N.Y., Coward, McCann, 1961.

Phillips Elite Directory, New York, Phillips Andrade & Co., 1874-5.

Phisterer, Frederick, compiled by, *New York in the War of the Rebellion*, 3rd edition, Albany, J. B. Lyon Co., State Printers, 1912.

Porter, Kenneth Wiggins, *John Jacob Astor, Business Man*, Cambridge, Mass., Harvard University Press, 1931.

Riis, Jacob, *How the Other Half Lives*, New York, Sagamore Press, 1957 (originally published 1890).

Bibliography

Sampson, Anthony, *Anatomy of Britain,* London, Hodder & Stoughton Ltd., 1962.

Schleich, Karl, *Die Astorstiftung von Walldorf in den letzten 25 Jahren 1921–1945,* 1946.

Schriftgiesser, Karl, *Families,* New York, Howell Soskin, 1940.

Scott, J. D., *Life in Britain,* New York, William Morrow & Co., 1956.

Scoville, Joseph A. (pseudonym Barrett, Walter), *The Old Merchants of New York City,* New York, M. Doolady, 1872.

Smith, Matthew Hale, *Sunshine and Shadow in New York,* Hartford, Conn., J. B. Burr Publishing Co., 1880.

Social Register, New York, 1891, 1892, 1920, 1958, 1961, 1963, 1965.

Spooner, Walter W., ed., *Historic Families of America,* Vol. 3, New York, Historic Families Publishing Association, 1908.

Stokes, I. N. Phelps, *The Iconography of Manhattan Island, 1498–1909,* Vol. III, New York, Robert H. Dodd, 1928.

Stryker, Rev. Peter, *A Discourse. The Lower Depths of the Great American Metropolis,* Delivered in 34th Street Reformed Dutch Church, New York, Apr. 29, 1866.

Sutton, Horace, *Confessions of a Grand Hotel: The Waldorf-Astoria,* New York, Henry Holt & Co., 1951.

Tebbel, John, *The Inheritors,* New York, G. P. Putnam's Sons, 1962.

Terrell, John Upton, *Furs by Astor,* New York, William Morrow & Co., 1963.

Thomas, Lately, *Sam Ward "King of the Lobby,"* Boston, Houghton Mifflin, Co., 1965.

Tully, Andrew, *Era of Elegance,* New York, Funk & Wagnalls Co., 1947.

Van Rensselaer, Mrs. John King, *Newport Our Social Capital,* Philadelphia, J. B. Lippincott Co., 1905.

Van Rensselaer, Mrs. John King, in collaboration with Van de Water, Frederic, *The Social Ladder,* New York, Henry Holt & Co., 1924.

Wector, Dixon, *The Saga of American Society,* New York, Charles Scribner's Sons, 1937.

Worden, Helen, *Society Circus,* New York, Covici Friede, 1936.

The following newspapers and periodicals have been consulted from nineteenth century back files (wherever possible) to the present day:

American Newspapers: *Christian Science Monitor,* New York *Daily News,* New York *Herald Tribune,* New York *Journal American,* New York *Mirror,* New York *Sun, The New York Times,* New York *World-Telegram & Sun.*

British Newpapers: *Daily Telegraph & Morning Post,* London *Daily Mirror, Sunday Telegraph, Times* of London.

American Periodicals: *American Heritage, Atlantic Monthly, Collier's, Cosmopolitan, Current Opinion, Harper's Weekly, Hobbies, Holiday, Ladies Home Journal, Literary Digest, Magazine of American History, McClure's Magazine, Moody's Magazine, The Nation, The New Yorker, Newsweek, Saturday Evening Post, Time, Town & Country, Vogue, World's Work.*

British Periodicals: *The Economist, Guardian, The Queen, The Spectator, Saturday Review.*

Index